The Complete Illustrated
Thorburn's Birds

The Complete Illustrated

THORBURN'S BIRDS

with text and illustrations by
ARCHIBALD THORBURN
Fellow of the Zoological Society

SELECT
EDITIONS

This edition published 1990 for Selectabook Ltd,
Devizes, Wiltshire, by Wordsworth Editions Ltd,
8b East Street, Ware, Hertfordshire.

Copyright © Wordsworth Editions Ltd 1989.

ISBN 1-85326-922-0

Printed and bound in Spain by Gráficas Estella SA.

PREFACE

THIS work has been designed mainly with the purpose of providing, as far as I have been able, sketches in colour from life of our British birds, including not only the resident species but also in most cases those which have more or less regularly or even rarely visited us from abroad. Having for many years past been making studies from life with this object in view, the present seemed a fitting time for carrying out the project, and where it was not possible to obtain living birds for the drawings, I have filled in the gaps from the best preserved specimens I could procure.

I have endeavoured, where space permitted, to represent as many species as possible of the same family, on the same plate, and drawn to the same scale.

This not only enables me to make the volumes of a convenient size but also gives the reader an opportunity of comparing the various proportions and divergence of colour in closely related birds.

Being more familiar with the brush than with the pen, it was at first my intention that this book should be simply a sketch-book of British Birds, practically without letterpress; but as the work proceeded, I was induced to write a short description of each of the various species represented, giving rough notes, as far as possible, of the distribution, nest and eggs, food, song, and habits of the different birds.

This letterpress is admittedly and of necessity largely a compilation; for at the present day it is not easy to supply much original matter, and I have inserted, in addition to that which has already appeared in print, such notes as I have been able to add from my own observations and those of my friends. For full and more scientific accounts of the birds included in this book, I would refer my readers to some of the standard literature on the subject, which has been freely used by me in preparing the letterpress—viz. the fourth edition of Yarrell's *British Birds;* Macgillivray's *British Birds;* Lord Lilford's *Coloured Figures of the Birds of the British Islands,* and his *Birds of Northamptonshire and Neighbourhood;* Mr. Dresser's *Birds of Europe,* and his *Manual of Palæarctic Birds;* Mr. J. G. Millais' *The Natural History of British Surface-feeding Ducks; British Diving Ducks;* and *The Natural History of British Game Birds;* Howard Saunders' *Manual of British Birds* (2nd edition); Seebohm's *British Birds;* also *A Hand-list of*

PREFACE

British Birds, by Hartert, Jourdain, Ticehurst, and Witherby ; Witherby's *British Birds*, and others.

The task, otherwise so difficult, of noting the occurrence of rare stragglers, has been made much easier by the accurate records of rare visitants in the two last mentioned works.

I have adopted as far as possible the classification and nomenclature of Howard Saunders' Manual, making some slight alterations in the classification to suit the requirements of the plates.

I owe a debt of gratitude to the Hon. W. Rothschild for kindly lending me specimens from his collection, to complete the details in the plumage of various birds, which I could not otherwise have obtained, and my thanks are also due to Dr. Hartert for the trouble he has taken in selecting these.

My friend Mr. J. G. Millais has freely given me the run of his collection, and has looked over the letterpress besides providing me with various notes, and I am under much obligation to Mr. G. E. Lodge and many other friends, especially to Mr. Robert J. Howard, without whose advice and assistance the book could not have been produced in its present form.

A. T.

HASCOMBE,
GODALMING, *July* 1914.

PREFACE TO THE NEW EDITION

IN the new edition of this work now published are given two additional plates, in which I have taken the opportunity of showing some rare warblers that have recently visited the British Islands, apparently for the first time. Besides these, are included drawings of various subspecies and racial forms, such as the Willow-Tit, Irish Coal-Tit, Hebridean Song-Thrush, etc., these birds of late years having aroused a good deal of interest among ornithologists.

I have also been able to represent some rare species in winter plumage, from the specimens obtained in the Scottish Islands.

A. T.

HASCOMBE,
GODALMING, *September* 1917.

CONTENTS OF VOL. I.

Order PASSERES.

CONTENTS

Order PASSERES.

FAMILY **TURDIDÆ**.   SUBFAMILY *TURDINÆ*.

THE MISTLE-THRUSH.

Turdus viscivorus, Linnæus.

PLATE I.

The Mistle-Thrush, Mistletoe-Thrush, or Stormcock, the largest of our native species, may be found in meadows, woodlands, and gardens throughout the year. There it seeks its food of worms, snails, and larvæ, supplemented in autumn and winter by various berries, including among others those of the mistletoe.

The name Stormcock happily describes the character of this Thrush. Often long before the coming of spring, he may be seen, perched high up on some tall tree, pouring forth his wild and broken song, at one moment loud and clear, then again lost in the rush of the wind among the branches.

The sketch for the accompanying drawing was taken from a bird, singing in the teeth of a north-easterly gale, among the topmost boughs of an old ivy-covered oak.

Though usually a shy and wary bird, he is bold and fearless in defence of nest and young, fiercely attacking any prowling magpie or other intruder upon his domain, whom he pursues with loud and strident cries. The nest is made outwardly of grasses, to which moss and wool are sometimes added. Inside this structure a layer of mud is spread, with a final lining of finer grasses. Placed on a branch or in the fork of a tree, it contains four or five eggs, greenish- or reddish-white in ground colour, blotched with ruddy-brown and lilac.

The Mistle-Thrush inhabits the greater part of Europe, breeding as far north as Norway; in Asia ranging eastwards to Lake Baikal, while in winter it is found in India, Persia, and North Africa.

It may easily be distinguished from the Song-Thrush by its larger size, bolder carriage, greyer colouring, and by having the axillaries white, instead of buffish-yellow.

THE SONG-THRUSH.

Turdus musicus, Linnæus.

PLATE I.

Though subject to a partial migration during the autumn months, the Song-Thrush is resident and common in most parts of the British Islands. Numbers of this species, however, bred in Northern Europe, visit our shores in autumn, travelling mostly by night; while many of our home-bred birds leave us at the same time for the Continent, returning in spring. It breeds in Norway, thence southwards throughout a great part of Europe, and across Siberia as far as Lake Baikal.

The Song-Thrush breeds early in the year, rearing more than one brood during the season, and builds its nest in almost any shrub, hedge, or furze-bush. The nest is skilfully constructed of dead grass-stalks, roots, &c., the cup-shaped interior being lined with rotten wood and dung, which becomes quite water-tight when dry. The beautiful greenish-blue eggs, spotted with black and dark brown, vary in number from four to six.

The food of the Song-Thrush consists of worms, insects, larvæ, and snails, varied with fruit and berries in their season.

Its presence is often made known in the garden by a tapping sound, as it batters a snail against some convenient stone, to which it will return again and again with fresh victims.

This Thrush is the Mavis of Scotland, while it is also known as Throstle in many places.

The song, composed of various loud clear notes, repeated several times in succession, is continued throughout the greater part of the year, and may often be heard late in the evening, until darkness sets in.

The female is slightly smaller and paler in colour than the male.

THE REDWING.

Turdus iliacus, Linnæus.

PLATE I.

The Redwing, a winter visitor to our shores from Scandinavia and Iceland, usually arrives about the middle of October, travelling in flocks, when the plaintive call-note may often be heard at night as the birds pass overhead.

Early in April it returns to its breeding quarters in Northern Europe. According to information supplied to Mr. Hewitson by Wooley, as quoted in the 4th Edition of Yarrell (p. 269) by Professor Newton, it " makes its nest near the ground, in an open part of the wood, generally in the outskirts, on a stump, a log, or the roots of a fallen tree, sometimes amongst a cluster of young stems of the birch, usually quite exposed, so as almost to seem as if placed so purposely, the walls often supported only by their foundation. The first or coarse part of their nest is made for the most part of dried bents, sometimes with fine twigs and moss ; this is lined with a layer of dirt, and then is added a thick bed of fine grass of the previous year, compactly woven together, which completes the structure."

The eggs, usually six in number, are very like those of the Blackbird, but smaller. The ground colour is pale green, closely marked with reddish-brown. While with us the Redwings remain in flocks, and being more dependent on a diet of worms and grubs, than on berries, are among the first to suffer from a severe spell of frost and snow. The Redwing haunts the open fields and meadows during the day, roosting by night among evergreen shrubs and trees. The full clear song is only heard in its summer haunts, but Mr. J. G. Millais has kindly given me the following note of its song in this country: " Before leaving us in the middle of April, male Redwings assemble in parties of ten to fifty and indulge in a chorus of song so subdued that it is not heard unless the observer is close at hand."

The Redwing is rather smaller than the Song-Thrush, and may be readily distinguished from it, by the conspicuous light streak along the side of the head above the eye, and by the chestnut-red patch on the flanks, this colour being repeated on the underwing coverts and axillaries.

The female is a little duller in colour than the male.

THE FIELDFARE.

Turdus pilaris, Linnæus.

PLATE I.

Arriving about the same time as the Redwing, the Fieldfare is another of our winter visitors from Scandinavia, and leaves us in April or the beginning of May. It breeds in companies, the nest being placed in the fork of a birch or other tree, sometimes only a few feet from the ground. The birds are very noisy when their nests are approached, and utter harsh cries. The eggs, four to six in number, resemble the Blackbird's, being bluish-green, marked and blotched with reddish-brown. The song is described by Seebohm (*British Birds*, p. **232**) as "a wild desultory warble."

The Fieldfare is a shy and wary bird, the flocks in open weather frequenting wide meadows and grass lands, while feeding on worms, insects, and grubs. In times of frost or snow they come into the hedgerows, outskirts of copses, and even gardens, subsisting then on berries. Though more hardy than the Redwing, they soon feel the stress of weather, and numbers often perish.

The female resembles the male in colour.

Pl. 1.

Mistle-Thrush

Black-Throated Thrush
♂ & ♀.

Song-Thrush

Fieldfare

Redwing

THE BLACK-THROATED THRUSH.

Turdus atrigularis, Temminck.

PLATE I.

This rare straggler from Western Siberia has been taken thrice in England, the first having been shot near Lewes, Sussex, in December 1868, the second in Kent, January 1909, and the last in the same county, March 1911. In Scotland one was obtained near Perth in February 1879.

Mr. H. L. Popham, who took the first authentic eggs of this species in Siberia, says (*Ibis*, 1898, p. 494): "Although several pairs were nesting in the same locality, they were not by any means in colonies, like the Fieldfares. I obtained my first specimen at Yeniseisk, but did not meet with this Thrush again till we came to Inbatskaya, where I took five nests, each containing six eggs, which vary considerably. Two clutches have the markings of the Mistle-Thrush, but the ground colour is of a deeper blue; other clutches are very much of the type of the Blackbird, and in one of these latter a single egg has the markings of the Mistle-Thrush type. The nests, composed of dry grass with a lining of mud and an inner lining of broad dry grass, were all placed in small fir-trees close to the stem (except one, which was on the top of a stump) at heights varying between 3 feet and 6 feet." He also states, "When singing, the male whistles a few notes at a time, somewhat like a Song-Thrush with considerable variation, but does not repeat the same phrase two or three times."

THE DUSKY THRUSH.

Turdus dubius, Bechstein (1795).

PLATE 2.

An example of the Dusky Thrush was shot near Gunthorpe, Nottinghamshire, on 13th October 1905, this being the only occurrence of the species in the British Islands.

In summer it inhabits Siberia, moving southwards in autumn, to winter in China and North-western India.

Mr. Dresser, in his *Manual of Palæarctic Birds*, pp. 13-14, writes: "This species frequents woodlands, usually pine, larch, and spruce groves, and differs little from its allies in its general habits."

The nest, he says, "resembles that of the Fieldfare, is strongly built and lined with fine grass and dry larch needles."

The four or five, rarely six, eggs are also the same as those of the Fieldfare.

The female resembles the male, but is duller and paler in colour.

WHITE'S THRUSH.

Turdus varius, Pallas.

PLATE 2.

The first recorded example of White's Thrush in the British Islands was shot at Heron Court, near Christchurch, Hampshire, in January 1828; since that time nineteen others have been obtained at different times, fifteen of these in England, one in Scotland, and three in Ireland. They were nearly all procured in winter.

Named after White of Selborne, this bird is a native of Eastern Siberia, Northern China, and Japan, migrating in winter to Southern China and sometimes as far as the Philippines.

According to Mr. Dresser (*Manual of Palæarctic Birds*, p. 17), "fully authenticated eggs have not yet been obtained, though eggs said to be those of this species, all differing from each other, have been sent from three sources."

This species is one of the "Ground" Thrushes, seeking its food, of various insects and grubs, amongst dead leaves in shady woods. It is larger than the Mistle-Thrush, and its size, beautiful golden colour, crescent-shaped bars of black, and tail of fourteen feathers instead of twelve, distinguish it from all our other Thrushes.

The axillaries are black and white.

The female resembles the male, but is hardly so bright in colour.

THE SIBERIAN THRUSH.

Turdus sibiricus, Pallas.

PLATE 2.

One of these rare Siberian Thrushes is said to have been killed in the winter of 1860-61, in the neighbourhood of Godalming, Surrey. Although the genuineness of this specimen has been doubted by some authorities, Lord Lilford says "the probability is strongly in favour of its having been a *bona fide* traveller, and not an 'escaped' bird."

This species inhabits Eastern Siberia, wintering in China, Burma, Sumatra, and Java.

Mr. H. L. Popham writes (*Ibis*, 1898, pp. 494–495): "The neighbourhood of Toorukhansk appears to be their headquarters. The eggs, which place the identity of my supposed eggs of 1895 beyond doubt, can readily be distinguished from those of other Thrushes nesting in the same locality by their pale greyish-blue ground colour; one clutch has the ground colour very pale blue-green, and is covered all over the surface of the shell with minute reddish spots. I have never observed this Thrush in the pine forests, but always in the willows fringing the shore and islands, on the topmost boughs of which the male sits and whistles a few rich notes without any variation, but darts down out of sight at the slightest alarm. It is rather later in nesting than the other Thrushes, and was not seen at Yeniseisk." He describes the nest as "a rather untidy structure of dry grass, built in the fork of a willow a few feet from the ground, not so bulky as a Fieldfare's, with a scanty wall of mud and an inner lining of coarse dry grass."

The food, which is similar to that of other Thrushes, is always obtained on the ground.

The general colour of the female is buff and olive-brown, shading into white on the lower parts. The throat, as well as the flanks, speckled and barred with brown.

THE BLACKBIRD.

Turdus merula, Linnæus.

PLATE 2.

This handsome species, with velvety-black plumage and "orange-tawny bill," is to be found in almost every garden and shrubbery throughout our islands. It is also widely distributed in Europe, Asia, and Africa. The nest, made of grasses, twigs, moss, and leaves, with a layer of mud, is lined with grass and placed in some bush or hedge. The eggs, varying in number from four to six, are bluish-green, freckled with reddish-brown.

The fine melodious notes of the Blackbird, begun early in the year, especially if the weather be mild, are continued through the greater part of the summer.

At times he is a good mimic, and will imitate the voices of other birds. I have heard one, which haunted a garden, finish off his own familiar song with some of the musical notes of the Australian Piping Crow, learned from some captive birds in an aviary near by.

The Blackbird is an early riser, and leaves the shelter of the hedgerows and bushes at the first streak of dawn, to seek the worms, grubs, and insects which are its principal food, although in late summer and autumn various fruits and berries are consumed.

THE RING-OUZEL.

Turdus torquatus, Linnæus.

PLATE 2.

Unlike the Fieldfare and Redwing, the Ring-Ouzel is a summer visitor to our islands, arriving in April, about the time the others leave us. Passing through the cultivated country, it makes its home among the rocky hillsides and high moorlands. It breeds in many districts in England, Wales, and Ireland, while it is common in Scotland in places suited to its habits. Abroad the Ring-Ouzel breeds in Northern Europe, migrating to spend the winter in the countries by the Mediterranean.

The nest, which is very like the Blackbird's, is placed under a bank or over-hanging rock, and contains four, or occasionally five, eggs, bluish-green in ground colour, blotched and speckled with reddish-brown.

The food consists of worms, grubs, and insects, varied at times with fruit and berries, especially those of the rowan-tree.

The Ring-Ouzel has a wild and sweet song, harmonising well with his surroundings, as he delivers it from some crag or stone on the mountainside. The female is duller in colour than the male, and has a less conspicuous gorget. A race of the Ring-Ouzel, the *Turdus alpestris* of C. L. Brehm, having the pale margins to the feathers on the underparts broader than those in our bird, and marked in the centre with white, has twice or thrice occurred in England. This form inhabits the mountains of Southern and Central Europe.

THE ROCK-THRUSH.

Monticolo saxatilis (Linnæus).

PLATE 2.

The first British example of the Rock-Thrush was obtained in Hertfordshire in May 1843, and two or three more have since been taken. It is a native of Southern and Central Europe, North-west Africa, and Asia Minor, ranging across Asia to Northern China, while it migrates southwards in winter.

The nest, built of dead grasses and roots, with a lining of finer grasses and rootlets, sometimes of hair and feathers, is placed in a hole or cranny in an old wall or under a fallen rock.

Seebohm writes (*British Birds*, p. 284): "The eggs of the Rock-Thrush are four or five in number, of the same beautiful bluish-green as those of the Song-Thrush, but slightly paler and rounder; indeed they are almost intermediate between a Song-Thrush's and a Starling's. The markings are confined to a very few faint light-brown specks, usually on the larger end; but the eggs are very often spotless."

The female is mottled brown, lighter on the underparts, which are whitish or buff, marked with broken crescent-shaped lines of brown.

Pl. 2

Siberian Thrush   White's Thrush   Dusky Thrush
Ring-Ouzel   Blackbird   Rock Thrush

THE WHEATEAR.

Saxicola Œnanthe (Linnæus).

PLATE 3.

The Wheatear, a summer visitor to the British Islands, usually arrives in March, migrating southwards in autumn to spend the winter in the tropical parts of Africa. Abroad during summer, it has a wide range over Europe, Iceland, Greenland, and across Siberia to China.

The nest, composed rather loosely of dead grasses, mixed sometimes with small roots and moss, and having a lining of hair and feathers, is placed in a hole in a wall, a crevice under a rock, or within a deserted rabbit-burrow. The eggs, varying in number from four to seven, are in colour light greenish-blue, occasionally marked with tiny purple specks.

Stony hillsides and high grassy uplands are its favourite haunts. In former days it was much sought after as a table delicacy, and vast numbers were trapped, by means of horse-hair nooses, by the shepherds of the South Downs.

A large race of this species, differing from ours also in its brighter colour, touches our shores on its way to breed in Greenland, and is known as the Greenland Wheatear.

THE ISABELLINE WHEATEAR.

Saxicola isabellina (Rüppell).

PLATE 3.

Only four examples of this Wheatear have been taken in the British Islands, the first shot at Allonby, in Cumberland, on 11th November 1887, a second at Rye Harbour, Sussex, 17th April 1911, a third at the same place on 28th March 1912, and the last on 10th May 1912, near St. Leonards-on-Sea.

This is an Eastern species, ranging in summer from South-eastern Russia across Asia to Northern China, wintering in Arabia and India, while it appears to be resident in Egypt, and southwards to Abyssinia, as well as in Palestine and Persia.

The nest is usually placed underground in the empty burrow of some small animal, and contains from four to six pale blue eggs.

The Isabelline Wheatear frequents barren sand-covered regions, also bush-covered slopes, and occasionally fir woods. It is said to have a powerful song, and its food consists of insects.

The female resembles the male, but is duller in colour. Although the Isabelline Wheatear is very like the female of our Common Wheatear, it may be distinguished by having a smaller patch of white at the base of the tail feathers.

THE BLACK-THROATED WHEATEAR.

Saxicola occidentalis, Salvadori.

PLATE 3.

This handsome species, the *Saxicola stapazina* of Vieillot, is a summer visitor to Southern Europe, moving southwards to warmer regions in winter. It was first known as a British bird on 8th May 1875, when a specimen was shot near Bury, Lancashire. A second example was obtained near Lydd, Kent, on 23rd May 1906, and a third, the first recorded in Scotland, on Fair Isle, Shetlands, September 25, 1907; while two more were shot near Winchelsea on 16th and 19th May 1912.

A female of either this species or the Black-eared Wheatear was also obtained on St. Kilda, September 21, 1911.

Dr. Hartert, who considers these two birds, viz. the Black-throated and Black-eared Wheatears, to be one and the same species, states (Witherby's *British Birds*, vol. iv. p. 131): "An unbiassed and careful study of a large series of skins, and last, but not least, my own personal observations in company with the Hon. W. Rothschild in Algeria, have confirmed Pastor Kleinschmidt's suspicion and the observations of Messrs. Schiebel and Reiser."

The nest, loose in texture, is made of dead grasses and bents, and placed in a hole or cranny among rocks or ruined masonry. The eggs, varying in number from four to five, are in colour pale green, speckled and marked with brown.

In its habits and food this species is like the Common Wheatear.

The female has the upper part of the back tawny-brown, with the rump white, as in the male, the tail also being similar. The throat is dull white, and the underparts buffish-white.

THE BLACK-EARED WHEATEAR.

Saxicola stapazina (Linnæus).

PLATE 3.

This bird, either closely related to or the same as the Black-throated Wheatear, does not differ from the other in its food, nest, or habits. It has been obtained four times in England, the first near Polegate, Sussex, May 28, 1902, the second shot near Hoo, Sussex, May 22, 1905; another near Pett, Sussex, September 9, 1905, and a fourth obtained at Winchelsea on May 2, 1907.

According to Mr. Dresser (*Manual of Palæarctic Birds*, p. 38), "the female has the dark portions of the plumage brownish-black, the crown, nape, and back brownish-grey," and the habitat of the species is given as "S. Europe, Asia Minor, Palestine, Persia, Morocco, Algeria, Egypt, and Arabia, migrating further south in winter."

THE DESERT WHEATEAR.

Saxicola deserti, Rüppell.

PLATE 3.

The Desert Wheatear has been obtained six times in the British Islands, the first near Alloa, Clackmannan, on November 26, 1880, the second on the Holderness coast, Yorkshire, October 17, 1885, the third near Arbroath, Forfar, December 28, 1887, a fourth on the Pentland Skerries, June 2, 1906, while another was shot in Norfolk, October 31, 1907, and the last at Scotney, Kent, on May 21, 1913. The home of this bird lies more to the south than that of the Black-throated and Black-eared Wheatears. It ranges from North Africa southwards and eastwards across the deserts to Abyssinia, and through Asia Minor, Arabia, and Persia as far as Afghanistan and India. It inhabits dry and sandy wastes, and builds its nest in holes and fissures among rocks or underground. The eggs are of a pale bluish-green colour, speckled with reddish-brown.

The female has no black on the throat, is duller and greyer than the male, has the black portions of the wings brown, and the rump tinged with sand-colour.

THE EASTERN PIED WHEATEAR.

Saxicola pleschanka (Lepech).

PLATE 3.

A female of this species was taken on the Isle of May on 19th October 1909. Mr. Dresser, in his *Manual of Palæarctic Birds*, p. 32, gives its habitat as "Cyprus, the Crimea and the lower valley of the Volga, east to Kashmir, south-eastern Siberia, Tibet, Mongolia, and northern China, wintering in N.W. India, Abyssinia, and Arabia, and occasionally in Gilgit."

It appears to be more inclined to perch on trees and bushes than the other Wheatears, and builds its nest in holes and crannies among rocks and stones. The eggs are a delicate blue in colour, sometimes, but not always, marked with small reddish spots.

Lord Lilford, in his list of the birds of Cyprus (*Ibis*, July 1889), says: "This is the characteristic Chat of Cyprus; so far as my observation goes it mostly frequents the neighbourhood of towns, and is especially common near Larnaca."

The female is dull brown on the upper parts.

THE BLACK WHEATEAR.

Saxicola leucura (Gmelin).

PLATE 3.

The Black Wheatear is resident in Portugal and Spain, and along the northern shores of the Mediterranean to Sicily, some birds wintering in North Africa—a pair of these birds were observed in the neighbourhood of Rye Harbour, on August 31, 1909, and were afterwards shot, the male ·on September 2, and the female on the 16th. On Fair Isle, Shetlands, a male was seen several times, but not obtained, between the 28th and 30th September 1912.

According to Colonel Irby (*The Ornithology of the Straits of Gibraltar*, 2nd ed., p. 41), "the Black Wheatear is a common and conspicuous bird at Gibraltar, and to be seen throughout the year.

"The nest is sometimes in clefts of rocks, so deep as to be inaccessible. Mr. Stark took a nest on the 25th of April, near Gibraltar, containing four pale blue eggs hard sat on, marked with a zone of light reddish-brown spots.

"The nest was very large, loosely built with grass and heather-roots, lined inside with finer grass, two or three feathers of the *Neophron*, and one bit of palmetto fibre.

"The name of *pedrero* is applied to this bird from their curious habit of placing small stones as a foundation to their nest, and frequently, as when open to view, making a sort of wall or screen of stones in front of the nest."

The Black Wheatear inhabits stony places. The female differs from the male in having the black parts brown, while the white is not so pure.

Pl. 3.

Pied Wheatear
Isabelline Wheatear
Black-throated & Black-eared Wheatear
Black Wheatear   Stonechat

Wheatear ♂♀♀
Desert-Wheatear
Eastern Stonechat

A. Thorburn 1913

THE STONECHAT.

Pratincola rubicola (Linnæus).

PLATE 3.

This little bird may be seen on most of our furze-clad commons, perched on the top of a prickly spray or on a stalk of dead bracken. In the British Islands it is a resident species, frequenting the more sheltered parts of the country in winter. On the Continent the Stonechat is found occasionally as far north as Southern Sweden, and ranges through Europe to the Mediterranean, some wintering in Africa and Asia Minor.

The nest, carefully hidden at the foot of dense furze-bushes or among other vegetation, is made of dead grasses and moss, with a lining of finer grass, hair, and feathers. It contains five or six pale greenish-blue eggs, marked at the larger end with spots of reddish-brown.

The Stonechat has a pleasing little song, sometimes uttered when on the wing, and its characteristic alarm note, resembling the sound produced by hitting one stone with another, may be often heard as the bird flits from bush to bush.

The Eastern form of Stonechat, of which a sketch is given on Plate 3, has once been taken near Cley, Norfolk, on September 2, 1904; whilst another was obtained on the Isle of May on October 10, 1913. It differs from our bird in having more white on the rump. It ranges from Eastern Europe across Asia to Japan, migrating southwards to winter in India.

THE WHINCHAT.

Pratincola rubetra (Linnæus).

PLATE 4.

The Whinchat, sometimes called "Utick" from its call-note, is one of our summer visitors, arriving in April and leaving us in October.

Although fairly common in many parts of the kingdom, and widely distributed, it is absent or local in others. The nest, placed on the ground and concealed among rough grass and herbage, is composed of dry grasses and moss, and lined with finer fibres and hair. The four to six eggs are greenish-blue, spotted with rusty-red dots.

It feeds on various insects, grubs, and wireworms. The Whinchat has a low sweet song, sometimes heard when the bird is fluttering in the air.

Macgillivray says: "When one approaches their nest, they evince great anxiety; but at first keep at some distance, perch on the top twigs of the bushes, and at short intervals emit a mellow plaintive note followed by several short notes resembling the ticking of a clock, or that produced by striking two pebbles together, and at the same time jerk out their tail and flap their wings."

In the female the colours are duller, the eye-stripe being yellowish, the upper breast having some small spots, and the primary coverts less white than in the male.

THE REDSTART.

Ruticilla phœnicurus (Linnæus).

PLATE 4.

The Redstart is a conspicuous bird, on account of his bright and strongly-contrasted colouring, and his curious habit of spreading and flirting the feathers of the tail, which is at the same time moved upwards and downwards. A summer migrant, it reaches the British Islands in April, returning south in autumn.

The Redstart can hardly be called a common bird, but is widely distributed, though local, in many parts of England and Scotland ; much rarer in Ireland.

Abroad this species ranges from northern Scandinavia southwards to the Mediterranean, and across Siberia as far as Lake Baikal, wintering in Africa and Persia.

The nest, which is loosely made of moss, dead grasses, and rootlets, lined with some hairs and feathers, is placed in a hole in a wall or tree, and contains six or seven eggs, resembling those of the Hedge-Sparrow, but of a paler blue. Occasionally they are marked with small reddish dots.

The Redstart frequents gardens and orchards, and is often found near ruins and old ivy-covered walls, or among the rocks and birch-trees by the side of a Highland loch.

Its food consists of insects and grubs, and the song, though short, is soft and pleasing.

The female lacks the bright colouring of the male, the upper parts generally being of a brownish-grey, and the chestnut tail of a duller tint.

THE BLACK REDSTART.

Ruticilla titys (Scopoli).

PLATE 4.

Much less common than the preceding species, the Black Redstart regularly visits the south coast of England in autumn while migrating, sometimes spending the winter there, although not, as far as is known, breeding in this country.

Abroad this species occasionally ranges as far north as Scandinavia, and is found southwards to the Mediterranean and North Africa, wintering still further southwards in Africa. Eastwards it reaches the Ural and Asia Minor.

In summer the Black Redstart is a common and familiar bird in the Swiss valleys, frequenting the neighbourhood of villages and cowsheds.

The nest is placed under the eaves of buildings, or in a hole in some wall or rock, and is composed of dead grasses, moss, and rootlets, and lined with hair and feathers.

The eggs, varying in number from four to six, are mostly pure white, though occasionally marked with brown spots.

According to Seebohm (*British Birds*, p. 294), "Its song is very simple, consisting only of three or four melodious notes. Like the Robin it is constantly in the habit of drooping its head and slightly lifting its wing, whilst the tail is suddenly jerked up and half expanded."

Like the Common Redstart, its food consists of flies and various other insects and larvæ.

THE ARCTIC BLUETHROAT.

Cyanecula suecica (Linnæus).

PLATE 4.

This form of the Bluethroat, with a chestnut spot, set in the azure gorget, breeds in northern Scandinavia, Russia, and Siberia, migrating in autumn to spend the winter in China, India, and Africa.

On passage many pass along our east coast, mostly in autumn, though sometimes in spring, and great numbers visit Heligoland at the same time.

During the breeding season the Arctic Bluethroat frequents swampy forest ground, and in its nesting habits and character is very like a Robin. The nest, built of dead grasses and roots, with a lining of rootlets and hair, is concealed in some cavity in the side of a hillock, and contains five or six eggs.

According to Séebohm (*British Birds*, p. 273), "They are greenish-blue, more or less distinctly marbled with pale reddish brown, and are very similar to the eggs of the Nightingale."

The food consists of various insects, grubs, and earth-worms, and sometimes of seeds.

The Arctic Bluethroat is a loud and sweet singer, and is said to approach the Nightingale in the richness of his song.

In colour the females resemble the males in the greyish-brown of the upper parts, but are usually greyish-white on the chin and lower breast, with a band of dusky-brown across the chest. In some old females, however, the blue and chestnut colour is more or less displayed.

THE WHITE-SPOTTED BLUETHROAT.

Cyanecula leucocyana, Brehm.

PLATE 4.

Ranging more to the west than the preceding species the White-spotted Blue-throat is found during summer in Central Europe, breeding in Holland and Germany, and, according to Mr. Dresser (*Manual of Palæarctic Birds*, p. 62), "wintering in Asia Minor, Palestine, and North Africa; Asia as far east as India."

Its habits, food, and song, as well as the nest and eggs, are the same as those of the Arctic Bluethroat; the females being also alike.

In this species the white spot on the throat is sometimes absent.

THE REDBREAST.

Erythacus rubecula (Linnæus).

PLATE 4.

This familiar and best known of all our birds, with its confiding manners and sweet song, hardly needs description. Although the Redbreast or Robin haunts our gardens and homesteads all the year round, and appears to be always with us, yet a migratory movement takes place in autumn, when many birds, moving southwards, cross the Channel. Abroad the Redbreast has a wide range over Europe and Asia.

The nest, made of moss and withered leaves, with a lining of hair and feathers, is placed in a hedgerow, bank, or within some cavity in a wall. The five to seven eggs are white, marked and speckled with red; occasionally without any markings.

As soon as the moult is completed, in early autumn, the Redbreast again begins his song, which is continued through the winter. During September, when the majority of birds are silent, this plaintive strain is very beautiful.

The food of the Redbreast consists of insects and worms, varied with fruit and berries.

Though sometimes rather duller, the female does not otherwise differ from the male in colour. The young in their first plumage are spotted with yellowish-brown, and show no orange on the breast.

25

Pl. 4

Redstart   Redbreast

Black Redstart   Whinchat   Nightingale

White-spotted Bluethroat   Arctic Bluethroat

Archibald Thorburn
1913

THE NIGHTINGALE.

Daulias luscinia (Linnæus).

PLATE 4.

The unrivalled song of the Nightingale, delivered throughout the greater part of the night, as well as during the day, has made the bird celebrated from the earliest times. The male birds, which arrive in this country a week or more before the females, reach us about the middle of April, and, apparently, return year after year to the same spot. The general distribution of the Nightingale in England seems to be roughly as follows. The eastern parts of Devonshire, Somerset, and the south of Glamorgan. In the valley of the Wye, through Hereford, Shropshire, Staffordshire, and Derbyshire, extending a few miles beyond York, in all of which districts it is scarce and local. Southwards in the midland, southern, and eastern parts of the country it becomes more plentiful, and is abundant in some districts. It has once occurred in Scotland, one example having been taken on the Isle of May on May 9, 1911.

Abroad the Nightingale is found over a great part of Europe, from Northern Germany to the Mediterranean countries, while it spends the winter in Africa.

The nest is placed on the ground, or just above it, and is constructed of dead leaves, mostly of the oak, and withered grass, with a lining of fine rootlets, grasses, and occasionally horse-hair. The eggs, four or five in number, are usually olive-brown, or sometimes bluish-green, marked with reddish-brown.

The Nightingale loves the thick undergrowth of tall hedges, coppices, and shrubberies, and is fond of thick cover in the neighbourhood of streams.

The food consists of worms and various insects, as well as fruit and berries.

It seems surprising how little Nightingales are affected by cold; late at night on May 18, 1913, I heard two birds in full song, although the thermometer stood at 38 degrees, and the wind was bitterly keen. In June the Nightingale ceases to sing.

The female does not differ from the male in colour.

A larger and greyer species, having a somewhat harsher song, and known as the Thrush Nightingale or "Sprösser," *Daulias philomela*, has once been obtained on Fair Isle, Shetlands, May 15, 1911. A sketch of this bird is given on Plate 5.

It is found in Northern and Eastern Europe.

26

Subfamily SYLVIINÆ.

THE WHITETHROAT.

Sylvia cinerea, Bechstein.

PLATE 5.

This summer migrant, the type of the Sylviidæ or Warblers, arrives about the same time as the Nightingale.

An active and restless little bird, it soon makes its presence known by its joyous song, among the trees and brambles of some coppice, or by the roadside hedges.

The notes are often uttered during flight, as the bird rises with a curious flapping action of the wings to a moderate height, and descends again to his perch.

Abroad the Whitethroat is found from Scandinavia southwards to the Mediterranean, also in Asia, Asia Minor, and Palestine, wintering in Africa and the Canaries.

The nest is lightly and neatly constructed of fine grass stalks, with a lining of finer bents and horse-hair. The eggs, varying from four to six in number, are greenish-white, speckled with greyish-green and purplish-grey.

The food consists mainly of insects and grubs, though sometimes fruit and berries are eaten.

The female is duller in colour, and has the head browner than in the male.

THE LESSER WHITETHROAT.

Sylvia curruca (Linnæus).

PLATE 5.

The Lesser Whitethroat may be distinguished from the preceding species by its slightly smaller size, dark ear-coverts, general greyer colour of those parts which are rufous in the other, and by having the feet and legs slaty-grey instead of brown.

Less abundant than the Greater Whitethroat, it confines itself more to the midland and southern parts of England, becoming rarer in the west and in Scotland.

On the Continent the breeding range of the Lesser Whitethroat extends from Norway to the Mediterranean, and eastwards to the Ural. It winters in Africa.

The nest is placed in some thick cover, and is made of dry bents and grasses, with a lining of hair. The four or five eggs are greenish-white, spotted and blotched with brown.

The song of this bird is superior to that of the Common Whitethroat, and its habits are more shy and retiring.

The food of both species is the same.

The colour of the female is rather duller than that of the male.

THE ORPHEAN WARBLER.

Sylvia orphea, Temminck.

PLATE 5.

Four examples of this southern Warbler have been recorded in England.

Abroad it is found in Central and Southern Europe and North Africa, wintering still further south on the latter continent.

Lord Lilford, in his book on British Birds, describes it as being common in Spain, especially in the neighbourhood of Madrid and Aranjuez. He says: "The nest is very much more substantially built than that of the other Warblers of this family; the eggs much resemble those of the Lesser Whitethroat. The song of this bird, though more powerful than that of our Blackcap, cannot, in my opinion, be compared with it for melody or sweetness, in fact, I have always been puzzled to know why the name of Orpheus should have been bestowed on this species."

The female is duller in colour than the male, the head being greyish-brown instead of black.

THE SARDINIAN WARBLER.

Sylvia melanocephala (Gmelin).

PLATE 5.

Only one example of the Sardinian Warbler has been obtained in Great Britain, a male having been killed near Hastings on June 3, 1907.

According to the authors of *A Hand-list of British Birds*, p. 71, this species " Breeds in south Europe, Asia Minor, and north-west Africa, and winters partly in same countries, partly in Sahara, Palestine, and Nubia."

The Sardinian Warbler resembles the Blackcap in its habits.

Colonel Irby, who was well acquainted with this bird, writes in *The Ornithology of the Straits of Gibraltar* (2nd ed., p. 54) : " The earliest egg laid was on the 12th of March." Speaking of the nest, he goes on to say : " This was built in a small rose-bush, and was spoiled by a gale of wind, which blew all the eggs out of it, being the only one I ever saw in what could be called an open bush. All the others were placed in thick bushes, generally box, about two to four feet from the ground, and were formed of grass with a few bits of cotton-thread, lined with hair ; but they also nest at some height on boughs of trees. The eggs vary in number from three to five. The male assists in incubation.

" This bird is, like the Blackcap and Garden-Warbler, very fond of figs and grapes and all kinds of fruit."

The female is duller and browner in colour than the male.

THE BLACKCAP.

Sylvia atricapilla (Linnæus).

PLATE 5.

The Blackcap reaches this country early in April, and usually leaves in September, though it has been known to winter here. Abroad it is widely spread over Europe during summer, from Scandinavia to the Mediterranean, being also found in North Africa. It spends the winter in Central Africa.

This bird is unobtrusive in its habits, and builds its nest of dead grasses and bents, with a lining of horse-hair, in some shady bush.

It feeds on insects, fruit, and berries.

The Blackcap's beautiful song has been truly described by White of Selborne as "a full, sweet, deep, loud, and wild pipe; yet that strain is of short continuance and his motions are desultory; but when that bird sits calmly and engages in song in earnest, he pours forth very sweet, but inward melody, and expresses great variety of soft and gentle modulations, superior perhaps to those of any of our Warblers, the Nightingale excepted."

This passage has been often quoted, but it stands unrivalled as the best description of the Blackcap's song.

Unlike its congeners, the female Blackcap is larger than the male.

THE GARDEN-WARBLER.

Sylvia hortensis, Bechstein.

PLATE 5.

Arriving after the Blackcap, the Garden-Warbler is seldom noticed before the first week in May.

In England it is widely distributed, though local, becoming much scarcer in the south-west and in Wales.

In Scotland it has not been known to breed north of Perthshire, south of which county it nests in different localities, more frequently in the Lothians and Clyde districts.

It is rarer in Ireland.

On the continent of Europe it is widely distributed, and winters in Africa.

The nest is usually placed in the shade of thick brambles, briars, or bushes, and is composed of stalks of grass, sometimes with the addition of moss, and lined with fine roots and hair.

The four or five eggs are dull white, blotched with different shades of brown and spots of ash colour.

The food consists of insects, fruit, and berries.

This species is more often heard than seen, owing to its shy and skulking ways, and unobtrusive colouring.

In Surrey I have not noticed that it is more partial to gardens than other places, in fact it seems tȯ prefer the cover of tall hedges and copses.

The song, though resembling the Blackcap's, lacks its richness and tone.

The female is very like the male in colour, but slightly paler.

Pl. 5.

Whitethroat
Blackcap
♂ & ♀   Barred Warbler
Thrush-Nightingale

Lesser Whitethroat
Orphean Warbler
Sardinian Warbler   2/3
Garden-Warbler

THE BARRED WARBLER.

Sylvia nisoria (Bechstein).

PLATE 5.

At one time only known as a rare straggler to the British Islands, this species has during the last few years been met with in considerable numbers, mostly in autumn.

It breeds in Central and South-eastern Europe, wintering in Central Africa.

The Barred Warbler seeks the shelter of thick coverts and thorn-brakes, where the nest is placed.

This is a more substantial structure than that of most of the Warblers. Seebohm, in his *British Birds* (vol. i. p. 388), describes it as "composed of dry grass-stalks and roots, with generally some small-leaved plants, cobwebs, thistle-down, or other woolly material mixed with it." The four or five eggs, laid towards the end of May, are buffy-white, marked with grey.

Its food consists mostly of insects and fruit.

The song, Seebohm says, "resembles that of the Whitethroat, some of its notes being quite as harsh as those of that bird; but the finest parts are almost as rich as the warble of the Blackcap."

The female resembles the male in colour.

SUBALPINE WARBLER.

Sylvia subalpina, Bonelli.

PLATE 6.

Only two specimens of this delicately tinted little bird have been obtained in the British Islands, the first on the island of St. Kilda in June 1894, and another, an adult male, on Fair Isle, Shetland, on May 6, 1908. It is a South European species, common in some of the Mediterranean islands, and inhabiting also Spain, Portugal, Italy, and south-eastern France. It winters in Africa.

Howard Saunders, in his *Manual of British Birds* (2nd ed., p. 54), says: "The nest, of dry grass with a finer lining, is placed in a low bush"; and he describes the four to five eggs as varying "from greenish-white with brown spots, to reddish-white with violet-brown spots and streaks."

The food consists of insects.

Colonel Irby says, in *The Ornithology of the Straits of Gibraltar* (2nd ed., p. 53): "I saw eight or ten among the flowers and trees on the Alameda de Apodaca at Cadiz; they were exceedingly tame, and I watched them for a long time hopping about in and out among the flowers like a common Wren."

In colour the female is brownish above, and tawny-white on the throat and breast.

THE DARTFORD WARBLER.

Sylvia undata (Boddaert).

PLATE 6.

The Dartford Warbler is easily distinguished from the Subalpine Warbler by the tail being longer in proportion to the wing, by its much darker colour, and the absence of the white streak under the eye.

It was first noticed as a British bird near Dartford in 1773. Since then it has been found in many other districts, mostly in the southern and south-western counties. Unlike the other birds of this family, the Dartford Warbler lives throughout the year among the tall furze-bushes and heather on our commons and heaths, although sometimes in winter resorting to the turnip fields.

Abroad it is found in many parts of Southern Europe, also in North Africa.

The nest is placed in thick furze, sometimes in tall heather amongst furze, and is lightly built of grass-stalks with some furze shoots and wool. It contains four or five eggs of a greenish- or buffish-white, with brown spots.

The food consists of insects and wild fruits.

The Dartford Warbler has not much of a song, and the alarm notes of a pair I had under observation lately, reminded me of the Whitethroat's. In habits it is a quick and restless little bird, often spreading and flirting its long tail as it perches on the topmost sprays of the furze-bushes. On the least alarm it hides immediately.

The female is slightly smaller and duller in colour than her mate.

THE YELLOW-BROWED WARBLER.

Phylloscopus superciliosus (J. F. Gmelin).

PLATE 6.

The first British example of the Yellow-browed Warbler was obtained by the late John Hancock, in Northumberland, a few miles north of the mouth of the Tyne, in September 1838. Since that date a considerable number have been recorded, along our eastern coasts at different times, and especially on the Isle of May and Fair Isle, nearly all during the autumn migration. Numbers have also been taken on Heligoland at the same time of the year (Gätke). Its summer home is in Siberia, and it winters in India and China. Seebohm found it near the Yenesey, and describing the nest in his *British Birds* (vol. i. p. 449), says : " It was built in a slight tuft of grass, moss, and bilberries, semi-domed, exactly like the nest of our Willow Warblers. It was composed of dry grass and moss, and lined with reindeer-hair." The six or seven eggs are white, spotted at the larger end with reddish-brown.

Mr. H. L. Popham, writing in *The Ibis* (1898, p. 496), says : " It is quite the commonest of the small forest birds. It arrived at Yeniseisk on June 1, and subsequently (till the limit of trees was reached) was daily heard and seen working its way up the willows and firs in search of food. It is a lively and tame little bird, but the song becomes rather wearisome."

The Yellow-browed Warbler is insectivorous.

It may be distinguished from the other Warblers by the distinct pale yellow eye-streak, extending from the base of the bill to the nape, and by the two bars of a like colour across the wing ; there is also an inconspicuous stripe of dull brownish-green along the top of the head.

In the female the colours are similar to those of the male.

PALLAS'S WILLOW-WARBLER.

Phylloscopus proregulus (Pallas).

PLATE 6.

One example of this rare Warbler was recorded by the late T. Southwell (*Zoologist*, 1896) as having been shot at Cley-next-the-Sea on October 31, 1896.

Pallas's Willow-Warbler spends the summer in east Siberia, where it breeds, migrating for the winter to southern China and India.

One specimen has been obtained and another seen on Heligoland.

According to Mr. Dresser (*Manual of Palæarctic Birds*, p. 105): "Its nest is placed on the branch of a tree near the stem, is oven-shaped, constructed of grass-bents and moss and lined with feathers and horse or cattle hair, and its eggs which are deposited in May or June are white dotted and spotted with violet, ash-grey, and red, the spots being frequently collected round the larger end."

It has a loud and melodious song, and frequents wooded districts.

THE GREENISH WILLOW-WARBLER.

Phylloscopus viridanus, Blyth.

PLATE 6.

Mr. G. H. Caton Haigh shot the only British specimen of this Warbler which has been obtained, at North Cotes, on the Lincolnshire coast, on September 5, 1896. Unknown in the western part of Europe, it is found during summer in Russia, Siberia, and Turkestan, migrating for the winter to India.

The eggs of this bird are unknown.

It resembles our Willow-Wren, but differs in having only one whitish bar across the wing.

THE DUSKY WARBLER.

Phylloscopus fuscatus (Blyth).

An example of the Dusky Warbler (recorded in the *Scottish Naturalist*, 1913, pp. 271–3, by Mr. W. Eagle Clarke) was obtained on Auskerry (Orkneys) early in October 1913.

This rare wanderer, apparently never before taken in Europe, inhabits Siberia during the summer months, passing southwards in autumn to spend the winter in southern China and India.

The nest, hidden among herbage on the ground, or close to it in a bush, is domed and has the entrance at the side, the structure being composed of dead grasses and moss, with a lining of feathers. The eggs are white, without markings.

As the only example of this species was recorded after the Warbler plates had been reproduced, a sketch of the bird is given with the drawing of Tengmalm's Owl on Plate 27, Vol. II.

THE CHIFFCHAFF.

Phylloscopus rufus (Bechstein).

PLATE 6.

This is the earliest of all our summer Warblers, sometimes reaching our shores in the beginning of March, though usually about the end of that month. Common in the southern and western parts of England, it becomes rarer or more local in Norfolk, Lancashire, and part of Yorkshire, its numbers again increasing in the north of England, but diminishing in Scotland. It is widely spread over Europe, wintering on both sides of the Mediterranean.

In habits it seems more partial to the upper branches of tall trees than its near relation, the Willow-Wren, and may often be heard in such situations delivering its double notes of *chiff, chaff*, which compose its song, and from which it has derived its name. Often the bird will add a number of low chirping notes after the others. The latest date on which I have heard its song was the 2nd of October.

It often enters gardens in search of the caterpillars and insects on which it feeds.

Hidden among herbage, the domed nest, with the entrance at the side, is usually placed just above the ground, and is composed of dry grass and moss, with a lining of feathers. The five or six eggs are white, with dark purplish-red spots.

In appearance the Chiffchaff is very like the Willow-Wren, but differs in being rather smaller, slightly browner in colour, and the legs are of a darker brown. The wing also is more rounded in form, the second primary being about the same length as the seventh, while in the Willow-Wren the second is intermediate in length between the fifth and sixth.

There is a slightly larger and paler form, known as the Northern Chiffchaff, *P. abietina* (Nilsson), which has once occurred in the Isle of Wight, and also the Siberian Chiffchaff, *P. tristis*, Blyth, several of which have been obtained on migration in Scotland.

The last-mentioned form is distinguished from our bird by the browner colour of the upper parts, and by the absence of any yellow beneath, except on the under tail coverts and axillaries.

The sexes are alike in plumage.

Pl. 6.

Subalpine Warbler.

Dartford Warbler.   Willow-Wren.

Wood-Wren.

Yellow-browed Warbler.

Pallas's Willow-Warbler.

Greenish Willow-Warbler.

Chiffchaff. $\frac{2}{3}$

THE WILLOW-WREN.

Phylloscopus trochilus (Linnæus).

PLATE 6.

The Willow-Wren, often called Willow-Warbler, arrives just after the Chiffchaff, about the beginning of April. It is much more abundant than either the Chiffchaff or the Wood-Wren, being common in most parts of the country, haunting woodlands, gardens, and other like situations. It is widely spread over Europe, from the North Cape to the Mediterranean, ranging eastwards into Siberia and wintering in Southern Europe and Africa.

The nest, concealed by herbage and made of grass and moss, with a lining of finer grasses, horse-hair, and feathers, is placed on the ground, and, like those of the Chiffchaff and Wood-Wren, is domed. The five to eight eggs are white, with light red to purplish-red spots.

The food, similar to the Chiffchaff's, is composed mostly of insects, in autumn varied with fruit and berries.

On its arrival it is partial to birch woods and young plantations of larch, where its joyous and most pleasing notes may be constantly heard.

Mr. J. Burroughs has happily described these: "The song of the Willow-Warbler has a dying fall; no other bird-song is so touching in this respect. It mounts up round and full, then runs down the scale, and expires upon the air in a gentle murmur." It is delivered with short intervals, the bird flitting about and picking up its insect food between the snatches.

The sexes are alike in plumage, but the young are much more brightly coloured.

In autumn many of these birds may be seen about our gardens, even in large towns.

Two specimens of a Willow-Wren, known as Eversmann's Warbler (*Phylloscopus borealis* [Blasius]) have been taken in Scotland. In this species the bill is rather thick and heavy, and the colour duller than in our Willow-Wren. Its summer home is in Northern Europe and Siberia, and the bird winters in Southern Asia.

THE WOOD-WREN.

Phylloscopus sibilatrix (Bechstein).

PLATE 6.

The Wood-Wren is the largest and the brightest coloured of the three closely related species, and arrives in its summer quarters later than the others, usually towards the end of April.

Though local it has a wide range throughout the country, and is not uncommon in well-timbered districts.

As a nesting species it is rare in Ireland. The Wood-Wren is found in summer over the greater part of Europe, and winters in North Africa.

In shape and outer materials the domed nest is very like those of the Chiffchaff and Willow-Wren; is lined with hair and fine grass, but contains no feathers. The eggs, five to seven in number, are pure white, spotted with dark red.

This bird, besides being larger, is easily distinguished from the other two by its longer and more pointed wing, the greener tint of the upper parts, the bright lemon-yellow eyestreak, and the pure white of the lower breast.

The Wood-Wren lives, like its allies, on insects and berries. It is usually to be found in woods of beech or oak, when its characteristic song, beginning with the syllables *twee, twee, twee,* and ending with a succession of trilling notes, may often be heard; during the song the bird makes a quivering movement of the wings.

According to Mr. J. G. Millais, the female has far less yellow and is less rich in colour on the back than the male.

THE RUFOUS WARBLER.

Aëdon galactodes (Temminck).

PLATE 7.

This southern species has been taken five times in the British Islands : the first was shot on September 16, 1854, near Brighton ; the second at the Start in Devonshire ; the third at the Old Head of Kinsale in September 1876 ; the fourth near Slapton, Devonshire, on October 12, 1876 ; and the fifth, and last, in September 1913 at Brede, Sussex.

It is plentiful in the southern parts of Spain and Portugal, though rare in Italy, and is also met with in North Africa.

Lord Lilford found it not uncommon in Andalucia, haunting gardens and vineyards, and he states that the Rufous Warbler "seems to find some special attraction about the plants of prickly pear which is so abundant in Andalucia."

It winters in Africa.

The tamarisk tree furnishes the favourite site for the rather large nest, lined with wool and other soft materials, prominently placed on some branch or in a fork. To the other materials comprising the nest, a piece of cast serpent's skin is usually added.

The eggs, varying in number from four to five, are in ground colour light grey, marked with brownish-ash and violet-grey.

The Rufous Warbler is insectivorous and has a rather low, sweet song. Canon Tristram, in *The Ibis* for 1882 (p. 409), describes its characteristic habit of "expanding, jerking, and fanning its tail, with its conspicuous white bar."

The female is slightly paler in colour than the male.

Two examples of the Eastern form of this Warbler are recorded as having been obtained in England.

RADDE'S BUSH-WARBLER.

Lusciniola schwarzi (Radde).

PLATE 7.

One example of this rare Warbler, from south-eastern Siberia, was shot by Mr. G. H. Caton Haigh on October 1, 1898, near North Cotes, Lincolnshire.

According to the late E. W. Oates (*Fauna of British India*, vol. i. pp. 399-400), this species is migratory, visiting the southern half of Burma, Pegu, and Tenasserim ; also south China.

He found this Warbler, on the two occasions he met with it, in bushes, and describes it as feeding "a good deal on the ground, its strong tarsus being suited to this mode of life."

The nest and eggs of this Warbler are unknown.

Its brief but rather loud song is wanting in quality.

THE ICTERINE WARBLER.

Hypolais icterina (Vieillot).

PLATE 7.

The first example of the Icterine Warbler was shot at Eythorne, near Dover, on June 15, 1848.

Since that date about twenty others have been recorded in Great Britain.

In summer this species is found over the greater part of Europe, and it winters in Africa.

The well-built, cup-shaped nest is placed in a tree or bush, and is composed of grasses, wool, moss, &c., with a lining of hair.

According to Seebohm (*British Birds*, vol. i. p. 383): "The eggs are four or five in number, very rarely six. They are brownish pink in ground-colour, evenly spotted and more rarely streaked with very dark purplish brown, which occasionally approaches black."

Describing the song he says: "It has great power, wonderful variety, and considerable compass, but is singularly deficient in melody."

This bird feeds on insects, fruit, and berries.

It is closely related to the Melodious Warbler, but is slightly larger and rather brighter in colour, whilst the wing is longer in proportion to the tail. The bastard primary is also smaller.

In colour the female resembles the male.

THE MELODIOUS WARBLER.

Hypolais polyglotta (Vieillot).

PLATE 7.

The Melodious Warbler has thrice been obtained in England, viz. at Burwash, Sussex, April 30, 1897; Ninfield, Sussex, May 10, 1900; and Looe, Cornwall, May 12, 1905.

This species has a less northern and more western range than the preceding, being found, principally during the breeding season, in Portugal, Spain, western and southern France, and Italy. It winters in Africa.

Colonel Irby (*The Ornithology of the Straits of Gibraltar*, p. 65) describes it as "exceedingly plentiful near Gibraltar. . . . The birds frequent trees and bushes, especially willows and sallows; and the nest, neatly built and cup-shaped, in a great measure composed of sallow-cotton and thistle-down, is placed in bushes and usually contains four pinkish-tinted eggs, marked with blackish spots."

The song, according to H. Saunders (*Manual of British Birds*, 2nd ed., p. 78), is far finer, but less loud than that of the Icterine Warbler.

THE REED-WARBLER.

Acrocephalus streperus (Vieillot).

PLATE 7.

This species is a regular summer visitor, arriving in England towards the end of April. It is locally common in many parts, where the surroundings suit its habits, and is usually to be found among reed-beds or where willows fringe river margins. It is very rare north of Yorkshire, while only two authentic occurrences of the bird have been noted in Scotland on migration (Fair Isle, autumns of 1906 and 1909), and one in Ireland, October 1908 (Rockabill Light).

This species is found practically over the whole of Europe, except the extreme north; also in South-western Asia. It winters in Africa.

The deep cup-shaped nest of the Reed-Warbler is beautifully constructed of fine grasses and the flowering tops of reeds, wool, moss, &c.

Stevenson, in his *Birds of Norfolk* (vol. i. p. 116), says: "The ordinary number of reeds selected is three, round which the materials are firmly woven, so as to include them all in the structure, whilst the nest is placed, with instinctive judgment, neither low enough to be affected by the rising of the water, nor yet high enough to be influenced too powerfully by the wind. Occasionally a nest may be found on four reeds; and I once found one on five, and another on two; but these cases are rare." The four or five eggs are a pale greenish-white, marked with greenish-brown and grey.

The bird is of an active and restless disposition, and its song, consisting of various notes rapidly delivered, is not altogether unmusical. It is continued till late in the evening, while in calm, still weather it is often heard during the night.

It feeds on water insects of various kinds and their larvæ, sometimes during autumn taking fruit and berries.

The sexes are alike in plumage.

Pl. 7.

Melodious Warbler.   Icterine Warbler.
Rufous Warbler.   Radde's Bush-Warbler.
Marsh-Warbler.   Reed Warbler.

THE MARSH-WARBLER.

Acrocephalus palustris (Bechstein).

PLATE 7.

This bird so much resembles the preceding species that it was not until attention was drawn to the difference by Mr. Harting and other ornithologists, that it was given a place on the British list. There is now little doubt that the bird visits England annually. The Marsh-Warbler arrives late in May, and, so far as we know at present, is a scarce and local species, nesting in the midland, southern, and south-eastern counties. Abroad it reaches as far north as Denmark and eastwards to Persia, wintering in Africa.

Although closely resembling the Reed-Warbler in outward appearance, the Marsh-Warbler differs considerably in habits, and in its song which is much more striking and melodious. The colour of the upper parts is slightly more olive and less rufous than in those of the Reed-Warbler; while its legs and feet are fleshy-brown, whereas in the other they are slaty-brown.

The nest is usually placed in rank herbage or bushes, generally near water, but not over it, and is more or less lightly constructed of grass-stalks and lined with horse-hair. The eggs, varying in number from five to seven, are white, spotted and blotched with olive-brown.

Its food consists of insects, and also of berries.

The sexes do not differ in colour.

One specimen of Blyth's Reed-Warbler, *Acrocephalus dumetorum*, was shot on Fair Isle, Scotland, in September 1910.

This species differs from the Reed-Warbler in having a shorter second primary feather, and in the colour being more of an olive-brown.

THE GREAT REED-WARBLER.

Acrocephalus turdoides (Meyer).

PLATE 8.

This Warbler, although nesting yearly in the neighbourhood of Calais, and common in Belgium, Holland, and many other parts of Europe, south of the Baltic, is a rare visitor to England. The first example was shot by Mr. Thomas Robson, near Newcastle, in May 1847, and about nine others have since been recorded. In autumn the Great Reed-Warbler migrates to its winter quarters in Africa.

The favourite haunts of this bird are the beds of tall reeds, among the stems of which its deep cup-shaped nest, composed of reed-tops and grasses, is woven. The four to five eggs are pale blue with a greenish tinge, marked with ashy-grey and dark olive-brown.

Lord Lilford writes (*Birds of Northamptonshire and Neighbourhood*, vol. i. pp. 117-118): "The Reed-Thrush is not a bird likely to escape observation, from his incessant, chattering song, which resembles that of our common Reed-Warbler (*Acrocephalus streperus*), but is much more powerful, and is varied with occasional croaking notes like those of the edible frog, which reptile is often found in great abundance in the haunts of this species. I believe that these birds are never found far from the reed-beds which are their favourite resorts, and amongst which it is often very difficult to obtain more than a casual glimpse of the bird as it flits chattering from one perch to another. In the early morning they come to the tops of the reeds to sing, and no one who has not visited a well-frequented haunt of this species would believe what a confused din can be produced by a dozen or so of Reed-Thrushes, in concert with a sprinkling of the amphibious vocalists above mentioned."

The food of the Great Reed-Warbler consists of insects, sometimes in autumn varied with berries.

The sexes do not differ in colour.

THE SEDGE-WARBLER.

Acrocephalus phragmitis (Bechstein).

PLATE 8.

The Sedge-Warbler arrives in this country during the last half of April, usually a little earlier than the Reed-Warbler. It is by far the most numerous of the aquatic Warblers and breeds over the greater part of the mainland of England and Scotland, and also in the Orkneys. It is found in Barra, Outer Hebrides, although absent in the Shetland Islands. Abroad it has a wide range from Norway southwards to central Italy, and eastwards through Russia to Siberia, wintering in Africa.

The nest, composed of grasses and moss, with a lining of finer material, horsehair, and feathers, contains five or six eggs, in ground colour buff, spotted with brown or olive-buff, often streaked with dark, hair-like lines.

It feeds on insects, and according to Naumann, in autumn it also eats elderberries.

The Sedge-Warbler is an active restless bird, and has a harsh chiding song which may be heard day and night, and into which it introduces various imitations of the notes of other species. A characteristic of this bird is its habit of breaking out into song, if suddenly disturbed by a stone being thrown into the cover where it is concealed.

It haunts sedgy and marshy ground, but may be found in hedges and plantations far away from water.

The Sedge-Warbler is easily distinguished from the Reed- and Marsh-Warbler by the very distinct yellowish-white streak above the eye, and by the dark brown feathers forming longitudinal stripes on the crown of the head.

The female resembles, but is rather duller in colour than the male.

THE AQUATIC WARBLER.

Acrocephalus aquaticus (J. F. Gmelin).

PLATE 8.

The first authentic example of the Aquatic Warbler was discovered in the collection of the late Mr. Borrer, of Cowfold, Sussex, by Professor Newton. This bird had been shot on October 19, 1853, near Brighton, and had long been considered as only a brightly-coloured specimen of the Sedge-Warbler. Since that date, however, a number of other specimens have been recorded. Abroad it is found during the breeding season in the central and southern parts of Europe, and is said to winter in Africa.

According to Mr. Dresser (*Manual of Palæarctic Birds*, p. 123): " It breeds in May, and its nest, which resembles that of the Sedge-Warbler but is smaller, is constructed of plant stems and bents, and a few rootlets, worked together with insect webs and intermixed with plant cotton, and lined with horsehair."

The number of eggs varies from four to five. Seebohm describes them (*British Birds*, vol. i. p. 359) as : " Brownish white in ground-colour, thickly mottled and clouded over the entire surface with yellowish brown, and sometimes with one or two streaks of dark brown."

The song resembles that of the Sedge-Warbler, but is inferior.

Its food consists of insects.

This bird is easily distinguished from the other by the broad, buff streak running through the centre of the crown. It is shy and retiring in its habits, escaping observation by creeping among the reeds and tangled vegetation of marshy ground.

The female does not differ from the male in colour.

THE GRASSHOPPER-WARBLER.

Locustella nævia (Boddaert).

PLATE 8.

The Grasshopper-Warbler is a local but widely distributed species over England, Scotland, and Ireland, and has been recorded as nesting "as far north as Elgin" (*A Hand-list of British Birds*, p. 62). According to Howard Saunders (*Manual of British Birds*, 2nd ed., p. 89), "Northumberland and Durham are two of the counties in which it is abundant in some summers."

In Europe it ranges as far north as Norway and southwards to Spain, where it sometimes passes the winter. It is also found during this season in North Africa.

The cup-shaped nest is made of dead grass and moss, sometimes with the addition of withered leaves, and lined with finer grasses. It is carefully hidden among dense herbage, such as brambles, furze-bushes, &c., and when disturbed the bird glides off with a mouse-like action before taking wing. The four to seven eggs are of a delicate pinkish-tinted white, spotted with red-brown dots, and having paler underlying markings.

The earliest date on which I have heard the song of the Grasshopper-Warbler in Surrey was on 26th April, and it leaves us in September.

Once heard, its peculiar reeling notes can never be mistaken for those of any other bird, and although called the Grasshopper-Warbler, the noise produced is much louder and more continuous than that made by the insect.

Its food consists of insects and their larvæ.

In habits it is an extremely shy and skulking bird, and may best be observed in the very early. morning, when it often leaves the shelter of the thick undergrowth, where the nest is hidden, and sings on the upper twigs of the brambles and bushes.

The sexes do not differ in plumage.

PALLAS'S GRASSHOPPER-WARBLER.

Locustella certhiola (Pallas).

An example of this rare Warbler was found dead at the Rockabill Lighthouse, near Dublin, on September 28, 1908. Its summer haunts are in Asia, ranging from the river Yenesei and the Altai mountains eastward to the Pacific. Passing through China on migration, it winters in India, Burma, and the Malay Archipelago.

Pallas's Grasshopper-Warbler is decidedly larger than our bird, and in colour is blackish-brown and reddish-brown, streaked with dark on the upper parts; the underparts being white, tinted with buff on the breast, flanks, and under tail coverts. The tail feathers are tipped with white.

The sexes do not differ in colour.

THE LANCEOLATED WARBLER.

Locustella lanceolata (Temminck).

This is another rare straggler from Siberia, which winters in India, Burma, and the Andaman Islands. The first recorded specimen was shot by Mr. G. H. Caton Haigh, at North Cotes, Lincolnshire, on November 18, 1909, while two others have since been recorded.

Though smaller than the Grasshopper-Warbler, the general colour of the upper parts of this bird resembles that of the other, but the dark stripes are more distinct and the underparts are strongly streaked with dark.

The colours are alike in both sexes.

Pl. 8.

Sedge-Warbler

Cetti's Warbler

Grasshopper-Warbler

Great Reed-Warbler

Savi's Warbler

Aquatic Warbler

SAVI'S WARBLER.

Locustella luscinioides (Savi).

PLATE 8.

Although in former days this bird was without doubt a regular visitor during the summer months to the fens of the eastern counties of England, and bred there ; its nest being well known to the marsh men of those parts ; it has now vanished entirely from its old haunts, the last having been obtained in Norfolk in June 1856. Since that date only one other example has occurred in Great Britain, viz. on Fair Isle, Shetlands, in May 1908.

The earliest known example of Savi's Warbler was got in Norfolk early in the last century, and was erroneously considered by Temminck, to whom it was submitted, to be a variety of the Reed-Warbler, although later he seems to have had a confused impression that it was Cetti's Warbler. In 1824 the Italian naturalist Savi made it clear, from specimens obtained in Italy in 1821, that this was a distinct species, and it has, therefore, been named after him. In Europe this bird is found in the marshes of Holland, France, Spain, Italy, and portions of Russia.

In habits it is usually shy and retiring, but in the early morning the males utter their reeling grasshopper-like song from the top of some tall reed. Professor Newton says (Yarrell's *British Birds*, 4th ed., vol. i. p. 393): " It used to arrive in the Eastern Counties, according to Mr. John Brown's information, about the middle of April, and at its first coming was not shy ; but, when settled in its home and during the breeding-season, was not much seen. Its song was a long, smooth trill, pitched higher, but possessing more tone than that of the Grasshopper-Warbler, and, like that bird's, chiefly heard early in the morning or at nightfall."

Colonel Irby, describing nests found in Andalucia, says (*The Ornithology of the Straits of Gibraltar*, 2nd ed., p. 60): " The nests were all alike, loosely and clumsily built, solely constructed of dead sledge, often placed so close to the water that the base was wet ; they were always in the open marsh, none, that we saw, under bushes or in tall rushes or reeds, and the single nest that was not in sedges was in a tuft of the spiky rush so common in wet ground."

The eggs, varying in number from four to five, are whitish, speckled with small spots of brown.

54

CETTI'S WARBLER.

Cettia cettii (Marmora).

PLATE 8.

This species, distinguished from other European Warblers by having only ten tail feathers instead of 'twelve, has twice occurred in Sussex, May 1904 and September 1906, the only records in Great Britain. Its home is in Southern Europe and North Africa, ranging eastwards to Central Asia.

Colonel Irby, describing the breeding habits of Cetti's Warbler, says (*The Ornithology of the Straits of Gibraltar*, 2nd ed., p. 62): "These nests, extremely difficult to find, are built of bits of small sedges, intermingled with willow-cotton, and chiefly lined outside with strips of the stems of the *Epilobium*, inside with fine grass, a few hairs, and bits of cotton at the top. Those nests built in bushes are chiefly constructed with grass and cotton, and are entirely lined with hair."

The nest is cup-shaped, and generally contains five eggs, of a beautiful pink colour.

Its song, though short, is clear and melodious.

The sexes are alike in colour.

Subfamily REGULINÆ.

THE GOLDCREST.

Regulus cristatus, K. L. Koch.

PLATE 9.

The Goldcrest or Golden-crested Wren, the smallest of our British birds, is a common species in most parts of the country, wherever there are woods of larch and pine.

It is scarce or absent in the Outer Hebrides, Shetlands, and Orkneys. Abroad it has a wide range all over Europe and across Asia.

The beautiful spherical nest, generally suspended from the underside of a branch of the spruce, larch, yew, or cedar, is made of green moss and spiders' or other webs, with a lining of feathers and a few fine bents. I have one now in my garden, in a Deodar cedar, fixed to small bunches of its needles, which are fastened down by bands of caterpillar web to the sides of the nest, thus suspending it under the branch.

The eggs, varying in number from five to eight and occasionally ten, are brownish- or reddish-white in ground colour, with minute specks of reddish-brown.

The Goldcrest is a hardy little bird, and even in the coldest weather seems content with the insect food it obtains in the shelter of plantations and gardens, where it may often be seen and heard till darkness begins to set in on winter evenings.

Being exceedingly tame and confiding, it will approach fearlessly within a few feet of anyone who remains still.

The high-pitched call-note, which is uttered incessantly while feeding and creeping about the branches, has been aptly described by Macgillivray as being like that of the Shrew-mouse.

It begins to sing early in the year, and its melodious though tiny song is very pleasing.

The Goldcrest is active and restless, sociable in its habits, and ranges through the woods in company with Tree-Creepers and various Tits.

In autumn large flocks of immigrants often arrive on the east coast of England and Scotland.

The female resembles the male, although the colours are less brilliant, the crest being lemon-yellow. This is absent in the young bird.

56

THE FIRECREST.

Regulus ignicapillus (C. L. Brehm).

PLATE 9.

The Firecrest or Fire-crested Wren was first recorded as a British bird in 1832, an example having been killed by a cat in a garden near Cambridge. Although some doubt has since been expressed as to the genuineness of this occurrence, many Firecrests have since been recorded, mostly during the months from late autumn till spring; chiefly in the south and west of England and the east coast.

In Europe the Firecrest does not range so far north as the Goldcrest, but is found in the central and southern parts, and also in Asia Minor and Algeria.

The nest is composed of similar materials to those of the Goldcrest, and the eggs, varying from seven to ten in number, are redder in colour.

The Firecrest differs from the Goldcrest by having the black bands alongside the crest continued across the forehead, by a distinct dark streak passing through and beyond the eye, the ear coverts being slaty-grey, bordered by a dark line below. The crest is also of a deeper orange, and the general colour of a brighter olive-green.

The female is duller in colour than the male, and the young at first are without the crest, but show the black bands on the head.

Subfamily ACCENTORINÆ.

THE HEDGE-SPARROW.

Accentor modularis (Linnæus).

PLATE 9.

This familiar little bird, also called "Dunnock," is well known all over the British Islands, except in some of the Outer Hebrides and Shetlands. Although a resident throughout the year, a migratory movement has been observed in autumn and spring, and, according to Gätke, numbers visit Heligoland. It is also widely spread over Europe.

A glance at the head and bill will suffice to show that the Hedge-Sparrow has no relationship whatever to the House-Sparrow, and to emphasize this fact it has been named by some authors Hedge-Accentor.

Lord Lilford says (*Birds of Northamptonshire and Neighbourhood*, vol. i. p. 102) "in habits, food, and conformation this little bird has no affinity with what are properly called Sparrows, but I believe that in old times the term Sparrow was used merely to convey the idea of a small bird, as, for instance, Brook-Sparrow, Reed-Sparrow, and (a name I once heard) Moor-Sparrow, as applied respectively to the Reed-Bunting, Reed- and Sedge-Warblers, and Meadow-Pipit."

The nest, often begun in March, is placed in any low bush or hedge, very often in a pile of faggots or pea-sticks, and is made of twigs, roots, dead grasses, and green moss, with a lining of hair and wool. The beautiful turquoise-blue eggs vary in number from four to six.

The food consists of insects and larvæ, with seeds of grasses, &c., and in winter the birds fearlessly approach house doors in search of crumbs and refuse.

The song is short, but sprightly and pleasing, and is kept up through a great part of the year. Macgillivray mentions that it may sometimes be heard at night, a statement which I can confirm.

He also says: "In dry sunny weather in summer I have watched them basking on the road near a hedge. They would stand quite motionless, their legs much bent, their tail touching the ground, their wings spread a little, and their plumage all ruffled; and thus they remain a long time, seeming to enjoy the heat exceedingly, and suffering a person to approach very near them, before they fly off."

The sexes are alike in plumage.

THE ALPINE ACCENTOR.

Accentor collaris (Scopoli).

PLATE 9.

The first recorded examples in England of the Alpine Accentor were two birds seen in and about the gardens and buildings of King's College, Cambridge, in November 1822, one of which was shot.

A single bird had been previously killed in Essex in 1817, although not recorded until 1832.

There are altogether about twenty authentic records of this bird in Great Britain.

The Alpine Accentor is an inhabitant of the high mountain ranges of Central and Southern Europe, varying the altitude of its haunts according to the season, and it is always an exceedingly tame and confiding bird.

The nest is built in May among the rocks and stones, and according to Professor Newton (Yarrell's *British Birds*, 4th ed., vol. i. p. 299) "is formed of rootlets, grass, moss and wool, and lined with hair. The eggs are four to six in number, of a fine light greenish-blue."

Its food consists of seeds and insects.

Seebohm states in his *British Birds* (vol. i. p. 502): "The song is described as something like that of the Lark ; and the male is said frequently to ascend thirty or forty feet into the air, and then descend again, singing like a Tree-Pipit or a Snow-Bunting. At other times they will sit motionless for a long time basking in the sun on a rock, with head drawn in, plumage puffed out, and wings and tail depressed." This basking habit, which Macgillivray noticed in the Hedge-Sparrow, seems common to both species.

The only personal acquaintance I have had with the Alpine Accentor was many years ago in Switzerland, near the top of the Rigi, where I had the opportunity of watching an old bird, followed by a fully-fledged young one. They were easily approached, and were hopping and flitting about among the rocks and patches of half-melted snow, where gentians were flowering.

The sexes do not differ in colour.

59

Family CINCLIDÆ.

THE DIPPER.

Cinclus aquaticus, Bechstein.

PLATE 9.

The home of the Dipper or Water-Ouzel is by the banks of rapid rivers and brawling streams, and wherever they occur the Dipper may be looked for along their margins.

In England and Wales it is resident where the surroundings suit its habits, while in Scotland it is plentiful.

The nest of the Dipper is placed on some ledge of rock over water, in a hole in a wall by a mill dam, or sometimes behind a waterfall. It is outwardly constructed of moss, with an inner structure of grasses lined with dead leaves. The five or six eggs are pure white.

The food of the Dipper consists of water-beetles, caddis worms, fresh-water mollusca, and various insects, many of which are harmful to fish spawn. Macgillivray states: "As to the ova and fry of the salmon, there is no evidence whatever that the Dipper ever swallows them." Having closely studied from nature the habits of this bird, he says: "It plunges into the water, not dreading the force of the current, dives and makes its way beneath the surface, generally moving against the stream and often with surprising speed.

"It does not, however, immerse itself head foremost from on high like the Kingfisher, the Tern, or the Gannet, but either walks out into the water, or alights upon its surface, and then plunges like an Auk or a Guillemot, slightly opening its wings, and disappearing with an agility and a dexterity that indicate its proficiency in diving.

"I have seen it moving under water in situations where I could observe it with certainty, and I readily perceived that its actions were precisely similar to those of the Divers, Mergansers, and Cormorants, which I have often watched from an eminence as they pursued the shoals of sand-eels along the sandy shores of the Hebrides. It, in fact, flew, not merely using the wing from the carpal joint but stretching it considerably and employing its whole extent, just as if advancing in the air. . . .

"The assertion of its walking in the water, on the bottom, which some persons have ventured, is not made good by observation."

The male and female are alike in plumage.

The Black-bellied Dipper, *Cinclus melanogaster*, the Scandinavian form of our bird, has been several times recorded in England. In this, the chestnut on the breast is absent, or only slightly defined.

According to Dr. Hartert (Witherby's *British Birds*, vol. iv. p. 136), "Irish Dippers differ from English and Scotch ones."

60

Pl. 9

Goldcrest
Firecrest
Wren
Alpine Accentor.

Nuthatch
Hedge-Sparrow
Dipper

Archibald Thorburn
1915

Family SITTIDÆ.

THE NUTHATCH.

Sitta cæsia, Wolf.

PLATE 9.

This bird may be said to be common in localities suited to its habits, over central and southern England, becoming scarcer as one goes northwards, and is very rare in Scotland.

One individual seen in Ireland, in 1911, had probably been introduced.

When making its nest, this bird usually selects a hole in a tree, and cleverly fills in the entrance with wet clay, until the size suits its requirements. A rough nest is made within the cavity, composed of dead leaves, or scales from the bark of pine trees, which contains six or seven eggs, in colour creamy-white, blotched with reddish-brown.

According to Mr. J. G. Millais, "the call-note of the Nuthatch is a rather soft 'twit-twit,'" and another note is the loud "quoit-quoit," which has been accurately described by the Rev. C. A. Johns in his *British Birds in their Haunts* as being "precisely like the sound made by a pebble thrown so as to bound along ice." In spring, during the pairing season, the courting note is a long musical trill.

In autumn and winter its principal food consists of various nuts, acorns, haws, &c., and at other times of insects.

It has a characteristic habit of fixing a nut in some chink or crevice in a tree, and striking and hammering at the shell with its strong pointed bill, soon extracts the kernel. The noise made by this tapping will often betray its whereabouts.

The Nuthatch is an active, restless bird, creeping about the branches of tall trees, as much at ease when its head is pointing directly downwards as in any other position.

The female is slightly duller in colour than the male.

Family TROGLODYTIDÆ.

THE WREN.

Troglodytes parvulus, K. L. Koch.

PLATE 9.

This well-known and attractive little bird is common all over Great Britain and Ireland, while island forms, differing somewhat in size and colour, are resident in St. Kilda and the Shetlands. Its range also extends more or less throughout Europe.

The Wren usually begins its nest in April, and selects various sites, such as hedge-banks, overhung with roots of trees, or among ivy on walls, in crevices in rocks, and in evergreens. The structure is domed, with a small entrance at the side, and is made of moss, leaves, dead grass, &c., with a lining of hair and feathers. Some observers have noticed that the bird chooses materials which harmonise with the surroundings of the nest and help to conceal it. I have seen one, however, constructed almost entirely of the fronds of dead bracken, and built in a yew hedge.

Several more or less completed nests are often found in the vicinity of the one where the young are reared; for what purpose has never been satisfactorily explained.

The eggs vary in number, the usual complement being from six to eight or even nine. In colour they are white, generally dotted with red spots. The young remain in the nest until they can fly well, when, if alarmed, they will leave it and scatter in all directions.

The food consists mostly of insects, although fruit and seeds are sometimes eaten.

It seems to be able to obtain a living even when snow is on the ground; at such times it will creep among the shelter afforded by shrubs and plants in gardens and hedgerows, seldom appearing to suffer.

The song of the Wren is loud and penetrating, and is continued through the greater part of the year, its cheering notes being often heard on bright winter mornings.

The female is like the male in colour, but rather duller.

Family PANURIDÆ.

THE BEARDED TITMOUSE.

Panurus biarmicus (Linnæus).

PLATE 10.

The Bearded Titmouse or Bearded Reedling, though apparently much like the Titmice in many of its habits and actions, has no real relationship to that family, and according to Professor Newton (Yarrell's *British Birds*, 4th ed., vol. i. p. 512) "must be regarded as the representative of a separate family to which he would apply the name *Panuridæ*."

Before the drainage of the fens, this bird was common in many of the reed-beds and marshes of England, but it is now confined as a resident almost, if not entirely, to Norfolk, where it is called by the fen-men the "Reed Pheasant."

It is also found in parts of Central and Southern Europe, where the surroundings suit its habits, and was at one time very plentiful in the reedy marshes of Holland. Eastwards it ranges through southern Russia and Asia Minor to Mongolia.

The nest, begun about the end of March or beginning of April, is built low down among sedge and herbage near the water, and is made of the blades of the sedge and reed plants, with a lining of the feathery reed tops. The eggs, varying in number from five to seven, are white, with broken streaks or speckles of reddish-brown.

The Bearded Titmouse breeds twice in the year, and when the nesting time is over the birds collect and rove about the reed-beds in parties; flitting from one feeding ground to another, uttering the while their musical, ringing notes. As soon as the food in one clump of reeds is exhausted, they move on to a fresh cluster, climbing up and down the stems with great agility and searching them closely for insects. They also eat small molluscs, whilst in winter the seeds of the reed are sought for.

These birds show great affection, a pair often sitting close together while preening each other's feathers.

Family PARIDÆ.

THE LONG-TAILED TITMOUSE.

Acredula caudata (Linnæus).

PLATE 10.

The Long-tailed Titmouse has been separated by naturalists from the rest of the family, as it differs in many particulars, and is easily distinguished from the true Tits by its extremely long graduated tail.

The Long-tailed Titmice inhabiting Northern and Central Europe have the head pure white, without any black; this race was obtained on one occasion in Northumberland, and is said to have occurred once in Kent.

The Long-tailed Titmouse, also called Bottle-Tit, is resident and common throughout the greater part of the British Islands, with the exception of some of the northern and treeless districts. It is found abundantly in larch and birch woods, and about tall hedgerows and plantations, often coming into gardens in woodland neighbourhoods.

The nest is usually placed in some thick furze-bush or tall thorn-hedge, or it may be built in a fork on the stem of a birch tree. It is oval in shape, with a small hole at the side near the top of the dome, and is most beautifully constructed of lichens, green moss, and cobwebs, woven and felted together, and thickly lined with many feathers. According to Macgillivray, as many as 2379 have been found in one nest. The eggs vary in number from six to eleven or even more. These are white, finely speckled with red.

The birds feed on insects and larvæ, and when the young have left the nest, the families keep together until the following spring. Parties of a dozen or more may be seen at any time during the autumn and winter, constantly uttering their soft chirping notes as they make their way through the woods. They twist and climb all over the thinner twigs and branches, intent on food, and although often scattered, never seem to lose touch or get out of hearing of each other. These parties are often accompanied by other species of Tits, and also by Goldcrests and Tree-Creepers.

The female resembles the male in colour, but has more black on the head.

THE GREAT TITMOUSE.

Parus major, Linnæus.

PLATE 10.

The Great Titmouse or Ox-eye is more or less common over the greater portion of our islands, with the exception of the northern and western parts of Scotland, where it is rare. It is found throughout Europe from as far north as Lapland to the Mediterranean, and also in North Africa and Asia.

The Great Titmouse is a strikingly handsome bird, active and often aggressive in its habits, and is fond of wooded and cultivated districts, gardens, and orchards.

In early spring, before the leaves have opened, its loud and resonant song may constantly be heard. This is quite distinct from that of any other British bird, and has been compared to the sound of a file in sharpening a saw. The bird is also a mimic, and imitates the alarm notes of other species.

The nest is placed in many different situations, often in a hole in the trunk of a tree, or in a wall; sometimes in a pump or greenhouse chimney, while it is one of the first birds to take possession of a nesting-box. I have seen it turn a Blue Titmouse out of one of these boxes and drive the owner away.

The nest is made of a quantity of green moss, in which is placed a warm lining of hair, wool, and feathers. It contains from six to eleven or twelve eggs, which are white, with reddish spots. The female sits very close, and will allow herself to be touched with the hand without leaving the nest.

The chief food of the Great Titmouse consists of insects, but the bird is more or less omnivorous. In autumn it is fond of nuts, especially beech mast, picking them off the trees and flying to some convenient perch to open them. It is said to attack and kill smaller birds, and is partial to meat of any kind.

The colours of the female resemble those of the male, but are less bright, and the black stripe running through the centre of the breast and underparts, which distinguishes the Great Titmouse from its congeners, is narrower and less extended.

THE COAL-TITMOUSE.

Parus ater, Linnæus.

PLATE 10.

This Titmouse is found in most parts of the British Islands, and wherever pine woods occur it may be said to be abundant.

The Coal-Titmouse, or closely related races of the same species, is also met with over a great part of Europe and Asia.

The form of this bird with olive-brown back (the *Parus britannicus* of Messrs. Sharpe and Dresser) is the more common, while the grey-backed Continental race has occurred in Norfolk, and this or intermediate forms are found commonly in Scotland.

At a meeting of the British Ornithologists' Club, in December 1910, Mr. W. R. Ogilvie-Grant exhibited and described a new species of Titmouse from Ireland (*Parus hibernicus*), two specimens of which he discovered among some birds forwarded to the Natural History Museum by Mr. Collingwood Ingram (*Bulletin, B.O.C.*, xxvii. p. 37). These differ principally from our Coal-Titmouse in having the light patches on the sides of the head and nape pale mustard-yellow.

It is, however, a matter of opinion as to whether this should be accepted as a new species or not.

The nest of the Coal-Titmouse, begun early in spring, is situated in a hole in a wall or tree, often underground in some disused burrow of mouse, rabbit, or mole, and is made of moss, wool, hair, and other materials. It contains from six to eleven eggs, which are white, dotted over with red.

The food consists mainly of insects, but it also eats seeds and nuts, and in winter it will come readily to bones and pieces of fat.

In spring it sings a pleasing little ditty, and, like the other Tits, is restless and ever on the move. Although mostly found in pine woods, it may often be seen among birches and alders, as well as in gardens and shrubberies.

The male is slightly brighter in colour than the female.

THE MARSH-TITMOUSE.

Parus palustris, Linnæus.

PLATE 10.

The Marsh-Titmouse, which, like the Coal-Titmouse, is subject to colour variations, though not by any means rare, is perhaps less frequently met with in England than most of its congeners.

In Scotland it is scarce and local, while in Ireland it has only rarely been recorded.

The Marsh-Titmouse inhabiting Scotland is apparently the race with a dull black crown to the head, known as the Willow-Tit, which form is also resident in England.

The nest is usually placed in a hole in the stump of an old willow or other tree, or sometimes underground in a disused mouse hole, and is composed of moss, willow-down, wool, and hair. It contains from five to eight eggs, which are white, spotted with red.

About the end of March 1914 a pair of Marsh-Titmice began to dig out a nesting hole in an old rotten post which had been used to support some netting in my garden. Near the top of this a shaft was carried downwards within the post, to the depth of several inches, with two small entrance holes about three inches apart, one above the other.

The numerous chips which were dug out during the operation were strewn about on the ground below, without any attempt at concealment. Unfortunately the birds abandoned the site before the excavation was completed.

Although frequenting willow trees near water, the Marsh-Titmouse is just as often found among woods and plantations in dry situations.

In spring this bird has some pleasing notes which may be described as a song, and its call-note is very distinct from that of the other Titmice. In actions and habits it very much resembles the rest of its family, clinging in various attitudes to the twigs and branches as it searches for insects.

The sexes are alike in plumage.

Pl. 10.

Archibald Thorburn

Marsh-Titmouse.   Long-tailed Titmouse.   Bearded Titmouse.
        Great Titmouse.   ♂ & ♀
Coal-Titmouse.   Crested Titmouse.   Blue Titmouse.

THE BLUE TITMOUSE.

Parus cæruleus, Linnæus.

PLATE 10.

This little favourite is resident and widely distributed throughout the country, becoming scarce or local in the Orkneys, Shetlands, and north-west of Scotland. Abroad it is spread over almost the whole of Europe, and it ranges eastwards as far as Persia.

It is the most common and best known member of the Titmouse family, and may be met with all the year round in gardens, orchards, and woodland country.

It nests in April, and usually chooses a hole in a tree or some cavity in a wall, though various other and often strange sites are selected in which to rear its young.

The nest is made of moss, wool, hair, and feathers, and contains from six to ten eggs—sometimes more—which are white, spotted with rusty-red.

The Blue Titmouse lives principally on insect food, and is of great service to the gardener in ridding the fruit trees of grubs and other pests. Expert and skilful in securing its prey, the larvæ hidden in buds and foliage have little chance of eluding its sharp eyesight.

In spring it produces, like the other Titmice, a little song, in addition to its usual alarm and call notes, and in autumn small parties may often be seen about the woods, mixed up with other Tits, Goldcrests, and Tree-Creepers.

The sexes are similar in colour, although the male is rather the brighter of the two.

THE CRESTED TITMOUSE.

Parus cristatus, Linnæus.

PLATE 10.

As a resident species the Crested Titmouse is confined to the natural pine forests which cover the valley of the Spey in Scotland, although it has occurred as a wanderer in other parts of that country. Several stray specimens have been also recorded in England, while it has a wide range over Europe.

Lord Lilford, in his work on British Birds, quoting a letter from Lieut.-Colonel Irby, says: "The Crested Titmouse is common in the Spey district, where there are old and decayed pine-trees, but is very local—found in one small valley and absent in the next. A hole about eight inches deep and enlarged at the bottom is excavated vertically in a rotten fir-stump or decayed alder, and the nest, which is very scant, consists of moss lined with hair or felt; the usual complement of eggs is four." The eggs are generally laid about the end of April or beginning of May, and are white, dotted with red.

It feeds on insects, larvæ, and berries. I have observed the bird in autumn on one or two occasions in its Scottish haunts; its actions and general bearing much resembled those of the Blue Titmouse, and it allowed a near approach.

The call-note is difficult to describe, but once heard, cannot be mistaken for that of any other Titmouse. According to Mr. J. G. Millais, it has a twittering note, like the call-note of the common Canary.

The sexes are alike in colour.

Family CERTHIIDÆ.

THE TREE-CREEPER.

Certhia familiaris, Linnæus.

PLATE 11.

The Tree-Creeper is not uncommon in districts suiting its tree-loving habits throughout the British Islands, although rare in the Shetlands and Orkneys, and unknown in the Outer Hebrides. Either this species, or closely related races, also inhabit Europe, Asia, Africa, and America.

It breeds early in the year, and the nest may be looked for behind a piece of bark which has become more or less detached from the trunk of a tree, in thatch, wood-stacks, or in crevices under the eaves of buildings. It is usually composed of twigs, grasses, and moss, and lined with feathers, wool, and pieces of bark.

The six to nine glossy white eggs are spotted with rusty-brown and purplish-red. This tiny bird, one of the smallest of our native species, is retiring and unobtrusive in its ways, and may be found in wooded localities, wherever there are good-sized trees. Diligently searching the trunks and branches for the spiders and insects on which it lives, it begins operations near the roots and works its way upwards, moving round and round the tree as it ascends. As soon as one has been thoroughly explored, it quickly flits to another and repeats the same movements. It always appears to be absorbed in its occupation, paying little heed to anyone who does not approach too near, and constantly utters a rather shrill and squeaking cry.

The long curved claws and stiff pointed feathers of the tail are a great help to the bird when climbing up the trees and creeping along the branches.

The female does not differ from the male in plumage.

THE WALL-CREEPER.

Tichodroma muraria (Linnæus).

PLATE 11.

On October 30, 1792, Robert Marsham, of Stratton-Strawless in Norfolk, wrote to Gilbert White of Selborne, describing a specimen of the Wall-Creeper which had been shot by his man, whilst flying about his house. This was the first authentic record in England of this bird, which has since been obtained four times, viz. one in Lancashire, May 8, 1872; another near Winchelsea, about 1886; one near Hastings, December 1905; and the last, recorded by Mr. H. W. Ford-Lindsay in Witherby's *British Birds* (vol. vi. p. 218), was obtained within the ruins of Camber Castle, Sussex, on November 1, 1912.

Abroad the Wall-Creeper is found among the mountain ranges of Central and Southern Europe, and in winter may sometimes be seen climbing about the walls of old buildings in southern France and Italy. It is also met with in Asia and in Northern Africa.

The nest, placed in rock crevices which are often inaccessible, is described by Seebohm (*British Birds*, vol. i. p. 520), from a specimen in his collection, as follows: " Its chief material is moss, evidently gathered from the rocks and stones, intermingled with a few grasses, and compactly felted together with hairs, wool, and a few feathers. The lining is almost exclusively composed of wool and hair, very thickly and densely felted together." The eggs are white, minutely spotted with reddish-brown, and vary in number from three to five.

Lord Lilford, in his book on British Birds, says: " My own acquaintance with the Wall-Creeper was first formed high up in the Italian Alps during the month of August; I found it in small family-parties, generally frequenting precipitous faces of rock; the birds examine every nook and crevice, not, as in the case of the Woodpeckers, by continuous climbing, but by a series of short hops in some degrees resembling the method of progression of the Nuthatch; the birds thus observed by me appeared to be perfectly fearless of man, probably from their small acquaintance with him, and permitted a very close observation of their habits; they seemed to find abundant food in the crannies and small fissures of the limestone upon which I could hardly bear my hand in the full blaze of noon; after carefully examining one of these localities the bird would flit with a very peculiar butterfly-like flight to the lower end of another crevice in the rock. I never saw one of them progress head downwards or sideways, and the only sound that I heard from them was a rapidly repeated single note somewhat resembling that of the Wryneck."

The female resembles the male, but in summer has less black on the throat.

71

Family MOTACILLIDÆ.

THE PIED WAGTAIL.
Motacilla lugubris, Temminck.

PLATE II.

The Pied Wagtail, although common and resident throughout the British Islands, is subject to a partial migration southwards in autumn. According to Lord Lilford, "its range appears to be virtually limited to our islands and the extreme west of the continent of Europe."

The nest, built of moss, grass-stalks, and roots, and lined with hair, is placed in a cavity under some bank or rock, in thatch, or perhaps more often in thick ivy against a wall. It is usually begun in April, and contains from four to six eggs, in colour white, speckled with grey.

The food of this bird consists mainly of insects, and it is a most expert flycatcher.

On June 7, 1913, I observed one which was feeding its young in a nest placed close to my window, cleverly seizing these insects, although its bill already held a plentiful supply. Sometimes only half a minute elapsed between the visits of the female to the nest, and she occasionally wetted the food in a drinking pan before taking it to the young.

The Pied Wagtail is met with in fields and gardens; riverside meadows are also favourite haunts, and in autumn many feed along the seashore.

It is a strikingly beautiful bird, the various tones of black, white, and grey being strongly contrasted.

In spring it has a pleasing though short song.

This Wagtail may be distinguished in summer plumage from the so-called White Wagtail—the next species to be described—by having the back black instead of grey. In winter the black mantle of the former changes to grey, when both species are much alike.

The female has the back grey, marked with dark feathers.

72

THE WHITE WAGTAIL.

Motacilla alba, Linnæus.

PLATE 11.

This species is a fairly common spring visitor to our shores, passing southwards again in autumn, and is found over the greater part of Europe, where it is the common form of Pied Wagtail. Apparently, from want of observation, it was unknown as a British bird until Mr. Bond found it nesting at Kingsbury Reservoir, near London, in May 1841.

The situations selected for the nest are like those chosen by the Pied Wagtail, and the eggs are very much the same.

In habits it is not to be distinguished from the other, and their notes are also alike.

The female has the colours duller, and less black on the head than her mate.

THE GREY WAGTAIL.

Motacilla melanope, Pallas.

PLATE 11.

This very graceful bird, though smaller than the Pied Wagtail, has greater length of tail, and its elegant shape and beautifully contrasted colours make it one of the most attractive of the family.

It is resident in the British Islands, having a partial migration southwards in autumn. It is also not uncommon on high ground in Central and Southern Europe, its most northerly range on the continent being south Sweden.

During summer the usual haunts of the Grey Wagtail in our islands are the wild and hilly parts of the northern and western counties of England, as well as in Wales; also over the greater part of Scotland, where it may be found nesting by the sides of rocky burns, often far up among the hills. It is likewise common in Ireland.

The nest is placed in a hollow under an overhanging rock, or among grass and stones, and is made of grasses, moss, and wool, with a lining of hair. The five or six eggs are greyish-white, spotted with greyish-brown.

Macgillivray says: " Its flight is rapid and performed in large curves. When alighting it spreads out its tail, displaying the lateral white feathers, which then become very conspicuous, and when standing it vibrates its body continually, so that the tail, which it now and then spreads by a sudden jerk, is always in motion. . . . Its food consists of insects of various kinds, which it usually picks up from the ground, although it often performs a short aerial excursion in pursuit of them."

Its sharp and clear note somewhat resembles that of the Pied Wagtail.

The female is duller in colour than the male, and has little or no black on the throat, both sexes being much alike in winter.

Pl. 11.

Wall-Creeper (summer & winter)
Pied Wagtail.
White Wagtail
Grey-headed Yellow Wagtail.

Tree-Creeper
Blue-headed Wagtail
Grey Wagtail.
Yellow Wagtail.

THE BLUE-HEADED WAGTAIL.

Motacilla flava, Linnæus.

PLATE 11.

It was first made clear by Gould in 1832 that the Blue-headed Wagtail, which is the Continental form of our common Yellow Wagtail, was distinct, and he therefore separated the two birds.

It has a wide range over Europe, and is also found in Asia and America, wintering in Africa.

The Blue-headed Wagtail is now known to be a more or less regular spring visitor to our islands, a few remaining to nest, especially in parts of Sussex and Kent. It has also been known to breed in Durham and Wiltshire.

Mr. Dresser states (*Birds of Europe*, vol. iii.): "The present species (*Motacilla flava*) which may be considered the typical form, is during the breeding season found in Central Europe, while in the high north *Motacilla viridis* alone occurs."

The food of this Wagtail consists of flies and other insects, and in its habits it is very like the others, haunting marshy ground and grass lands, especially where there are cattle. It has a twittering song.

The nest, built in May, is made of roots, bents, dry grasses, and moss, with a lining of hair and some feathers. It is placed on the ground among long grass and other herbage, and contains from four to six eggs, which are buffish-white, clouded with yellowish-brown.

A variety of this Wagtail, the *Motacilla beema* Sykes, known as Sykes' Wagtail, has once occurred at Rottendean, Sussex, in April 1898. This has the cheeks and lower part of the ear-coverts white, and the grey on the top of the head and nape are paler than in the Blue-headed Wagtail.

The other forms of this Wagtail, which have visited the British Islands, and are all closely related, are as follows :

The Grey-headed Yellow Wagtail (*Motacilla viridis*, Gmelin), (figured on Plate 11), a northern race, found in Scandinavia and ranging across Russia to Siberia; it has the top of the head dark slaty-grey, almost black ear-coverts, and is without the eye-stripe. Several examples have been recorded.

The Black-headed Wagtail (*Motacilla melanocephala*, Lichtenstein), a southern form inhabiting South-eastern Europe and Asia in summer, and spending the winter in Africa and India.

This has the crown, sides of the head, and back of neck black, without any eye-stripe. The first example in England was shot in Sussex in 1903, and two or three others have since been recorded.

The Ashy-headed Wagtail, *Motacilla cinereicapilla*, Savi. This form has a slaty-grey crown, ear-coverts black, and is without the eye-stripe. It inhabits the Mediterranean countries, and winters in Africa. Two English examples have been recorded.

THE YELLOW WAGTAIL.

Motacilla raii (Bonaparte).

PLATE 11.

This species is a common summer visitor to many parts of the British Islands, reaching our shores in spring, leaving in the autumn, and wintering in Africa.

It is the representative in Western Europe of the Blue-headed Wagtail, previously described, only differing from it in the colour of the head, the crown being of a yellowish-green.

Its habits are precisely the same, usually seeking its food in fields among grazing cattle, where a plentiful supply of flies and other insects may be found.

The nest, placed on the ground, is built of dead grasses and fine roots, and lined with hair. The five or six eggs are greyish-white, mottled with yellowish-brown.

Describing its notes, Lord Lilford says (*Birds of Northamptonshire and Neighbourhood*): "The Yellow Wagtail has more of a song and altogether more musical notes than either the Pied or Grey species."

The female is browner on the back than the male, paler on the underparts, and has the eye-stripe more of a buff-colour.

THE TREE-PIPIT.

Anthus trivialis (Linnæus).

PLATE 12.

The family of Pipits, closely related to that of the Wagtails, contains a large number of species.

The first of these to be considered is the Tree-Pipit, a regular summer visitor, more or less common in many parts of the country, with the exception of western Cornwall and the northern parts of Scotland. It has not been recorded in Ireland. Over Europe and Asia it has a wide range, and winters in the southern parts of Europe, Africa, and India.

The Tree-Pipit usually arrives about the middle of April; the earliest date on which I have observed it, in Surrey, was the third of that month.

It likes a more or less open, though wooded country, with good-sized trees; and also frequents orchards.

The same or succeeding pairs of birds return year by year to certain spots, near which they nest, with extraordinary regularity.

The nest is cleverly concealed and placed on the ground. It is made of dead grasses, moss, and rootlets, and lined with fine grass and some hair. The eggs, numbering from four to six, vary much in colour. Howard Saunders says (*Manual of British Birds*, 2nd ed., p. 132), "some being greyish-white, mottled with deep brown; others rich reddish-brown; some almost lilac pink; and again a not uncommon variety resembles the egg of the Reed-Bunting."

The Tree-Pipit soon makes its presence known by its striking and characteristic song. Perched on the upper branch of a tree, it suddenly springs upwards and outwards in a slanting direction, remaining quite silent until about the turning point, when it begins its song. This is continued as the Tree-Pipit descends with open wings, outspread tail directed upwards, and feet hanging down below the body, until it regains its footing, close to the branch from which it started; or on another at some distance. As far as I have observed, this point is left undecided until after the bird has begun to sing. It is also often heard singing while perched upon a tree.

The actions of the Tree-Pipit are nimble and active, and it runs swiftly along the ground after insects, on which it feeds.

The sexes are much alike in colour.

THE MEADOW-PIPIT.

Anthus pratensis (Linnæus).

PLATE 12.

The Meadow-Pipit or Titlark is resident and well known all over the British Islands, being also widely distributed throughout the greater part of Europe and in many portions of Asia. Some winter in North Africa. It is a common bird on our pastures, wastes, and moorland country; in winter leaving the high ground and bleak hillsides for lower and more sheltered localities. Some pass out of this country in autumn, returning in spring.

The nest, usually placed in some hollow on a bank, or on flat ground, and concealed among grass and heather, is made of grasses, and lined with finer material of the same kind and hair. The five or six eggs vary a good deal in colour, but usually have a brownish- or greyish-white ground, dotted with purplish-grey or reddish-brown.

Though often seen on a wall or rock, the Meadow-Pipit seldom perches on trees, and seeks its food of insects, small worms, and snails, and also seeds on the ground.

It sings while descending after an upward flight, in the manner of the Tree-Pipit, although it sometimes utters a few *cheeping* notes during the ascent. The song is distinctly inferior to that of the Tree-Pipit, and may occasionally be heard while the bird is perched on a stone. Its ordinary call is a shrill and rather melancholy squeaking note, frequently uttered.

The Meadow-Pipit is slightly smaller than the other, and may be distinguished from it by its much longer and straighter hind claw.

The sexes are alike in colour.

THE RED-THROATED PIPIT.

Anthus cervinus (Pallas).

PLATE 12.

The first authentic occurrence of the Red-throated Pipit was one obtained on Unst, Shetlands, in 1854, and not identified until many years afterwards. Two other supposed examples, one captured near Brighton in March 1884, and the other shot at Rainham, Kent, in April 1880, are now considered to be only brightly-coloured specimens of the Meadow-Pipit (Witherby's *British Birds*, vol. ii. p. 278).

A number of undoubted examples, however, have since been noted.

In summer the Red-throated Pipit inhabits the far north of Europe and Asia, wintering in India, China, and North Africa.

Seebohm found it plentiful in Siberia, and describes the nest as being " placed in recesses on the sides of the tussocky ridges which intersect the bogs," and "entirely made of dry grass, the coarser pieces being used for the foundation and the finest reserved for the lining." According to Mr. Dresser (*Manual of Palæarctic Birds*, p. 214): " The eggs vary considerably, some having the ground colour greenish grey, others brown, some are rich reddish-brown, the colour of old mahogany, others dull brown, and others again greenish-grey, closely spotted with brown, and I have seen some with large brown scratches like those on the eggs of the Lapland Bunting."

The food is similar to the Meadow-Pipit's, but it has a finer song than that species.

In the female the reddish-chestnut colour is confined to the throat, and does not extend to the breast, as in the male.

THE TAWNY PIPIT.

Anthus campestris (Linnæus).

PLATE 12.

This species is an irregular autumnal migrant to England, some thirty or forty examples having been obtained, mostly in Sussex.

It is said to visit the north of France and Holland annually in summer, and is also found over the greater part of Europe, and ranges eastwards into Asia, wintering in India and North Africa.

It is a bird of the desert wastes and uncultivated country, and, according to Lord Lilford: " In comparison with the other species of the genus *Anthus*, this is a shy and retiring bird, chiefly remarkable for its loud single alarm-note."

He describes a nest he found in Spain as follows—" it was placed between two large clods of sandy earth, near a horse-track, was composed of dry root-fibres, lined with goat's hair, and contained four eggs of a dull creamy white profusely blotched and streaked with ash-grey markings."

The male and female are alike in colour.

RICHARD'S PIPIT.

Anthus richardi, Vieillot.

PLATE 12.

This Eastern species of Pipit breeds on the steppes and marshy lands of Central and Northern Asia, wintering in China and India. Although not breeding in Europe, it has a wide range there, and has occurred many times in England, seldom in Scotland, and only twice in Ireland.

According to Seebohm, it nests late in May or early in June, as its breeding-grounds are covered with snow until that time.

It builds its nest on the ground, and the five or six eggs are dull white, spotted and blotched with different shades of brown.

It feeds on worms and insects.

In habits Richard's Pipit is said to be very shy and wary, and difficult to approach within gunshot.

It is partial to well-watered country, being frequently found in wet meadows and grass-lands.

It is by far the largest of the Pipits visiting Great Britain, and has a very long hind claw.

The female does not differ from the male in plumage.

Pl. 12.

Rock Pipit.
Tawny Pipit.
Meadow-Pipit.

Richard's Pipit.

Tree-Pipit.
Red-throated Pipit.
Alpine Pipit.

$\frac{2}{3}$

THE ALPINE PIPIT.

Anthus spipoletta (Linnæus).

PLATE 12.

A few years ago the Alpine or Water-Pipit was considered an unusual visitor to England, but of late it has been frequently seen and obtained on migration, mostly in Sussex.

Its summer home is among the mountains of Central and Southern Europe, and across Asia, while in winter it visits Africa, India, and China.

When its high summer haunts are free from snow, the Alpine Pipit returns to them, and there on the ground, among rocks and stones, the nest is placed. It is made of dead grasses, moss, and small roots, and lined with hair or wool. The four or five eggs are greyish-white in ground colour, and blotched with olive-brown.

Seebohm compares its song to that of the Meadow-Pipit, but says it " is louder‧ though not so sweet."

The sexes do not differ in colour.

Referring to the name of Alpine Pipit, Lord Lilford, in his work on British Birds, says : " I have adopted the above designation for this species in preference to that of *Water*-Pipit, for the simple reason that all the European species of the genus *Anthus* frequent the sea-shores and alluvial flats in autumn and winter, and are, with very few exceptions, at all seasons fond of the neighbourhood of water, whilst the present bird, during the breeding-season, is seldom, if ever, to be met with, except among mountains of a considerable elevation."

An example of the American Water-Pipit (*Anthus ludovicianus*) occurred in St. Kilda in the autumn of 1910.

This species breeds in the Arctic portions of north-eastern Siberia and Northern America, and winters as far south as Central America.

It is rather larger than *A. spipoletta*, and more tawny on the underparts.

THE ROCK-PIPIT.

Anthus obscurus (Latham).

PLATE 12.

This bird is resident and common along all the rocky parts of our coasts, inhabiting the mainland as well as the islands, and during the autumn and winter months it also frequents the low-lying shores and mud-flats. It is found, in suitable localities, over the greater part of Europe.

The Scandinavian race of Rock-Pipit, visiting our shores on migration, has a vinous-chestnut tint on the breast, and the throat less spotted during the breeding season, but otherwise does not differ from the ordinary form.

The nest is placed close to the sea, among tufts of thrift, or under a stone, and is composed of dead grass—sometimes partly of seaweed—and often, but not always, lined with hair. The eggs vary in number from four to five, and varieties of colour occur. They are often of a greyish or greenish tint in ground colour, blotched with olive-brown.

The food consists of insects, larvæ, and tiny shellfish; the little black flies, so plentiful about decaying seaweed, forming a large part of its diet.

The song is delivered on the wing, the bird rising in the air and then descending, after the manner of the Meadow-Pipit.

The shrill call-note also resembles that bird's, and is frequently uttered as it flits about the rocks and seaweed with an unsteady wavering flight.

The sexes are alike in colour.

THE GREAT GREY SHRIKE.

Lanius excubitor, Linnæus.

PLATE 13.

The Great Grey Shrike is a not very uncommon autumn and winter visitor along the eastern parts of England and Scotland, occasionally occurring in spring, and very rarely during summer.

It is also found over a great part of Europe, ranging eastwards as far as western Siberia.

The large and bulky nest is made of twigs, dead grass, and moss, with a lining of wool, hair, and feathers, and is placed in a fork of a branch, at some distance from the ground. It contains five or six eggs, greenish-white in ground colour, and blotched with olive-brown and purplish-grey.

The Great Grey Shrike is in character bold and aggressive, and preys largely on small birds and mice, besides beetles, moths, and grasshoppers.

It has a habit, in common with the other members of the Shrike family, of fixing its victims on a sharp thorn or between two twigs, and, in consequence, has acquired the name of " Butcher-bird."

When on the look-out, it usually perches on some bare branch of a tree or tall hedge, ready to avoid danger or to pounce on any prey within reach.

According to Seebohm (*British Birds*, vol. i. p. 600): "The song is something like that of a Starling"; and it has also a rather harsh alarm-note.

There are two forms of the Great Grey Shrike, both visiting this country, viz. *Lanius excubitor*, the one drawn on the plate, having white bases to the quill feathers of the wing, which extending to the secondaries, make a double bar.

In the other form, known as *Lanius major*, the white is confined to the primary quills alone.

The female resembles the male, but has faint greyish-brown bars on the breast.

THE SOUTHERN GREY SHRIKE.

Lanius meridionalis, Temminck.

One example of this species was obtained in Sussex in January 1911.

It is resident in Spain, Portugal, and southern France, and resembles the bird just described, but has the white above the eye extended to the base of the bill, and the breast tinged with pink.

THE LESSER GREY SHRIKE.

Lanius minor, J. F. Gmelin.

PLATE 13.

Of much rarer occurrence than the Great Grey Shrike, the present species has been recorded sixteen times in England, and once on Fair Isle, Scotland.

The Lesser Grey Shrike is a summer visitor to many parts of Central and Southern Europe, with the exception of Spain, ranging eastwards into Asia, and wintering in South Africa.

The nest, built of twigs, roots, grasses, and flowering plants, with a lining of wool, hair, and feathers, is often placed in a fruit tree or poplar, and contains from five to seven eggs, which are a delicate bluish-green in ground colour, spotted and blotched with brown and grey.

The song is described by Seebohm (*British Birds*, vol. i. p. 604) as "a not unmusical chatter, something like the twitter of the Swallow or Starling, but louder and mixed with some harsher notes."

The bird is easily distinguished from the Great Grey Shrike by its smaller size, pale salmon-tinted breast and flanks, and by having the forehead black. In the female this part has less black, but otherwise the sexes are much alike.

THE RED-BACKED SHRIKE.

Lanius collurio, Linnæus.

PLATE 13.

The Red-backed Shrike is a regular summer visitor to England, arriving in May, being rather unevenly distributed over the central and southern counties, and is not uncommon in Wales. It is rare in Scotland, and has only thrice occurred in Ireland.

The nest, which is rather large, is composed of roots, stout grass-stalks, and moss, and lined with wool and hair. It may be sought for in some thick thorn-hedge or bush, and contains from four to six eggs; these vary in colour, being often greenish-grey, blotched with brown, or with the ground colour salmon-pink, with purplish and red markings.

The Red-backed Shrike feeds on various beetles, humble bees, grasshoppers, and other insects; often on mice and small birds, and, like the other Shrikes, frequently fixes its prey on a thorn, before tearing it to pieces.

It usually takes up its station on an exposed branch or twig in a tall hedge or bush, watching with sharp eyes any passing quarry and darting after it in pursuit. While perched it frequently flirts its tail from side to side, and upwards and downwards, at the same time spreading and closing the feathers.

When crossing a field from one high thorn fence to another, the Red-backed Shrike will fly in a straight course, not far from the ground, and on arriving at the opposite hedge, darts suddenly upwards to the topmost branches.

The alarm-note is harsh, but the song is not unpleasing.

THE WOODCHAT.

Lanius pomeranus, Sparrman.

PLATE 13.

Over forty examples of this Shrike have been recorded in the British Islands, most frequently in the south-eastern parts of England.

It is not uncommon in France and Germany, becoming abundant in Spain and other portions of Southern Europe, and winters in Africa.

The nest, constructed of grass and other herbage, is conspicuously placed on a branch or in a fork, usually not far from the ground, and contains about five eggs. These are very like those of the Red-backed Shrike, but the red variety is not often met with.

The Woodchat is by no means shy or wary, and its strongly-contrasted colours make it conspicuous, as it sits on some exposed branch in a tree.

Like the other Shrikes, it has a harsh call-note, but the song is low and pleasing.

The female is not so brightly-coloured as the male, the upper parts, which are black in the latter, being brown tinged with reddish.

Pl. 13.

Red-backed Shrike, ♂ & ♀.   Great Grey Shrike
Woodchat Shrike.   Masked Shrike   Lesser Grey Shrike

THE MASKED SHRIKE.

Lanius nubicus, Lichtenstein.

PLATE 13.

A specimen of the Masked Shrike was obtained in Kent in July 1905. This is a summer visitor to South-eastern Europe, Asia Minor, and south-western Persia, wintering in Africa, to the eastward of Tripoli, and in Arabia.

It builds a compact and neatly-made nest of roots and grasses, lined with finer materials, which contains four to seven eggs, in ground colour dull olive-green, spotted with brown.

The Masked Shrike is insectivorous, feeding mostly on beetles, and is shy in its habits, keeping to the thick cover of bushes.

It is said to have a pleasant song.

The female resembles the male, but has the dark parts browner in colour.

Family ORIOLIDÆ.

THE GOLDEN ORIOLE.

Oriolus galbula, Linnæus.

PLATE 14.

The Golden Oriole, one of the most beautiful of our birds, is a regular summer visitor to the south-western portions of England, occurring more sparingly in other parts.

A fair number usually reach the Scilly Islands during the month of May.

It is common in many parts of Europe, and winters in Africa.

The Golden Oriole has been known to breed several times in England, and would do so more frequently if left alone.

Lord Lilford describes the nest (*Birds of Northamptonshire and Neighbourhood*, vol. i. p. 86) as "very unlike that of any other European bird, being composed entirely of wool and long sedge grass, and placed in the horizontal fork of a branch, generally but not always, at a considerable height from the ground, and difficult of access, from being at or near the extremity of a long and slender bough." The four or five glossy white eggs are marked with reddish-purple spots.

The food consists of insects, grubs, and various fruits.

The Golden Oriole has a loud flute-like call, with a much harsher note at times, and haunts the open parts of shady woods and trees in gardens and shrubberies.

In the female, the upper parts are olive-green, becoming yellower near the tail, the throat and underparts whitish with dark streaks, and the wings of a dark brown ; the flanks and under tail coverts being yellow.

Family AMPELIDÆ.

THE WAXWING.

Ampelis garrulus, Linnæus.

PLATE 14.

The summer haunts of the Waxwing are the forests of northern Scandinavia, Russia, and Asia, whilst a more or less extended southward and westward movement takes place in winter.

It has long been known as a visitor to our islands, having been first mentioned by Sir Thomas Browne of Norwich, who, writing to his friend, Merrett on September 16, 1668, says: "Garrulus Bohemicus probably you haue a prettie handsome bird with the fine cinnaberin tipps of the wings some wch I haue seen heere haue the tayle tipt with yellowe wch is not in the discription" (*Notes and Letters on the Natural History of Norfolk*, with notes by Thomas Southwell, p. 68. Jarrold & Sons, 1902).

Nothing was known about the nest and eggs of the Waxwing until the year 1856, when John Wooley obtained them from his collectors in Russian Lapland.

The nest is placed on the branch of a fir or birch, and is principally made of the lichen called tree-hair and twigs; and the eggs, varying in number from five to seven, are described by Mr. Dresser (*Manual of Palæarctic Birds*, p. 250) as "pale blue with pale purplish shell-markings and black surface-spots, but occasionally the ground colour is warm-pinkish."

In summer the food of the Waxwing consists of insects, and in autumn and winter of hips and haws, the fruit of the berberry and other trees.

Seebohm compares the note of this bird to that of the Blue Tit.

The female resembles the male in colour.

Family MUSCICAPIDÆ.

THE SPOTTED FLYCATCHER.

Muscicapa grisola, Linnæus.

PLATE 14.

This is one of the later summer migrants, usually arriving about the middle of May. It is fairly common in most parts of the British Islands, and has a wide distribution throughout Europe, wintering in Africa.

The nest of the Spotted Flycatcher is usually placed in a creeper or fruit tree trained on a wall, or on the trunk of a large tree; but various and sometimes curious sites are selected.

It is composed of fibrous roots, moss, &c., and lined with wool and hair; and contains from four to six eggs. These are bluish-white or greenish in ground colour, marked with reddish-brown.

Its food consists of flies and other insects, although in autumn berries are sometimes eaten.

The Spotted Flycatcher has a little low-toned song, which is not often heard, but its rather sharp call-note is frequently uttered. This bird is fond of gardens, and parks where there are tall, old trees, and when feeding, takes up its station on a bough or post, from which it darts after any passing insect, the snap of its bill being often heard as the prey is secured.

The sexes are alike in colour.

THE BROWN FLYCATCHER.

Muscicapa latirostris, Raffles.

PLATE 14.

The Brown Flycatcher has only once been taken in England, an example having been shot near Lydd in Kent, May 21, 1909. This is also the first occurrence of the bird in Europe.

According to the late E. W. Oates (*Fauna of British India*, vol. ii. p. 35): "It occurs in Ceylon and the Andamans. On the Himalayas it is a summer visitor as far west as Chamba, and it is found in the other portions of the Empire chiefly in winter, but some birds appear to be resident in certain parts all the year round, for I have seen a specimen obtained in Ceylon in June.

"This Flycatcher has a wide range, being found from Japan and Eastern Siberia to the Philippines and Java."

The sexes do not differ in plumage.

THE PIED FLYCATCHER.

Muscicapa atricapilla, Linnæus.

PLATE 14.

The Pied Flycatcher is much less common than the Spotted Flycatcher, and is very local in its distribution. It seems to be more frequently met with in the Lake Districts of Westmorland and Cumberland, and in parts of Wales, where it breeds regularly every year.

It is rare in Scotland, whilst in Ireland only a few examples have been taken, mostly at the lighthouses, on migration.

It is widely spread over Europe during summer, and winters in Africa.

The Pied Flycatcher usually builds its nest, composed of grass and roots, with a lining of hair, in a hole in a tree or wall, and lays five or six very pale blue eggs. Sometimes these are spotted with tiny specks of reddish-brown.

Seebohm, describing this species in his book on *British Birds* (vol. i. pp. 329–330), says: " In many of its movements the Pied Flycatcher resembles its dingy congener.

" Far more of a restless species than a shy one, it may frequently be seen hovering, in butterfly-like flight, in the air. Sometimes it sits quietly on some decayed limb, ever and anon uttering its call-notes and incessantly jerking its tail and half opening its wings, as though anxious to sally into the air. Its food consists almost entirely of insects, especially flies and gnats, which it often takes from the leaves of the forest-trees whilst hovering daintily above them."

THE COLLARED FLYCATCHER.

Muscicapa collaris, Bechstein.

PLATE 14.

This is a near ally of the Pied Flycatcher, and, as may be seen on looking at the plate, differs from it in having a broad white collar right round the neck, and the patches of white on the forehead and wing primaries are larger.

Only two examples of this bird have been recorded in England, both having been shot at Winchelsea, one on the 12th, and the other on the 13th May 1911. It is a summer visitor to Central and Southern Europe and Asia Minor, spending the winter in Africa.

The females of the two species closely resemble each other.

Pl. 14

Waxwing.   Spotted Flycatcher.

Red-breasted Flycatcher.

Pied Flycatcher.

Collared Flycatcher. Golden Oriole.

Brown Flycatcher.

$\frac{2}{3}$

THE RED-BREASTED FLYCATCHER.

Muscicapa parva, Bechstein.

PLATE 14.

This little bird, which in colour much resembles a Robin, occasionally reaches our islands while migrating.

The first example obtained was shot near Falmouth in January 1863.

It is found during summer over a great part of Central and Southern Europe, ranging eastwards to Siberia, and wintering in Africa and India.

The nest, placed in a hole in a tree, is built of moss and lichen, and lined with grass and hair. It contains from five to seven eggs, in ground colour a pale bluish-green, speckled with reddish-brown.

It is said to be fond of shady woods where beech and fir abound, and in its habits is active and restless.

This Flycatcher has a pleasing song, and, like its relations, captures flies and other insects on the wing.

The female has the breast reddish-buff, and lacks the bluish-grey on the sides of the head, which contrasts so well with the reddish-orange on the breast of the male.

Family HIRUNDINIDÆ.

THE SWALLOW.

Hirundo rustica, Linnæus.

PLATE 15.

The Swallow arrives in our islands early in April, about the 10th of that month being the usual time; and takes its departure in September and October.

It is widely distributed over Europe, ranging eastwards as far as Manchuria, wintering in South Africa, India, China, and southward to the Malay peninsula.

In May the Swallow begins its nest, which is placed in various sites, often on the rafters of sheds and outbuildings, or in chimneys. The eggs vary in number from four to six, and are white, marked with brownish-red spots.

Gilbert White, who has given one of the best descriptions of the habits of this bird, says: "In general with us this *hirundo* breeds in chimneys; and loves to haunt those stacks where there is a constant fire, no doubt for the sake of warmth. Not that it can subsist in the immediate shaft where there is a fire; but prefers one adjoining to that of the kitchen and disregards the perpetual smoke of that funnel, as I have often observed with some degree of wonder.

"Five or six or more feet down the chimney does this little bird begin to form her nest about the middle of May, which consists, like that of the house-martin, of a crust or shell composed of dirt or mud mixed with short pieces of straw to render it tough and permanent; with this difference, that whereas the shell of the martin is nearly hemispheric, that of the swallow is open at the top, and like half a dish: this nest is lined with fine grasses and feathers, which are often collected as they float in the air."

The song consists of a succession of soft twittering notes.

The insect food on which it subsists is taken during flight, as the bird sweeps along, sometimes just above the ground.

The sexes are alike in colour.

THE RED-RUMPED SWALLOW.

Hirundo rufula, Temminck.

PLATE 15.

Two examples of this very handsome Swallow have been obtained in Great Britain, the first shot on Fair Isle, Shetlands, in June 1896, and recovered ten days later, and the second on Romney Marsh in May 1909.

It is found in the southern and south-eastern parts of Europe, in Asia Minor, and over a great portion of Asia, as well as in Africa.

Canon Tristram says (*Ibis*, 1867, p. 362): "The nest is a beautiful structure, composed of the same materials as that of the House-Martin, but is invariably attached to the flat surface of the underside of the roof of a cave or vault. It is of the shape of a retort, with a bulb of the size of a Thrush's nest, large and roomy, the neck or passage for entrance being sometimes a foot or more in length; the inside of the clay chamber is warmly lined with feathers."

The eggs, four or five in number, are pure white, without spots.

THE MARTIN.

Chelidon urbica (Linnæus).

PLATE 15.

The Martin, which haunts the eaves of our houses, very often in the midst of towns and villages, and hence often called the House-Martin, is easily distinguished from the Swallow by its conspicuous white rump, and arrives shortly after the other bird. It is found throughout the greater part of the British Islands, becoming less frequent and more local in the north and north-western portions, and in Ireland.

Abroad it has a wide range from Scandinavia to the Mediterranean, and ranges eastwards into Asia. It winters in Africa, south of Abyssinia.

A short time after their arrival the Martins either take possession of their old nests of the previous year, repairing them where necessary, or begin the work of building new ones. Great care and labour is bestowed on the foundations of the new nest, the birds first examining various sites, apparently testing them by fixing small pieces of mud to different parts of the walls of the house they have chosen on which to place their nest.

This is composed of mud, strengthened with grass-stalks or pieces of straw, with a lining of straws, feathers, and other soft material.

If provided with small pieces of cotton wool, thinned out and made very light so that they float away in the air, the Martins will readily take these on the wing, usually rising to the wool from below.

From their manner of seizing this material, it is probable that they take their prey in a similar way, as small gnats and flies would be more easily seen against the sky from beneath.

The eggs are pure white, and vary from four to five in number.

The Martin has a soft and very pleasing twittering song.

The sexes are alike in colour.

THE SAND-MARTIN.

Cotile riparia (Linnæus).

PLATE 15.

This little bird usually arrives before any of its congeners, often before the end of March, and is easily distinguished from them by its smaller size, duller colour, and uncertain wavering flight—"wheeling and gliding in untraceable mazes" as Macgillivray puts it. It is widely distributed over the British Islands and through the greater part of Europe, being also found in Asia. It winters in Africa, India, and in South America.

Sand-Martins nest in colonies, and selecting some steep bank or cutting, excavate holes, digging into the sand or earth with their tiny bills, which seem inadequate tools for such a purpose. On attaining a depth of about two feet, sometimes more, sometimes less, in a dug-out recess at the end of the shaft, the nest is placed. It is made of dried grasses, with a lining of feathers, and contains four or five pure white eggs.

Like the other members of its family, it lives on insects, and is fond of the neighbourhood of water. When the time approaches for their departure, great numbers collect together, roosting on trees by the river sides, and leave early in September.

The female does not differ from the male in colour.

Family FRINGILLIDÆ.   Subfamily FRINGILLINÆ.

THE GREENFINCH.

Ligurinus chloris (Linnæus).

PLATE 15.

This is a common and abundant species in almost every part of the British Islands, and is also widely distributed in Europe.

The nest, usually begun in April, is situated in a hedge or thick bush, and is composed of roots, twigs, green moss, and wool, with a lining of finer materials of the same kind, feathers, and hair. The five or six eggs are a delicate greenish-white in ground colour, spotted and marked with rusty-brown and purplish-grey.

The song of the Greenfinch is rather poor and feeble, but to some ears is not unpleasing; it is sometimes delivered while the bird is on the wing. It has also a curious prolonged call-note.

This is a useful bird in the garden, destroying a great number of caterpillars and harmful insects, and during the winter months it feeds on seeds and berries of various kinds.

Its favourite summer haunts are gardens and shrubberies, whilst in autumn and winter it collects in flocks about the fields and farm steadings.

In colour the female is much duller than the male.

THE HAWFINCH.

Coccothraustes vulgaris, Pallas.

PLATE 15.

The Hawfinch, at one time considered a rare bird in many parts of England, though local, has greatly increased in numbers of late years, and according to Howard Saunders (*Manual of British Birds*, 2nd ed., p. 171) "the nest has been found in every county in England, excepting Cornwall." It is also resident, but rarer, in Scotland, and only known as a wanderer to Ireland.

The rather level nest, usually placed in some fruit tree, is made of twigs and lichen, with a lining of rootlets and some hair. The four to six eggs are in ground colour greenish-blue or light olive-green, with spots and streaks of dark brown.

The Hawfinch is a shy and retiring bird, and likes well-timbered and sheltered ground. It will often enter gardens, especially at the time of year when green peas are ready, of which it is extremely fond. It also feeds on the hard seeds of various trees, such as beechmast and haws, eating only the kernels of these.

The song is feeble, but it has a very distinct call-note.

In winter the bill of the Hawfinch is of a pinkish horn colour, changing in the breeding season to a steely-blue, with dark tip.

Most authorities give the colour of the eye as greyish-white, but this appears to be incorrect, as far as the living bird is concerned.

My friend, Mr. Robert J. Howard, of Shearbank, Blackburn, first drew attention to the fact, and I therefore give below his notes on the subject, which were published in the second edition of Mr. F. S. Mitchell's *Birds of Lancashire*, edited by Howard Saunders (p. 66): "The irides, in a live bird, are not greyish-white but vinaceous. On August 7th, 1884, my male Merlin dashed from his bath at the Hawfinch which Billington brought from Redscar. I picked the bird from the cage-floor, as it was dying, and paid particular attention to the colour of the irides; the bright madder-brown got gradually lighter, until at last—before the bird was cold—it had faded away, and the colour could only be described as a greyish-white. I had often held the bird in my hand, so that I could closely examine the eyes, and found the colour arranged in concentric circles, those near the pupils being brightest; the intensity of colour varied when I teased the bird."

In an adult living bird I myself examined, the irides were a pale rather chocolate-coloured brown, which at times changed in intensity; and it would be interesting to know if at any period during life these are greyish-white.

The female is duller in colour than the male, and has less black on the throat.

Pl. 15.

ed. rumped Swallow.　　　　Sand Martin.

Swallow.　　　　　　Siskin.　　　　　　　Martin.

Goldfinch.　　　　　Hawfinch.　　　　Greenfinch.

THE GOLDFINCH.

Carduelis elegans, Stephens.

PLATE 15.

In former days, when less land was under culture, and in consequence thistles and other seed-bearing weeds were more numerous, the Goldfinch was a common bird in most parts of Great Britain.

Owing to the higher cultivation of the land, and also to the ravages of bird-catchers, its numbers rapidly decreased, until it was practically extinct in many places.

However, of late years it seems to be again on the increase in most parts of the country, except in Ireland.

It is found throughout the greater portion of Europe, as well as in Asia and Africa.

The nest of the Goldfinch is a beautiful structure of moss, lichens, rootlets, and grass, woven together and lined with down, feathers, and hairs ; and is placed in a fruit tree or in some shady oak, chestnut, or plane. The four or five eggs are greyish- or bluish-white, marked with brownish-purple.

During summer the Goldfinch feeds principally on insects and larvæ, and in the autumn and winter months on seeds of various kinds, such as those of the knap-weed, thistle, dandelion, and other weeds.

The teasel is a great attraction to the Goldfinch, and it makes a charming picture to see a flock of these dainty little birds, busily engaged in extracting the seeds while clinging to the prickly tops ; then suddenly flitting with twittering notes to another plant. In autumn a good many birds cross the Channel and winter abroad.

The song, begun early in spring, is sweet and pleasing.

The female is much like the male, but is duller, with less red on the throat.

THE SISKIN.

Carduelis spinus (Linnæus).

PLATE 15.

In England and Wales this small Finch is best known as a winter visitor, although nesting in some localities.

It is more numerous in Scotland, breeding freely in many places; and is also resident in Ireland.

The skilfully concealed nest is usually placed in a fork on the branch of a pine or spruce, at some height from the ground, and is composed of twigs, rootlets, and moss, and lined with feathers and hair.

The five or six eggs are pale bluish-green, with speckles and markings of reddish-brown and pinkish-grey.

According to Seebohm (*British Birds*, vol. ii. p. 94): "The song of the Siskin is not very powerful but is very pleasing—a succession of very rapid notes, some possessing considerable melody. It is an extremely industrious singer, and may be heard all the year round except in the moulting season."

The food consists mainly of seeds and buds of trees, especially those of the birch and alder, varied with insects in summer.

The Siskin resembles the Goldfinch in many of its actions, and, like that bird, is very easily tamed.

The female is less brightly coloured than the male, having altogether less yellow in her plumage, and lacking the black on the head and throat.

THE CITRIL FINCH.

Chrysomitris citrinella (Linnæus).

PLATE 16.

This species is resident in the mountainous parts of Southern and Central Europe, and one example was taken in Norfolk in January 1904. This is the only occurrence in the British Islands.

Mr. Dresser, in his *Birds of Europe* (vol. iii.), quoting some notes received from Howard Saunders, says: "The nest is warmly lined, but larger than, and quite different from, that of the Serin Finch; the eggs are nearly as large as those of the Goldfinch, but somewhat resemble miniature Greenfinches' eggs."

In summer the Citril Finch is found high up in forest districts among the mountains, and is common in Switzerland, and also in Baden and other parts of Germany.

The female resembles the male in colour, but is duller.

THE SERIN.

Serinus hortulanus, K. L. Koch.

PLATE 16.

Over twenty examples of this little Finch have been noted in the British Islands, while it is common in many parts of Central and Southern Europe, and also in North-west Africa.

The nest, according to Seebohm (*British Birds*, vol. ii. p. 85), "is generally built in fruit-trees, but frequently in other small trees and shrubs." It is neatly built of rootlets, stalks of grass, thistle-down, and wool, with a softer lining of similar materials. The four or five eggs are white, with a greenish tinge, spotted and marked with reddish-brown.

Lord Lilford, in his work on British Birds, says : "The Serin is exceedingly common in Southern and Central Spain, and in general habits somewhat resembles the Goldfinch ; the nest, however, is composed of different materials, and the song consists of a sharp sibilant murmur, much inferior to the pleasant notes of that bird."

In colour the female is duller than the male, and is more streaked with brown.

THE HOUSE-SPARROW.

Passer domesticus (Linnæus).

PLATE 16.

The House-Sparrow may be said to be the best known of our British birds, and no one, either in town or country, need be without the opportunity of studying its appearance and habits.

It is found almost everywhere in the British Islands, although absent in some of the high bleak districts in Scotland and Ireland. It is also widely spread over Europe.

The large and bulky nest, made of any suitable material that may come to hand, such as straws, grass-stalks, shreds of carpet, rags, &c., with a soft lining of feathers, is placed either in trees or in some hole, cavity, or any snug recess in a building, high enough to be out of the reach of anyone standing on the ground. The five or six eggs are greyish-white, blotched and spotted with pale grey and greyish-black.

There is no doubt the House-Sparrow hinders the increase of the Martin. Having had the nests of the latter bird under observation for some years, I have noticed that the attacks of the Sparrow are usually begun very early in the morning by the males, who appropriate the nests before they are quite completed, and if it has been so far finished, as to be inconvenient to the intruder, the entrance is enlarged.

During the summer months the House-Sparrow destroys great numbers of insects and grubs, for the food of themselves and young, which in autumn and winter principally consists of seeds and grain. At harvest time, when most of the young birds can fly well, large flocks of these and their parents leave the neighbourhood of houses and betake themselves to the corn-fields.

The House-Sparrow is a bold clever bird, and in spite of many enemies holds his own.

THE TREE-SPARROW.

Passer montanus (Linnæus).

PLATE 16.

This species may easily be distinguished from the House-Sparrow by the uniform reddish-brown colour on the crown of the head, dark spot in the centre of the white cheeks, and also by its smaller size. Unlike the House-Sparrow, the sexes do not differ in colour.

The Tree-Sparrow is widely spread over the British Islands, though local, and is not nearly so common as the other species. It is also found throughout the greater part of Europe, and has a wide range in Asia.

It usually nests in some hole, high up in a decayed tree, several pairs often associating together. The nest, composed of dead grasses and feathers, contains about six eggs ; these are greyish-white in ground colour, mottled with brown.

In its habits the Tree-Sparrow is lively and active, though somewhat shy ; in winter often frequenting stackyards in company with other birds.

According to Lord Lilford (*Birds of Northamptonshire and Neighbourhood*, vol. i. p. 182), " The ordinary notes of the Tree-Sparrow are sharper and more shrill than those of the House-Sparrow, to which, however, they have a great resemblance ; at the pairing-season we have occasionally heard a sort of prolonged chatter from the male bird."

The food consists of seeds and insects.

THE CHAFFINCH.

Fringilla cœlebs, Linnæus.

PLATE 16.

This gay and sprightly bird is very common in every part of the British Islands, wherever woods and cultivated country are found. In late autumn our home-bred birds form flocks and roam about the country, while large numbers arrive at the same time from abroad.

It is also found plentifully throughout Europe.

The nest, which is a beautiful structure, is composed outwardly of green moss, grey lichens, and grasses, deftly woven together, with a lining of wool, feathers, and hair; and is placed in a fruit or other tree, not far from the ground. The four, five, or six eggs are in ground colour a pale blue with a greenish tinge, spotted and marked with reddish-brown.

The Chaffinch during the summer months feeds largely on insects and grubs, whilst in winter seeds of various kinds are eaten. It is of the greatest service to the gardener, and in early summer may be seen searching for caterpillars on the trees in orchards and gardens.

Its blithe and joyous song is continued throughout the spring and early summer, and though short, is repeated many times in succession.

It was long ago observed by Gilbert White and others, when the flocks of Chaffinches were about in the autumn and winter, that a separation of the sexes had occurred. It was due to this fact that the name of *cœlebs*, or bachelor, was given by Linnæus, on account of the large companies of cock birds seen consorting together.

The general colour of the female Chaffinch is brownish-olive, tinged with grey, the bars on the wings being less distinct than in the male.

Pl. 16

Mealy Redpoll.   Serin.
Lesser Redpoll   Citril Finch.   Linnet
Brambling (summer & winter)   Tree Sparrow.
Chaffinch.   House Sparrow. (♂ & ♀)

THE BRAMBLING.

Fringilla montifringilla, Linnæus.

PLATE 16.

The Brambling is a more or less regular winter visitor to our shores, usually arriving on our north-east and east coasts in October, and leaving again in spring.

Abroad the summer haunts of this species are far to the north, and its nest may be looked for among the forests and birch-clad hillsides in Scandinavia and northern Russia. This is placed on a fir or birch, usually in a fork, and resembles in appearance that of the Chaffinch, although somewhat larger.

It is composed of birch bark, green moss, and lichens, with a lining of wool, hair, and feathers. The eggs, usually six in number, are the same in colour and markings as the Chaffinch's.

According to Seebohm, the song of the Brambling is "a short low warble," and it has also a prolonged call-note, which has been compared to that of the Greenfinch.

The number of Bramblings which visit us varies from year to year; sometimes large flocks make their appearance, frequenting the beech-woods along with Chaffinches, and feeding on the fallen beechmast.

They also eat insects and seeds.

As may be seen from the plate, the winter and summer plumage of the male Brambling differ a good deal, the rich blue-black head and mantle of the breeding season being replaced by duller and more patchy feathers in autumn.

The female is altogether duller and greyer than the male, the back and head being brownish instead of black.

THE SNOW-FINCH.

Montifringilla nivalis, Linnæus.

PLATE 17.

This Alpine bird, an inhabitant of the mountains of Southern Europe, has twice been shot in England, the first at Rye Harbour, Sussex, in February 1905, and the other at Paddock Wood, Kent, in December 1906.

The nest is placed in some crevice of a rock or building, and is composed of dead grass-stalks and fine roots, lined inside with hair, feathers, and wool, and contains four or five pure white eggs.

It feeds principally on insects and seeds; and the bird may often be seen flitting about among the rocks and stones on the barren mountain slopes which it frequents.

The female resembles the male, but is duller in colour, and has less black on the throat.

THE LINNET.

Linota cannabina (Linnæus).

PLATE 16.

The Linnet is a common and well-known bird in the British Islands, and may be observed in most parts of the country where there are large furze-covered commons and waste lands. After the breeding season a good many of our birds move southwards and cross the Channel.

It has a wide range in Europe, Asia Minor, and Asia.

The nest is usually placed in a thick furze-bush, sometimes in a hedge of yew or other evergreens in gardens, and is made of grass-stalks, wool, and moss, lined with hair. It contains from four to six eggs, in ground colour bluish-white, with blotches, spots, and streaks of ruddy-brown and purplish-grey.

The Linnet has a pleasing modulated song, and a rather plaintive call-note.

The food consists of various seeds and berries.

Although this bird is known as the Red, Grey, or Brown Linnet, these different names refer to one and the same species, and it is difficult to say why so much variety of colour should occur. In autumn the crimson on the breast and head of the brightly-coloured males almost disappears, whilst the female has none of that colour in her plumage at any time of the year.

THE MEALY REDPOLL.

Linota linaria (Linnæus).

PLATE 16.

The Mealy Redpoll, which is subdivided by naturalists into several subspecies or forms, inhabits the northern portions of both hemispheres, and visits more or less irregularly the northern and north-eastern parts of Great Britain in autumn and winter.

Its breeding haunts are among the birch woods or about the boundaries of forest growth in the northern districts of Europe and Asia, which it leaves in autumn for warmer climates.

According to Mr. Dresser (*Manual of Palæarctic Birds*, pp. 315–316), "It breeds in the high north, and places its nest, which is a neat structure of fine birch-twigs, vegetable stems, and moss, carefully lined with plant-down and feathers, in a tree generally about 10 feet from the ground, but rarely on or close to the ground." The five or six eggs are greenish-blue in ground colour, marked with rufous-brown.

Other Arctic races of the Redpoll are : The Greenland Redpoll, *Linota hornemanni*, nesting in Greenland, Iceland, and Spitzbergen, which is larger and altogether paler in colour than the one just described.

Also *Linota holboelli*, *Linota rostrata*, and *Linota exilipes* (Holboell's, Greater, and Hoary Redpoll), all closely related to each other, and occasionally visiting us during the autumn and winter months.

The female of the Mealy Redpoll is smaller than the male, and has only a small amount of red on the head, without any on the breast.

113

THE LESSER REDPOLL.

Linota rufescens (Vieillot).

PLATE 16.

The Lesser Redpoll, a resident species in the British Islands, is smaller and more ruddy in colour than the Mealy Redpoll, and although local in its distribution is widely spread over the country.

Some of our birds are said to migrate in winter, and in Europe it has not been recorded north of the Baltic.

The nest is placed in a bush or tree—often an alder or willow—and is composed of twigs, stalks of dead grass, and moss, and is warmly lined with willow-down or cotton grass.   The eggs, varying in number from four to six, are of a pale bluish or greenish colour, spotted with reddish-brown.

The food of the different races of Redpoll consists of buds of trees, especially those of the birch and alder, and also of various seeds.

Seebohm, in his *British Birds*, describes the song of the Lesser Redpoll "as a short monotonous trill, clear, shrill, and not altogether unmusical."

In winter large flocks visit the birch and alder trees, where they may be seen climbing about the twigs, picking out the seeds and buds, incessantly uttering their twittering notes.

After moulting in autumn, the male shows hardly any crimson in the colour of his plumage.

The female is duller in colour, the red being confined to the crown of the head.

THE TWITE.

Linota flavirostris (Linnæus).

PLATE 17.

Compared with the Lesser Redpoll in breeding plumage the Twite is a much more sober-coloured bird, having none of the crimson tints on the head and breast, and at all times may be distinguished by its more lengthened tail and proportionally slimmer form.

The Twite, sometimes called the Mountain-Linnet, is an autumnal visitor to the southern parts of England, though resident and breeding in the northern counties; whilst in Scotland and Ireland it is more or less common. Abroad it breeds in Scandinavia, and on migration occurs in many parts of Europe.

The Twite usually builds its nest either on the ground or close to it, and in its construction uses as material fine roots and grass-stalks, lining it with wool, feathers, thistle-down, and hair. The four to six eggs are pale greenish-blue, marked and streaked with reddish-brown.

Its food usually consists of seeds of various kinds, and its twittering call-note may be frequently heard as it flits among the grass and heather on moors and rocky hillsides.

Macgillivray says: " In the Hebrides it is plentiful and in winter frequents the corn-yards in large flocks, clinging to the stacks of oats, and picking out the seeds. . . . Its flight is rapid and undulated, and it wheels over the fields previous to alighting, uttering a soft twitter at intervals."

The female resembles the male in colour, but has none of the carmine tint on the rump.

THE BULLFINCH.

Pyrrhula europæa, Vieillot.

PLATE 17.

The Bullfinch is resident and more or less common in those parts of the country suited to its habits, throughout the British Islands. In the northern and eastern portions of Europe, and in Siberia, a larger and more brilliantly coloured race is found, known as the Northern Bullfinch, the *Pyrrhula major* of Brehm, which has been recorded several times in Great Britain ; although doubts have been expressed as to the genuineness of some of these occurrences, owing to the number of birds imported by dealers.

On the continent of Europe our smaller bird may also be found in the central, southern, and western portions.

The nest of the Bullfinch is of peculiar construction, being composed of slender twigs and fine roots, intertwined so as to form a kind of platform, in the centre of which is a cup-shaped depression, and occasionally a little wool or hair is placed within this interior.

It is generally built in an evergreen bush or tree, not far from the ground, and contains from four to six eggs, in ground colour greenish-blue, with spots and streaks of violet-grey and dark purplish-brown.

The food consists of the young buds of the larch and other trees, varied with the seeds of wild plants, such as the dandelion, chickweed, groundsel, &c.

The song of the Bullfinch is low and very soft in tone, and so is its piping call-note.

The bird is shy and retiring in its habits, haunting thick copses and well-timbered ground, shrubberies, and gardens ; the pairs usually keeping company throughout the year.

THE SCARLET GROSBEAK.

Pyrrhula erythrina (Pallas).

PLATE 17.

Of late years a good many examples of the Scarlet Grosbeak—till recently only known as a very rare visitor to Great Britain—have been observed or obtained. Its breeding grounds appear to be Russia, Siberia, and the mountainous parts of Central Asia, whilst in winter it is found throughout a great portion of India and China.

The nest is placed in the forked branch of a bush, and is composed of dead grass-stems and small roots, with a lining of hair. The eggs, varying in number from four to six, but usually five, are greenish blue, marked with spots of reddish- or blackish-brown.

Seebohm, in his *British Birds*, describes the song as "a loud clear whistle," and the food consists of various seeds, berries, and buds.

The red colouring is absent in the plumage of the female, which is in general of a neutral brownish tint, the wings and tail being darker, the throat and underparts dull white or buffish, with dark streaks on breast and flanks.

THE PINE-GROSBEAK.

Pyrrhula enucleator (Linnæus).

PLATE 17.

The Pine-Grosbeak is an irregular and very uncommon visitor to Great Britain from the forests of pine and spruce in Scandinavia, northern Russia, and Siberia, where in summer it nests and rears its young, moving as winter approaches to more temperate regions.

The nest is generally placed on the branch of a fir, close to the trunk, and is constructed much in the same manner as the Bullfinch's, of intertwisted twigs, with the interior lining of roots or grasses and lichen. The eggs, usually four in number, are greenish-blue in ground colour, marked with brownish-purple or dark brown.

The food of the Pine-Grosbeak consists of the seeds of the pine and fir, berries and buds of various trees, and also of insects.

Seebohm, who studied the bird in its native haunts, describes its song (*British Birds*, vol. ii. p. 43) as "very melodious, not very loud or long, but flute-like," and the call-note as "a plaintive single note."

Although apparently shy and retiring in its disposition, the Pine-Grosbeak is said to be easily approached, and its character is tame and unsuspicious.

The female differs from the male in having none of the carmine-red in her plumage, the edges of these feathers being of a golden yellow, and the back of the bird a slaty-grey.

THE CROSSBILL.

Loxia curvirostra, Linnæus.

PLATE 17.

The Crossbill is best known in England as an irregular visitor during the autumn and winter months, often arriving in large flocks, and keeping more or less to districts where there are woods of larch and pine. At times, however, the birds remain and breed in suitable localities.

In the northern parts of Scotland the Crossbill is resident throughout the year, and it is also widely spread over Europe.

The nest, begun very early in the year, is usually placed on the branch of a pine or fir, and is built of twigs and lined with grass and wool. The four, occasionally five, eggs are in ground colour whitish or pale greenish-blue, marked with different shades of reddish-brown.

The main food supply of the Crossbill consists of the seeds of the larch and spruce fir, as well as berries, pips, and insects.

The song is soft and low in tone, and the call-note, as the birds flit from tree to tree, is sharp and clear.

The points of the Crossbill's upper and lower mandibles are placed athwart each other, in some individuals crossing to the right, in others to the left, and form a well-adapted tool wherewith to open the cones and extract the seeds of conifers.

According to Professor Newton (*Dictionary of Birds*, p. 115), the young "on leaving the nest have not the tips of the bill crossed."

Mr. Knox, in his *Autumns on the Spey* (pp. 34–35), has happily described the actions of a flock of Crossbills as follows: "After close observation, I noticed that they seldom attempted to operate upon a cone on the exact spot where it grew, but after snapping one off from a slender terminal twig, each bird would hop or fly to the central part of the branch, and in parrot-like fashion hold it in his foot, but more frequently *under* it, as a hawk holds a small bird when in the act of devouring it, and quickly inserting his bill between the scales, split them open by means of that wonderful tool, and extract the seeds with the greatest facility. Occasionally a cone would fall to the ground just as it was snapped off; but, in such a case, a fresh one was instantly selected, no further notice being taken of the one that had dropped."

The colour of the female is a yellowish-green, and the males, after moulting in captivity, never regain their red plumage.

A form of our Crossbill, distinguished by having a larger and stouter bill, and known as the Parrot-Crossbill (*Loxia pityopsittacus*, Bechstein) has been obtained in the British Islands. This is an inhabitant of the pine regions of Scandinavia and the northern parts of Russia.

THE TWO-BARRED CROSSBILL.

Loxia bifasciata (C. L. Brehm).

PLATE 17.

The Two-barred Crossbill, whose summer home is in the pine-forest regions of northern Russia and Asia, has occurred a good many times in the British Islands, and may be distinguished from our bird by the double bars on the wings.

Mr. Dresser writes in his *Birds of Europe:* "The nest closely resembles that of *Loxia curvirostra*, but is smaller, and somewhat slighter in structure; and the eggs are somewhat darker in ground-colour than those of that species, and smaller in size, but otherwise closely resemble them."

In habits these two species are very much alike.

The female has no red in her plumage, being principally of a greenish-grey, tinged with yellow on the upper parts, and greyish-white and yellowish below.

Pl. 17.

Corn Bunting.
Black headed Bunting.
Bullfinch (♂ ♀).
Twite.
Pine Bunting.
Two barred Crossbill.
Crossbill.
Snow Finch.
Scarlet Grosbeak.
Pine Grosbeak.

Subfamily EMBERIZINÆ.

THE BLACK-HEADED BUNTING.

Emberiza melanocephala, Scopoli.

PLATE 17.

Some eight or more examples of this rare Bunting have been recorded as occurring in the British Islands, the first having been shot near Brighton in November 1868.

The summer home of the Black-headed Bunting is in South-eastern Europe, where it is common in many parts; it ranges also through Asia Minor as far as Baluchistan, and winters in India.

Seebohm writes (*British Birds*, vol. ii. p. 167): "The nest of the Black-headed Bunting is seldom placed at any great height above the ground; it is very frequently in a small bush, but the favourite situation is amongst trailing plants such as clematis, briars, and vines. In the gardens near Constantinople it is built principally amongst the rows of peas and beans.

"Canon Tristram states that he has frequently found it on the ground. It is rather a bulky structure, and though neatly finished inside, has a somewhat loose and ragged appearance outside. The foundation is made of dry grass, thistle-leaves, and other coarse material; but the main portion of the nest is constructed entirely of the yellow dry stalks of various small flowering plants, the seed-capsules on which are the most prominent object, and conjoined with the stiffness of the stalks, which prevents them from bending easily, gives the nest a very slender and unfinished look." The lining is of finer material and hair.

The four or five eggs are greenish-blue, marked with ashy-brown, without the lines and scratches found on those of the other European Buntings.

The food consists of insects, seeds, and fruit, and its song, though short, is said to be more musical than that of the Yellow Bunting.

In the female the upper parts are brown, with darker streaks; rump tinged with yellow; throat and belly whitish; breast and flanks buff, with dark streaks; and the under tail coverts suffused with yellow.

THE YELLOW-BREASTED BUNTING.

Emberiza aureola, Pallas.

PLATE 18.

Three examples of this brilliantly coloured wanderer to Europe have been obtained in England, all having been shot in Norfolk : the first on September 21, 1905, at Cley; the second on September 5, 1907, near Wells; and the last on September 4, 1913, again at Cley.

The breeding range of this bird stretches from northern Russia right across Siberia as far as Kamchatka, whilst in winter it migrates as far to the south as the Malay Peninsula.

According to Mr. Dresser (*Manual of Palæarctic Birds*, p. 349), it "frequents bush-covered plains on the outskirts of the forests, willow-thickets in damp places, and occurs in the mountains to an altitude of 5000 to 6000 feet, and in the winter frequents reed- and rush-beds.

"Its song, which is short but pleasant, is uttered from the top of a bush or a plant-stem, and it is said to be a most industrious songster."

The nest, built either on the ground or in some shrub, is composed of dead grasses and roots, with a lining of hair. The four or five eggs are grey tinged with green, obscurely shaded with a darker tint, and marked with a few indefinite brown scratchy lines.

The female has none of the rich black and chestnut on the head which distinguish the male.

The upper parts of the bird are greenish-brown, with dark stripes on the back, whilst the lower portions are pale yellow, streaked on the flanks.

She has also a broad yellowish-white eye-stripe.

THE PINE-BUNTING.

Emberiza leucocephala, S. G. Gmelin.

PLATE 17.

One example of the Pine-Bunting was obtained on Fair Isle, Shetlands, in October 1911. In summer it breeds in Siberia, from the Ural eastwards, migrating southwards to spend the winter in China and among the Himalayas. It only rarely visits Europe.

The nest, composed of the stems of grasses and other plants, with a lining of hair, is placed on the ground beneath a bush or clump of grass. The eggs, varying in number from four to six, are described by Mr. Dresser (*Manual of Palæarctic Birds*, p. 360) as "dull white, pale bluish white, or rose-white, with faint violet-grey shell-markings and marblings, and blackish brown surface-lines or spots."

It haunts the edges of birch and pine woods and bushy ground.

The general colour of the female is composed of different shades of brown and grey, and she has none of the beautiful chestnut on the head and throat which decorates the male.

THE CORN-BUNTING.

Emberiza miliaria, Linnæus.

PLATE 17.

The Corn-Bunting, sometimes called the Common Bunting, although only common in those parts of the country which suit its habits, is nevertheless widely spread throughout our islands.

It is also found over the greater part of Europe, from southern Scandinavia to the Mediterranean.

The nest, which is usually placed on the ground and hidden under a tussock of grass, or sometimes in young corn, is rather large, and is loosely constructed of grass-stalks, roots, and moss, with a lining of hair. The five or six eggs are dull white, shaded with lilac, and blotched and streaked with dark brown.

This Bunting does not usually lay its eggs until late in May.

In summer the food consists chiefly of insects, but later in the autumn and winter seeds of weeds, and also grain, are eaten.

The song, delivered while the bird is perched on a tall thistle or other plant, often from a wall or telegraph wire, consists of a succession of rather harsh scraping notes, the last one prolonged.

The Corn-Bunting haunts open arable land, particularly if near the sea, and is fond of dusting itself on roads.

The sexes do not differ in the colour of their plumage.

THE YELLOW BUNTING.

Emberiza citrinella, Linnæus.

PLATE 18.

The Yellow Bunting or Yellow Hammer is resident and common in most parts of the British Islands, and is widely spread over Northern and Central Europe and Asia.

The nest is generally placed on or close to the ground, hidden among grass and herbage, and is composed of dead grasses, roots, and moss, with a lining of fibrous rootlets and hair. The four or five eggs are purplish-white, marked with curious dark streaks and scribbles, and clouded with reddish-purple.

In summer the food of the Yellow Bunting consists principally of insects, at other times seeds of different weeds and grain are eaten.

The song is less harsh than that of the Corn-Bunting, and is a pleasing ditty, though rather monotonous. Late in summer, during hot weather, when the singing of most birds has ceased, it is often the only music to be heard, and is delivered while the bird sits on a wall or tree.

The Yellow Bunting is partial to cultivated ground, and in winter large flocks visit the farm-steadings, along with various Finches.

The female resembles the male, but is much duller, and more darkly streaked on the upper parts.

THE CIRL BUNTING.

Emberiza cirlus, Linnæus.

PLATE 18.

In Great Britain the Cirl Bunting is more or less confined to the southern parts of England, and only occurs in Scotland and Ireland as a rare vagrant.

On the continent it is found over Central and Southern Europe.

The nest, sometimes placed in a furze-bush or juniper, at others in a roadside bank amongst shrubs and vegetation, is composed of grasses and moss, with a lining of hair. It generally contains five eggs, in ground colour white, tinged with lilac, and spotted and streaked with brownish-black.

The food of the Cirl Bunting is similar to that of the other species of this family, and the song resembles the Yellow Bunting's, but lacks the prolonged drawn-out note at the end.

In habits it is not so sprightly and brisk as that bird, and is easily approached; it frequents enclosures and cultivated land, and in winter may sometimes be seen in flocks.

The female is not so brightly coloured as her mate, having only a pale yellow streak over the eye, without the black and yellow on the head and throat.

THE ORTOLAN.

Emberiza hortulana, Linnæus.

PLATE 18.

The first British specimen of the Ortolan was taken in Marylebone Fields in the year 1776 or thereabouts. Since that time a good many have been obtained in England on the eastern and southern coasts.

On the mainland of Scotland it is very rare, although it appears to visit Fair Isle, Shetlands, regularly during the spring and autumn migrations, whilst in Ireland it is said to have been taken once, but the record is doubtful.

Abroad it is a summer visitor to many parts of Central, Eastern, and Western Europe, making its way to Africa to spend the winter.

The nest is placed on the ground, hidden among corn, grass, or other vegetation, or sometimes beneath a bush.

It is constructed of dead grasses and roots, with a lining of finer materials and hair, and contains four or five eggs; in ground colour pale grey, with a purplish tinge, spotted and blotched with purple-brown.

Its food consists of seeds and insects, the young being reared on the latter.

Seebohm describes its "plaintive monotonous song," which, he says, "begins somewhat like that of the Yellow Hammer, but ends quite differently" (*British Birds*, vol. ii. p. 154).

The Ortolan frequents open wooded country, roadsides, and gardens; and during migration large numbers are caught in nets, and fattened on oats and millet, to be used as a table delicacy.

The female resembles the male, but the colours are duller and paler, and the head is streaked.

THE MEADOW-BUNTING.

Emberiza cia, Linnæus.

PLATE 18.

This species inhabits the central parts of Europe and the countries bordering the Mediterranean, ranging westwards as far as Portugal.

Five examples have been taken in England, four of these in Sussex and one in Kent.

Colonel Irby, describing the habits of the Meadow-Bunting in his work, *The Ornithology of the Straits of Gibraltar*, 2nd ed., p. 110, says: It "is a common and, like most of the Buntings, a stupidly tame bird, as far as my experience goes, living about stony, rocky, and hilly ground. . . . In April they frequent the slopes and tops of the sierras, nesting during that month."

The Meadow-Bunting builds its nest, which is similar to the Yellow Bunting's, on the ground, and lays four or five eggs, greyish in ground colour, and darkly marked with undulating lines running into each other.

Like its congeners, it feeds on seeds and insects, and its song also resembles that of the Yellow Bunting.

The female is much duller in colour than the male, whilst the stripes on the side of the crown and face are absent.

THE SIBERIAN MEADOW-BUNTING.

Emberiza cioides, Brandt.

PLATE 18.

One example of this Eastern species was obtained at Flamborough, Yorkshire, in November 1886.

It inhabits eastern Siberia, and is also widely spread through Turkestan, Mongolia, Manchuria, and Corea, spending the winter in China.

According to Mr. Dresser (*Manual of Palæarctic Birds*, p. 365): "The nest is a light but tolerably strong structure of dry grass-bents lined with finer bents, horse- or cattle-hair, and is placed on the ground in a depression and usually at the foot of a bush." The four or five eggs have the ground colour violet-white, marked with spots and broken lines of dark brown.

This Bunting is said to have a pleasing song.

The female is more soberly coloured than the male, and has not the bright chestnut tints on the head and gorget.

THE RUSTIC BUNTING.

Emberiza rustica, Pallas.

PLATE 18.

About a dozen examples of this rare Bunting have occurred at different times in the British Islands, the first near Brighton in October 1867, and the latest on Fair Isle, Shetlands, in May 1913.

The breeding haunts of the Rustic Bunting reach from Finland across northern Russia to eastern Siberia, whilst in autumn it makes its way southwards to spend the winter in China, Japan, and Turkestan.

It frequents wet forest ground, and according to Mr. Dresser (*Manual of Palæarctic Birds*, p. 363) it makes "a rather loose nest of wiry grass-bents and depositing in June 5 to 6 eggs greenish grey in colour with olivaceous brown blotches and without any scratchy lines."

Von Middendorff describes its song as rich and melodious.

In the female the black portions of the head and ear-coverts are dark brown, broken with buff; and the plumage is altogether duller than in the male.

THE LITTLE BUNTING.

Emberiza pusilla, Pallas.

PLATE 18.

The first specimen of the Little Bunting obtained in the British Islands was one caught near Brighton in November 1864. It has since occurred a good many times, and seems now to be a more or less regular autumn visitant to Fair Isle, Shetlands.

This is an Arctic species; in summer breeding in northern Russia and Siberia, passing southwards in autumn as far as China, India, and the Andaman Islands.

Seebohm, describing its habits, writes (*British Birds*, vol. ii., p. 145): "It was most common in the pine- and birch-forests, and was frequently seen feeding on the ground on the mossy and marshy open spaces in the woods, on the swampy edge of the forest tarns, searching for insects in company with Green and White Wagtails, Temminck's Stints, Fieldfares, Blue-throated Warblers, and other Arctic birds."

The nest, the same author says, "was nothing but a hole made in the dead leaves, moss, and grass, copiously and carefully lined with fine dead grass," and the five eggs were in ground colour "pale grey, with bold twisted blotches and irregular round spots of very dark grey, and equally large underlying shell-markings of paler grey."

The Little Bunting feeds on seeds and insects, and the song has more resemblance to a Warbler's than a Bunting's.

In the female the plumage generally is duller than that of the male.

stic Bunting.   Little Bunting.   Yellow Bunting or Yellow Hammer.
    Cirl Bunting. Yellow-breasted Bunting. Reed-Bunting.   Lapland Bunting.
Siberian Meadow-Bunting. Meadow-Bunting.   Snow-Bunting.
                    Ortolan.   (Summer & Autumn)

THE REED-BUNTING.

Emberiza schœniclus, Linnæus.

PLATE 18.

The Reed-Bunting, sometimes misnamed the Black-headed Bunting, and also known as the Reed-Sparrow, is a resident species and is found in localities suited to its habits in most parts of the British Islands. It has also a wide range throughout Europe.

The Reed-Bunting is an early breeder, the nest being sometimes begun in March. This is usually placed on the ground, though I have once found it in Scotland built in a fir, a few feet above the ground.

It is composed of dead grasses, flags, and moss, with a lining of the feathery tops of reeds, fine grasses, and hair. The five or six eggs are pale brown, blotched and streaked irregularly with dark brown or black.

The food, like that of the other Buntings, consists of seeds and insects.

During the summer months this species frequents the banks of sluggish streams and marshy reedy ground; and the rather harsh song, consisting of several notes, with the last one prolonged, is uttered as the bird clings to a tall reed or willow sapling.

In winter a good many Reed-Buntings leave their summer haunts and betake themselves to the fields, where they feed with other species.

The head of the male at this time of the year has the black more or less obscured by brownish margins to the feathers.

The female is by no means so brightly coloured as the male, the head being reddish-brown, streaked with darker brown, and having a whitish eye-stripe.

THE LARGE-BILLED REED-BUNTING.

Emberiza pyrrhuloides, Pallas.

This large race of Reed-Bunting, with a thicker and heavier bill than our bird, and paler in colour, has twice been taken in England, viz. near Lydd, Kent, in May 1908, and again at Rye, Sussex, in April 1912. The former appears to belong to the Western, and the latter to the Eastern form of this Bunting.

THE LAPLAND BUNTING.

Calcarius lapponicus (Linnæus).

PLATE 18.

The first occurrence of the Lapland Bunting in England was noted by Selby in the year 1826. Since that time, however, it has often been taken, while in autumn flocks have been observed on the east coast.

The summer home of this Bunting is in the far north, where it breeds within the circumpolar regions, moving southwards in autumn to pass the winter in warmer latitudes.

The nest is placed in some depression on the ground by the side of a hillock or tuft of grass, among marshy wastes, beyond the region of forest trees; with here and there a few stunted birches or willows. It is built of dead grass-stems, moss, and roots, and, according to Seebohm, is "profusely lined with feathers." The eggs vary in number from four to six, and in ground colour are pale brown or grey, blotched and streaked with darker brown.

The food of the Lapland Bunting, like that of its allies, consists of seeds and insects, and the song is usually delivered while the bird is in the air.

In the female those parts of the head and breast which are black in the male are streaked with dark brown or black on a ground of buff; the chestnut at the back of the neck being duller, and also streaked.

THE SNOW-BUNTING.

Plectrophenax nivalis (Linnæus).

PLATE 18.

This truly Arctic species, whose summer home is in the circumpolar regions, and which has been found breeding further north than any other bird, yet nests, at high elevations, as far southwards as the Grampian Mountains in Scotland.

Colonel Feilden found a nest and eggs as near to the Pole as Grinnell Land, and during summer it is widely spread over Iceland, Spitzbergen, Nova Zembla, and the barren Arctic wastes.

On the mainland of Scotland the nest is placed high up on the mountainsides, under stones or in some cleft in a rock, and is built of dry bents and moss, with a lining of hair and feathers. The eggs, varying in number from four to six, are in ground colour white, with a bluish tinge, spotted and marked with brownish-red and black.

Mr. J. G. Millais tells me that the song of the Snow-Bunting "is very wild and sweet and has more continuance and variety than any of the other Buntings. In the long summer evenings in Iceland I have heard the male Snow-Buntings singing for hours. They usually sit on a high rock and sing in close vicinity to the sitting female."

In late autumn and winter large flocks of these birds arrive on our coasts, and feed along the sandy beaches, among the stranded seaweed.

Dr. Saxby writes : "Seen against a dark hillside or a lowering sky, a flock of these birds presents an exceedingly beautiful appearance, and it may then be seen how aptly the term 'snowflake' has been applied to the species. I am acquainted with no more pleasing combination of sight and sound than that afforded when a cloud of these birds, backed by a dark grey sky, descends, as it were, in a shower to the ground, to the music of their own sweet tinkling notes."

The food of the Snow-Bunting consists principally of insects and the seeds of various grasses.

In breeding plumage the female has broad grey margins to the black feathers of the head, neck, and back, which give a dull look to the bird compared to the male.

Family STURNIDÆ.

THE STARLING.

Sturnus vulgaris, Linnæus.

PLATE 19.

The Starling is widely distributed over the British Islands, and is one of our most common birds. Abroad it is found in the Faroes—where a broader-billed race than ours occurs—and from northern Scandinavia southwards to the Mediterranean countries.

The large and rather slovenly nest is placed in a hole in a trunk of a tree, wall, or cliff; in thatch, under the eaves of houses and outbuildings; sometimes even in thick ivy growing on the walls of a dwelling. It is composed of dead grasses, straws, roots, and moss, roughly lined with some feathers and hair. The eggs, varying in number from four to six or seven, are pale blue, without any markings.

The song, often heard during the winter months as well as at other times, is delivered as the bird sits perched on some tree or building, and consists of various chattering notes, combined with some which are really musical.

As he sings the Starling has a habit of flapping and closing his wings, at the same time expanding his crest and the feathers of the throat.

During the past fifty years this bird has greatly increased in numbers, and although at times helping itself freely to cherries and other fruit, any damage done is more than paid for by the destruction of countless insects and larvæ.

In autumn vast numbers of Starlings find their living in the fields and pastures, and as evening deepens the flocks resort to some favourite roosting-place, such as evergreen shrubberies or reed-beds.

As the various packs unite, they perform wonderful aerial evolutions before finally settling down for the night.

The female resembles the male, but the tints are duller, and the light spots are larger. For some time after leaving the nest the young are of a uniform blackish-brown colour, marked underneath with greyish-white.

136

THE ROSE-COLOURED STARLING.

Pastor roseus (Linnæus).

PLATE 19.

This beautiful bird, an irregular wanderer to our shores, was unknown as a British species until 1742. Since that date it has frequently been noticed as a visitant to our shores.

Its breeding headquarters are in Western Asia, although sometimes vast numbers nest in Southern Europe, and migrating eastwards, pass the winter in India.

The favourite food of the Rose-coloured Starling, or Rose-coloured Pastor as it is sometimes called, is the locust, which accounts for the erratic movements of this species.

An account is given in the *Zoologist* for 1878, p. 16, furnished by Edoardo de Betta, of a great visitation of these birds to the castle of Villafranca in Italy during the summer of 1875.

Arriving at first in small numbers, they rapidly increased until it was estimated that some twelve or fourteen thousand birds had occupied the building.

They at once began their nests, and as soon as the young were able to fly, disappeared as suddenly as they came.

The nest, loosely constructed of dead grasses, is sometimes placed in a cranny or recess in a wall, at others among heaps of stones on the ground, and contains five or six smooth and shining bluish-white eggs.

The notes of this bird are very like the Starling's.

The female resembles the male in colour, but is duller.

Family CORVIDÆ.

THE CHOUGH.

Pyrrhocorax graculus (Linnæus).

PLATE 19.

This bird, unfortunately rapidly decreasing as a British species, still lingers on some of the sea cliffs in the south-western parts of England and Scotland, on the coasts of Wales and Ireland, and in the Isle of Man and other islands.

It also occurs in many parts of Europe, where it can find localities suited to its habits, and in Africa and Asia.

The nest, placed in some recess or fissure in rocks, or among ruins, is built of sticks, with a lining of wool and hair. The four or five eggs are dull white, marked with streaks and spots of ashy-grey and light brown.

The food consists of grubs, insects of various kinds, and seeds.

The birds have a shrill and penetrating cry.

It is one of the most beautiful members of the Crow family, on account of its elegant shape, velvety plumage shot with purple and green reflections, and scarlet bill and legs.

The plumage of the sexes is alike.

Pl. 19.

Starling. (summer & winter)   Rose-coloured Starling.
Nutcracker   (adult & young)
        Jay.   Chough.

THE NUTCRACKER.

Nucifraga caryocatactes (Linnæus).

PLATE 19.

The earliest known occurrence of the Nutcracker in the British Islands was one obtained in Wales in October 1753, and recorded by Pennant. Since that date a good many have been noticed, mostly in England.

Abroad it breeds among the pine forests in the mountainous parts of Central and Southern Europe, and ranges eastwards across Siberia.

The Siberian form has a longer and more slender bill than the one inhabiting Europe, and as it is apparently this race which most commonly visits England, I have represented it in the plate.

Little was known of the nest and eggs of the Nutcracker until 1862, when they were obtained on the Danish island of Bornholm, lying to the south of Sweden in the Baltic; although an egg had been procured in the lower Alps by the Abbé Caire as far back as 1846.

Like the Jay, the Nutcracker becomes extraordinarily shy and silent during the nesting time, which begins very early in the season before the winter's snow has melted in the forests, where the nest is built on the bough of a pine, at a moderate height from the ground.

The nest, composed of sticks, with a lining of grasses and moss, contains from three to five eggs, pale bluish-green in ground colour, spotted and freckled with olive-brown.

The Nutcracker feeds on the seeds of coniferous trees, nuts, berries, and insects, whilst in manner of flight and tone of voice it resembles the Jay.

The female is indistinguishable from the male in colour.

THE JAY.

Garrulus glandarius (Linnæus).

PLATE 19.

The Jay is a resident and fairly common bird in the woodland districts of England and Wales, though much scarcer and more local in Scotland and in Ireland. Over the greater part of Europe it is also found, where the surroundings suit its habits. It is said to have been more plentiful formerly in our country, before the days of game preservation; nevertheless, owing to its intelligence and wariness, it still holds its ground, wherever there are large tracts of wood and coppice.

I have lately had under observation a nest of the Jay, which was placed in a Scotch fir, about ten feet from the ground, and built in a fork where the branches join the trunk. It was composed of twigs of the birch and other trees, with a lining of finer twigs of birch and roots. The five or six eggs are greenish-white, minutely speckled with olive-brown.

While the nest is being made, and until the young have left it, the parent birds are never heard and seldom seen, approaching it silently by roundabout ways, unless the nestlings are interfered with, when the female utters harsh screams and at times a curious cat-like call.

In the nest which I observed the young were also absolutely silent, unless handled or alarmed by anyone climbing their tree. The colour of their eyes was a bluish-grey, not brown, as it is sometimes said to be.

The food of the Jay consists of various nuts and berries, also of the eggs and the young of other birds.

Its usual call-note is harsh and strident, and sometimes the notes of other birds are imitated.

The female is rather duller in her plumage than the male.

In Ireland the general colour of this species is said to be of a warmer tint.

THE MAGPIE

Pica rustica (Scopoli).

This handsome bird is a resident species and widely distributed in many parts of the British Islands, though scarce and rapidly diminishing where game preserving is general.

Abroad it is found over the greater part of Europe, from northern Scandinavia to the Mediterranean.

The Magpie, like the Jay, breeds early in the year, usually in March, and builds its large domed nest of sticks arranged on a groundwork of earth and clay with a lining of rootlets or grasses, which is placed in the fork of a tree, or in some tall thorn hedge. The eggs vary in number from six to nine, and are generally of a pale bluish-green, speckled with umber brown.

The food consists of grubs, eggs, young birds, rats, mice, and carrion of various kinds.

The notes of the Magpie, softer in tone than those of the Jay, are, as Macgillivray describes them, "a sort of chuckling cry or chatter." Always shy and watchful, and never off its guard, it frequents woods, meadows, and cultivated ground, especially those fields surrounded by trees and tall hedges, to which it retreats on the first suspicion of danger.

In thick covert, if a fox be about, its presence is often betrayed by the incessant chattering of the watchful bird.

The male and female are alike in colour, though she may be a little duller.

Pl. 20.

Magpie.   Raven.   Jackdaw.

THE JACKDAW.

Corvus monedula, Linnæus.

(Frontispiece.)

The Jackdaw is a common and well-known bird throughout the greater part of the British Islands, often to be seen in company with Rooks. It is also found all over Europe, in Asia, and North Africa.

It makes its nest in hollow trees, crannies and holes in the stonework of churches, ruined castles, and other buildings; sometimes in cliffs, or even underground in rabbit burrows.

This is usually a large structure composed of sticks, snugly lined with wool and fur, and holds from four to seven eggs, greenish- or bluish-white in ground colour, marked and blotched with black or purplish-brown.

The call-note of the Jackdaw is a sharper and shorter caw, or rather *cae*, than that of the Rook, and the birds may easily be distinguished when flying in company overhead by their smaller size and different note.

It lives on much the same diet as its larger relation, viz. insects, worms, grubs, &c., and also on eggs when they can be obtained.

The Jackdaw is a sociable bird, seeking its food in fields and meadows, as well as by the sea, in companionship with its fellows.

The female is very like the male in colour, except that she has a less noticeable collar of grey.

THE RAVEN.

Corvus corax, Linnæus.

(*Frontispiece.*)

The Raven still lingers as a breeding species in some of its ancient haunts along the southern and south-western coasts of England, nesting also in Cumberland and Wales, as well as in some of the wilder parts of Ireland.

In Scotland it is much more numerous, especially in the western islands and among the wilds of the Highland deer forests.

This wanderer over the face of the earth is found all over Europe, and has a wide range in Asia and America, it also inhabits Greenland.

The nest, begun in February, is usually placed on an inaccessible ledge of rock, although in former days, when the Raven bred in the wooded districts of England, it was generally built in some tall tree, and so situated that it could hardly be reached from below.

It is composed of dead sticks of various sizes, with a warm lining of wool, feathers, fur, or the hair of deer. The eggs, varying in number from three to six, on rare occasions seven, are bluish-green in ground colour, marked and blotched with greenish-brown and grey.

The Raven's voice is distinct and may be recognised at a great distance, the harsh double croak being often heard when the bird itself seems a mere speck against the sky.

Its food consists of carrion of all kinds, such as sheep and lambs which have died on the hill or fallen over a precipice, dead fishes cast ashore by the sea, and also sometimes of grain, nothing coming amiss to this omnivorous bird.

In character and intelligence the Raven stands first among his kind, and endowed with wonderfully keen eyesight and a hardy constitution, he is able to find a living where most birds would starve.

The male and female are alike in colour, and pair for life.

END OF VOL. I.

CONTENTS OF VOL. II.

CONTENTS

Order PASSERES.

FAMILY CORVIDÆ.

THE CARRION-CROW.

Corvus corone, Linnæus.

PLATE 21.

The Carrion-Crow is resident and not uncommon in many parts of England and Wales, and although a shy and wary bird, it is known to inhabit the London parks. Roughly speaking, from the Borders to the central portions of Scotland, this crow is still plentiful, while it occurs along the eastern side as far as Sutherland, but it is either rare or altogether absent in the northern and north-western parts, where its place is taken by the Hooded Crow. In Ireland it is seldom found.

According to the new "List of British Birds" published by The British Ornithologists' Union (2nd ed. 1915), the latest and most authoritative work on the subject, to which I am indebted for much information, "the typical form of the Carrion-Crow breeds commonly in western Europe as far east as the Elbe, in Switzerland, Bohemia, the highlands of Austria and upper Italy. It occurs occasionally in other parts of Europe." Its range extends eastwards to western Siberia, where Seebohm found it interbreeding with the Hooded Crow.

Breeding later in the year than the Rook or Raven, the Carrion-Crow has its nest completed by the end of April, either building a new one or returning to its home of former years. This is usually placed in a tree or on some ledge of rock, and is built of sticks and warmly lined with moss, wool, feathers, and hair. When the nest has been occupied for several years in succession, it becomes large and bulky owing to the frequent addition of materials. The eggs, varying in number from four to six, have the ground colour of a pale bluish-green, spotted and blotched with umber- or olive-brown and shades of purplish-grey.

Like the rest of its family, the Carrion-Crow will eat almost any food which comes to hand, and devours great numbers of the eggs and young of other birds, sometimes also attacking and killing leverets and even newly-born lambs when it gets the opportunity. It keenly searches the sea-shore for mussels and other shell-fish, of which it is extremely fond, and in order to open these easily will rise to some height and drop its booty on a stone or rock, thus fracturing the shell. The ordinary cry of the Carrion-Crow is a harsh grating croak, varying in tone, but not so deep as the Raven's nor so soft as the Rook's.

In its habits this bird is more or less solitary, scouring the countryside in search of food, generally in pairs, as it probably mates for life. At times, however, when food is abundant in any particular locality, or when their numbers are not kept down, Carrion-Crows will collect in flocks. The sexes do not differ in plumage.

THE HOODED CROW.

Corvus cornix, Linnæus.

PLATE 21.

This species, also known as the Grey or Royston Crow, is a common autumn and winter visitant to England, being more numerous in the eastern counties, where it may be seen from September to April; although its wanderings extend to many inland districts in England, it is but seldom found in Wales. There is little doubt that these winter visitors to our shores come from Northern Europe. In Scotland the Hooded Crow is a resident, being plentiful all along the western coast and islands, as well as in the northern districts, while it is not uncommon among the deer-forests of the central Highlands. It also nests in the Isle of Man. In Ireland this species is plentiful and remains throughout the year. Abroad it is found over a great part of Europe, principally in the northern and eastern portions, ranging through Siberia to the Yenesei, and either this or a closely related race is resident in some of the Mediterranean islands, Egypt, and Palestine.

The nest, constructed of the same materials as that of the Carrion-Crow, is built in a tree or on a rocky cliff, while the colour and markings of the four or five eggs are exactly like those of the latter bird. According to Professor Newton (Yarrell's *British Birds*) the two species only differ in their colour, their habits, voice, and nidification being precisely alike, but Lord Lilford and other authorities have noted a distinct difference in their cries. There is no question, as mentioned before in the article on the Carrion-Crow, that in places where the two species overlap they interbreed, and hybrids in intermediate states of plumage have often been obtained.

The Hooded Crow, like its congeners, lives on eggs, young or wounded birds, carrion of all kinds, and on the deer-forests feeds largely on the offal left on the hill or in the burns after a stag has been killed. It haunts the sea-shore to obtain any dead fish left by the tide, and may often be seen there stalking about in its sedate manner, in company with gulls and other shore birds, occasionally giving a little quick sidelong hop when any titbit attracts its notice. It has the habit, in common with the Carrion-Crow, of getting at the contents of the larger shell-fish by rising to a height and dropping them on a stone. Owing to its marauding habits it is trapped, shot, and destroyed on every possible occasion by gamekeepers and others; nevertheless it seems able to hold its own.

The colours of the male and female are alike.

THE ROOK.

Corvus frugilegus, Linnæus.

PLATE 21.

This bird, the best known and most abundant of the Crow family in the British Islands, is widely distributed, being less plentiful in the northern parts of Scotland, although found nesting as far north as the Orkneys, as well as on some of the Outer Hebrides and islands off the west coast of Ireland. Its breeding range extends over the greater part of Europe, from Scandinavia and northern Russia as far south as Biarritz in France and Modena in Italy, and eastwards to the Crimea. After the nesting season a certain migratory movement takes place among our home-bred birds, some apparently crossing to the Continent; while birds in the northern portion of Europe migrate southwards as winter approaches as far as the Mediterranean countries. Many of these migrants come over to winter with us, leaving our shores again in March and April for Scandinavia.

The Rook is peculiarly regular in its habits, returning year after year early in February to its old familiar haunts, although the nests are not usually completed until the middle of March. The favourite site for a rookery is among the topmost branches of tall elms or other trees in parks, or in the neighbourhood of cultivated ground, but other situations are often chosen, even in the midst of large towns.

As the season advances the rookery becomes a noisy and busy scene and the birds have no scruples in robbing an unguarded nest of its building material, causing in consequence much uproar and disturbance.

The bulky nest is composed of sticks and twigs, either dead or gathered fresh from the trees, and lined with fine roots, straws, grass, and sometimes wool. It contains five or six eggs, in ground colour pale greenish-blue, blotched and marked with greenish-brown.

The familiar caw of the Rook is known to everyone, and while pairing and nest building is in progress the babel of various cries and murmurings

3

Pl. 21.

Carrion Crow.   *Rook.*   *Hooded Crow.*

is continuous and incessant, yet to those who have become accustomed to the sound, and from association, it is most pleasing.

The Rook is more or less omnivorous, worms, grubs, and insects being its staple diet, while it has gained the reputation of being an inveterate egg-stealer when opportunity offers, especially in times of drought, which cause a scarcity of worms and larvæ. It also causes a good deal of harm owing to its partiality for seed-corn and potatoes, but no doubt some of the damage done is compensated for by the quantity of insect pests destroyed, and it is an open question whether the Rook is beneficial to the agriculturist or not.

Although always, comparatively speaking, at our doors and affording many opportunities of studying its ways, the Rook has many unexplained habits and customs: sometimes a large flock will perform curious aerial evolutions, which I have heard described as "weaving," the individuals crossing and recrossing each other's tracks while circling at a great height in the air.

Young Rooks, up to the time of their second moult, have the base of the bill sheathed with bristly feathers, similar to those on the bills of the adult Carrion and Hooded Crows.

On reaching maturity, however, these feathers in the Rook are either shed or worn off by abrasion, caused by the bird's habit of digging in the soil for its food, leaving bare a large portion of the skin around the base of the bill, which forms a ready means of distinguishing the adult Rook from its congeners. The male and female are alike in colour.

THE SKY-LARK.

Alauda arvensis, Linnæus.

Plate 22.

Hardly any bird is better known, or so famed in poetry and song, and few more widely distributed through the length and breadth of our land, than the Sky-Lark. Countless numbers arrive on our shores during the autumn and winter months from Northern and Central Europe, while at the same time many of our home-bred birds, as well as immigrants, leave us during the cold season, moving southwards and westwards.

The Sky-Lark is found breeding all over Europe, but the race which inhabits southern Italy, South-eastern Europe, and the Mediterranean islands is said to be slightly different to the typical form. About the end of February or beginning of March the flocks break up and pairing begins, although they do not usually commence their nesting duties until the middle of April.

The nest is always placed on the ground, frequently in a slight depression in the soil concealed by a tuft of herbage on some grassy upland, or perhaps more often among growing corn, which affords a safe retreat. It is composed of dead grasses, with a lining of finer fibres, and contains four or five eggs, occasionally only three; in ground colour greyish, with closely distributed olive-brown freckles and markings. Two broods are reared in the season, most of the young birds leaving the neighbourhood as soon as they are able to do for themselves. The food consists of the seeds of weeds and other plants, as well as greenstuff, insects, and small worms; in time of snow they are often hard pressed for nourishment.

The most striking act in the life history of the Sky-Lark is his wonderful song, made even more effective by the manner in which it is delivered. This joyous and "heart-lifting" lay fills the air as the bird ascends higher and higher till almost out of sight, "melting in the flood of light," and is continued while he floats downwards, head to wind, when he ceases and drops like a stone.

5

The song does not last for many minutes at a time, often for only two or three, and may sometimes be heard while the bird is perched on a post or bush or even on the ground.

When feeding Larks run swiftly and nimbly among the herbage, not hopping like so many other small birds, and their long rather straight hind claw is well adapted to assist them in passing over the grass. They have a characteristic habit of standing erect, with raised crest, as shown in the plate, and on other occasions will crouch, when they are easily overlooked owing to their colour harmonising so well with the ground.

When migrating Sky-Larks appear to be very much attracted by any brilliant light, and great numbers out of the countless migratory flocks are lost at the lighthouses on our coasts.

On one occasion when I was working at night close to a lighted window, a Lark arrived out of the darkness and fluttered against the glass, until it was opened, when the bird entered the room. This habit has been taken advantage of by the invention of an unsportsman-like appliance, known as a lark-glass, which, attracting the birds, allowed them to be easily shot by a gunner stationed near.

Sky-Larks are fond of dusting their plumage, and also of bathing. The sexes are alike in colour.

Pl. 22.

Sky-Lark.
Shore-Lark.
Crested Lark

Wood Lark.
Short-toed Lark.
White-winged Lark.
Black Lark (summer & winter)

THE WOOD-LARK.

Alauda arborea, Linnæus.

PLATE 22.

This species, easily distinguished from the Sky-Lark by its smaller size, shorter tail, and more strongly marked light-coloured eye-streak, is local in its distribution, and much less plentiful than the other.

It has been noticed chiefly in the southern and south-eastern districts of England, being rare in the middle and northern parts, while it is only locally distributed in Wales, and rarely seen either in Scotland or Ireland.

It is said to have decreased in numbers of late years, and is now unknown in some of its former haunts.

Throughout Europe it is found from the central parts of Scandinavia as far south as the Mediterranean and eastwards to the Ural Mountains.

According to Professor Newton in his edition of Yarrell's *British Birds*, the Wood-Lark breeds early in the year, sometimes about the middle of March.

The nest is placed in a slight hollow on the ground, concealed by a grass tuft or small shrub, and is made of bents with some moss, and lined with finer grasses; the materials being more firmly compacted together than in the nest of the Sky-Lark. The four or five eggs are pale yellowish- or greenish-white, spotted and marked with reddish-brown and violet-grey, while sometimes the markings blend into each other, forming a zone at the larger end.

This species is more insectivorous than the Sky-Lark; in summer grass-hoppers form a considerable part of its food, but seeds are eaten during the winter months, at which time the birds may be seen in small flocks, and have a habit of squatting close to the ground in order to escape observation.

The Wood-Lark is one of our finest songsters, its flute-like notes being sweet and melodious, sometimes given as the bird perches on a branch, at others delivered while it circles or hovers in the air. Its favourite haunts are among the uncultivated parts of the country, and although not actually inhabiting woods, it is seldom found far from trees, and is partial to open spaces skirted by plantations in dry and sandy situations.

The sexes do not differ in colour.

7

THE CRESTED LARK.

Alauda cristata, Linnæus.

PLATE 22.

Although fairly common as near our shores as the north of France, as well as in Holland and Belgium, the Crested Lark is only a rare straggler to England, the latest occurrence I have heard of being one seen this summer (1915) by Mr. J. G. Millais near Horsham. Subject to variations both in form and colour, this bird is found in suitable localities throughout Europe, as well as in North Africa and Asia.

The nest is generally placed on the ground, the slight depression caused by a hoof-print being often made use of, but Naumann says it is occasionally built on an old earth wall or among the thatch of a shed in the fields. It much resembles the Sky-Lark's, and contains four or five eggs, pale yellowish or greenish-white, spotted with olive-brown and violet-grey.

Its food is also like that of other Larks.

The soft pleasant song is delivered either from the ground or in the air.

It is a very tame and confiding bird, often frequenting the neighbourhood of villages and showing little fear of man, and when dusting itself on sandy ground or roads it will, if disturbed, merely fly a short distance and then alight. The female differs little from the male, being only slightly smaller.

THE SHORT-TOED LARK.

Alauda brachydactyla, Leisler.

PLATE 22.

This little Lark has occurred about a dozen times in England, and has also been obtained on five occasions on Scottish islands, viz. Fair Isle, the Orkneys, and Outer Hebrides, and once in Ireland. It is common as a breeding species in Southern Europe, especially in the open tracts of uncultivated and sandy country of central and southern Spain, and also in North Africa, as well as Asia.

The nest is situated in a hollow or hoof-mark in the sand, or under the shelter of a clod in fallow land, and is slightly constructed of grass-bents with a lining of hair, and sometimes two or three feathers. The eggs, usually four or five, are white, thickly freckled with ashen-brown.

The Short-toed Lark lives principally on seeds, and has a pleasing but somewhat feeble song, uttered sometimes while the bird is soaring aloft, sometimes on the ground. There is no difference in the colours of the sexes.

THE WHITE-WINGED LARK.

Alauda sibirica, J. F. Gmelin.

PLATE 22.

The first occurrence of this Eastern species noted in England was a bird caught alive near Brighton in November 1869, which had been consorting with some Snow-Buntings. Since that date five others have been obtained in Kent and Sussex. It breeds among the steppes of southern Russia, where it is quite common, and also in Asia from Turkestan to Siberia, migrating southwards and westwards in autumn.

The nest, usually begun in May, is built like those of its congeners on the ground in some small depression, sheltered by a grass tuft or bush. The eggs vary in number from three to five, and in colour are yellowish-white, with markings of dull brown and lilac-grey.

Little is known of its habits, and I can find no information about its food, which probably is similar to the other Larks'. It frequents open country, and according to Pallas is often to be seen by roadsides, where it sings while fluttering in the air after the manner of the Sky-Lark, but with a shorter and somewhat different strain.

The female is duller in colour than her mate, and lacks the bright rufous tints on the head and other parts.

10

THE BLACK LARK.

Alauda yeltoniensis, Forster.

PLATE 22.

A small flock of this large-billed and very striking species visited the borders of Sussex and Kent in January 1907, of which four were obtained, the last being shot on 18th February of that year. Previous to their arrival the weather had been very cold and stormy. The Black Lark lives among the steppes of southern Russia, and east of the Caspian Sea as far as the Yenesei, wandering occasionally in winter to Europe.

The nest is loosely constructed and placed on the ground. It contains four or five eggs, in colour white, mottled with umber-brown and grey.

Its food consists of seeds, especially those of the salt-flavoured plants of the steppes, and in time of snow, when pressed for nutriment, it frequents roads in company with flocks of other species.

Its song is said to resemble the Sky-Lark's, and like the Shore-Lark it leads a wandering life in winter, but little is known of its habits.

The female during summer has the upper-parts light buffish-brown, with darker markings of brown, is rufous on the lower part of the back, while some of the primaries and tail feathers are edged with white. In winter the general colour is more bleached and hoary.

THE SHORE-LARK.

Otocorys alpestris (Linnæus).

PLATE 22.

The Shore-Lark has long been known as a winter visitor to our islands, the first having been obtained in March 1830 on the Norfolk coast. Of late years, during the months between autumn and spring, its visitations have greatly increased, and may now be considered as annual along the east coast and as far north as Fair Isle, Shetlands. It has never been recorded in the west, and only once in Ireland.

During winter the Shore-Lark seems to lead a wandering life, and in summer is found over a great part of Northern Europe, mainly beyond the Arctic Circle, and also in Northern Asia and America.

The nest is invariably built on the ground, usually in some slight depression or among stones, being lightly made of grass and bents, and lined inside with the hair of the reindeer or with willow-down. The number of eggs varies from three to five, and their colour is pale greenish-white, closely and irregularly marked with dull brown; occasionally the markings form a zone at the larger end.

The Shore-Lark breeds twice yearly, the broods afterwards forming flocks. Its food consists of seeds and insects, and its song, though brief, is full of melody, the birds singing in the air as well as on the ground. It is not shy and may be seen about the villages and towns of Northern Europe.

The female is rather smaller, has less black on the head, and is duller in colour than the male.

Order PICARIÆ.

FAMILY CYPSELIDÆ.

THE SWIFT.

Cypselus apus (Linnæus).

PLATE 23.

This summer visitor to our islands often arrives in the south of England at the end of April, at which time I have seen it in the Isle of Wight, but in Surrey the date of its coming is usually early in May. It leaves us rather suddenly and mysteriously about the middle of August or a little later, without the noticeable gatherings so often displayed by the Swallows and Martins before taking their departure. There are few parts of the country where it is not more or less plentiful, except in some portions of northern and western Scotland. It is widely spread over Europe during the summer, as far north as Scandinavia and Russia, while in winter it retires to Africa and Madagascar.

It haunts the neighbourhood of towns and villages, the nest being placed in some recess or crevice in the darkness beneath the thatch or tiles of cottages and houses, under the beams on the roofs of churches, and sometimes in crannies in the rocky faces of cliffs; a very small opening is sufficient for the entry of the bird, which can squeeze itself through a tiny crevice; according to Gilbert White they even turn their bodies edgeways to effect their purpose. For the construction of the nest the bird collects some straws, grass, wool, or feathers, gathered while on the wing, and glues these together with a glutinous secretion from the salivary glands. The two white eggs are rather rough in texture and elongated in form; they are usually laid at the end of May or beginning of June, and unless some accident happens no second brood is reared in the season, while birds have been known to abandon their young rather than delay their departure.

The shrill ringing scream of the Swift is a familiar summer sound, as the birds dash in their wild career, the clamour varying in intensity as they wheel

13

Pl. 23.

Swift   Needle-tailed Swift. Nightjar.   Alpine Swift.
Red-necked Nightjar.   Egyptian Nightjar.

round and about the steeples and buildings; they show a marvellous power in guiding and controlling their flight, at times moving with rapid beats of their wings, then again gliding in long sweeps and curves. Their energy appears to be untiring, and they do not seem in any way affected by heavy rain.

During the long days they are capable of remaining on the wing from early morning till dark, and towards evening, when the young are able to look after themselves, the birds may be seen circling at an incredible height; whether for recreation or after their food, which consists entirely of insects, it would be difficult to say.

It has been stated and is a common belief that owing to its great length of wing the Swift is unable to rise from a flat surface, but this has been proved to have no foundation in fact, from the observation of competent authorities. When they first arrive, Swifts are in the perfection of plumage, with a beautiful gloss on their feathers, but before they leave us they become faded and bleached. The sexes are alike in colour.

The Swifts have now been entirely separated by naturalists from the Swallows and Martins, as it has been proved that they have no relation whatever to these birds.

The foot of the Swift is of peculiar construction, having the four toes, which are short and strong, all directed forwards, and the tarsus very short and feathered in front. This formation enables the bird to cling with great ease to the rough surface of a wall or rock when alighting at the nest.

THE ALPINE SWIFT.

Cypselus melba (Linnæus).

PLATE 23.

The Alpine or white-bellied Swift was unknown in the British Islands until the summer of 1829, when the first example was obtained off the Irish coast. Some twenty-five others have since occurred in England, one in Wales, and three in Ireland.

This species is a summer visitor to the mountainous districts of Central and Southern Europe and North Africa, migrating in autumn to South Africa and Ceylon. It also breeds eastwards as far as the Himalayas.

The Alpine Swift builds its semi-circular nest within some cranny or recess in inaccessible rock faces or in the walls of lofty buildings, the old cathedral tower at Berne before it was removed having been one of their breeding stations. The nest is composed of straws, grasses, feathers, and other materials, gathered on the wing, the mass being united by saliva. The dull white eggs are generally two in number.

The cry of this Swift is loud and more powerful than that of our common bird, and its food is the same, consisting entirely of insects. Its powers of flight are even more striking, as it dashes and wheels at lightning speed, while it is easily distinguished on the wing by its large size and white underparts. There is no variation in the colour of the sexes, but in the young the feathers are edged with dull white.

THE NEEDLE-TAILED SWIFT.

Acanthyllis caudacuta (Latham).

PLATE 23.

This bird, an extremely rare straggler from Eastern Asia and Australia, has only twice been obtained in England, and has never hitherto been seen in Europe. The first was shot at Great Horkesley, near Colchester, in July 1846, and the other near Ringwood, Hampshire, in July 1879, the last having had a companion which was not secured. The breeding range of this large and long-winged Swift extends from eastern Siberia southwards through Saghalien, Manchuria, Mongolia, and Japan, while the bird spends the winter in Australia and Tasmania.

General Prjevalsky found these birds breeding in river cliffs and in hollow trees, several pairs generally nesting in close proximity; their notes are said to be weak, more like a Swallow's than the common Swift's. The eggs are white, and the bird subsists entirely on insects. The male and female are alike in colour.

FAMILY **CAPRIMULGIDÆ.**

THE NIGHTJAR.

Caprimulgus europœus, Linnæus.

PLATE 23.

The Nightjar, also called Fernowl and Goatsucker, and known in many country places by its old name of Puckeridge, usually arrives in England about the middle of May, though I have seen one near Hascombe, Surrey, which I put up from the shelter of some furze bushes in a disused sandpit on 29th April 1909. During summer it is widely distributed over our islands, and leaves us in September for Africa, the latest date on which I have seen it in Surrey being the 13th of that month. In Europe it ranges as far north as Scandinavia and southwards to Spain.

The Nightjar makes no nest, laying its two eggs on the ground, usually in a clearing among trees, but sometimes in the open, sheltered by furze, brambles, or bracken ; the eggs, which are elongated in shape, are white, marbled and veined with different shades of brown and violet-grey. One brood only is reared in the season, and in their first downy stage, before attaining their powers of flight, the young often move a short distance from their birthplace, and are fed by their parents until after they are able to fly.

The food consists of insects, large moths and cockchafers forming a good part of it ; these are caught on the wing during the hours of twilight and darkness, the wing cases and other indigestible portions being ejected in the form of pellets from the mouth.

Perched on a bare branch, the bird utters his loud and singular vibrating song, which often lasts for several minutes at a time, and has been likened to the whirr of a spinning machine. It is usually heard between twilight and dawn, but is said t have been noticed occasionally in the daytime. Often when on the wing in early summer the male gives out a sharp whistling note, and at times produces a rather loud clap by the striking together of its wings after the manner of a pigeon.

17

During daylight the Nightjar drowses with closed eyelids, either crouching on the ground or on the bough of a tree, usually perched so that the body of the bird is placed lengthways in a parallel line with the branch, and not across it; as far as I have been able to observe, with the head held higher than the body. It seems to delight in the warmth of the sun, and may often be seen basking and dusting on sandy footpaths or in sheltered corners, and the curiously mottled and protective colouring of the bird makes it difficult to see when at rest. When disturbed during the day, as it flops into the quietness of some shady retreat, one can form no idea of its wonderful powers of flight as displayed during the dusk of evening, when the birds are fully awake, swooping with marvellous speed in pursuit of their prey, or toying and twisting in the air and chasing one another.

The foot of this bird is extremely small, and no satisfactory reason appears to have been discovered for the curious pectinated or comb-like edge on the inner side of the middle claw, unless it be to enable the bird to sit more securely when settled along a branch.

The female resembles the male in colour, but is slightly less rufous, and is without the bold white spots on the three first quill feathers of the wing and the two outermost feathers on each side of the tail.

THE RED-NECKED NIGHTJAR.

Caprimulgus ruficollis, Temminck.

PLATE 23.

The only British example of this beautiful Nightjar was shot on 5th October 1856 at Killingworth, near Newcastle, and recorded by the late John Hancock. It is common in many parts of southern Spain and Portugal, and also in Morocco, while a paler form of the same bird occurs in Tunisia and Algeria.

Lord Lilford says, in his work on British Birds, "it is very common in most parts of Andalucia during the summer months, especially frequenting the sandy pine-woods, though by no means infrequently met with also in the scrub-grown wastes." He also states that in comparison with the common Nightjar "there is a very perceptible difference between the churring' notes of the two species."

Their eggs are very much alike in colour, and there is apparently very little difference in their food and habits.

The sexes are similar in the colour of their plumage, both having the white spots on the three outer primaries, and broad white tips to the two pairs of outer tail feathers.

THE EGYPTIAN NIGHTJAR.

Caprimulgus ægyptius, Lichtenstein.

PLATE 23.

The Egyptian or Isabelline Nightjar is another rare species, one example only having been obtained in England. This was shot near Mansfield, Nottinghamshire, by the gamekeeper of Mr. J. Whitaker, of Rainworth Lodge in that county, on 23rd June 1883, and is now in his collection.

This species is found in Egypt and Nubia, and across South-western Asia to Afghanistan and Baluchistan. It makes no nest, the two eggs, in ground colour a dingy yellowish- or greyish-white, with pale ashen-grey mottlings, being placed on the desert sands.

The male and female are alike in colour, and both lack the white wing and tail spots, so marked in both sexes of the Red-necked Nightjar, and also in the male of our common bird.

FAMILY **PICIDÆ.** SUBFAMILY *IŸNGINÆ*.

THE WRYNECK.

Iÿnx torquilla, Linnæus.

PLATE 24.

This summer visitor to England usually arrives in the first or second week in April, the earliest date on which I have noted it in Surrey being the 4th of that month, while it takes its departure in September. Coming usually about the same time as the Cuckoo, it is often called the Cuckoo's mate, and in my neighbourhood it is known to country people as the "rinding bird," from its arrival coinciding with the time of rinding or stripping of bark from the oak.

It is not an uncommon bird in the south-eastern counties of England, but is scarcer in the west and very rare in the north, while in Scotland and Ireland it is only known as a passing migrant.

It breeds throughout the greater part of Europe, and in many of the temperate portions of Asia, retiring for the winter months to tropical Africa.

Not till some time after its arrival does the Wryneck begin its nesting operations, although it may be seen about the neighbourhood of its nesting hole as soon as it reaches this country. It returns year by year to the same spot, and generally selects some hole in a fruit or other tree in which to deposit its eggs, and if it once takes to a nesting-box will return regularly to it. I have had many opportunities of watching a pair which have taken possession of one fixed to the boarding of a shed in my garden.

They frequent the neighbouring trees for some time before the eggs are laid, and were it not for the peculiar notes of the male, which bear a strong resemblance to the cry of a Kestrel or Hobby, and are delivered as he sits stolidly on the bough of a tree, the birds might easily pass unnoticed, so quiet and unobtrusive are their actions.

No materials are gathered on which to lay the eggs; they are merely placed on the wood within the hole, although if the site has been previously occupied

21

by any nest-building bird, they are laid on the top of this ready-made structure. In number the eggs vary from seven to ten, but if these be removed the bird will continue to lay, as many as forty-two having been recorded as taken from one nest by Mr. Norgate between 29th May and 13th July, 1872. The eggs are pure white.

The food consists almost entirely of insects, the bird being especially fond of ants and their pupæ, hence the old Norfolk name of "Emmet eater." The curiously long and pointed tongue is beautifully adapted for this purpose, having ducts which convey a sticky secretion to the sharp and hard tip, which enables the bird to capture its prey with great ease and rapidity.

The Wryneck has a singular habit from which it takes its name, of turning and twisting its head and neck if disturbed in its nesting-hole or taken in the hand, and it will feign death when captured in order to effect its escape.

This last-mentioned ruse was noticed long ago by Sir Thomas Browne, of Norwich, who in his notes on birds found in Norfolk speaks of the Wryneck, or "Hobby bird," as he calls it, "as maruellously subiect to the vertigo." By way of repelling an intruder it will also utter a sharp hissing sound, which, coming from the darkness of its retreat, often gives the impression that a snake has sheltered therein. The young also make a similar noise when disturbed.

The female resembles the male in colour, but is slightly duller.

THE GREEN WOODPECKER.

Gecinus viridis (Linnæus).

PLATE 24.

The Green Woodpecker, the most common of the three species inhabiting this country, is plentiful in many of the wooded districts of the southern and midland counties of England, though scarce in the northern parts, and hardly known in Scotland or Ireland. It is found over the greater part of Europe, ranging as far north as Norway and the neighbourhood of Petrograd, while it also inhabits parts of Asia.

The nest is placed within the hollow core of a decaying branch or trunk of a tree, one of the softer-wooded kinds, such as the elm, ash, poplar, or willow, being preferred to the beech or oak. Into this a circular hole is cut by the chisel-like bill of the bird, running in a horizontal direction until the rotten wood is reached, when a cavity is dug out in which to lay the eggs. The chips of wood are thrown out at the entrance as the birds proceed with their work, the litter at the roots of the tree affording a good indication of where the nest is. The five or six eggs, which are of a beautiful shining white, are laid either on the bare floor of the hole, or on some of the chips which may not have been removed.

The food of the Green Woodpecker consists of insects of various kinds, ants and their pupæ being much sought after; on such occasions the bird may be seen hopping in a curious, ungainly manner on the ground. When searching for timber beetles and grubs in trees, it begins near the ground and works upwards, usually in a spiral course, with short quick jumps, using its tail as a support, and inserting its tongue into the cracks and openings in the bark as it ascends, while it occasionally stops to cut away a piece of bark or decayed wood which conceals some delicacy within.

The Green Woodpecker, or Yaffle as it is called in country places, on account of its loud laughing cry, which has a fine joyous ring in it, especially during the breeding season, is shy and solitary in its habits, and haunts the neighbourhood of old timber trees in parks and woods, though it may sometimes be seen in the open. When in fear or distress the bird utters piercing and discordant cries, such as I have heard when one has been chased by a Sparrow-Hawk. It is easy to distinguish the bird at a considerable distance when on the wing, as it alternately rises and falls during flight.

The female differs from the male by having less red on the head, and none on the dark patch at the base of the bill, which is entirely black.

THE GREAT SPOTTED WOODPECKER.

Dendrocopus major (Linnæus).

PLATE 24.

The Great Spotted Woodpecker, or, as it is often called, the Pied Woodpecker, is much less common than the species last described, although it is not so scarce as many people suppose, owing to its shy and retiring habits. It is widely distributed over England, where there are sufficient trees to suit its requirements, but becomes rarer in the northern counties. In Scotland it breeds as far north as Dunkeld, while it has not been known to nest in Ireland, although it has been obtained there. It is found over a considerable part of Europe, ranging as far north as Scandinavia and Russia, but these European birds which frequently migrate to our shores are said to belong to a different race.

This Woodpecker either makes for itself a nesting-hole in a tree, or occupies a ready-made cavity which is often enlarged to suit the bird's requirements, oaks being frequently selected. The five to seven eggs are either laid on the bare wood or on chips left in the hole, and are pure white in colour.

In spring the bird produces a loud jarring note, caused by the rapid tapping of the bill against a bough, which is used as a sounding-board, the strokes being delivered so rapidly as to be almost invisible. Mr. J. G. Millais informs me that he does not think this species makes the long rattle of the Lesser Spotted Woodpecker, but only a short one, while the calling note is " Pleek-Pleek-Pleek-Pleek "; it also makes a single flute-like note when flying.

This bird appears to be much less insectivorous than the Green Woodpecker, and although insects no doubt compose the bulk of its food, it undoubtedly feeds largely on nuts and berries, and I am assured by a friend in my neighbourhood that the young, after they have left the nest, have come to the green peas in his garden.

The female differs from the male in having no red on the head, while the young, as shown in the plate, has the whole crown of that colour.

Pl. 24.

Wryneck.   Green Woodpecker.
ser Spotted Woodpecker. ♂ & ♀.   Great Spotted Woodpecker. (adult ♂ & young)
            Kingfisher.   Roller.

THE LESSER SPOTTED WOODPECKER.

Dendrocopus minor (Linnæus).

PLATE 24.

This little bird, which should more properly be called the Barred Woodpecker, appears to be much more common than its larger relation just described, and is frequently to be heard, though not so often seen, in the southern and midland parts of England and the adjoining counties in Wales. In the north of England it becomes scarce, while it has only once occurred in Scotland, and in Ireland the records of its capture are not to be relied upon.

In Europe the Lesser Spotted Woodpecker is found as far north as Scandinavia and Russia, and ranges eastwards across parts of Siberia and Central Asia to Japan. It also inhabits North and North-west Africa.

In May the glossy white eggs are laid in its nesting-hole, which is similar, but, of course, smaller than the other species, and generally situated at a good height from the ground. They are placed on the bottom of the cavity, in which chips are sometimes left, and vary in number from five to eight.

This species is said never to eat fruit or seeds, but feeds on the insects caught on the trees it frequents.

Both sexes have a short call-note, rapidly repeated, and make besides the loud jarring sound somewhat resembling but more prolonged than the Great Spotted Woodpecker's, produced, according to Mr. J. G. Millais, by rapid hammering of the bill in a hole, which may be compared to a long-drawn guttural R. He also tells me that it utters a high-pitched note when flying.

The bird is active and restless in its habits, and usually haunts the upper branches of tall trees, especially those that are dead or decayed. In the young male the crown of the head is red, as in the adult bird, while the young female has only the front of the head of this colour.

Several other species of Woodpecker, native to foreign countries, are said to have been taken here, but the records are either unreliable or refer to escaped birds.

Family **ALCEDINIDÆ**.

THE KINGFISHER.

Alcedo ispida (Linnæus).

PLATE 24.

This beautiful bird, renowned for the gem-like brightness of its plumage, is found over the greater part of the British Islands, and although well known, is not by any means common, owing to the persecution it receives on account of the value of its feathers for the dressing of artificial flies, and the demands of millinery; it is also much sought after as a subject for the taxidermist, and a good many are destroyed by the owners of fishings.

In Europe it ranges from Scandinavia and Russia to the Mediterranean.

The Kingfisher generally chooses for its nesting site a steep bank by a pond or riverside, in which by digging with its bill it excavates a tunnel with an upward slope, penetrating about two feet into the soil, although the distance varies. The entrance is narrow, but is made wider and rounded at the extremity in order to accommodate the sitting bird and nestlings.

There is no real nest, the eggs, which are glossy white and from six to eight in number, being merely laid on an unsavoury deposit of fish-bones cast up in the form of pellets by the birds. Amid these unpleasing surroundings the eggs are hatched, and as the young gain strength they come to the mouth to receive the small fish brought in rapid succession by the parents.

After leaving the nest, and before they are able to fend for themselves, the little birds form a charming picture as they sit on a bough waiting to be fed. The food consists of small fish, such as minnows, stickle-backs, and other kinds, as well as tadpoles and aquatic insects; small crustaceans are also said to be taken. The Kingfisher's mode of fishing is to remain motionless on the bough of a tree, post, or some other point of vantage, until its prey comes within reach, when with a sudden dash into the stream it is secured, carried to a branch, and speedily killed by a few sharp strokes against the perch, when with a dexterous movement it is so held as to be always swallowed head foremost. Sometimes the bird may be seen hovering over the water before darting at its prey.

The note of the Kingfisher is a shrill cry, several times repeated, and has been likened to that of our common Sandpiper.

The flight is straight and rapid, usually carried out close to the water and following the turnings of the river, though the bird will often travel some distance over ground away from any stream. During the greater part of the year it is rather a solitary bird, and suffers much during severe weather owing to its food supply being cut off by the freezing of the waters, and at such times it commonly makes its way to the sea-shore.

The sexes are alike in colour, the female being perhaps slightly duller.

26

Family CORACIIDÆ.

THE ROLLER.

Coracias garrulus, Linnæus.

PLATE 24.

Since Sir Thomas Browne recorded the occurrence of this gaily-painted species in Norfolk, now more than two hundred and fifty years ago, a large number have reached our shores, over a hundred having been noticed, mostly in the southern and eastern counties of England, while it has also visited the Orkneys and St. Kilda, though owing to its brilliant plumage few of these visitants have escaped destruction.

During summer it is found over a great part of Europe, being plentiful in the Mediterranean countries, and in North-west Africa. It also visits western Siberia, and winters in South Africa and India.

The Roller generally selects for its nest a hole in a tree, or in some bank or cliff, but a cavity in a ruined wall is also sometimes chosen. A light fabric is put together of twigs and dead grasses, in which it lays from four to six shining white eggs, globular in shape.

It feeds chiefly on grasshoppers, beetles, and other insects captured on the ground, and, according to Lord Lilford, it occasionally takes frogs and small reptiles.

Its notes are harsh and discordant, and it is by nature a shy and wary bird, constantly flitting from branch to branch or swooping to the ground to capture its prey, and haunting more or less open country.

At times, especially during the breeding season, it performs somersaults and other curious gymnastic antics in the air, hence its name of " Roller."

It usually selects a dead bough or some isolated tree-top as a look-out station, from which it sallies after food.

There is no difference between the male and female in colour, but the immature birds are duller.

Pl. 25.

Cuckoo. (adult & young). Great Spotted Cuckoo
American Yellow-billed Cuckoo. Bee-eater. Hoopoe

A. Thorburn. 1914.

THE BEE-EATER.

Merops apiaster, Linnæus.

PLATE 25.

Some forty examples of this rare visitant to the British Islands have been obtained, one of these having occurred as far north as the Shetlands. It is plentiful in the south European countries, and is found eastwards as far as western Siberia, Afghanistan, and Kashmir.

The new B.O.U. "List of British Birds" (2nd ed. 1915) states that "occasionally it is found breeding to the north of its range as far as Silesia and has wandered to almost every part of Europe." It migrates for the winter to tropical and South Africa and India. The Bee-eater usually breeds in colonies, boring deep holes in river banks, and sometimes in open and uneven ground. Referring to the latter breeding-places, Colonel Irby says (*The Ornithology of the Straits of Gibraltar*, 2nd ed., p. 132): "The shafts to these nests are not usually so long as those in banks of rivers, which sometimes reach to a distance of eight or nine feet in all; the end is enlarged into a round sort of chamber, on the bare soil of which the usual four or five shining white eggs are placed." The same writer observed that the bills of the birds, after boring the holes, "are sometimes worn away to less than half their usual length."

The food consists of winged insects, such as bees and wasps, while its note, according to the late Howard Saunders, is "a sharp *quilp*."

The female is not so bright as the male, and has the two central tail feathers shorter.

THE HOOPOE.

Upupa epops, Linnæus.

Plate 25.

This bird is a regular spring visitor to the southern parts of England, and were it not for the constant and senseless persecution it receives at the hands of the collector and others, would no doubt breed annually in this country. It is known to have done so on several occasions, but very few of the birds which visit us escape destruction, as they are very tame and confiding and have little fear of man.

It was evidently more often seen in former days than at present, as Sir Thomas Browne in his list of birds found in Norfolk, written some two hundred and fifty years ago, quaintly describes it as " Upupa or Hoopebird so named from its note a gallant marked bird wch I have often seen & tis not hard to shoot them."

The Hoopoe is a common species in Southern Europe, and breeds throughout the continent, ranging as far north as south Sweden, inhabiting also western Siberia and other parts of Asia, including north-western India. It usually nests in a hole in a tree, such as the ash or willow, or in a cavity in a rock or wall, the few twigs, grasses, &c., which compose the nest being set in an accumulation of ordure. From four to seven eggs are laid, of a pale greenish-blue, which soon lose their beautiful colour.

It feeds on insects, worms, and grubs, sought for among manure in pasture lands and roads. The singular and far-reaching note of the Hoopoe is a hollow-sounding whoop, repeated several times in succession.

The birds pass a good deal of their time on the ground, where they "march about in a stately manner," as Gilbert White observes, at times erecting their showy crest if alarmed or excited and when first alighting.

The female is hardly so brightly coloured as the male.

29

THE CUCKOO.

Cuculus canorus, Linnæus.

PLATE 25.

Looking over my notes, kept for a number of years, on the first arrival of the Cuckoo in the neighbourhood of Hascombe, Surrey, I find the earliest date is the 10th of April, the bird usually arriving shortly after that time.

Mr. J. G. Millais tells me that he saw and heard one in Warnham Park, Sussex, as early as 31st March, which he believes is the earliest authentic date known : this was recorded in *The Field* at the time.

The males, who come before the females, soon announce their presence by their well-known call, which, continuing throughout the month of May, becomes hoarse before ceasing in June. Towards the end of July or early in August the old birds disappear, the young following them later.

Soon after its arrival it spreads over the country, reaching the northern parts of Scotland shortly after the beginning of May.

During summer it visits the whole of Europe, ranging, according to the late Howard Saunders (*Manual of British Birds*, 2nd ed., p. 287), "almost to the North Cape in Norway, nearly as far north in Russia, and across Northern Asia up to lat. 67°," while in winter it migrates to South Africa, India, and other parts of Southern Asia.

Owing to the Cuckoo's strange habit of entrusting the care of its eggs and young to foster-parents of other species, it has long attained a notoriety possessed by few other birds.

As is now well known the female lays her egg on the ground, and taking it in her bill deposits it in the nest of some other bird ; perhaps the most favoured are those of the Pied Wagtail, Meadow- and Tree-Pipit, Reed-Warbler, Hedge-Sparrow, and other soft-billed birds. The eggs are remarkably small for a bird of the Cuckoo's size, and vary a good deal in colour and markings, but apparently

Pl. 26.

Long-eared Owl.

Barn-Owl.

Tawny Owl.

Short-eared Owl.

each female always produces eggs of the same type. These may be greenish- or reddish-grey, with close specklings of darker shades, or occasionally pale blue, and sometimes, but not always, resemble the colour of the foster-parent's eggs. Not long after being hatched, the young Cuckoo contrives to hoist its fellow-nestlings on to its back, which for the first twelve days or so has a convenient hollow, and with more or less violent efforts heaves them one by one over the edge of the nest.

The familiar song of the Cuckoo need not be described, but I have never come across any account of the curious fact that it appears to be uttered with the bill closed, as when a pigeon coos. My attention was first drawn to this by the late J. Wolf many years ago, and I have since had opportunities of verifying it. The sketch of the adult bird in the plate was taken from life with the aid of a field-glass, and shows the attitude assumed when the notes are given. The bird sits in a more or less horizontal position, with wings drooped below the tail, which is spread and slightly raised, while a swaying motion is given to the body and the throat is puffed out.

The female does not usually differ from the male in colour, but occasionally is tinged with rufous on the breast; it appears always to be less numerous than the other sex, and leads a wandering life. She has not the loud "plain song" of her mate, but utters a kind of note, which Seebohm compares to the sound of bubbling water.

THE GREAT SPOTTED CUCKOO.

Coccystes glandarius (Linnæus).

PLATE 25.

This large Cuckoo is a very rare visitor to the British Islands, four specimens only having been recorded, viz. the first captured on Omey Island, off the Connemara coast, about 1842, the next near Bellingham, Northumberland, another on the Denes, Yarmouth, and the last seen at the Skellig Rock, county Kerry, by the lightkeeper there. The Great Spotted Cuckoo is found in South-western Europe, particularly Spain and Portugal, ranging across Asia Minor to Persia. It also inhabits North Africa, retiring in the winter to tropical and South Africa.

It is said always to place its eggs in nests belonging to the Corvidæ (Irby); the colour is pale bluish-green, spotted with reddish-brown and purplish.

Howard Saunders describes the note of the male as a harsh "*kark-kark*," and the female's as "*burroo-burroo.*"

The sexes are alike in colour, but the young bird has the head and nape much darker, with tawny-buff on the throat and breast, and chestnut on part of the primaries.

THE AMERICAN YELLOW-BILLED CUCKOO.

Coccyzus americanus (Linnæus).

PLATE 25.

This species during the breeding season inhabits the temperate parts of North America, and migrates by way of the West Indies and Central America to pass the winter in South America. It has occurred about a dozen times in the British Islands.

Unlike our common Cuckoo, it makes its own nest and rears its young, although the egg has been found on rare occasions in the nests of other species. The eggs, seldom more than four in number, are pale green in colour.

Its notes, according to Macgillivray, resemble the word *cow*, repeated eight or ten times, and the sexes are alike in colour.

One example of the American Black-billed Cuckoo, *Coccyzus erythrophthalmus* (Wilson), has been recorded in our islands, this having been shot at Kilbead, county Antrim, Ireland, about 25th September 1871.

As its name implies, this species inhabits North America and Canada, migrating in the autumn to South America. It resembles the species last described in its habits and nidification, but differs in colour, having the bill entirely black, the orbits red, a more decided brown on the back, and is without the chestnut on the primaries.

Pl. 27.

Hawk Owl.

Tengmalm's Owl (with Dusky Warbler)

Scops Owl

Snowy Owl ♂

Little Owl.

Order STRIGES.

FAMILY STRIGIDÆ.

THE BARN-OWL.

Strix flammea, Linnæus.

PLATE 26.

The Barn, White, or Screech-Owl, as it is variously called, is a fairly common bird throughout the British Islands, although scarce in northern Scotland. It has a very wide geographical range in both the old and new worlds, and shows some variation in colour, the race inhabiting southern Sweden, Denmark, and Central Europe having a darker breast than our bird.

This species dislikes sunlight and therefore selects for its nesting-place some dark retreat in the walls or under the roof of old buildings, church towers, or in hollow trees, while dovecots are often chosen. For several years in succession a pair occupied a dovecot in my garden, and I noticed what they most appreciated was to have within their dwelling as little light as possible. By placing an inverted wooden box in the darkest corner, to which access was obtained by a hole in the side, the owls were induced to breed regularly, always, however, leaving their home after the young were able to fly in August, and returning early in spring. The eggs, which are pure white, usually number six or more and are placed among old castings, without any nest. As soon as the first one or two are laid, the bird begins to sit, and thus the young are hatched at various times, the eldest of the family helping to incubate the later eggs.

The owlets, at first clad in white down, are fed through the evening and night, but I have found dead mice beside them in the daytime. During the day, as well as by night, they utter a curious sound, like that made by the valve of a cistern.

The food consists almost entirely of mice, rats, voles, bats, and shrews, the Sparrow being the only bird whose remains I have found at the nest referred to. They seem able to bear great heat without any inconvenience, as when a July sun was beating on the roof of their dwelling the heat inside was suffocating.

About the time of twilight when the mice come out to feed and play, the owls begin their hunt, beating along the hedges and among orchard trees with noiseless flight not far from the ground, and dropping suddenly on their unsuspecting prey; at times they utter a weird harsh cry, which can be heard a long way off.

The female resembles the male, and as is the case with most birds of prey, is the larger bird.

Several occurrences of the Dark-breasted race, which inhabits Central Europe, south Sweden, and Denmark, have been noted.

34

THE LONG-EARED OWL.

Asio otus (Linnæus).

PLATE 26.

This species, a resident in the British Islands, frequents woods of pine and fir, while in autumn its numbers are much increased by others which reach our eastern counties from abroad. It is widely distributed over Europe, inhabiting also North Africa and many parts of Asia.

The Long-eared Owl appropriates the former nest of a Magpie, Crow, Jay, or Woodpigeon, and sometimes the "drey" of a squirrel; these are made to suit the convenience of the bird by the addition of twigs or some soft material such as rabbit's fur. In March it lays its smooth white eggs, from four to six in number, and according to Mr. S. E. Brock (*Zoologist*, 1910, p. 117), incubation lasts twenty-eight to thirty days.

Occasionally this species nests on the ground, when the nest resembles the Short-eared Owl's. It preys on rats, voles, and mice, while a considerable number of small birds, as well as beetles, are taken.

Being nocturnal in its habits, it usually passes the day close to the trunk of a tree, and if disturbed has a quaint way of raising its ear-tufts, contracting the feathers of the body, which at the same time is stretched out to much more than its usual length, while the bird peers with half-closed eyes at the disturber of its peace below.

Mr. R. J. Howard, who has provided me with a number of notes on the Owls and other birds of prey, which I have freely used, informs me that in the breeding season the call of the male is "hoo-hoo-hoo," repeated very slowly; when the birds are disturbed at their nests the cry is a loud "wack-wack," while that of the nestlings is a loud mewing.

The young often leave the nest before they are able to fly, and climb to it again aided by their bills. There are grey as well as rufous phases of plumage of the Long-eared Owl.

35

THE SHORT-EARED OWL.

Asio accipitrinus (Pallas).

PLATE 26.

Avoiding woodlands, this species is much more a bird of the open than the other British Owls, frequenting stubble and turnip-fields, moors, furze-covered slopes, and marsh-lands. It breeds regularly in many places in Great Britain, but much less frequently to the south of Lancashire and Yorkshire than in the north, while in Ireland it never nests. In all three countries it is not uncommon as a bird of passage from autumn to spring, and as numbers often arrive from oversea at the same time as the Woodcocks, it is sometimes called the Woodcock-Owl. It is widely distributed over both hemispheres, inhabiting Europe, Asia, Africa, and America.

The Short-eared Owl breeds late in the year, laying its creamy-white eggs in a slight cavity among sedges or heather. They usually number from four to eight, occasionally amounting to ten or twelve. It is well known that under the stimulus of an abundant food supply the number of eggs laid is largely increased. The young ramble a considerable distance from the nest before they are fully fledged.

The food consists largely of voles, field-mice, rats, small birds, occasionally of fish, bats, beetles, and large moths. During the periodical vole plagues, Short-eared Owls flock to the infested districts, and remain as long as food continues plentiful. They may frequently be seen hunting during daytime with a buoyant unsteady flight, and do not seem inconvenienced by bright sunlight.

The note of this Owl when disturbed is somewhat similar to that of the Long-eared species.

Mr. R. J. Howard tells me that "when stooping down to examine a full-fledged young Short-eared Owl—one of a nest containing seven young and an addled egg—a parent bird struck him a resounding smack on the head, leaving marks of the claws on his hat. The following season at this spot, a bird, presumably the same, struck his claws into the nape of the neck of the gamekeeper, covering his collar with blood. On this Lancashire moor, which has been planted by the Liverpool Corporation, all Owls and Kestrels are strictly preserved for the purpose of keeping down the voles and field-mice, which do great damage to the young forest trees. A large handful of castings taken here on the 24th May consisted altogether of the remains of Short-tailed Voles and one Shrew. There were no remains of birds. Four pairs of Short-eared Owls reared broods on this moor in each of the seasons mentioned above."

The sexes are alike in colour.

36

Pl. 28.

Eagle Owl. ♀

THE TAWNY OWL.

Syrnium aluco (Linnæus).

PLATE 26.

This species, also called the Brown or Wood-Owl, is resident in many parts of Great Britain, and of late years has been introduced into Ireland. It is scarce in the north of Scotland, but seems to be the most abundant of the Owls in most parts of that country. It inhabits the greater portion of Europe, occurring as far north as Scandinavia and south to the Mediterranean. It ranges eastwards to Siberia, and is also found in Persia, Asia Minor, and Syria.

The Tawny Owl loves the shade of old and ivy-covered trees, and early in the year lays its eggs within a hollowed trunk or in the old nest of a Crow or Rook, although it will occasionally use a rabbit-hole or even the bare ground. The eggs vary in number, from three to five or six, and are rounded in shape and pure white in colour.

Its well-known hooting note, which has been rendered as " whoo hoo," is often heard more frequently during the autumn and winter months than in summer.

The food of this species consists chiefly of rats, mice, voles, small birds, and occasionally fish, and it should be carefully protected.

A phase of this Owl sometimes occurs of a much greyer tone of colour than the better known tawny form.

TENGMALM'S OWL.

Nyctala tengmalmi (J. F. Gmelin).

PLATE 27.

Tengmalm's Owl, a rare visitant to Great Britain, has been recorded about twenty times in England and four in Scotland. Although migratory in autumn and winter, its home is in the forest regions of Northern Europe, and high up on the wooded mountain-sides of the central and eastern portions of that continent, while it also ranges into Siberia.

Its four to six—occasionally ten—white eggs are laid, according to Wooley, either in holes of trees or in the nesting-boxes placed by the Lapps for the use of Golden-eye and other ducks, and it is said to occupy the deserted nest of the Black Woodpecker.

Its food consists of lemmings and other small mammals, as well as birds and beetles.

Wheelwright, in his notes on the ornithology of Lapland, describes its note as a " very musical soft whistle."

The ear orifices in most Owls are not symmetrical, but the late Professor Collett has drawn attention to the fact that this want of equality extends to the skull in this species.

It may readily be distinguished from the Little Owl by its rather dense but downy plumage, and the thick covering of feathers on legs and toes.

THE LITTLE OWL.

Athene noctua (Scopoli).

PLATE 27.

It is hard to say whether the Little Owl has ever reached this country unassisted, the first having been taken alive near the Tower of London in 1758. As far back as 1843 Waterton is known to have turned out five near Wakefield, and since then large numbers, imported alive from the Continent, have been liberated by the late Lord Lilford in Northamptonshire, Mr. Meade-Waldo in Hampshire, and Mr. St. Quintin in Yorkshire, whence it has spread far and wide.

It inhabits Europe from as far north as the Baltic to the Mediterranean, slightly different races being found in North Africa and Western Asia.

The eggs, white in colour and numbering three to five, are placed within a hollow tree or in some cavity in walls or rocks, or even in a hole underground.

A great part of the food consists of insects, mice, and small rodents, but owing to its custom of often hunting in daylight, many small birds are caught and killed; it is therefore much disliked by other birds, and I once saw as many as seven different species clamouring round their enemy.

It has a monotonous double note.

This Owl was accounted by the ancient Greeks as the bird of Pallas Athene, and hence its likeness is often to be found on their coins.

THE SNOWY OWL.

Nyctea scandiaca (Linnæus).

PLATE 27.

This fine species is a circumpolar bird, breeding among the Arctic wastes of both hemispheres, and leaving its more northerly quarters in the winter to escape the rigours of the climate and consequent want of food.

About twenty examples have been taken in England, and more than that number in Ireland, while in the north of Scotland, especially in the Orkneys, Shetlands, and Outer Hebrides, it may be considered an annual visitor.

It breeds on the open fjelds and tundras away from forest growth, the nest being often a mere depression in the moss-covered ground, though sometimes, according to Seebohm, made of "a few lichens, mosses, and feathers." It contains from six to eight or even more creamy-white eggs, the incubation period being just five weeks.

The Snowy Owl feeds chiefly on the lemming and other small mammals, but does not, however, confine its diet to these, preying also on Ptarmigan, Willow-Grouse, and Arctic hares, and hunting by day as well as by night. Mr. Millais says: "In Iceland the Snowy Owl preys largely on fish. I have seen them catching quite large char."

During the breeding season the male is very bold and fierce, and will attack anyone approaching the nest. The cry is loud and harsh. Both sexes show a great variety in the markings of their plumage, but the females are more strongly barred with dark than the males. The latter are sometimes almost entirely white, showing only a few brownish-black spots on their snowy feathers.

THE HAWK-OWL.

Surnia funerea (Linnæus).

PLATE 27.

The Hawk-Owl, of which there are two forms, one inhabiting Northern Europe and Asia, and occasionally occurring in Alaska; and the other a native of North America—the *Surnia ulula caparoch* of trinomialists—is a rare visitor to the British Islands. Of the latter race, which differs mainly from the European bird in having the transverse bars on the breast broader and of a ruddier colour, four examples have occurred, while about an equal number of the former have been recorded.

The European Hawk-Owl lays its eggs, which are white in colour and number from five to eight, in a hole in a decayed pine or fir, or in the nesting-boxes of hollowed trunks set up by the peasants of Scandinavia for ducks.

It preys on lemmings, mice, and other rodents, as well as birds, such as the Ptarmigan, Willow-Grouse, and Siberian Jay.

According to Mr. G. E. Lodge—who, having had good opportunities of watching the habits of this species in Norway, obligingly lent me a series of sketches done from life, which were invaluable to me when painting the picture— the Hawk-Owl usually takes up a position on the bare upper branch of a pine, keeping the body and tail in a much more horizontal position than other Owls, and with head pressed downwards watches with its keen yellow eyes for some movement that might betray the whereabouts of the prey below: they are very fearless, and often show a considerable amount of bold curiosity on the sight of a human being, frequently flying straight towards one, and settling on the top of a fir, either large or small.

The Hawk-Owl has a weird strange cry, and does not avoid sunlight.

Like the other Owls, the female is larger than the male, but shows no appreciable difference in colour.

THE SCOPS-OWL.

Scops giu (Scopoli).

PLATE 27.

Nearly sixty examples of this little tufted Owl, the smallest known in this country, have occurred in the British Islands since 1805, when it was first noticed in Yorkshire. It is common during summer in Southern and South-eastern Europe, and, according to the B.O.U. "List of British Birds" (1915), it extends its migrations to "Holland, Belgium, northern France, Germany, and Switzerland."

It also breeds in Asia Minor, Palestine, and North-west Africa, migrating during winter still farther south in Africa.

The Scops-Owl usually nests within a hollow tree, and lays five or six pure white eggs.

It is almost entirely insectivorous, and is seldom seen abroad during the hours of daylight, which it spends in drowsy sleepiness, usually perched close to the trunk of a tree.

It has a curious monotonous cry, constantly repeated, resembling the syllables *kew-kew*.

I am indebted to my friend, Mr. G. E. Lodge, for kindly lending me a sketch, taken from life, which I made use of for the plate.

THE EAGLE-OWL.

Bubo ignavus, T. Forster.

PLATE 28.

The Eagle-Owl, one of the strongest and most rapacious of the birds of prey, has occurred at various times in Great Britain, and although specimens obtained or seen in the Orkneys, Shetlands, the mainland of Scotland, and eastern parts of England were no doubt genuine visitants from Scandinavia, birds recorded elsewhere may have escaped from captivity, as it is often kept as a caged bird.

This species inhabits the wooded mountainous regions of Europe, from Scandinavia and northern Russia to the Mediterranean shores, and other forms have been recognised in Asia and North Africa.

It breeds early in the year, and lays its eggs, usually two or three in number, rounded in shape, and white in colour, in the deserted dwelling of some other bird in a tree. Often ledges of rock in sunny quarters on steep mountain-sides are chosen, or situations on the ground at the roots of trees, but in these places the bird does not construct a nest of its own, although often a kind of bed, on which the owlets repose, is formed by the accumulation of castings and fur.

The Eagle-Owl usually rests during the day in some dark and shady retreat, sallying forth in the evening in search of food. Owing to its size and strength it can without difficulty master birds as large as the Capercaillie, and hares, rabbits, and other game, besides young fawns, form a large part of its food.

Its deep sonorous note, often heard in the breeding season, resembles its German name " *Uhu*."

Pl. 29.

Griffon-Vulture
Egyptian Vulture. (adult & young)

Order ACCIPITRES.

FAMILY VULTURIDÆ.

THE GRIFFON-VULTURE.

Gyps fulvus (J. F. Gmelin).

PLATE 29.

An immature specimen of this Vulture was captured near Cork Harbour in the spring of 1843, and another is recorded by Howard Saunders as having been seen near Southampton Water many years later. It is a common bird in many parts of the Spanish Peninsula, and is found across Southern Europe to the Ural Mountains, also in northern India and a great part of Africa.

The Griffon is gregarious during the breeding season, and builds its nest of sticks and grass on the ledges of cliffs or in rocky cavities; it lays one or two eggs, generally white, but sometimes blotched with reddish-brown.

The bird feeds on the carcases of animals, discovered not by scent but by its wonderful power of sight, each individual while aloft not only searching the ground, but keeping its eye on any tell-tale movements of its neighbours.

The female is rather less in size than the male.

THE EGYPTIAN VULTURE.

Neophron percnopterus (Linnæus).

PLATE 29.

Two immature Vultures of this species were seen at Bridgewater Bay, Somersetshire, in October 1825, one of which was killed, and many years later, on 28th September 1868, another was obtained at Peldon, Essex.

It has a wide range over Southern and Eastern Europe, being found as far east as north-western India, and over a great part of Africa. It appears to be migratory in many places, and usually is seen in pairs.

The nest is made of sticks and any kind of odds and ends the bird can find, and is generally placed on a ledge or in a cavity in a cliff, occasionally in trees. The two eggs are creamy-white in ground colour, marked with brownish-red.

The bird feeds on reptiles, carrion of all kinds, and any filthy garbage it may come across, and therefore makes itself a most efficient scavenger in hot climates, where those useful members of society are non-existent. In character it is timid and cowardly.

THE MARSH-HARRIER.

Circus æruginosus (Linnæus).

PLATE 30.

The Marsh-Harrier, known to fenmen as the Moor-Buzzard, although still occasionally visiting the British Islands in spring and autumn, has almost vanished as a resident species. It is possible, however, that a pair or two may linger among the bogs of Ireland.

At one time this fine bird was common in the fens and marshy districts of our eastern counties, and in places suited to its habits in Dorset, Devonshire, and other parts of south-western England. It is still plentiful among the marshes of Central, Southern, and Eastern Europe, and also inhabits North Africa and Asia.

The nest is usually placed on or near the ground among reeds, sedge, and rushes, and is built of dead reeds, sedge, and grasses. The eggs, bluish-white in colour, and occasionally having faint brownish markings, are four or five in number.

The greater part of the Marsh-Harrier's food consists of frogs and other reptiles, eggs, nestlings, and disabled waterfowl or Snipe, which are pounced upon as the bird slowly quarters the ground in regular beats, flying low down and moving backwards and forwards with steady flaps of its broad and long wings. Lord Lilford states (*Birds of Northamptonshire and Neighbourhood*) that "the female whilst sitting, is fed by the male bird, who hovers over the nest and drops the prey to his mate."

It is only the fully adult male which shows the distinctive grey colouring on the wings and tail, as represented in the plate. The female has the tail and underparts brown, with some creamy-white on the shoulders of the wings. The second figure in the background gives the plumage of the young in the first year, with the conspicuous light buff-coloured head, which gave it the name of Bald Buzzard.

It may be noted here that the Harriers have a distinct frill of small close-set feathers passing from the sides of the head round the neck, causing a resemblance to the facial disc of the Owls, but according to Professor Newton (*Dictionary of Birds*): "No osteological affinity, however, can be established between the Harriers and any section of the Owls, and the superficial resemblance will have to be explained in some other way."

45

THE HEN-HARRIER.

Circus cyaneus (Linnæus).

PLATE 30.

This Harrier, which shows such a marked difference in the size and colour of the sexes as to have caused them at one time to be considered different species, is resident, though yearly diminishing in numbers, in some of the wilder parts of the British Islands. A few still breed in the Orkneys, Outer Hebrides, and Ireland, and within recent years it is said to have nested in England, as well as in Wales. It has a wide breeding range in Europe, from as far north as Scandinavia and Russia to Spain and Italy, whilst in winter it visits North Africa and Asia.

The Hen-Harrier haunts rushy, furze-covered land or moors and hill-sides clothed with heather and broom, and nests on the ground, sometimes under cover of a furze-bush or among tall heather, at others on the bare hill-side. The nest is built of sticks and sedges, being more lightly constructed if placed in the latter situation than in others, when it is often composed of a mass of dead herbage. From four to six eggs are laid, bluish-white in colour, and occasionally, but not always, marked with rust-coloured freckles.

The Hen-Harrier feeds on mice and other small mammals, reptiles, birds and their eggs, on which it pounces unexpectedly, and, unlike the Marsh-Harrier, does not hesitate to chase and strike down birds as large as the Red-Grouse.

When seeking its prey it shows wonderful command of flight, quartering the ground with great exactness as it flies with measured beats of the wings close to the ground, hovering as something catches its eye, or sailing gracefully over a hedge.

Macgillivray, who knew this bird well, has given a good description of its habits.

The female, known as the Ring-tail, is much larger than her mate.

Pl. 30

Montagu's Harrier. ♂ & ♀.   Marsh-Harrier. (adult ♂ & young)   Hen-Harrier. ♂ & ♀.

MONTAGU'S HARRIER.

Circus cineraceus (Montagu).

PLATE 30.

Colonel Montagu, from whom this species takes its name, was the first to distinguish it from the Hen-Harrier, having published an account of his discovery in his *Ornithological Dictionary* in 1802. It is a migratory bird, visiting the fenny districts of the eastern counties of England every summer and breeding regularly there when left undisturbed, and occasionally in other parts, as it did in Surrey in 1907. It is only a rare visitant to Scotland and Ireland, only about seven having occurred in the former, and a dozen in the latter country.

This species is plentiful in suitable localities over a great part of Europe, North-west Africa, and Asia, and spends the winter in Africa and India.

It makes a slight nest of twigs and dry grasses among furze or heather in open places, or of sedges in the fens, and lays four or five eggs of a very pale bluish-green, occasionally marked with some rust-coloured spots.

Montagu's Harrier much resembles the Hen-Harrier, but is slightly less in size and more slender in shape, while having its wings of more proportionate length, and therefore showing more buoyancy of flight.

Howard Saunders has pointed out in his *Manual of British Birds* that Montagu's Harrier "may infallibly be recognized by the outer web of its 5th primary having no emargination."

It lives principally on frogs, lizards, and other reptiles, as well as on eggs, small mammals, and birds.

A very dark brown or black form of this Harrier often occurs, which in a live specimen belonging to the late Lord Lilford, had the eyes as dark, if not darker, than a Falcon's, instead of the usual yellow colour.

THE COMMON BUZZARD.

Buteo vulgaris, Leach.

PLATE 31.

The days when the Buzzard could be considered common in the British Islands have long since passed, though it is still a resident, but in diminishing numbers, in parts of northern and western England, in Wales, central and western Scotland, and the Inner Hebrides, where its plaintive wailing notes may yet be heard.

It is found over the greater portion of Europe, ranging as far eastwards as Poland and southwards to Spain ; while many migrate in winter to Africa.

In hilly districts its home is usually on a ledge of a bush-covered cliff, scattered here and there with a birch or rowan, but in woodland country the nest, which is made of sticks and heather, with a lining of dead grasses and wool, is placed in the fork of a tree. It contains three or four eggs, in ground colour dull white, spotted and streaked with rich reddish-brown, and showing pale lilac shell-markings.

This Buzzard when beating the country-side for food, flies not far from the ground, and pounces on its prey, which consists mainly of small mammals, such as field mice and moles, young rabbits, frogs, insects, and earthworms, and it is therefore not detrimental to game. Although active enough when in search of food, it appears to be sluggish at other times, and will often sit for a long time on the branch of a tree or on some rock from which it can command a wide view. At times it flies at a great height, moving gracefully in circles, when it is often mistaken for the Golden Eagle, although it may always be distinguished, if near enough, by the white patches under the wings.

The Common Buzzard shows great variation in colour among different individuals, some being more or less a uniform dark brown with a beautiful plum-coloured gloss, and others much marked with white on the breast and lower parts.

THE ROUGH-LEGGED BUZZARD.

Buteo lagopus (J. F. Gmelin).

PLATE 31.

This species, easily distinguished from the Common Buzzard by its feathered tarsus, and in the adult by the creamy-white on the head, and lighter tail, is a more or less regular autumnal and winter visitor to Great Britain, mostly to the eastern parts, where numbers of immature birds have sometimes been observed. It has never been known to breed in the British Islands, the accounts of its having done so being unreliable, but it nests in Northern Europe and Asia, whence it wanders southwards in autumn.

The nest, placed in a tree or ledge of rock, is built of sticks and twigs, sometimes with some lichen added, and contains from three to five eggs, which though subject to some variation in colour, are similar to the Common Buzzard's.

In our country the Rough-legged Buzzard is partial to open country, especially warrens and wastes overrun with rabbits, on which it preys, as well as on mice, reptiles, wildfowl, and other birds.

During the breeding season it is said to utter a plaintive wailing note, likened to the mewing of a cat.

THE SPOTTED EAGLE.

Aquila maculata (J. F. Gmelin).

PLATE 31.

Some eight or nine examples of this Eagle have occurred in England, three of these having been shot in the autumn of 1891 in Suffolk and Essex, while two others have been obtained in Ireland.

Naturalists have distinguished two distinct races of this species, one considerably larger than the other, and, according to Howard Saunders, those visiting the British Islands have been "chiefly—if not entirely"—the larger. The two forms have a wide distribution over Europe, North Africa, Western Asia, China, and India.

The Spotted Eagle builds its nest, which is large and very flat, high up on big trees, and generally lays two eggs, in colour dull white, streaked or spotted with brownish-red.

It appears to live chiefly on reptiles, small mammals, and water-birds, and utters a shrill cry.

Immature examples of the larger race seem for the most part to be those which have reached our coasts, and I have therefore given a picture of one of these, which vary somewhat in colour. When fully adult, the colour becomes a paler brown, with only a few small spots on the lesser wing-coverts.

Pl. 31.

A. Thorburn. 1914

Rough legged Buzzard.   Spotted Eagle.   Common Buzzard.

THE GOLDEN EAGLE.

Aquila chrysaëtus (Linnæus).

PLATE 32.

This grand bird, although now confined as a resident to the wildest parts of the Highlands of Scotland, yet at one time had its eyrie in England. Willoughby described a nest found in the Peak of Derbyshire in 1668, and also records that in his time it bred on the Snowdon Hills. It lingered much later in the Lake District and on the Borders, where, Bewick states, it formerly bred on the steepest part of Cheviot, while over the border, in Scotland, eyries are said to have been occupied "for some years after 1850 in Ayrshire and Kirkcudbrightshire" (Howard Saunders's *Manual*, 2nd ed.).

The Golden Eagle inhabits Europe, where it is found in mountainous districts, as well as North Africa, Asia, and America; and various races, showing difference in size and colour, have been distinguished.

Very early in the year the royal birds prepare their nest, usually returning to one occupied in previous seasons, which is situated on a ledge in the steep and rocky face of a precipice or inaccessible walls of some wild corrie among the hills. The site is chosen so that a projecting crag shelters the eggs and young from the weather. Occasionally the nest is so placed that it is not difficult to reach it from below, and I have seen one only about twenty feet above a broken, grassy slope, while others, again, are placed in trees. Outwardly the eyrie is constructed of sticks, forming a rough platform, on which are put pieces of heather and other material, and in the centre is a cup-shaped depression, small in proportion to the rest of the nest, which is lined with the flattened blades of the wood-rush (*Luzula sylvatica*), a common plant on the Scottish mountains. The eggs are laid early in April, and are usually two, though three may sometimes be found. They vary considerably in colour and markings, even in the same nest, and may be dull white, with either a grey or buffish tinge and mottled with shades of reddish- or purple-brown, while others, again, are sometimes pure white. The young, clothed at first in white down, are carefully fed and tended by the parent birds, who remove the feathers and fur from game before presenting it.

THE GOLDEN EAGLE

The Golden Eagle feeds principally on the Mountain Hare, but Grouse and Ptarmigan are also taken, as well as lambs and very young red-deer calves. It will also feast on dead sheep and stags which have been left out on the hill.

I have had a good many opportunities of watching this fine bird, when sketching in lonely places among the deer-forests : they may sometimes be seen in pairs, but more often alone, beating the slopes of the mountains at some height from the ground, and ready at any moment to swoop down on some helpless victim who may be attempting to escape observation by crouching among the rocks and heather. Often the Eagle's approach may be known before he comes in sight, by the appearance of terrified packs of Grouse or Ptarmigan who fly before him at their utmost speed.

One can form no idea of the lightness and buoyancy of the Eagle's flight until the bird has been seen at freedom in his own domain, and it is an inspiring sight to watch him on a bright sunny day soaring in wide circles as he ascends to a great height, his broad motionless wings outstretched to their full extent, and with an upward curve at their ends, supporting him without effort. While the bird is aloft, the curious notched pinion feathers may be clearly seen, separated like the fingers of a hand.

Like Hawks, the Golden Eagle is sometimes chased and annoyed by lesser birds, such as Curlews and Rooks, but, on the other hand, is sometimes very bold, attacking and attempting to beat over precipices unwary calves of the red-deer, which are sometimes surprised in difficult places.

The Golden Eagle may always be distinguished from the White-tailed or Sea Eagle by having the legs feathered right down to the yellow toes, while the latter bird has the lower half of the tarsus bare.

There is also a difference in the structure of their feet ; these in the Golden Eagle are covered with a network of little plates as far as the last joint, on which there are four or sometimes three broad scales. On the other hand, the White-tailed Eagle has broad scales along nearly the whole upper part of the toes.

THE WHITE-TAILED EAGLE.

Haliaëtus albicilla (Linnæus).

PLATE 33.

The White-tailed or Sea Eagle, once numerous in the Highlands and northern parts of Scotland, as well as in Ireland, and known in former days to nest in England, seems to have disappeared altogether as a resident species except in the Outer Hebrides. Until recently it bred in the Shetlands, but according to *Bird Notes and News* published this spring (1915), by the Royal Society for the Protection of Birds, the last remaining bird there is one very old solitary female, who still haunts the old nesting-place, "but when last seen was flying out to sea mobbed by Carrion-Crows."

In autumn and winter individuals—mostly immature birds—visit us from abroad, which are often mistaken for Golden Eagles. It has a wide range over Northern Europe and Asia, and nests as far south as Albania.

The eyrie is built on a high cliff overlooking the sea, or inland on a rocky ledge, and sometimes on a tree, or even on the ground. The materials of the nest are similar to those used by the Golden Eagle, and the two eggs, pure white in colour, are laid in March or April.

In character it is less bold than the last-mentioned bird, and feeds largely on fish and carrion along the shore, where its loud yelping cry could be heard in former days. Rabbits are also a favourite food, and shepherds used to suffer from its depredations in lambing time.

The sexes are alike in colour, but the young differs from the adult by having a dark tail.

Pl. 32

Golden Eagle (adult & young)

A.Thorburn 1914

THE OSPREY.

Pandion haliaëtus (Linnæus).

PLATE 33.

The Osprey, at one time a regular visitant during the summer months to many a Highland loch, and returning year after year to the same eyrie, has now deserted its two last well-known strongholds, viz. Loch an Eilan in 1903, and Loch Arkaig in 1911. Whether it may still nest elsewhere is not known, and without doubt the destruction of this fine bird as a breeding species was caused partly by the greed of egg collectors, and also by the wanton shooting of both old and young birds during their migration southwards in autumn, and of the former when they return in spring. Migrating Ospreys still occur, however, during those seasons in the British Islands, including Ireland, though they have never been known to breed there. Elsewhere this species has almost a world-wide distribution, but has not been recorded in Greenland or Iceland.

The nest is a large piled-up structure, built of sticks and turf, on the flattened top of which is formed a small moss-lined cavity to receive the eggs. These are generally three in number, and vary a good deal in colour, the usual type being white or buffish-white in ground colour, marked with spots and blotches of deep reddish-brown, sometimes with underlying shell-markings of violet-grey.

In Scotland the site selected in most cases was the top of some ruined building, by the side or surrounded by the waters of a loch, the summit of a steep conical island rock, or the upper branches of a tall old pine.

A large extent of water, well stocked with fish; solitude and freedom from molestation, seem essential to the Osprey, which obtains its prey by a sudden plunge into the water, after hovering Kestrel-like at some height above the surface, while should the fish be within easy reach, it wets little more than its feet in the process. These are wonderfully adapted to the purpose of securing their slippery quarry, being armed with long curved claws, while the under-surface of the toes, the outer one of which is reversible, are rough and studded with pointed scales. The legs are strong and muscular, the thighs, unlike those of most raptorial birds, being clothed with short close feathers to withstand the wet.

The female is larger than the male, and is more marked with brown on the breast.

53

THE GOSHAWK.

Astur palumbarius (Linnæus).

Plate 34.

This forest-loving species is now only a rare visitant to Great Britain, a few, for the most part immature birds, occasionally reaching this country, generally in the eastern parts.

Colonel Thornton, in his *Northern Tour* published in 1804, states that he had seen nests and obtained a nestling from the old pine forests of Rothiemurchus and Glenmore, showing that the Goshawk bred a little previous to that date in the Spey district.

In Europe it frequents wooded country from Lapland and Russia southwards to the Mediterranean, and eastwards to the Caspian Sea.

The nest is built by the bird itself, high up in some tree on the edge of the forest, and is composed of sticks and twigs, and often occupied by the same birds for many successive years, and as material is annually added, it frequently attains a great size. The four eggs are very pale bluish-green, occasionally showing spots of reddish-brown.

The Goshawk, which resembles its diminutive relative the Sparrow-Hawk, is bold and predatory, and has a curious wild expression in its eye. It preys on squirrels, hares, rabbits, as well as on game and other birds, and is much esteemed as a trained bird by falconers, being well adapted for work in an enclosed country. Though the male is superior to the female in speed, he is much inferior in size and strength, but both have great courage and show an almost incredible lust for killing.

THE SPARROW-HAWK.

Accipiter nisus (Linnæus).

PLATE 34.

In spite of incessant persecution the Sparrow-Hawk still holds its own in districts where there are large tracts of woodland, especially in those where game is not strictly preserved. Except in the extreme north, it breeds throughout Europe, though sparingly in Spain and Italy, while in Asia it ranges as far east as Japan and southwards to the Himalayas.

Mr. R. J. Howard has provided me with the following account of the habits of this species : " It usually builds its own nest of twigs broken by itself from the branches. Should the first clutch of eggs be robbed the bird will then probably take possession of the nest of some other bird, and in it lay her second clutch. The eggs, from four to six, sometimes seven in number, are round in shape, bluish-white, blotched more or less with reddish-brown, and are laid on alternate days.

"Incubation lasts thirty to thirty-two days. The difference in size of the young is, I think, sexual, rather than due to age; for a young female almost covered with down will be about double the weight of her brother who is more advanced in feather.

"As is the case with almost all birds of prey, the female remains in the neighbourhood of the nest to brood and protect the young, whilst the cock does the hunting. He brings food to a spot within gunshot of the nest, calls to the hen, who flies to him and takes the quarry, already plucked and frequently headless, to the nest, where she breaks it up and feeds the young. Should the hen be killed whilst the young are too small to tear the food for themselves, I think they would perish from hunger, for although the cock would bring birds to the nest, ready plucked, his instinct would carry him no further. A gamekeeper shot a cock Sparrow-Hawk in the evening, having killed the hen the day before. The young in the nest were surrounded with small birds which had been brought in by the cock. All were more or less plucked, the heads of some having been pulled off. I saw and counted these: one House-Martin, one Wren, several Wagtails, Blue Tits, Chaffinches, &c., twenty-one small birds in all. I have other somewhat similar records, but not with so many small birds collected.". . .

"The short round wings and the large tail enable the bird to thread its way through thick cover in a wonderfully rapid manner. The long slender legs give it a good reach, and the long flexible toes, armed with claws as sharp as needles and also furnished with elongated, indiarubber-like pads, enable it to secure a grip on the feathered body of its quarry that is seldom relaxed so long as life is left in the poor victim. It takes any bird up to or exceeding its own weight which it can catch ; the female can and does kill Woodpigeons."

The female is very much larger than the male, and in old age often assumes the colour of her mate.

Pl. 33.

A. Thorburn
1914.

White-tailed or Sea Eagle.
(adult & young)

Osprey.

$\frac{1}{5}$

THE KITE.

Milvus ictinus, Savigny.

PLATE 35.

In old days the Kite, often called Glead or Gled from its graceful gliding motion during flight, was everywhere abundant in our country, and appears to have been common in many places till the early part of last century. Now it is only known as a breeding species in certain parts of Wales, but according to the B.O.U. "List of British Birds" (1915), it "is said to have nested in Devonshire in 1913." Elsewhere in Great Britain it is now only an uncommon visitant, and does not appear to occur in Ireland, but it has a wide range over Europe, as well as North Africa and Asia.

The nest is generally built high up in the fork of a tall tree, and is composed of sticks and various odd pieces of rubbish, waste paper, and rags. The eggs, usually three in number, are dull white, with blotches and streaks of rust-colour.

The Kite will eat anything in the way of food which comes easily to hand, including offal of all kinds, reptiles, small mammals, and birds. Formerly, when it was abundant, it made sad havoc among the young chickens in the poultry yard, and to prevent its depredations on the Scottish crofts, where the rents were paid with pullets, children were generally posted on the watch to "sheu the Glead" (Mudie).

On the wing the Kite is a most graceful bird, often sailing in wide circles and guiding its flight by its long forked tail. It was much prized for sport in the old days of falconry, being looked upon as the special quarry of kings, and hence the epithet "royal" was applied to it.

It has a plaintive mewing note. The male is rather brighter than the female in colour, and a little less in size.

THE BLACK KITE.

Milvus migrans (Boddaert).

PLATE 35.

This migratory species, smaller and duller in colour than our **Kite, though** by no means black, may easily be distinguished by its shorter and less forked tail, and has twice occurred in Great Britain, the first example at Alnwick, Northumberland, in May 1866, and the other near Aberdeen in April 1901. It breeds principally in Central and Southern Europe, as well as in Asia and North Africa.

Lord Lilford says, in his work on British Birds, "the present species generally nests in pine-trees, poplars, or willows, at a considerable height from the ground : several pairs are often to be found breeding in close vicinity."

The two eggs resemble those of the Red Kite, and both birds live on much the same kind of food, although the Black Kite is more partial to fish.

The sexes are alike in colour.

THE HONEY-BUZZARD.

Pernis apivorus (Linnæus).

PLATE 35.

The Honey-Buzzard is a migratory species which at one time appears to have been a regular summer visitor to England, though it apparently was never plentiful. Their nests have been recorded in wooded districts as far north as east Ross-shire and Aberdeenshire, while between fifty and sixty years ago it bred annually in the New Forest, and would do so still if not constantly persecuted and destroyed. It is well known during summer in most parts of Europe, from Norway, Sweden, and Russia to northern Spain and Italy, ranging eastwards to western Siberia, and wintering in Africa and Madagascar. When passing to and fro between Europe and Africa, the birds have been described as flying in large flocks, which pass continuously for several days.

The Honey-Buzzard selects for its home a tall beech or oak, and builds its nest—often placed on the foundations of an older one of some other species—of sticks, lined with beech twigs and fresh green leaves of the same tree.

The late E. C. Newcome, as quoted in the fourth edition of "Yarrell," observed that in France the young when in the nest were sheltered by a bower of leafy boughs, a fact which has not been noticed in our country. The two or three eggs are buffish-white in ground colour, blotched or thickly clouded with various shades of rich brownish-red.

The Honey-Buzzard is an entirely harmless species, its principal food consisting of the grubs of wasps and wild bees, obtained by digging out the combs with its powerful feet, which enable it to excavate deeply into the ground ; worms, caterpillars, frogs, lizards, and mice are also eaten. It is very nimble and can run with great speed on the ground, which peculiarity was noticed long ago by Willoughby.

In the *Victoria History of the County of Sussex* Mr. J. G. Millais has given an interesting account of a tame Honey-Buzzard, which would perch on his hand, whence it would sweep after and capture passing bees or wasps, following the latter insects to their nest in order to dig out the comb. It appeared to be quite indifferent to the attacks of the insects, which were unable to penetrate the armour of its feathers.

The Honey-Buzzard is subject to great variety of colouring, which is more evident in immature specimens. The white-headed form shown in the plate was taken from a beautiful living bird of the year, in the late Lord Lilford's collection, which was very confiding and gentle in its manners, perching freely on any person's arm, and living on a diet of bread and milk. It frequently uttered a peevish wailing cry.

58

Pl. 34.

A. Thorburn 1914

Sparrow-Hawk. (♂ & ♀)

Goshawk (adult & young)

THE GREENLAND FALCON.

Falco candicans, J. F. Gmelin.

PLATE 36.

This truly noble bird, one of the three large northern Falcons belonging to the group formerly known as " Jer," or " Gyr," is, as its name implies, a native of northern Greenland, breeding also within the Arctic Circle in North America.

The late John Hancock was the first to point out that it may be distinguished at all ages from the Iceland and Gyr-Falcon by the spots and markings telling dark against the light ground colour of white ; whereas in both the other forms the plan of colouring is reversed, these having a dark ground relieved with spots and markings of white or grey. Owing to the hunting grounds of the Greenland Falcon in the far north being frozen up in the winter months, and thus cutting short its food supply, a good many birds migrate southwards during the cold season, and thus it more often visits our islands, especially Scotland and Ireland, than the other two species, which live in a less severe climate.

The nest is placed on the rocky ledge of a cliff, sometimes on the former habitation of some other species, and usually contains four eggs, in ground colour reddish-orange, spotted over with reddish-brown or brick-red.

The Greenland Falcon is the most beautiful of our Hawks, with its full dark eye and snowy plumage, and was in great repute in the days of falconry, when it was flown at the larger kinds of quarry, such as Cranes and Herons, but its place has now been taken by the Peregrine for purposes of sport. In olden times so much value was set on this bird, that it was looked upon as a gift for kings. Falconers, skilled in trapping Hawks, were sent to Norway and Iceland to obtain it, and it seems always to have been more prized than the grey Falcons. The young bird has broad brownish markings above, and tear-shaped spots below, and the tail is barred with dusky brown.

THE ICELAND FALCON.

Falco islandus, J. F. Gmelin.

PLATE 36.

This species occasionally visits the British Islands in winter, though less frequently than the Greenland Falcon, and, like the other northern Falcons, shows considerable variations in colour in different individuals. In all these Falcons, however, when once they have attained their mature plumage, no alteration takes place in the type of markings or colour, a dark bird always remaining so, while a light one keeps the same phase of colouring during its lifetime.

This Falcon is a resident in Iceland and southern Greenland, the race inhabiting the latter country, known as *F. holboelli*, being whiter than the true Icelander, and is apparently intermediate between it and *F. candicans*.

In Iceland this species lays its eggs, which are similar to the Greenlander's, on ledges of cliffs, or in the unoccupied nest of a Raven or other bird. It often chooses inland situations, on precipices overhanging freshwater lakes, where it obtains an abundant supply of waterfowl and other birds. It was, like the species just described, much sought after in ancient times by falconers, but not prized so much as the more northern bird.

The young have the general plumage of the upper parts dark brown, with brownish-yellow edgings to the feathers, and the lower portions broadly marked with longitudinal bands of dark brown on a lighter ground.

THE GYR-FALCON.

Falco gyrfalco, Linnæus.

PLATE 37.

Two or perhaps three specimens only of the true Gyr-Falcon have occurred in England, the first, an adult bird, having been shot at Mayfield, Sussex, in January 1845. Inhabiting more southern regions than either of the other two northern Falcons, it appears to have less inducement to wander in winter from its haunts in Norway, Sweden, Lapland, and northern Russia, though it is said to occur in Greenland and Arctic America.

The adult birds may be distinguished from those of the Iceland Falcon by their darker colouring, especially on the head, by the dark moustacial patch, and also by their slightly smaller size. The immature birds are practically the same in colour in both species, as are likewise the eggs.

It breeds on cliffs like its congeners, and preys chiefly on wildfowl and Ptarmigan.

THE PEREGRINE FALCON.

Falco peregrinus, Tunstall.

PLATE 37.

The Peregrine Falcon still retains its old eyries in many parts of our islands, and though by no means common, is perhaps more numerous than our other large birds of prey, and in relation to its size is without doubt the most daring and fearless of them all. In ancient times, when, as now, its high courage, hardy constitution, and docility were greatly valued by falconers, its breeding-places were much more numerous and strictly guarded. During autumn a good many Peregrines, mostly birds of the year, known as "Passage Hawks," reach our country from abroad, usually following the hosts of migrating ducks from more northerly regions, and many of them take possession of a hunting ground and stay for the winter. As a resident or migrant the Peregrine is well known all over Europe from Scandinavia to the Mediterranean, within the area of which there resides a smaller form known as *F. punicus*; and, admitting different subspecies, it may be said to have a world-wide distribution.

The eyrie, often the former home of some other bird, is usually situated on some steep rocky cliff, either overhanging the sea or inland, while it is occasionally placed in trees. The same station—for the nest is merely a hollow scratched out on the earth-covered shelf, and surrounded by bones and castings—is often occupied for many successive years, even in some cases used by succeeding generations of Falcons for centuries; and if at any time one of the pair be destroyed, the survivor seems to have no difficulty in quickly obtaining another mate. The eggs are usually three or four in number, and vary in colour, some closely freckled with rich orange-brown, others with deep brick-red.

In hawking language the female is always known as the Falcon; the male, from his smaller size—considered as one-third less—being called the "Tercel" or "Tiercel." At the present time this noble form of sport, far from being extinct, is still carried on in various parts of the country where the open nature of the ground allows it to be practised with success.

The food of the Peregrine consists chiefly of waterfowl—including on occasions

Pl.35.

Black Kite.   *Kite.*

Honey-Buzzard. (2 varieties)

birds as large as wild Geese—Pigeons, Grouse, and other species, struck down while in full flight by a lightning stoop from above, the Falcon always striving to get above its quarry in order to deliver the fatal stroke: the velocity of this downward rush is almost incredible, and even during a "stern chase" the speed is extraordinary. I have seen one in full career after a small flock of Golden Plover, and never remember observing any birds fly so fast. From constant practice wild Peregrines are able, by skill and wing power, to capture the Peewit, which often baffles any but the best-trained Hawks by its rapid turns and shifts. When the Falcon takes to soaring, it can rise to an immense height, and frequently passes out of sight. This fine bird is ruthlessly and needlessly persecuted and done to death by many game preservers.

The late Lord Lilford, while stating that the Peregrine can and does take Grouse and Partridges when she gets a fair chance and is hungry, adds "but it must be remembered that as a rule she captures her 'quarry' in the air, and that our common game-birds just mentioned are of terrestrial habits and certainly by no means willing to take wing when a Falcon is in sight, but do their utmost to squat close and conceal themselves, so that they are by no means the habitual or even (in my opinion) a particularly favourite prey of the Peregrine."

Two examples of the American Peregrine or Duck-Hawk, *Falco anatum*, have occurred in England, the first shot by Mr. W. Whitaker, on 31st October 1891, at Newbold Verdon, near Market Bosworth, Leicestershire, and now in his possession, and the other netted on the Lincolnshire coast, 28th September 1910, and recorded by Mr. G. H. Caton Haigh. This race is said to be larger and darker than our bird, but according to Elliot Coues (*Key to North-American Birds*), it varies a good deal in size and colour. This Falcon inhabits the greater part of North America.

THE HOBBY.

Falco subbuteo, Linnæus.

PLATE 38.

This beautiful little Falcon generally arrives in England about the middle of May, and though by no means common, breeds more or less regularly in the southern and south-eastern counties, being less frequently met with farther north. It is also distributed over Europe and North Africa, across Asia to Kamchatka, while in winter it occurs in China and India.

The Hobby is often described as being like a miniature Peregrine, but the wings are proportionally longer, and the dark markings of the underparts are longitudinal in the adult Hobby, whereas in the Peregrine they form transverse bars.

It breeds late in the season, usually laying its three eggs in June. These are deposited in the unoccupied nests of Crows, Magpies, or other birds, and resemble the eggs of the Kestrel, though not of so bright a red, nor so boldly spotted.

Although it sometimes kills small birds, and can even with its wonderful wing power outmanœuvre and capture the Swift, the Hobby is largely insectivorous, feeding on dragonflies, beetles, grasshoppers, and other insects. Lord Lilford says (*Birds of Northamptonshire and Neighbourhood*): " In pursuit of its prey the rapidity of the Hobby is marvellous, and the manner in which it turns and mounts after making a stoop is quite unrivalled by any bird of prey with which I am acquainted."

The Hobby, however, when trained for purposes of sport, in spite of all its fine powers of flight, is not a success, for although it " waits on " beautifully, flies well to the lure, and is very docile, it is a poor *footer*.

The cry is very like the Kestrel's, and also resembles the Wryneck's, and the bird leaves us in September.

THE MERLIN.

Falco æsalon, Tunstall.

PLATE 38.

This little Falcon, the smallest of its kind inhabiting the British Islands, breeds more or less regularly on the moors of northern England, in Wales, Scotland, and Ireland; while their numbers are increased in autumn by the arrival of others from the continent of Europe, over which it has a wide range, especially in the northern and central portions, as well as in Central Asia. In winter it visits North Africa, northern India, and China.

The nest, if such it can be called, consists of a few twigs of ling arranged round a hollow scooped out in the ground, either among heath on the open moor or on a heathery brae by the side of a burn, while at times the eggs are laid on a rocky ledge or in the deserted home of a Crow or some other species in a tree. They are generally four in number, and of a rich red-brown or purplish-red colour.

The Merlin, for its size, is one of the boldest of our Hawks, and will attack birds twice its own weight, but its chief food consists of the smaller species, such as Meadow-Pipits, Larks, Thrushes, Snipe, and other waders.

About the month of October the Merlins leave the moors, some moving southwards, others merely descending to the coast, where they linger till the spring. When hunting they strive to take their quarry by surprise, sweeping along by the side of a bank or concealed by a fold in the ground, but though not so swift as the Hobby, the Merlin can usually outfly and overhaul without difficulty the smaller birds on which it preys. It seldom perches on trees; stones and rocks being its favourite resting-places, hence it is sometimes called the Stone-Falcon. The Merlin is docile and easily tamed, but in confinement is delicate and seldom lives beyond the first moult. It was, and still is, much esteemed by falconers as a trained Hawk, and can be flown with success at Larks and even larger quarry.

The females, like so many birds of prey, are larger than the males, and occasionally, when old, assume more or less the colours of the other sex.

Pl. 36

A. Thorburn. 1914

Greenland Falcon. ♀   Iceland Falcon. ♂

THE RED-FOOTED FALCON.

Falco vespertinus, Linnæus.

PLATE 38.

The Red-footed Falcon, which is closely related to the Kestrel, though resembling in build the Hobby, is a rare and irregular visitor to the British Islands, about forty examples having occurred therein. During summer it inhabits Eastern Europe and Western Asia, migrating in winter as far south as Central Africa. It is sociable in its habits, arriving at its breeding ground in flocks, and a number of nests are often occupied in the same tree.

The nests are not built by the birds themselves, but are the deserted homes of Rooks, Magpies, or Crows. The eggs, varying in number from four to six, are reddish-yellow, spotted and marked with reddish-brown.

It is perhaps more insectivorous than any of our Hawks, capturing much of its food on the wing, though it takes grasshoppers, beetles, and other insects on the ground, over which it can run with a nimbleness unusual in birds of prey.

It is said to be fond of marshy ground, sparsely scattered with timber, and its cry resembles the Hobby's.

THE LESSER KESTREL.

Falco cenchris, Naumann.

PLATE 38.

The visits of this small Falcon are few and far between, the number met with in England amounting to eight, while it has once occurred in Scotland and once in Ireland. It breeds in Southern Europe, from Spain, where it is extremely abundant, eastwards through Western Asia to Bokhara and Persia, and also in North Africa, migrating in winter to tropical and South Africa.

The Lesser Kestrel makes no nest, its eggs, usually four or five and paler in colour than the Common Kestrel's, are placed in holes in rocks, buildings, or ruins.

It lives on insects.

The female resembles that of the common species, but both sexes can be always distinguished from our bird by their white claws.

THE KESTREL.

Falco tinnunculus, Linnæus.

PLATE 38.

The Kestrel, by far the most numerous of our predatory birds, though resident in many parts of the British Islands, moves southwards in winter from its more northern quarters, and about this time also numbers reach England from the continent of Europe, where it has a wide range, while it is likewise found in Africa and Asia.

The Kestrel either takes possession of the deserted nest of a Crow or Magpie, or lays its eggs in a recess in the rocky face of a cliff, or in a hole in the wall of a ruin, and occasionally in a hollow tree. The four, five, or six eggs are closely dappled with various shades of rich reddish-brown, often on a creamy-white ground.

The Kestrel—or Windhover as it is often called, from its method of hanging in the air—hovers head to wind, either motionless or supporting itself with rapid beats of the wings, gliding quickly to another point as soon as it is satisfied that there is no mouse or other prey beneath, and repeating the operation until it finds some unsuspecting quarry on which it drops.

It is one of the least harmful and most useful of our raptorial birds, killing large numbers of mice and voles, as well as beetles and other insects, and although it occasionally takes small birds, its short toes are ill adapted to the capture of feathered prey.

The well-known cry has been syllabled as *klee, klee, klee.*

Very old female birds partially assume the male plumage, and have more or less bluish-grey on the rump and tail. I have shown one of these, in the plate, from Mr. G. E. Lodge's collection, who kindly lent it for the purpose.

Gyr Falcon.
♀.

Peregrine Falcon (adult & young
♂.

Pl. 38.

Hobby. ♂.

Merlin. (♂.♀.& young).

Kestrel. ♀.

Red-footed Falcon. (♂.& ♀.)

Lesser Kestrel. ♂.

Kestrel. ♂.

Order STEGANOPODES.

Family PELECANIDÆ.

THE COMMON CORMORANT.

Phalacrocorax carbo (Linnæus).

PLATE 39.

This bird is plentiful about our rocky coasts, being more common on the north-eastern shores of England and east coast of Scotland than the Shag or Green Cormorant, though the latter predominates in many parts of the west. The Common Cormorant is also widely distributed over Europe, Asia, and America, and even reaches Greenland. The birds usually nest in colonies on high rocks and cliffs by the sea, or occasionally inland on trees.

The nest is constructed of sticks, grass, seaweed, and various odds and ends, and contains from three to five eggs, which are coated with a white chalky substance, overlying the delicate greenish-blue shell. The blind and naked young, when first hatched, are slaty-black in colour.

The Common Cormorant, often called the "Great" or Black Cormorant, feeds on fish, caught with great dexterity, of which it requires a large amount to satisfy its ravenous appetite. The birds have a characteristic habit, when gorged and resting after a meal, of basking on some low rock, where they may be seen in groups, some of the party generally spreading their wings to the sun and wind so that they may dry.

In the plate the Cormorant is shown in nuptial dress, with the white filaments on head and neck, which are shed early in June.

The sexes are alike in colour.

THE SHAG, OR GREEN CORMORANT.

Phalacrocorax graculus (Linnæus).

PLATE 39.

This species, also sometimes called the Crested Cormorant, from the tuft of curved feathers on the crown, worn during the breeding season only, is common in rocky places on our western coasts and islands, and along the western shores of Europe from Norway to Spain and Portugal. It breeds on ledges of rock and among boulders, and often chooses a site within a dark and sea-washed cavern.

The nest is made of bits of turf, seaweed, and other materials, which soon become an evil-smelling mass. The three or four eggs are similar in colour and texture to the Common Cormorant's, and the young likewise are without any down when hatched.

The habits of the Shag, and its mode of catching fish by diving, are like those of the larger bird ; and both utter a croaking note.

The male and female do not differ in colour.

THE GANNET.

Sula bassana (Linnæus).

PLATE 39.

The Gannet is found breeding regularly on certain rocks and islands off our coasts, which it leaves as soon as the young are able to fly, while the rest of the year is spent at sea, where it leads a wandering life. In winter it ranges as far south in Europe as the Mediterranean, while to the north its breeding range extends to Iceland, the Faroes, and also to North America.

One of the best known breeding stations in Great Britain is the Bass Rock, off the Haddingtonshire coast, others being Suliskerry, some forty miles west of the Orkneys, Sulisgeir, Outer Hebrides, the St. Kilda Islands, and Ailsa Craig, at the entrance of the Firth of Clyde. Off the Welsh coast there is a breeding station on Grassholm, and two others in Irish waters, viz. the Bull Rock, county Cork, and the Skelligs, county Kerry.

About the end of March or in April the Gannets, or, as they are sometimes called, Solan Geese, collect at their nesting rocks, and construct their nests of sea-weed and grassy material, placing them on a ledge or among boulders. The eggs, like those of the Cormorant, are coated with a chalky substance, under which is the pale bluish-green shell, and number three or four. The young when hatched are blind, naked, and slaty-black in colour, but are soon clothed in thick white down.

The fish on which the Gannet lives are obtained by diving, and when occupied in this pursuit the birds follow the shoals, flying at a considerable height and then plunging downwards, at first with the wings held partly open, but on nearing the surface they are folded in just before the water is struck, when a jet of spray is thrown upwards. They only remain below for a few seconds, then rise and resume their fishing.

In the plate a bird in the dark speckled plumage of the first year is shown in the background ; this becomes lighter every season until the bird attains maturity, which, according to Howard Saunders, is in its sixth year.

Order HERODIONES.

Family ARDEIDÆ.

THE COMMON HERON.

Ardea cinerea (Linnæus).

PLATE 40.

The Common Heron is resident and widely distributed in the British Islands, being also found over the greater part of Europe, as well as in Africa, Asia, and Madagascar.

It breeds in colonies, and the nests, composed of sticks, with a lining of finer twigs and roots, are usually placed in tall trees or on cliffs, but are sometimes built on the ground.

These heronries, to which the birds return very early in the season, are often used for many years in succession. The three or four eggs are greenish-blue, showing a chalky surface.

The food, for the most part obtained at night, consists of various fish, reptiles, and small mammals.

The bird is extremely shy and wary in its habits; its usual mode of fishing is to stand immovable in some shallow until its unsuspecting prey comes within reach, when with a sudden stroke of the long bill the fish is caught between the mandibles and swallowed.

The cry is loud and harsh, and may often be heard as the birds fly to their feeding grounds in the evening.

The female is rather smaller and duller in colour than the male.

Pl. 39.

Cormorant. (adult & young)   Gannet. (adults & young)   Shag. (adult & young)

THE PURPLE HERON.

Ardea purpurea, Linnæus.

PLATE 40.

This handsome species is a rather rare visitor to our islands, some fifty specimens having been recorded at different times, which were mostly immature birds. It has more frequently been taken on the south-eastern coast of England than elsewhere. The Purple Heron is migratory, and frequents during the breeding season those marshy places where there are dense reed-beds, in many parts of Central and Southern Europe, as well as Africa, Asia, and Madagascar. It spends the winter in tropical and Southern Africa.

The nest is generally placed in thick reed-clumps, often on the bent down and matted stems just above the water, and is built of the dead stalks of the same plant and of sedges. The three to five eggs are the same in colour and texture as the Common Heron's, but are smaller.

It is very shy and skulking in its habits, and feeds principally on frogs.

According to Howard Saunders (*Manual of British Birds*), " the note is more guttural than that of its congener."

There is no difference in the colour of the sexes.

THE GREAT WHITE HERON.

Ardea alba, Linnæus.

PLATE 40.

Some seven examples of this beautiful Heron have been recorded in Great Britain, five of these having been obtained in England and two in Scotland. In Europe it haunts the marshes and waters of the south-eastern countries, and is also found in Southern Asia, and seemingly in North Africa.

The nest, placed in reed-thickets or in trees in swampy places, is built of sticks or dead reeds, and contains three or four eggs of a greenish-blue tint.

The bird is sociable in its habits, and its food is similar to the Common Heron's. According to Lord Lilford, in his work on British Birds, it resembles the latter bird in its general habits, " frequenting the open marshes and the margins of rivers and lakes in quest of food during the day and roosting in high trees."

The males are a little larger and have more fully developed dorsal plumes than the females, and both sexes are wantonly destroyed in great numbers, on account of these decorations, known as " Ospreys " in the millinery trade.

THE LITTLE EGRET.

Ardea garzetta, Linnæus.

PLATE 40.

This is an extremely rare visitant to the British Islands, apparently the only reliable record being one got at Countess Weir, on the Exe, Devonshire, on 3rd June 1870. Some others have been recorded as occurring in Yorkshire, Northamptonshire, and Sussex, but doubt has been expressed as to their authenticity. The Little Egret breeds in Southern Europe, as well as in Africa and the warmer parts of Asia; the European birds mostly wintering in Africa.

It breeds in colonies, and builds its nest, which is lightly made of sticks and reeds, in a bush or tree among the swamps; the eggs, usually four in number, are pale bluish-green.

This species is very clamorous and noisy at the breeding stations, the cry being harsh and discordant like that of its congeners, and like them it suffers much at the hands of the plume dealers.

It lives on small fish, reptiles, and water insects, and the sexes are alike in colour.

THE BUFF-BACKED HERON.

Ardea bubulcus, Audouin.

PLATE 40.

A specimen of this Heron was shot in October 1805 near Kingsbridge, Devonshire, the only one which has been obtained in the British Isles.

The Buff-backed Heron breeds in southern Spain, also inhabiting South-west Asia, Africa, and Madagascar.

It breeds among dense reed-beds and on bushes in marshy places, forming large colonies like its allies, and constructs its nest of sticks. The eggs, from three to five in number, are a delicate pale blue in colour.

Its principal food appears to consist of the ticks infesting cattle, and in consequence it may usually be found near the herds, but it also feeds on grasshoppers and other insects.

Its notes are harsh like those of other Herons.

In the autumn the buff-coloured plumes are moulted, and are not again assumed till the following spring. In the female these are less developed, and she is smaller than the male.

END OF VOL. II.

Buff-backed Heron.

Little Egret.   Purple Heron.

Common Heron.   Great White Heron.

CONTENTS OF VOL. III.

CONTENTS

Order HERODIONES.

Family ARDEIDÆ.

THE SQUACCO HERON.

Ardea ralloides, Scopoli.

PLATE 41.

Over sixty examples of this species have been recorded in the British Islands, the greater number of these having occurred in the southern and south-western parts of England, including the Scilly Islands. It has only been noted thrice in Scotland, and eight times in Ireland. During summer it visits the countries bordering the Mediterranean, as well as southern Russia, eastwards to the Caspian Sea, but is only occasionally seen in Central Europe, whilst it appears to be a resident in Africa.

This beautiful little Heron is usually found breeding in colonies, often in company with Night-Herons and Egrets, the nest being rather slightly constructed of twigs and placed on the boughs of trees or in bushes in marshy places or where floods have inundated the ground. In North Africa, it is said to nest on the ground among reed-jungles. The greenish-blue eggs vary in number from four to six. A large proportion of the food of this species consists of aquatic insects, but frogs, tiny fishes, and even small mammals are also eaten. A captive bird with which I was well acquainted passed a good deal of its time during sunny weather in stalking blue-bottle flies, which it approached in a crouching attitude with great caution, and when within striking distance, with a sudden dart of its bill, seldom failed to secure its victim.

The late Colonel Irby says (*The Ornithology of the Straits of Gibraltar*, 2nd ed., pp. 204–205): "On the Spanish side the Squacco Heron is entirely migratory, arriving during the month of April. They are common in the marisma of the Guadalquivir; but I never observed any near Gibraltar, nor did I ever see them following cattle, like the preceding species (Buff-backed Heron). They nest late in the season."

This bird is generally quiet and silent, spending a good part of its time with its neck drawn closely in after the style of a Bittern. The late Lord Lilford states that the only note he ever heard from this species was "a harsh rattling croak."

The female resembles the male, but the plumes on the back of the neck are not quite so long.

According to the late H. E. Dresser (*Birds of Europe*), "the fully adult dress is not assumed until the third year."

THE NIGHT-HERON.

Nycticorax griseus (Linnæus).

PLATE 41.

The Night-Heron has been known as a straggler to England since 1782, when it was first recorded, and since that date a good many have been obtained, mostly on the southern and eastern coasts, although a fair number have occurred inland. A few have been noticed in different parts of Scotland, one as far north as Aberdeen, and another on the Outer Hebrides, whilst in Ireland twenty-four have been observed.

It is known as a regular spring visitor to Central and Southern Europe, and has been recorded as far north as the Faeroes, inhabiting also more or less the whole of Africa and a large part of the temperate and southern regions of Asia. A closely allied form is found in America.

Regarding its nidification, Lord Lilford says (*Birds of Northamptonshire and Neighbourhood*, vol. ii. p. 125): "This species commences to nest about the middle of May, sometimes in congregations composed entirely of its own species, but, in my experience, most frequently in company with other members of the Heron family. The nests are slightly but solidly built of twigs and reed-stalks, and usually situated in low-growing bushes in marshy jungles, but occasionally in trees at a considerable height, and now and then among canes and reeds only a few inches above the ground or water. The eggs are generally four in number, and in colour are of the usual greenish-blue that prevails among the Herons."

The bird represented in the plate was drawn from a sketch of one in the Lilford aviaries, as it stood over its eggs, which were laid on the bare ground, two small twigs being the only material collected for the nest.

The rather melancholy "squak" which represents the Night-Heron's usual note is mostly heard after sunset, as the habits of the bird are entirely nocturnal; during the day it generally seeks the repose of shady willows and other trees, where it passes the time, sitting quietly on some bough.

The food consists of various aquatic insects, reptiles, and small fishes, in the capture of which the bird shows great activity.

The long white neck-plumes of the Night-Heron vary considerably in number; according to Lord Lilford there are usually five, while some birds have only two, and as many as ten have been noted. These are shorter in the female, and her colour is also duller.

The immature bird has the upper parts brown with lighter stripes and spots, and the pale underparts are streaked with dark.

3

THE LITTLE BITTERN.

Ardetta minuta (Linnæus).

PLATE 41.

Although only an occasional visitor to the British Islands, there is good ground for believing that this small species has nested in Norfolk as well as in other parts of England. It is rarer in Scotland, but some thirty occurrences have been noted in Ireland.

The Little Bittern is common during the summer months among the marshes of Central and Southern Europe and in North Africa, where it is also found in winter, whilst eastwards it ranges as far as North-west India.

The nest, built of twigs, dead reeds, and sedge, is usually placed just above the water, in dense reed-jungles or in tamarisks. The eggs, generally six in number, are dull white in colour, sometimes tinged with pale greenish.

Like the Common Bittern and Night-Heron, this species feeds at night, and lives on frogs, small fishes, worms, aquatic insects and their larvæ.

It passes the day lurking among the dense tangled growth of the marshes, and if suspicious of danger, is an adept at threading its way through the thick cover of its surroundings.

Lord Lilford states that "the only note I ever heard uttered by this species is, to my ear, best rendered by 'woogh,' 'woogh'—a sort of deep guttural cough."

The female differs from the male in being rather smaller, also in having the head brownish-black in colour, the cheeks and neck reddish-buff, and the back and scapulars dark chestnut with narrow margins of buff, while the underparts are buff streaked with brown.

THE COMMON BITTERN.

Botaurus stellaris (Linnæus).

PLATE 41.

The Bittern, whose name is familiar to most people, though but few have seen it at large or listened to its weird love-song, has occurred in most of the English counties, the dense reed-beds and sedgy bogs of East Anglia having been its chief stronghold in former times. Now it is principally known as a not uncommon winter visitor, and in recent years, where it has obtained sufficient protection from the egg-collector, is known to have reared its young, at least in one instance, in Norfolk as late as 1911.

The Bittern was plentiful as a resident in the fen districts until the first quarter of last century or even later, its disappearance as a breeding species having been hastened by the extensive draining of the marshes where it nested. It has been recorded in many parts of Scotland, mostly as an irregular visitor, and during winter it occurs in Ireland, more especially in the southern portions. Its range is wide over Europe, Asia, and North Africa.

The nest is placed among the cover of reed-jungles, and consists of a mass of the dead stems of water-plants. It contains four eggs, of a dull brownish-olive, without markings, laid early in the year, often in March. When sitting on her eggs, a captive Bittern which I had opportunities of watching, on being approached usually puffed out her feathers, appearing a much larger bird than she really was, as depicted in the plate.

The food consists of fishes, reptiles, and any small mammals up to the size of a Water-rat that can be reached with a quick lunge of its pointed bill, or even birds as large as a Water-Rail.

Mr. E. W. Wade, writing in *British Birds* (vol. i. p. 330), says: "The peculiar note from which the Dutch name (Roerdomp) is derived, is uttered as the bird sits in some reed-bed over the water. It resembles the bellowing of a bull, but with a deeper resonance. When heard at close quarters the bird seems to catch its breath three times, as if inhaling air, and then booms three or four times, the first boom sounding half-choked, the others clear and loud, after which it is silent for twenty minutes or half-an-hour. On wet days the note is oftener heard than on fine."

Living amidst the thick cover of lonely swamps the Bittern leads its solitary life, hiding among the reeds during the day, where it may easily be overlooked owing to the colour of its plumage harmonising so closely with its surroundings. Loth to leave its retreat by taking wing, if approached in its hiding-place the bird will immediately straighten itself out in an upright position, with its bill pointing to the sky, always facing the intruder, but moving so gradually that the motion is hardly perceptible. I have often watched a captive bird carry out this manœuvre, and was struck with the close resemblance the striped and barred feathering on the neck bore to withered reed-stems.

As evening deepens the Bittern becomes active, and may be seen passing from one reed-clump to another on noiseless wings.

The strange aloofness of this bird's character combined with its nocturnal habits, of which little appears to be known, have lent an interest to the Bittern which makes its very name attractive to the bird lover, and it is to be hoped that the attempts it has lately made to re-occupy some of its old haunts during the breeding season will lead to its increase.

The female resembles the male in colour, but is said by Montagu and others to be smaller.

Pl. 41.

Night-Heron

Little Bittern.   Squacco Heron

Glossy Ibis.

Common Bittern.   American Bittern.

THE AMERICAN BITTERN.

Botaurus lentiginosus, Montagu.

PLATE 41.

This New-World species has been recorded about forty times in the British Islands, the first having been killed in Dorsetshire in 1804. Curiously enough, it has apparently never occurred on the Continent of Europe, although it has visited Greenland. The home of this species is in America, its range extending over the greater part of that country. The late Howard Saunders states (*Manual of British Birds*, 2nd ed.), "When situated on dry ground the nest is a very slight structure of reeds and grass; but in places liable to inundations it is sometimes considerably elevated."

In colour the eggs closely resemble those of the Common Bittern, and, according to Seebohm, are from three to five in number.

The food consists chiefly of frogs and other reptiles, as well as fishes and small mammals.

The love-note differs from that of our bird, the sound having been compared to that caused by a mallet when driving home a stake in swampy ground.

In general, its habits and appearance resemble those of the Common Bittern, but it is rather less in size, the crown of the head is brown instead of black, the vermiculations are finer, and the quill feathers of the wing are a uniform slaty-brown without bars. According to Millais, its flight is also more rapid and it rises very swiftly.

Family CICONIIDÆ.

THE WHITE STORK.

Ciconia alba, Bechstein.

Plate 42.

The White Stork is an occasional straggler from the Continent of Europe to the British Islands, the greater number of the records coming from East Anglia, where some thirty have been noted, whilst its visits to Scotland and Ireland are few and far between, and although known for some centuries as a wanderer to our shores, it has never at any time nested here.

A summer visitant to many parts of the Continent of Europe, and ranging as far north as Norway and southwards to Spain, the White Stork also inhabits Asia and Africa, and winters in Central and South Africa, as well as in India.

The nest, composed of sticks, is generally placed on buildings, where, in Europe, the birds are often encouraged to make their homes by the fixing of a cart-wheel or some other staging. They will also build on wood- or straw-stacks as well as in trees. The eggs, usually four in number, are white in colour.

The food consists of worms, reptiles and insects, as well as young birds and small rodents, which the bird obtains in the pastures and marshes.

The White Stork appears to be voiceless, but in the breeding season makes a loud clatter by the striking together of the mandibles. According to the late Colonel Irby (*The Ornithology of the Straits of Gibraltar*), " Storks usually migrate in large flocks at a great height, with a gyrating flight."

The sexes do not differ in colour.

8

THE BLACK STORK.

Ciconia nigra, Linnæus.

PLATE 42.

Rarer than the last-mentioned species, the Black Stork has been recorded in England about twenty times, two of these having occurred in the Scilly Islands. According to the B.O.U. "List of British Birds," 2nd ed., it "breeds in Europe and Asia, ranging from southern Sweden and central Russia eastwards across Siberia, south of about 55° N. latitude, to Mongolia, southwards to Spain, Turkey, Palestine, Persia, Turkestan, and north China. In winter it visits Africa, ranging southwards to the Cape and to India." In habits it differs from the White Stork, avoiding the neighbourhood of human dwellings, and making its home in forests of tall trees near marshy ground, and sometimes on cliffs. The nest is built of sticks, with a lining of grass and moss, and occasionally the birds occupy the former habitations of other species. The eggs vary in number from three to five, and are a dull white in colour.

Howard Saunders states (*Manual of British Birds*, 2nd ed.), "When the shell is held to the light the lining membrane shows *green*, whereas it is yellowish in the egg of the White Stork."

The Black Stork feeds on frogs and other reptiles, fishes, and insects, obtained in the marshes. It makes a clattering sound with the bill, like that produced by its congener.

The male and female do not differ in colour, but the immature bird is of a brownish colour on the upper parts, with the feathers mostly margined with dull white.

Pl. 42.

Spoonbill.

White Stork.

Flamingo.

Black Stork.

$\frac{1}{6}$

THE GLOSSY IBIS.

Plegadis falcinellus, Linnæus.

Plate 41.

The Glossy Ibis ought by rights to have appeared on Plate 42 along with the Storks and Spoonbill, but to prevent it being represented on too small a scale I have placed it with the Bitterns.

Nearly every year this species arrives as a Bird of Passage on our coasts, generally coming in the autumn months, more often seen on the southern and eastern shores of England, ranging as far north as Yorkshire. About twenty have been noted at different times in Scotland, in addition to a flock of a similar number which was observed in the Orkneys in the autumn of 1907. About forty occurrences have been recorded in Ireland. The Glossy Ibis is widely distributed over the Old World, and is also found in the south-eastern United States, whilst a closely allied form inhabits the southern parts of the same region, and also South America.

During the breeding season the birds associate in large colonies ; their nests, composed of the stems of reeds and twigs, are placed low down on the branches of bushes among the marshes, or in thick reed-beds.

The eggs are a deep greenish-blue in colour, and are usually four in number.

The food consists of worms, crustaceans, water-insects, frogs, &c. Lord Lilford describes the only note he ever heard from these birds as "a decidedly corvine, prolonged, guttural croak."

Formerly the Glossy Ibis seems to have visited our shores more frequently than at the present time, as Lubbock, writing in 1845 of its occurrence in Norfolk, as quoted by Stevenson (*Birds of Norfolk*), stated that "fifty years back it was seen often enough to be known to gunners and fishermen as the black curlew."

Some twenty years ago the late Lord Lilford had a small flock of this species in his aviaries, and in his *Coloured Figures of the Birds of the British Islands* refers to the curious attitude they assumed in warm weather. I had opportunities of watching these birds as they stood in an upright position, with one side facing the sun, and the wing opened to its full extent and pointing upwards; they would bask in this manner, and seemed to enjoy the warmth on their bodies. When the wing is closed, the long axillaries usually protrude below the other feathers, as shown in the picture which was taken from one of the birds above referred to.

The sexes do not differ in colour, but the immature bird is of a dull blackish-brown, with some whitish streaks and patches on the head and neck.

Family **PLATALEIDÆ**.

THE SPOONBILL.

Platalea leucorodia, Linnæus.

PLATE 42.

Although the Spoonbill at one time bred in various English counties, including Norfolk, Suffolk, Sussex and Middlesex, as well as in Wales, it is chiefly known at the present time as a Bird of Passage in spring and autumn on the southern and eastern coasts, although it occurs as an autumn straggler in other parts. Professor Newton has proved that it nested in Norfolk in the reign of Edward I, and Mr. Harting in *The Zoologist* has shown that it also bred at Fulham in 1523, and near Goodwood in 1570, whilst Sir Thomas Browne, writing of it in 1688 in Norfolk, as quoted in Stevenson's *Birds of Norfolk*, says, "The Platea or Shovelard, which build upon the tops of high trees. They formerly built in the hernery at Claxton and Reedham ; now at Trimley, in Suffolk. They come in March, and are shot by fowlers, not for their meat, but for the handsomeness of the same ; remarkable in their white colour, copped crown and spoon or spatule like bill." The Spoonbill occasionally visits Scotland and Ireland, and is a summer visitant to Central and Southern Europe, having also a wide range over Asia and Africa. In winter it migrates from its more northern range to Central Africa and India. The birds usually breed in colonies, and place their nests, composed of a mass of dead reeds, on the mud among the thick cover of marsh vegetation, sometimes low down on the branches of willows and alders, or often in high trees. The eggs, generally four in number, are dull white, spotted and marked with rust-colour.

When seeking its food, which consists of small fishes, reptiles, molluscs, crustaceans, &c., the Spoonbill frequents open marshes and mud-flats, probing the soft ground with its peculiarly shaped bill.

Lt.-Commander J. G. Millais has kindly supplied me with the following note regarding this species in Africa. "I have observed a flock feeding in a semi-circle in shallow water. They advanced moving their bills from side to side like a mower cutting hay. The prey was some species of water insect."

It appears to be a more or less silent bird, but Seebohm states that it makes "a sharp snapping sound with its bill."

The female has a smaller crest, but otherwise does not differ much from the male. In winter the head plumes of both sexes show very little development, and in the young bird these feathers are absent.

12

Pl. 43.

White-fronted Goose.
Pink-footed Goose.

Grey Lag-Goose.
Bean-Goose.

Order ODONTOGLOSSÆ.

Family PHŒNICOPTERIDÆ.

THE FLAMINGO.

Phœnicopterus roseus, Pallas.

PLATE 42.

About fifteen occurrences of this beautiful bird have been recorded in Great Britain, but of this number three only appear to have been really wild birds. The first was captured and killed in Staffordshire in September 1881, the second shot near the Beaulieu River in Hampshire in November 1883, and the third seen near New Romney, Kent, in August 1884.

The Flamingo inhabits parts of Spain and southern France, thence eastwards in Asia to Lake Baikal, and southwards to India, and is found throughout the greater part of Africa.

A most interesting account of the nesting of the Flamingo has been given by Mr. Abel Chapman (*Ibis*, 1884, pp. 86–89), who was the first to give an accurate description of the manner in which the birds disposed of their long legs when sitting on the nests, which are merely circular platforms or bulwarks of mud raised a little above the surface of the shallow water, and varying in height from two or three inches to a couple of feet. Instead of standing astride the nest, as described by the old English navigator, William Dampier, Mr. Chapman has shown that the birds sit with "their long red legs doubled under their bodies, the knees projecting as far as beyond the tail, and their graceful necks neatly curled away among their back feathers, like a sitting swan, with their heads resting on their breasts."

The Flamingo breeds in large colonies, masses of nests being often crowded together in the shallow water of the lagoons.

The two eggs, with a rather chalk-like surface, are laid towards the end of May. The birds seem very partial to salt lakes, and obtain their food of tiny crustaceans by dabbling in the water, holding their heads and curiously formed bills in a reversed position while sifting the mud. The gaggling voice of this species resembles that of the Goose, and, like the latter bird, it adopts the same formation when flying.

The sexes do not differ in colour, but the female is smaller. The young take a considerable time before assuming the pink and scarlet of the old birds.

13

Order ANSERES.

FAMILY **ANATIDÆ**.

THE GREY-LAG GOOSE.

Anser cinereus, Meyer.

PLATE 43.

The Grey-Lag Goose, from which species our domestic bird is said to be derived, is the only resident wild Goose in the British Islands. Until about the beginning of last century it still bred in the English fens, but at the present time it is only known to nest in parts of north and north-western Scotland, viz. in the counties of Ross, Caithness and Sutherland, and on the Outer and some of the Inner Hebrides.

During winter its numbers are increased by immigrants, when it is more generally spread over the country, although always scarce on the east coast of Scotland.

It is now only a rather rare winter visitor to England, occurring more frequently in the southern and western parts than in the eastern counties, and the same may be said as regards Ireland. The Grey-Lag Goose breeds in Iceland and in various portions of the Continent of Europe from Scandinavia to Spain, ranging eastwards in Asia through Siberia as far as Kamchatka. In winter it is common in Southern Europe, North Africa, and parts of India. The Grey-Lag is the largest of the British wild Geese, the word *lag*, according to Professor Skeat (*Ibis*, 1870, p. 301), signifying late, last, or slow, which came to be applied to this bird because it lagged behind and nested in our fens when the other species left for their breeding stations in the far north. Professor Newton in his *Dictionary of Birds* quotes an interesting fact mentioned by Mr. Rowley (*Orn.*, Miscell. iii. p. 213), that to this day the tame Geese of Lincolnshire are urged on by their drivers with the cry of " Lag 'em, Lag 'em."

The nest, which is placed on the ground among grass and heather, is built of sticks, dead reeds and sedges, and the eggs, protected by down from the breast of the female, are dull creamy-white in colour.

Mr. Talbot Clifton has very kindly supplied me with some notes on the Grey-

THE GREY-LAG GOOSE

Lag Geese inhabiting South Uist, obtained from his gamekeeper, Murdoch MacDonald, a most careful observer. Owing to want of space I have been obliged to condense them as follows :

This Goose breeds in the Outer Hebrides, nesting on the islands of fresh-water lochs, and lays from four to eight eggs, the average number of the broods consisting of about five birds.

The female sits very closely on her eggs, almost allowing herself to be handled before moving off. They pair in March, and by the end of April or early in May the young are hatched. As soon as the latter are able to fly they come down to the low ground or "machars," where they choose a flat place as their camp. In this sanctuary they remain for a fortnight or so, and as soon as they have acquired their full powers of flight, move about in search of the best feeding ground. When the grain is ripe they frequent the harvest fields, but feed chiefly on grass and plant roots, and also in hard weather are seen among the turnips and in potato fields. Their usual feeding hours are in the early morning and again in the evening, the birds generally resting during the day on some fresh-water loch. They are difficult to stalk, as they always take care not to approach within range of any wall or dyke.

It is seldom possible to drive them twice over the same ground if they have once been shot at, as "they shy the place where they have been cheated, and change their course in the opposite direction." When a flock is feeding, one or two of the old birds are always posted as sentinels, who at once give the alarm if anything suspicious is seen or heard, when they all take wing to safer quarters. On moonlight nights they become much bolder, often at such times approaching steadings, but always taking their departure very early before anyone is astir.

Some twenty years ago my friend Mr. J. H. Dixon had a small flock of this species living in a semi-domesticated condition at Inveran, by Loch Maree. These birds roamed about at their own free will, and I have often seen them in company with wild Grey-Lags, which acquired a certain amount of tameness from association with the others ; and at times they might all be seen feeding in the fields near the house.

When travelling, this and other kinds of Wild Geese fly in a wedge-shaped formation. The four species drawn on Plate 43 represent what are known to shore-shooters as "Grey" Geese, who thus distinguish them from the so-called "Black" Geese (the Brent and Bernacle).

The colour of the Grey-Lag's bill is orange with a white nail, the latter forming a ready means of distinguishing it from the Pink-footed and Bean Geese, in both of which the nail is black. The sexes as in all our Geese do not differ in colour.

15

THE WHITE-FRONTED GOOSE.

Anser albifrons (Scopoli).

PLATE 43

This species is easily distinguished from the Grey-Lag by its smaller size, white forehead and orange legs, although in both the nail on the bill is white.

The black bars on the breast are strongly marked, whereas in the other there are only a few small dark spots.

Only known as a winter visitant to the British Islands, the White-fronted Goose is more numerous on the western portions than on the east coast, although, according to Millais, it is common in the Orkneys and Shetlands on migration in spring.

It is abundant in Ireland, more so than the other "grey" Geese.

The White-fronted Goose goes very far north to its breeding stations among the tundras and on the islands of Arctic Europe and Northern Asia, migrating in winter to the warmer parts of Europe, as well as to Egypt and India.

The nest does not differ from that of other members of the genus, and contains from four to six eggs, of a yellowish-white colour.

The bird feeds on grass, &c., and has been named "Laughing" Goose on account of its cry.

The Lesser White-fronted Goose, *Anser erythropus*, a smaller and darker bird, with the bill also smaller, and having the white on the crown extending farther backwards, breeds in northern Scandinavia, and has been recorded more than once in England. This was considered by Professor Newton and Howard Saunders as only a form of the White-fronted Goose, but others have given it the rank of a species.

THE BEAN-GOOSE.

Anser segetum, J. F. Gmelin.

PLATE 43.

This species differs from the Grey-Lag and White-fronted Geese in having a black nail on the point of the bill, which is orange as far as the nostrils, and then black at the base. Comparing it with the Pink-footed Goose, Lord Lilford says (*Birds of Northamptonshire and Neighbourhood*): " In appearance on wing, note, and habits—in fact, in almost every particular except that of size, and a few slight differences that are imperceptible at a distance—the Bean-Goose so closely resembles the Pink-footed that I could never be quite certain of distinguishing between them except when 'in hand,' and even in the latter case I have found that some of the external characters quoted by authors as distinctive are by no means constant. As a rule, I think that the Bean-Goose on its travels adheres more strictly to the single file or horizontal <-formation than other species."

The Bean-Goose visits us in the autumn, coming soon after harvest, and remaining through the winter. It is said to occur more frequently on the western coasts of England and Scotland than the eastern, and is common in Ireland. It goes north to breed in Kolguev, Novaya Zembla, and other lands within the Arctic Circle, returning to the more temperate parts of Europe and Western Asia for the winter.

According to Seebohm's *British Birds*, in the breeding season it "repairs to the lakes on the tundra, and chooses a hillock on the bank, or an islet in the lake itself where the rushes and sedge are tall enough to conceal the sitting bird. A slight hollow is scraped in the soil and lined with grass, moss, sometimes a few feathers, and always plenty of the light grey down of the bird itself." The eggs vary from three to four or even six in number, and are creamy-white in colour.

THE PINK-FOOTED GOOSE.

Anser brachyrhynchus, Baillon.

PLATE 43.

The late Mr. A. D. Bartlet has the credit of having first brought to the notice of British naturalists in 1839, that this short-billed species differed from the other "Grey" Geese, but he was unaware that it had been already distinguished by Baillon. As previously mentioned, it closely resembles the Bean-Goose, but may always be recognised by the shortness of its bill. According to Lord Lilford, the pink colour of the legs and feet is not constant, or to be certainly depended upon.

On the eastern coast of England it appears to be by far the most numerous species, being scarcer in the west and south.

The B.O.U. "List of British Birds" (1915) states that "it breeds in Spitsbergen, almost certainly in Iceland, and probably also in Franz Joseph Land. It winters in North-western and Western Europe."

Little appears to be known about the nest, but it is said to be so placed that the bird can obtain a wide view of its surroundings, and the eggs are described as being the same as those of the Bean-Goose in colour.

I have received from Mr. R. J. Howard the following notes describing the arrival of the Pink-footed Geese at the Ribble estuary on September 26, 1915, as seen by Mr. W. Pennington of Southport:

"The birds, about two hundred in number, were heard before they could be seen, so great was the height. They descended in small gaggles of eight or ten, led by a single bird, in a wide spiral, and were so tired, that they went straight to sleep and allowed the gunner to walk in the open almost within shot before they rose."

THE SNOW-GOOSE.

Chen hyperboreus, Pallas.

PLATE 44

This rare straggler to the British Islands, of which there are two forms, differing merely in size, visits us at irregular intervals, the greater number of those obtained having been captured or shot in Ireland, and all belonging to the smaller race, except one obtained near Belmullet, co. Mayo.

The larger race breeds in Arctic North America, migrating southwards in winter, whilst the summer home of the lesser appears to be eastern Siberia and western Arctic America. According to the late H. E. Dresser (*A Manual of Palæarctic Birds*), the Snow-Goose "breeds on the Arctic barren grounds near lakes, the nest being a hollow well lined with down, and the eggs, usually five in number, are white."

It feeds on grass and other vegetable matter, as well as on berries and shell-fish.

The bird shown on the plate was painted from a beautiful living specimen at one time in the Zoological Gardens of London.

The young are brownish-grey on the upper parts—the feathers on the back and wing coverts having darker centres—and dull white below.

Pl. 44.

Brent Goose.
Red-breasted Goose.

Bernacle Goose.
Snow-Goose.

A. Thorburn. 1915.

THE RED-BREASTED GOOSE.

Bernicla ruficollis, Pallas.

PLATE 44.

This beautiful species occasionally visits Great Britain during the winter months, two having been obtained about the same date (1776) in Middlesex and in Yorkshire, another at Berwick-on-Tweed (1818), a fourth in Essex (1871), and the last in Gloucestershire (1909). Others are said to have occurred in England.

In summer the Red-breasted Goose inhabits the tundras of western Siberia, nesting in the valleys of the Obi and Yenisei, and migrating in winter to the Caspian Sea and other parts of Asia. Occasionally it visits Western Europe, and in far-away times was certainly known to the inhabitants of Egypt, though rare in that country at the present time. The late Lord Lilford owned a specimen labelled "Alexandria, December 2nd, 1874," which was figured in his work on British Birds.

What is said to be one of the oldest, if not the oldest, picture in existence, painted some five or six thousand years ago, the well-known slab from a tomb at Maydoom, Egypt, gives a most accurate representation in colours of a pair of these birds. I have in my possession a photographic reproduction of this fresco in black and white, which shows that the painter must have drawn them from life and was familiar with the species. In the same group are also shown two of the Lesser White-fronted Geese and an equal number of a larger species, either the Grey-Lag or Bean-Goose, these last depicted in a most natural manner browsing on the herbage.

Mr. H. L. Popham found four nests of the Red-breasted Goose situated at the foot of cliffs on the Yenisei in 1895. The eggs varied in number from seven to nine, and were creamy-white in colour.

The bird feeds on grass and other herbage, and, according to Radde, who observed it during winter on the Caspian Sea, it associates in flocks, which frequent pastures by day and retire to the water at night.

Young birds in their first plumage lack the rich black and chestnut of the adults; the ear-patch is brown mottled with white, the neck and breast reddish-buff, and the upper parts, which are black in the old birds, are brown.

THE BERNACLE GOOSE.

Bernicla leucopsis, Bechstein.

PLATE 44.

Rather rare on the eastern coasts of Great Britain, the Bernacle is a common winter visitor to the Outer and Inner Hebrides, the western shores of Scotland, and north-western coast of England, becoming less numerous towards the south of the latter country. Large flocks visit the shores of the northern half of Ireland in winter, but seldom the south.

The Bernacle breeds within the Arctic Circle, on the eastern side of far-away Greenland, in Spitsbergen, and other remote regions. Little appears to be known about the nidification of this species, but Millais tells me, on the authority of the Danish explorer Mickelsen, that the latter found the Bernacle Goose breeding in colonies on steep cliffs in north-east Greenland.

The eggs laid by birds in captivity are white.

I am indebted to Mr. Talbot Clifton for some particulars regarding these birds in the Outer Hebrides, furnished by Murdoch MacDonald, gamekeeper, South Uist.

The Bernacles arrive there every year about the 25th October, and at first, owing, perhaps, to the number of young birds among them, are much tamer than they become at a later time.

After having rested for ten days or so, they begin to move about from one place to another, feeding during the day and also on moonlight nights. Their food consists entirely of grass.

Before leaving for their breeding grounds in the far north the birds become very wild, and at last congregate in one large flock on the extreme outermost point of land in the Atlantic, when they all take their departure together, between the 20th April and the end of the month. Occasionally birds which have been wounded remain throughout the summer, but these never breed.

It is hardly necessary to allude here to the quaint legend, popular in former days, of the generation of the Bernacle Goose from the shell-fish of the same name, attached to floating timber in the sea. Macgillivray describes the voice of this species as clear and rather shrill, and as coming agreeably to the ear when the cries of a large flock are heard at a considerable distance.

THE BRENT GOOSE.

Bernicla brenta, Pallas.

PLATE 44.

This salt-water species, in ordinary circumstances never leaving the sea-coast unless wounded, is by far the most numerous of the geese which come to our shores in the winter. According to Millais, the Brent is only a very rare straggler to the Orkneys and Shetlands, while its "most noteworthy resorts are the islands in the Cromarty and Moray Firths, where it is exceedingly abundant." It is also very numerous along the east coast to the south of England. The mud-flats near Holy Island, Northumberland, are a favourite resort, where vast numbers arrive during January and February. Large flocks also visit the Irish coasts. In spring the Brent Geese leave us for their breeding stations in the Arctic regions, including Spitsbergen, Novaya Zembla, Kolguev, Greenland, and eastern North America. There are two forms of this species, both of which visit the British Islands, one coming from America having the flanks and underparts of a lighter grey, and the other, a darker bird, from Arctic Europe and Asia.

The Black Brent, *B. nigricans*, found on the western side of North America and Arctic Asia, distinguished by a white collar almost encircling the neck, and by the black on the breast being more widely spread over the lower parts, is said to have been obtained on several occasions in England, but, according to the B.O.U. "List of British Birds" (1915), "its occurrence must be regarded as by no means proven."

Colonel Feilden, who found the nests of the Brent in Grinnel Land, describes them as being made of grass, moss, and the stems of saxifrages, and plentifully lined with down. The four or five eggs are creamy-white in colour.

The cries made by a flock of these geese have been often likened to the sound made by hounds, and no doubt gave rise to the superstition current in old days among country people, that packs of clamorous and shadowy spectre-dogs, known as Gabriel's Hounds, coursed through the air on cloudy nights.

Mr. Abel Chapman, who has given us an interesting account of the habits of the Brent in his *Bird-Life on the Borders*, says : " Speaking generally, they spend the night at sea and the day on the tidal oozes, but never (like the Grey Geese) go inland to feed on the fields, or travel a single yard beyond high-water mark."

Pl. 45.

Bewick's Swan.   Whooper Swan.
Mute Swan (adult & young).

THE BRENT GOOSE

Brent Geese are much sought after by punt-gunners, not only on account of the sport provided, but by reason of their excellence for the table. They are very wary and difficult of approach, unless tamed by severe weather.

Their food consists chiefly of the sea-grass *Zostera marina*, obtained on the mud-flats at low tide.

It is well known that wild fowl and other migratory birds fly at a great height when travelling, and move at an astonishing speed. Referring to this subject, a correspondent in the *Field* (December 4, 1915) gives some very interesting notes. He says, "While flying on duty between Béthune and La Bassée at a height of 8500 feet this afternoon (November 26), I was astonished to see a flock of about 500 ducks or geese passing over Béthune at least 3000 feet above the level of our machine. The wind was about 45-50 m.p.h. N.N.E., and the birds were travelling due south. They were flying at a tremendous speed, and were soon out of sight, as we were flying north." This shows that the birds were at an altitude of about two and a quarter miles, and probably quite out of sight from the ground.

THE WHOOPER SWAN.

Cygnus musicus, Bechstein.

PLATE 45.

Known also as the Whistling Swan, Wild Swan, and Elk, this fine bird is said to have bred in the Orkneys towards the end of the eighteenth century. Now it only visits the British Islands in winter, more often seen in Scotland than elsewhere, though considerable flocks sometimes frequent the shores of England in severe weather. It is rare in Ireland.

In spring the Whooper leaves us for its breeding grounds in Iceland and the northern parts of Europe and Asia. Seebohm, who found this swan nesting in the delta of the Petchora, says in his *British Birds*, "We found several nests between the 19th and 30th June; they were large structures, composed of dead sedge and coarse herbage, and concealed in the dense willow-scrub that covered most of the islands." The eggs vary in number from two to seven, and are creamy-white in colour.

The loud trumpet-like notes of the Whooper, from which it derives its name, are usually uttered on the wing.

The food consists chiefly of the roots of aquatic plants, which the birds obtain by plunging their heads and necks beneath the water. St. John noticed that when feeding they were usually surrounded by surface-feeding ducks, which secured the remains discarded by the larger birds.

This species, besides being about one-third larger than Bewick's Swan, may always be distinguished from the latter by the larger patch of yellow on the base of the bill, this colour extending below and beyond the nostril towards the tip and backwards to the forehead, whereas in Bewick's Swan the yellow does not reach the nostril, and the black extends along the whole length of the ridge of the upper mandible.

The immature bird is a dull brownish-grey colour, resembling the young of our common Swan, and has the bill of a greyish-flesh tint, with the margins and tip black.

When travelling, Wild Swans usually fly in a wedge-shaped formation, with their long necks outstretched to their full extent. The flying birds shown in the distance on Plate 45 were drawn from a sketch made in October 1890 of a flock of eight passing over the Moray Firth. The birds forming the sides of the wedge were unequal in number, five following the leader on one side and two on the other.

BEWICK'S SWAN.

Cygnus bewicki, Yarrell.

PLATE 45.

This Swan was first shown to be distinct from the last-mentioned species by Yarrell in 1829, and is said to have been also recognised about the same time by R. Wingate of Newcastle. It regularly visits Scotland, more particularly the Hebrides, and often in hard winters England and Wales. It is said by some to be rarer than the Whooper in the last-mentioned countries, but Lord Lilford considered that the one species was at least as common a visitor as the other in winter to the eastern coast and inland waters of England. In severe weather Bewick's Swan appears on the Irish coast in large flocks, and, according to Sir R. Payne-Gallwey, is more common than the larger species.

The summer home of Bewick's Swan is within the Arctic Circle in North-eastern Europe and Asia, but I find, according to my authorities, that its range lies more to the eastward than that of the Whooper.

The nests and eggs of the two species closely resemble each other, and I can discover no account of their habits differing in any particular. Seebohm describes the notes of Bewick's Swan as a "musical bark."

THE MUTE SWAN.

Cygnus olor (J. F. Gmelin).

PLATE 45.

It is not known with any certainty when the Mute or Tame Swan was first brought to England, but the date of its introduction is said to go as far back as the twelfth century, its first coming, like that of our common Pheasant, being wrapped in mystery. This species is the common Swan of our lakes and rivers, where large numbers live in a semi-domesticated condition; these are increased at times by the arrival of more or less wild birds from the Continent of Europe. There it breeds in many places in a perfectly wild condition, notably in Denmark, southern Sweden, Germany, Austria, and elsewhere.

The nest is a large piled-up structure of dead reeds and other vegetation, and contains from five to eight eggs of a greenish-grey colour. When the female is sitting I have noticed that the male is never far away, and on the nest being approached by anyone, he will boldly swim up and remain on guard near the spot until the intruder withdraws.

The Mute Swan is not always silent, as in the breeding season, according to Naumann, the bird utters a loud and trumpet-like note. In tame Swans the call notes are softer. It is easily distinguished from the two other species by the large black tubercle at the base of the upper mandible, the greater portion of the latter being of a deep orange colour.

What Yarrell described as a new species (*Proc. Zool. Soc.*, 1838, p. 19), which he named *Cygnus immutabilis*, commonly known by its English name of Polish Swan—though it seems to have had no connection whatever with the country its name suggests—is now considered to be only a variety of the Mute Swan.

It was supposed to differ from the latter bird in having, when adult, a smaller tubercle and slaty-grey legs and feet, the colour of the young being white instead of the usual brownish-grey of the other's cygnets.

Curiously enough, with one exception—a bird from the Lake of Haarlem in Holland—all the so-called "Polish" Swans have occurred in the British Islands.

26

THE COMMON SHELD-DUCK.

Tadorna cornuta (S. G. Gmelin).

PLATE 46.

The Common Sheld-Duck, known also by various local names, such as "Burrow-Duck," "Bar-Gander," "Sand-Goose," and others, is a resident species in the British Islands, and plentiful on many parts of our coasts, especially where there are long stretches of sandy shore and bent-covered dunes, being seldom found far from salt or brackish water. It has a wide range over Europe, from northern Scandinavia to the Mediterranean countries, and it also visits North Africa in winter. In Asia it inhabits localities which suit it as far east as Japan, and north to the southern parts of Siberia, while in the cold season its range extends to north India and China.

The seven to twelve creamy-white eggs are usually laid either within a rabbit burrow or in a cavity at the end of a tunnel excavated by the bird, a warm nest of dry bents and moss thickly lined with down being prepared for them.

The food consists mainly of sea-worms, molluscs and various small marine creatures, as well as sea-weeds, sought for by the bird on the flats at low-water.

Seebohm states that the call-note of both sexes is a "harsh quack," and that during the breeding season the male utters "a clear rapidly repeated whistle or trill." At all times the Sheld-Duck is a conspicuous and handsome bird, and readily recognised even at a distance by its strongly contrasted plumage. It is easily tamed, and is a favourite on ornamental waters. St. John, in his *Wild Sports and Natural History of the Highlands*, has given some interesting notes on their habits, telling us how, at low-tide, they obtain the sea-worms which form a good portion of their food. Locating their prey by the worm-casts, they pat the ground with their feet, thus causing the creatures to come to the surface. He also noticed how the sitting female always leaves her nest at low-tide, so as more easily to obtain her food. In colour she is rather duller than the male, and has only a trace of the knob at the base of the bill.

THE RUDDY SHELD-DUCK.

Tadorna casarca (Linnæus).

PLATE 46.

This species is a rather rare visitant to the British Islands, and was first recorded in 1776, when a specimen was killed near Blandford, Dorsetshire. On the Continent of Europe it favours the south-eastern parts more than the western, nesting, it is said, in some numbers on the Lower Danube, while a few breed in southern Spain. It inhabits North Africa, and has a wide range over Asia. In India, where it is plentiful, it is known as the " Brahminy Duck."

The Ruddy Sheld-Duck nests underground in various situations. The late Mr. Salvin and Canon Tristram found it breeding in crevices among cliffs, while such sites as burrows, hollow trees, and even the old nests of birds of prey are also chosen. Mr. E. H. Wilson (*A Naturalist in Western China*) says, " I once found a couple breeding in the margin of an alpine lake near Tachienlu, at 15,500 feet altitude." The eggs, varying in number from eight or nine to sixteen, are creamy-white in colour.

It has a loud uncouth cry, repeated several times, which has been syllabled as *Kark*.

The food consists of various aquatic insects, molluscs, grass, &c.

Unlike the Common Sheld-Duck, this species prefers inland lakes and rivers to the sea coast.

The female resembles the male in colour, but is without the narrow black collar.

THE MALLARD.

Anas boscas, Linnæus.

PLATE 46.

The Mallard, perhaps better known as Wild Duck, and the origin of our domestic species, is widely distributed not only in the British Islands, where it breeds in every county, but throughout the world. In winter the number of Mallards in our country is greatly increased by flocks arriving from the Continent of Europe, owing to the freezing of their northern feeding grounds.

The nest, built of grass and warmly lined with down, although usually hidden among reeds and other cover near water, is often situated on the tops of pollard willows or in hollow trees. The eggs, of a pale greenish-grey colour, vary in number from about seven to twelve.

The Mallard is more or less omnivorous, eating small fishes, molluscs, slugs, worms, &c., as well as vegetable products and grain, and it usually feeds by night. When on the coast the birds generally spend the day at sea or in the estuaries, resting and preening their feathers, and as soon as darkness begins, come in to the mud-flats and marshes, or to stubble or potato fields.

It is hardly necessary to describe the notes of this species, but those uttered by the drake are much lower and more husky than the duck's.

By nature the Mallard is shy and wary, and a flock will circle many times over a sheet of water before making up their minds to settle.

In days gone by great numbers of this species, as well as other ducks, were caught in decoys, an ingenious arrangement of reed-screens and netting, into which the birds were lured to their destruction.

Being a surface-feeder, the Mallard does not as a rule seek its food by diving, but according to Lt.-Commander J. G. Millais, our greatest living authority on all that pertains to the duck family (*The Natural History of British Surface-feeding Ducks*, p. 3), " The real exceptions to the rule are to be found in the immature birds —the birds three-quarters grown, and still unable to fly. At this stage of life the Mallard, encouraged by their attendant mothers, gain much of their food by diving."

The same author has given us a complete history of the curious change of plumage which takes place in the males of this species and other ducks during

Pl. 46.

Mallard (♂&♀)
Ruddy Sheld-Duck.

Gadwall. (♂&♀)
Common Sheld-Duck.

summer. It appears that this annual change into what is known as the eclipse plumage, which resembles more or less that of the female, commences in England as early as May 2cth and in Scotland about July 1st. By degrees all the gay colours disappear, being replaced by new feathers of brown and buff, and finally the quill·feathers of the wings are moulted, leaving the bird in a helpless condition as far as flight is concerned. Were it not for this protective colouring, the birds would have a poor chance of surviving during this critical period. It is not possible to give further details here, except to say that by October 1st the normal plumage of the Mallard has been entirely resumed.

The Bimaculated Duck, of Latham and other authors, figured by Bewick and described as a species, is now known to be only a hybrid, by some considered a cross between the Wigeon and Teal, but the late Lord Lilford, after handling a specimen caught in his decoy in December 1894, was satisfied that the parents were Mallard and Teal.

THE GADWALL.

Anas strepera, Linnæus.

PLATE 46.

This elegantly shaped, dull coloured species, though locally abundant in some favoured districts in winter, is otherwise a rather uncommon visitor to most parts of the British Islands. In Norfolk, where a fair number breed every year, it was originally established as a resident by the introduction of a pair of pinioned birds about sixty years ago, and large numbers now visit this county during the winter. It also breeds in Suffolk, and within the last few years has nested in southern Scotland, also coming to the western islands, especially Tiree, in the cold season, at which time it visits Ireland.

The Gadwall is found generally throughout Europe, breeding as far north as Iceland, while in winter many visit the basin of the Mediterranean and North Africa. It has also a wide range over Asia as well as in America.

The nest, built of dead grass and flags, is warmly lined with down and placed on dry ground, sometimes near, sometimes at a distance from the water. The eggs are buffish-white, and vary in number from eight to fourteen.

Lt.-Commander J. G. Millais says (*Natural History of British Surface-feeding Ducks*), "Although it will rest at sea by day, the Gadwall is even less a marine bird than the Mallard, yet in most of its habits it closely resembles that species; and, though not naturally so cunning as the wild duck or the Wigeon, is much more shy and retiring in its ways. It loves quiet and sheltered nooks, still waters and sluggish streams, where it feeds on a vegetable diet composed chiefly of water-plants, their seeds, and fresh-water molluscs. In summer it is very fond of insects, and spends much time in catching flies and water-beetles; but on the whole it is, except in the courting season, the most undemonstrative of ducks. Floating motionless in the shadows, or lying hidden in the reeds, the birds seldom attract the attention of the passer-by unless flushed from their shelter, which they are commonly loth to leave."

Lord Lilford describes the call of the male Gadwall as "a sharp shrill rattling note continually repeated, whilst the female responds with a 'quack' resembling that of the Wild Duck."

When at a distance on the water, the females of the Gadwall and Mallard look much alike, but the former may always be distinguished by the white speculum on the wing.

31

THE SHOVELER.

Spatula clypeata (Linnæus).

PLATE 47.

During the last forty years or so the Shoveler has greatly increased as a breeding species in the British Islands, especially in Scotland and Ireland, whilst in England it is best known as a spring and winter visitor, though nesting regularly in Norfolk and Lincolnshire, and more or less in many other counties. It breeds in Europe from about as far north as the Arctic Circle southwards to the Mediterranean countries and also in North Africa, but in the latter country it is more plentiful in winter. Eastwards across Asia it is found as far as Japan and southwards to India, whilst it has also a wide range in America. This species, according to Millais, "makes a deep nest of fine grass, and will place it in open grassy land near water, but not in rank vegetation. As a rule it is very well hidden, and, the parent bird sitting close, it is difficult to find." The eggs, varying in number from eight to fifteen, are greenish-buff in colour.

The Shoveler is a decidedly fresh-water duck, very seldom found on the sea, and obtains its food, consisting of water-insects, worms, molluscs, &c., as well as grasses, duck-weed and seeds, among the bogs and marshes of inland waters. It has a characteristic manner of feeding; plunging the broad and curiously shaped bill in the water, or holding it horizontally on the surface, it sifts the muddy liquid through the bristles with which the mouth is furnished.

The mated pairs in early summer may often be seen closely following each other in circles while feeding in this manner.

The Shoveler is a rather silent bird, but in the breeding season the male utters a low croaking note.

Teal. (♂&♀)   Shoveller (♂&♀)
American Blue-winged Teal. (♂&♀).   American Green-winged Teal.
Pintail. (♂&♀)

3

THE PINTAIL.

Dafila acuta (Linnæus).

PLATE 47.

The Pintail is a regular autumn and winter visitor to the British coasts, sometimes arriving in large numbers, and of late years some have remained to breed in Scotland, notably in the Orkneys, Shetlands, the Hebrides, and on Loch Leven, the first record of its nesting on this loch dating from 1898. On the Continent of Europe it is found breeding from as far north as Lapland to Spain, and in the cold season it visits North Africa. It has a wide range over a great part of Asia, as well as in America.

The nest, built of grass and sedge, and well supplied with down, is usually situated at some little distance from the water. The eggs vary in number from seven to twelve, and are usually buffish-green in colour.

The food consists mostly of water-plants, insects, and molluscs.

In the breeding season the male Pintail utters a double whistling note with a peculiar "*click*" in it, very similar to that of a drake Teal.

In disposition and habits this species is a very wide-awake bird, frequenting open and wide stretches of fresh water or the estuaries of the sea, and feeds by day as well as by night.

33

THE TEAL.

Nettion crecca (Linnæus).

PLATE 47.

The Teal is not uncommon as a breeding species in many parts of the British Islands, being more numerous in the northern counties of England and in Wales than in the south, whilst it is plentifully distributed over the bogs and mosses of Scotland and Ireland. In autumn and winter its numbers are much increased by birds arriving on our shores from Northern Europe, which gather in large flocks on the coast or make their way inland, according to the severity of the weather. Ranging through the whole of Europe, it visits North Africa in winter, is found over the greater part of Asia, and occasionally occurs in eastern North America.

The nest, placed on dry ground, occasionally at some distance from water, and usually amongst tall heather or other cover, is plentifully lined with down, and contains from eight to fifteen eggs, of a buffish-white colour tinged with green.

The male Teal, according to Millais, occasionally utters a low double whistle, and the female when frightened or anxious about her brood will emit a subdued little "quack."

The food is similar to that of other surface-feeding ducks.

Although its favourite haunts are bogs and fresh-water marshes, the Teal will resort to the estuaries and sea-coast in hard weather, at which times they are much harassed by punt-gunners, and at all times are a favourite prey of the Peregrine Falcon. When startled, they will rise suddenly and shoot upwards, flying at a great pace, and on such occasions do not afford an easy mark for the gunner.

The females are excellent mothers, and show great affection for their young.

THE AMERICAN GREEN-WINGED TEAL.

Nettion carolinense (J. F. Gmelin).

PLATE 47.

This species has thrice occurred in Great Britain, the first obtained in Hurst-bourne Park, Hampshire, about 1840, the next near Scarborough, Yorkshire, in November 1851, and the last on Kingsbridge estuary, Devonshire, on November 23, 1879. It is the representative of our European bird in America, and in summer is common in Canada and the United States, migrating in winter to the more southern parts of the New World.

The adult male is easily distinguished from the Common Teal by the white crescentic band on both sides of the breast, and by the absence of the white on the scapulars; the buffish lines on the head are also much less distinct, and the vermiculations on the flanks are finer. It requires an expert to distinguish the females of the two species, so closely do they resemble each other, whilst their nidification and habits in general are also alike.

Pl. 48.

Pochard. (♂ & ♀)

American Wigeon (♂ & ♀)

Wigeon. (♂ & ♀)

Red-crested Pochard (♂ & ♀)

Garganey. (♂ & ♀)

THE AMERICAN BLUE-WINGED TEAL.

Querquedula discors (Linnæus).

PLATE 47.

This little duck, commonly known as the Blue-winged Teal, is closely related to the Garganey, and judging from some live birds I had an opportunity of watching in the Zoological Gardens of London, is not unlike the Shoveler in its actions and manner of feeding. It has been obtained three times in the British Islands, viz. in Dumfriesshire, 1858, on the Dee estuary, Cheshire, about 1860, and at Ballycotton, co. Cork, in September 1910.

The Blue-winged Teal breeds in North America, especially from the Rocky Mountains eastwards, and in winter migrates to the warmer parts of the United States, Mexico, Central America, and the West Indies.

Its nest, eggs, and habits in general do not differ from those of its congeners.

THE GARGANEY.

Querquedula circia (Linnæus).

PLATE 48.

The Garganey or Summer Teal is a rather scarce spring visitor to England, arriving in small numbers about the beginning of March, and breeding regularly, though sparingly, in Norfolk, Suffolk, and Kent. Elsewhere in England it appears to be rare, but it has nested in other counties besides those mentioned. It visits Ireland occasionally, though never breeding there, and in Scotland is said to have occurred on some of the islands in the north and west. It has a wide range over Europe from the regions south of the Arctic Circle to the Mediterranean countries, and eastwards across Asia to Japan, visiting Africa and India in winter.

The nest, composed of grass and sedge, and warmly lined with down, is often placed at some distance from the water, and is well concealed, sometimes in the drier parts of marshes, sometimes in rough pastures. The seven to thirteen buffish-white eggs lack the greenish tint of the Common Teal's, having a more pronounced creamy colour.

This species feeds principally on tiny fishes and water-insects.

The curious grating rattle uttered by the male may be heard in the breeding season.

The late Lord Lilford in his *Birds of Northamptonshire and Neighbourhood* says, " A flock of Garganeys twisting among trees presents a very remarkable appearance, from the simultaneous flashing in the sun of the blue-grey coverts of the male birds amidst the pale green of the early spring foliage."

THE WIGEON.

Mareca penelope (Linnæus).

PLATE 48.

The Wigeon is a common winter visitant to the estuaries and shores of the British Islands, frequenting also inland waters and river valleys. It nests in various parts of Scotland, more often in the northern counties of that country than elsewhere, although in recent years its breeding range has extended more to the southwards, and nests have even been recorded in the north of England and in Wales. The Wigeon ranges far and wide over Europe, from about the Arctic Circle southwards, breeding in the northern portions and migrating to the more temperate parts in winter, when it also visits North Africa. A few are sometimes found on the coast of North America as well as in Alaska.

The nest, well hidden amongst the cover of rushes, rank grass or heather, and having a snug lining of down, usually contains from seven to ten cream-coloured eggs.

The favourite feeding grounds of the Wigeon are the *Zostera-covered* mud-flats on our coasts, this marine vegetation forming the principal part of their diet, although they also eat other aquatic plants as well as animal food. For a short period after their arrival the birds, which often congregate in enormous flocks, are less wary and unapproachable than they afterwards become, and at first feed by day, but when much persecuted they change their habits and become nocturnal.

The call-note of the male is a shrill double whistle.

THE AMERICAN WIGEON.

Mareca americana (J. F. Gmelin).

PLATE 48.

This New World species, common in various parts of America according to the season, and known there to sportsmen as " Bald-pate," breeds in the northern portions of that continent, whilst its southward migrations in winter extend sometimes to Guatemala and Cuba. It is said to have been found breeding in Iceland. The American Wigeon has rarely visited Great Britain, and some of the records are doubtful, or may possibly refer to escaped birds. Two specimens, a male and female, were discovered by the late Mr. Bartlet, mixed with some Common Wigeon, in the London market in the winter of 1837-38, another appeared in a Leeds game stall in February 1895, and the last obtained was shot on the island of Benbecula, Outer Hebrides, in January 1907.

This species appears to be more of a fresh-water duck than our bird, and is said to nest on high and dry ground at some distance from water among the cover of trees and bushes. The eggs resemble those of its European congener, being of a creamy-white colour.

THE RED-CRESTED POCHARD.

Netta rufina (Pallas).

PLATE 48.

All the ducks hitherto described may be classed as "surface-feeders," these usually seeking their food on or close to the surface of the water, whilst the Pochards and other species which follow obtain it more or less by diving, and are easily distinguished from the former by the large lobe on the hind toe.

The Red-crested Pochard is a rather uncommon autumnal and winter visitant to England, mostly appearing on the East Coast, and in Scotland and Ireland only two occurrences have been reported, one in Argyllshire and the other in Kerry. Its true home is in Southern Europe, the birds ranging eastwards to Central Asia, and in winter visiting India. Large numbers are found in North Africa during the cold season, in which country it also breeds.

The nest, hidden among flags and rushes near water, contains from six to ten eggs of a decided greenish stone-colour, paler and greener than those of the Common Pochard.

The late Lord Lilford describes the winter cry of this species as a "rattling croak," and the pairing note of the male as "a low whistle."

It feeds chiefly on the roots of aquatic plants and other vegetable matter, as well as on water-insects, crustaceans, molluscs, fishes, &c., obtained both by day and by night.

In disposition it is shy and timid, and loves the seclusion of large sheets of deep, still water.

THE COMMON POCHARD.

Fuligula ferina (Linnæus).

PLATE 48.

The Common Pochard, Red-headed Poker, or Dunbird, as it is variously called, though breeding in some favourable places in some of our English counties, especially those along the eastern coast, is better known in our islands as a common autumnal visitor, usually arriving in October and leaving in the spring. It breeds on many of the Scottish lochs, but seldom in Ireland.

This species is widely distributed over Europe and Asia, the birds which nest in the colder parts moving for the winter to the Mediterranean countries, North Africa, Egypt, India, China, and Japan.

The Common Pochard is a more or less fresh-water species, seldom visiting the sea unless under necessity, and is most at home on wide stretches of inland water where it can find shelter and protection.

The nest is placed among rushes and thick herbage near the water, and usually contains from seven to nine eggs of a dull greenish colour.

The food consists of the roots and other parts of various aquatic plants and their seeds, and also of molluscs, water-insects, &c., mostly obtained by diving.

The alarm call of both the male and female is a jarring croak, and the former also emits in the breeding season a soft whistle.

THE FERRUGINOUS DUCK.

Fuligula nyroca (Güldenstädt).

PLATE 49.

The Ferruginous Duck or White-eyed Pochard is only known as an occasional visitor in the British Islands, and has been recorded more often in the eastern and southern parts of England than elsewhere. It is however common in Central and Southern Europe, breeding in many parts of that continent and in North Africa, as well as in the temperate regions of Asia. It winters in Africa and India. Lord Lilford says in his work on British Birds, "I have met with the White-Eye in various parts of Southern Europe and North Africa, and discovered a nest in Andalusia in 1872; this nest was placed amongst high rushes at a short distance from a small fresh-water lake, and was composed of dry flags and rushes, and lined with thick brownish down and a few white feathers."

The number of eggs appears to vary between six and fourteen. The colour of these, according to Millais, is generally "pale brown, sometimes with a faint yellow or greenish tint."

The food consists of roots and shoots of different water-plants, insects, and molluscs.

Lord Lilford describes the call-note of this duck as "a harsh rattling mono-syllable, frequently repeated."

The White-eyed Pochard is said to be less shy of human beings than other ducks, is swift on the wing, and loves the seclusion of thick reed-beds and similar cover on fresh-water lakes and ponds.

An example of Baer's Pochard, *Nyroca baeri*, a Siberian species, was obtained on the Tring reservoirs, Hertfordshire, in November 1901. This bird had probably escaped from captivity.

Pl. 49.

Tufted Duck. (♂♀)   Ferruginous Duck. (♂♀)
Buffel-headed Duck. (♂♀)   Golden-eye (♂♀)   Scaup Duck. (♂♀)
Long-tailed Duck. (♂♀)

3

THE TUFTED DUCK.

Fuligula cristata (Leach).

PLATE 49.

During late years this handsome little duck has been increasing in numbers as a resident in all parts of the British Islands, so much so that it has been recorded as nesting over the greater portion of the United Kingdom. It is abundant in Scotland, being especially numerous on Loch Leven, and breeding plentifully every year on the islands of that historic lake. It is found over a great part of Europe, breeding in the northern districts of the Continent, speaking roughly, from Lapland southwards to Central Europe, whilst in winter it visits the Mediterranean countries and Northern Africa. It also inhabits a great part of Asia, and during the cold season migrates to India as well as to the islands of the Pacific.

The nest, sheltered by some bush or tuft of rushes, is built of dead grasses with a lining of down, and contains from eight to ten or even more eggs of a greenish-buff colour.

According to Mr. Whitaker, as quoted in Howard Saunders' *Manual*, the note of this species sounds as " *currugh, currugh,* uttered gutturally."

The food, partly vegetable, partly animal, consists chiefly of aquatic plants, insects, molluscs, tadpoles, &c., obtained by diving, in which art the Tufted Duck shows great proficiency.

THE SCAUP-DUCK.

Fuligula marila (Linnæus).

PLATE 49.

This marine species, common on many parts of our coasts and estuaries in winter, and much less often seen on inland waters, breeds throughout the greater part of the circumpolar regions of Europe, Asia, and America, and also within recent years a few nests have been identified in the north of Scotland, as well as in the Orkneys and Outer Hebrides.

The first authentic nest of this species found in the British Islands was that discovered by Mr. Heatley Noble on an island in a Sutherlandshire loch (*Ibis*, 1899, and the *Annals of Scottish Natural History*, 1899).

During the breeding season the Scaup frequents fresh-water lakes and rivers, and builds its nest among rushes or in rough grassy cover near water, and lays from six to ten or eleven eggs of a pale greenish-grey colour.

This duck is an expert diver, and obtains its food on the submerged mussel-beds or tangle-covered reefs, and in the summer months, when away from salt-water on its nesting ground, eats seeds of aquatic plants, small fishes, and insects. It is very gregarious in its habits, and utters a harsh, discordant croak.

THE GOLDEN-EYE.

Clangula glaucion (Linnæus).

PLATE 49.

The Golden-Eye, another of our autumn and winter visitants, is at that time fairly common on the salt-water estuaries, the brackish water of tidal rivers, and on many inland lakes and streams.

The summer home of the Golden-Eye is in Northern Europe, North Asia, and North America, but in the last-mentioned country a larger race represents our bird.

When the breeding season is over the birds move southwards to more temperate regions, and then visit other parts of Europe, North Africa, China, Japan, and India, whilst the American form winters in the southern regions of the New World.

The Golden-Eye usually occupies for its nesting site a hollow tree, and in Lapland logs are purposely hollowed out by the natives as breeding boxes. The eggs, varying in number from ten to a dozen, are of a bright, clear green colour.

The food is chiefly composed of the larvæ of water-insects, secured by the bird from under the stones when diving, also of mussels, tadpoles, and fishes.

Millais, in his *British Diving Ducks*, vol. i. pp. 90–91, has given us an interesting account of the Golden-Eye's methods when obtaining food. "In clear water it is easy to note the powerful strokes of the legs of these ducks, which seem to beat with great rapidity under water and much power. The stroke is more or less parallel to the wings, the head is held out straight in front. I have watched for hours the male Golden-Eye that lived for three years on the island below Perth bridge, and used to find his food at the bottom of the river in some 8 to 10 feet of water. In summer this water was as clear as crystal, and from the bridge above the observer could note every movement on the part of the bird. It always proceeded to a depth of 8 to 10 feet of water, and began to dive. On reaching the bottom it at once commenced to turn the stones over with the bill, and from under these, various water-insects were found or caught as they attempted to escape. Sometimes it would find a small batch of young fresh-water mussels, and these it would devour very quickly one after the other, like a duck taking grain out of a pan. It never stayed under water for more than a minute, even when finding food abundant in one spot, but came up, rested a moment or two on the surface, and dived again. All food was swallowed where it was found, and small pebbles and fairly large stones were pushed over in the search."

The Golden-Eye is known to fowlers in some places as " Rattlewing," from the curious whistling noise made by the wings of the bird in flight; whilst the females and immature males, under the name of " Morillon," were formerly, and in some cases even now, considered to be a different species.

THE BUFFEL-HEADED DUCK.

Clangula albeola (Linnæus).

PLATE 49.

I can find only two reliable records of this small American duck in Great Britain, the first shot near Yarmouth about 1830, and at present in the Norwich Museum, and another, now in the possession of Mr. J. Whitaker, of Rainworth Lodge, Notts, killed at Bridlington, Yorkshire, in the winter of 1864–65.

Some other specimens recorded are said not to be authentic. The Buffel-headed Duck breeds in the northern parts of the United States of America and in the Dominion of Canada, migrating in winter to the more southern parts of that Continent as far as California, Mexico, and Florida, as well as to the West Indies and the Bermudas.

Like the Golden-Eye, this species nests in holes in trees, often at some height from the ground, and lays from eight to ten eggs, which are buffish-white in colour.

In summer it lives on plants, worms, snails, &c., and when on salt water in winter, it eats shell-fish and other marine creatures.

It is usually a silent bird, merely uttering a low croak, and is known in America under the names of " Butter-ball," " Spirit Duck," and " Conjuror," the two last having been applied to this duck owing to the rapidity with which it disappears when diving.

THE LONG-TAILED DUCK.

Harelda glacialis (Linnæus).

PLATE 49.

This beautiful species is a winter visitant to the British Islands, arriving in considerable numbers in October and usually leaving in March. It is more abundant in the waters of the northern and western islands and along the coasts of Scotland and east coast of England than elsewhere, and is said to have nested in the Orkneys and Shetlands, which statement seems open to doubt.

The Long-tailed Duck breeds on the tundras of Northern Europe, Asia, and America, chiefly within the Arctic Circle, retreating in winter to more temperate climates.

The nest, usually hidden away among dwarf willows, rough grass, or other vegetation, and placed at various distances from fresh water, sometimes being close to it, at others at some little distance, contains from six to eight or even nine eggs, of a dull buff colour slightly tinged with greyish-green.

When feeding, according to Millais (*British Diving Ducks*), "Long-tailed Ducks seem capable of diving to a greater depth than most of the genus except the Eider, the Scaup, and the Velvet-Scoter; usually their feeding grounds are in ten to thirty feet of water, and they seem able to remain below in considerable currents. In diving they use the feet only, and turn and twist to avoid sea-weed with great skill."

Their food when off our coasts in winter consists principally of mussels and other shell-fish, as well as small crustaceans, and in summer the leaves and seeds of water-plants and also insects are eaten.

The cry of the drake is a loud and musical call, rendered by some authors as "calloo," but, according to Millais, "it is always the same, Ka-Ka-Coal-and-Candle-Light," and from its notes, various local names have been given to this bird, supposed to represent its voice.

The Long-tailed Duck is restless and active, and appears to be quite at home even among fairly heavy seas.

The winter plumage of this species, as shown on Plate 49, differs very much in colour from that assumed during the breeding season, which in the male is as follows: On the face a patch of brownish-grey, extending from the bill to the ear-

48

coverts, the part immediately around the eye being almost white; the rest of the head, neck, and breast are brownish-black, the scapulars and upper parts rufous with black centres to the feathers, and the rest of the plumage much the same as in winter.

The female in summer has the head and neck dark brown, with a light patch on the face corresponding in some degree to that in the male, the lower part of the breast brown and grey, and is elsewhere generally more rufous than in winter.

Pl. 50.

Harlequin Duck (♂♀)   Eider Duck. (♂♀)

King-Eider. (♂♀)

THE HARLEQUIN DUCK.

Cosmonetta histrionica (Linnæus).

PLATE 50.

The Harlequin Duck is an extremely rare visitor to the British Islands, and although most of the records of its occurrence are open to doubt, the male picked up on the shore at Filey, Yorkshire, in the autumn of 1862, now in the collection of Mr. J. Whitaker of Rainworth, Notts; and the two males obtained out of a party of three birds near the Farne Islands, Northumberland, in December, 1886, in the possession of Mr. R. W. Chase and the Rev. Julius Tuck, are well authenticated. In *British Diving Ducks*, Millais has added another record which he considers above suspicion, viz. "an adult male killed near the Farnes in December 1882 by one Cuthbertson, and now in the possession of Lord William Percy at Alnwick Castle."

This very conspicuous duck inhabits Iceland, where it is not uncommon as a breeding species, and is also found in eastern Siberia, Greenland, and over a great part of North America, being abundant in many places.

The nest is usually placed in holes, or under the cover of vegetation on the banks of some rapid stream, or on an island surrounded by rushing water, and contains from five to ten cream-coloured eggs, the normal number, according to Howard Saunders, being seven.

In winter the Harlequin Duck takes to the sea; seeking its food, which consists chiefly of shell-fish, crustaceans, and other marine creatures, by diving to the bottom, undeterred by the fear of breakers or rapid currents.

THE EIDER DUCK.

Somateria mollissima (Linnæus).

PLATE 50.

This truly marine duck, famed on account of the down provided by the female, with which she surrounds her eggs, is in England only known as a breeding species on the Northumberland coast, the Farne Islands, where it is known as St. Cuthbert's Duck, being its chief stronghold. In winter it appears off-shore in other parts of England, but only in small numbers in the south and west. In Scotland the Eider is much more plentiful, nesting freely along the coasts, and especially in the Orkneys, Shetlands, and Outer and Inner Hebrides, whilst in winter many arrive from the Continent of Europe. It is recorded as having bred for the first time in Ireland in 1912.

The Eider is widely spread over Northern Europe, in localities which suit its sea-loving habits, inhabiting also the islands of the Arctic Ocean, Iceland, and the Faeroes, but in winter many move southwards to more temperate regions. It breeds in northern Siberia, as far east as the Yenisei, other forms of the same species being found in Greenland, eastern and western North America, and North-east Asia.

The nest, composed of pieces of dead grass, sea-weed, or heather, is usually situated near the water in some depression in the ground among stones, or in a clump of marine vegetation, the warm lining of down, plucked from the breast and abdomen of the female, being added about the time the first clutch of eggs is completed. These, generally four or five in number, vary somewhat in colour, but are usually of a pale olive.

According to Millais (*British Diving Ducks*), Eiders in swimming and diving "are surpassed by no other species of diving ducks, being capable of holding their own in the roughest water, and diving to a great depth for food. It has been proved that they can take their food regularly at a depth of 25 to 35 feet and more without inconvenience."

The common salt-water mussel appears to be their favourite food, but various other shell-fish and crustacea are sought after and obtained on the bottom of the sea. In Scandinavian countries the bird is strictly protected on account of its valuable down, which is superior to that of other ducks.

The male Eider takes a long time before coming to maturity, the rich black and creamy-white plumage not being fully assumed until the third year.

THE KING-EIDER.

Somateria spectabilis (Linnæus).

PLATE 50.

This circumpolar species, whose breeding range extends through the arctic regions of Europe, Asia, and America to Greenland, visits warmer seas in winter, when it may be found off the coasts of Scandinavia and even in more southern parts of Europe.

The King-Eider is a rather rare visitor to the British Islands, four having been obtained and two others seen on the east coast of England, and a fair number taken or observed off the eastern shores of Scotland and in the seas surrounding the Orkneys and Shetlands, where its visits appear to be more frequent than elsewhere. Some five specimens have been recorded in Ireland.

The nest resembles that of our Common Eider, but, according to Millais, the down from the female is of a darker colour. The eggs, generally from four to five in number, do not differ from those of its congener in colour. Like our Eider it also obtains its food at some depth under water, feeding chiefly on molluscs and crustaceans.

The late H. E. Dresser, in pointing out the difference between the females of this species and the other, says (*A Manual of Palæarctic Birds*, p. 633), "The female differs from that of *S. mollissima* in being smaller, darker, and in having the central line of feathers on the upper mandible extending quite down to the nostrils."

Pl. 51.

Surf. Scoter.(♂♀).   Steller's Eider.(♂♀)

Common Scoter.(♂♀).   Velvet Scoter.(♂♀).

STELLER'S EIDER.

Somateria stelleri (Pallas).

PLATE 51.

Steller's Eider, another arctic species inhabiting the coasts of northern Siberia and North America, wanders southwards in winter, when it often visits the shores of Norway and the waters of the Baltic. It is a very rare visitant to the British Islands, only two specimens having been recorded; the first, an almost adult male, obtained at Caistor, Norfolk, in February 1830, and a younger bird of the same sex at Filey Brigg, in Yorkshire, in August 1845.

This beautifully marked little Eider takes after the other members of the genus in its habits.

According to Von Middendorff, who found these ducks breeding in some numbers on the Taimyr River in Siberia, as quoted by Dresser (*Birds of Europe*), "this bird places its nest in the moss on the flat tundras; it is cup-shaped and well lined with down, the male remains in the neighbourhood of the sitting female, who leaves the nest unwillingly, uttering a cry resembling that of our common Teal, but harsher."

It feeds chiefly on molluscs and crustacea, obtained by diving in deep water.

THE COMMON SCOTER.

Œdemia nigra, Linnæus.

PLATE 51.

The Common or Black Scoter is an extremely abundant autumnal visitant to the coasts of the British Islands. During that season and in winter enormous flocks may be seen in the English Channel and the North Sea, and in the summer months in much smaller numbers. It is not uncommon as a breeding species in the northern parts of Scotland, especially in Caithness and Sutherland, according to Mr. Heatley Noble, as quoted in Millais' *Diving Ducks*, being much more plentiful than generally supposed. It has also nested of late years on one of the Irish loughs.

The Common Scoter breeds chiefly in Northern Europe and Siberia, ranging in the latter country as far east as the Taimyr Peninsula, and in winter its visits extend as far south as the Mediterranean and North Africa.

The nest, composed of dead grasses, moss, &c., and warmly lined with down, is usually placed among heather, dwarf willows, or other cover—often on islands or by the side of a fresh-water loch—and contains from six to nine cream-coloured eggs.

It feeds mainly on shell-fish, the common mussel providing its chief supply when at sea, but crustaceans, insects, and worms are also eaten, as well as roots of aquatic plants.

According to Lt.-Commander Millais (*British Diving Ducks*, vol. ii. p. 59), "in winter the cry of both adult male and female and immature is a harsh grating call which is so common amongst other sea-ducks, but in spring the adult male utters a somewhat musical bell-like call, which is very difficult to render in words." The same author says: "With its powerful feet and legs the Common Scoter dives frequently when on feed, generally reappearing almost on the same spot; and where they are not constantly disturbed, they are seldom seen flying, but drift lazily about in great battalions when not on feed."

THE VELVET-SCOTER.

Œdemia fusca, Linnæus.

PLATE 51.

This sea-duck visits us in autumn in fair numbers, but it is not nearly so plentiful as the Common Scoter, and is more often seen off the eastern and southern coasts of Great Britain than in our western waters. It appears to be most numerous among the Orkneys, but never breeds in the British Islands, although a few odd birds have been seen occasionally on the east coast of Scotland during the summer months. The summer home of the Velvet-Scoter is in Northern Europe and western Siberia, where it frequents fresh-water lakes, which it leaves as winter approaches for the seas of Western Europe, and also the Black and Caspian Seas.

The nest, thickly padded with down, is generally placed in some hollow on dry ground, under the shelter of willow-scrub or bushes, sometimes, according to Seebohm, "on the tundras at some distance from water." The eggs, varying from eight to ten in number, are of a creamy-white colour.

The Velvet-Scoter, besides being more of a deep-sea diver, is able to withstand rougher and more exposed waters than the common species, and goes down to a considerable depth after its food of mussels and other marine creatures. It may easily be recognised by the white eye-spot and band of the same colour on the wings.

THE SURF-SCOTER.

Œdemia perspicillata, Linnæus.

PLATE 51.

A rare winter visitor to the British Islands, this American species has been more frequently obtained and seen off our western coasts than elsewhere, except in the Orkneys, where, according to Millais, no less than six specimens have been obtained. The Surf-Scoter inhabits North America, breeding in the arctic portions of that region, and migrating in winter as far south as the coasts of Lower California and Florida, in which season it also occasionally visits the Bermudas and Jamaica.

The late H. E. Dresser, in his *Birds of Europe*, quoting a communication received by him from Dr. Brewer, regarding the breeding haunts of this species, says, "The nest was snugly placed amid the tall leaves of a bunch of grass, and raised fully four inches above its roots. It was entirely composed of withered and rotted weeds, the former being circularly arranged over the latter, producing a well-rounded cavity six inches in diameter by two and a half in depth. The borders of this inner cup were lined with the down of the bird, in the same manner as the Eider Duck's nest; and in it lay five eggs, the smallest number I have ever found in any duck's nest, . . . of a uniform pale yellowish or cream-colour." Howard Saunders gives the number of eggs as from six to eight.

The food, like that of the other members of the genus, consists chiefly of shell-fish, obtained by diving to a considerable depth, the bird being quite at its ease among the roughest water.

THE GOOSANDER.

Mergus merganser, Linnæus.

PLATE 52.

Until some forty-five years ago, the accounts of the breeding of this very beautiful duck in Great Britain seem open to doubt, but Macgillivray believed that it nested near Loch Maddy, North Uist, in 1840. It is now known however to breed in various parts of northern Scotland, as well as in Perthshire and Argyll. Elsewhere in the British Islands the Goosander is only known as a winter visitor, and although frequenting estuaries, seems much more at home on rather large and clear, rapid rivers. During summer it inhabits Iceland and Northern Europe southwards to the lakes of Switzerland, many of the birds moving still farther south in the cold season. In Asia it ranges eastwards to Kamchatka and southwards to China and Japan. In Northern Europe the Goosander breeds in hollow trees or in nesting-boxes put up for the purpose by the peasants, but in Scotland the nest is usually placed in holes among rocks or peat and near running water. The eggs, from seven to twelve or thirteen in number, are creamy-white in colour.

The food of the Goosander consists almost entirely of small fishes, for the capture of which the saw-like bill, armed with small sharp projections, is beautifully adapted.

The usual cry of this species is a harsh guttural note.

Few of our wildfowl approach it in splendour of colouring, and I can think of no more beautiful glimpse of bird life than one I enjoyed on a winter's day many years ago when walking by the Tweed near Coldstream, of a flock sunning themselves on the ice-bound margin of the river.

Lt.-Commander J. G. Millais has kindly furnished me with the following notes on the Goosander: " The only known specimen of this bird in eclipse plumage (killed in Finmark) was figured in my work on the *Natural History of British Diving Ducks*. In September 1915 I killed four specimens in full eclipse in North-eastern Europe. At this season they are the most unapproachable of all water birds. As soon as the young are hatched, the adult males leave the breeding ground and make their way to the sea in parties in July, and then choose places on the coast where it is almost impossible to approach them without being observed. I have often seen them rise at a distance of half a mile. Drakes of all species are shy when in the eclipse dress, but Goosanders are the shyest of all birds, not excepting the Wild Geese."

THE RED-BREASTED MERGANSER.

Mergus serrator, Linnæus.

PLATE 52.

The Red-breasted Merganser is a winter visitor to the coasts of England, whilst in Scotland and in Ireland it is a resident, breeding on many inland sheets of water as well as by the sea. It is quite a common bird in suitable localities in north-western Scotland as well as in other parts, and I have often seen pairs frequenting Loch Maree in Ross-shire. It inhabits the northern regions of Europe, Asia, and America, ranging more towards the southern parts of those countries in winter.

The nest, situated among heather or some other thick vegetation, and often concealed in holes among rocks or in river banks, contains from five to ten eggs, in colour yellowish-buff tinged with green. The Red-breasted Merganser is an expert diver, and feeds on different kinds of small fishes, the sand-eel being a favourite when on salt water.

The harsh guttural cry of this species resembles that of the Goosander, but it is usually a silent bird.

Macgillivray says: "This bird flies with rapidity, in the manner of a duck, its wings whistling as it speeds along. It is very shy, vigilant, and active, so that the only good chance one has of shooting it on the water is either when it is floating with its head below, or just as it emerges after diving. Its flesh, however, is not in request, being tough, oily, and with what is called a fishy flavour. On ordinary occasions it rises from the water at a very low angle, striking the surface with its feet and wings, but it is able also to spring up directly either from the ground or from the water."

Like all the members of the genus, the Red-breasted Merganser has a toothed bill, and is hence often called "Saw-bill" by wild fowlers.

58

THE SMEW.

Mergus albellus, Linnæus.

PLATE 52.

The Smew is a rather late winter visitor to our islands, most commonly found on the eastern coasts of Great Britain, and annually visiting the southern coast of England, and, according to Millais, "it is not uncommon on the Inner Hebrides, but rare on the Outer Hebrides, Orkneys and Shetlands."

During the breeding season the Smew inhabits Northern Europe and Asia, ranging in winter as far south as the Mediterranean, also to India, China, and Japan.

The nidification of this species was long a mystery, until Wooley obtained the first eggs through one of his collectors, in Swedish Lapland, in June 1857. The cream-coloured eggs, which closely resemble the Wigeon's, generally vary in number from six to nine.

During its stay with us in winter the Smew usually haunts the salt-water estuaries, occasionally coming inland to sheets of fresh water and rivers, the beautiful full-plumaged adult males being less frequently seen, and much more difficult to approach than the less wary females and immature birds.

The food consists chiefly of small fishes, especially sand-eels when on the sea, which the bird has no difficulty in obtaining, as it is an accomplished diver.

As a rule, it is a silent bird.

Pl. 52.

Red-breasted Merganser.(♂&♀)

Hooded Merganser.(♂&♀)

Goosander.(♂&♀)

Smew.(♂&♀)

THE HOODED MERGANSER.

Mergus cucullatus, Linnæus.

PLATE 52.

This North American species is a very rare visitor to the British Islands, only four well-authenticated examples having occurred on our coasts. The first of these was obtained in the Menai Straits, North Wales, in the winter of 1830–31, a pair were shot by Sir R. Payne-Gallwey in Cork Harbour in December 1878, who also obtained a female on the north coast of Kerry in January 1881. Other specimens are said to have occurred in Ireland as well as in England.

The Hooded Merganser is plentifully distributed in summer over many parts of North America, ranging in winter as far south as Mexico, Cuba, and the West Indies.

Millais, in describing the habits of this species in *British Diving Ducks*, says: "Unlike the Goosander and Red-breasted Merganser, which delight in rushing streams and sea estuaries and bays, the Hooded Merganser loves the quiet lakes and pools of forest country. I have found it in British Columbia and Ontario in much the same habitat as the Buffle-headed Duck. They are often found on the same lakes as the Dusky and Wood Ducks, although not actually consorting with those species. They seem to be altogether a more delicate form of Merganser than the other species, and avoid rough winds and exposed situations of all kinds, spending the day in exploring the depths of some quiet pool for fish and water-insects."

This species breeds in hollow trees, and lays from five to eight pale creamy-white eggs.

Order COLUMBÆ.

Family COLUMBIDÆ.

THE WOOD-PIGEON.

Columba palumbus, Linnæus.

PLATE 53.

The Wood-Pigeon or Ring-Dove, known in the northern parts of our country as Cushat, is an abundant species throughout the British Islands and over a great part of the Continent of Europe, ranging, according to the B.O.U. "List of British Birds" (1915), to North-east Persia and North-west Africa.

The nest, containing the two white eggs, is lightly constructed of sticks, and usually placed in trees, conifers being more often favoured than others, though evergreens, including ivy on buildings, are often chosen.

The well-known notes of the Wood-Pigeon, which produce a pleasing reverberation of sound, especially when heard in woods of tall pines, are familiar to everyone, but what I take to be the true love-song of the male is entirely different, being much softer in tone and more blended. I was not aware of this until I became possessed of the very tame and fearless bird from which the drawing on Plate 53 was taken. This bird I kept for some years in an aviary, and he always assumed the crouching attitude depicted when uttering these love-notes, while the pupils of the eyes contracted until sometimes they were mere specks. At other times he would emit the ordinary Ring-Dove notes, but never, as far as I could see, with his body held in this characteristic position. I believe that this constitutes "the display" of the male when courting, but, owing to their shyness, I have never had an opportunity of witnessing it in a wild bird. My pigeon seemed to prefer the company of human beings to that of his own kind, and often began to coo when closely approached, and would allow himself to be handled.

In autumn vast flocks of this species come over to us from the Continent of Europe, particularly when there is a good "beech-mast year," the seeds of the beech, as well as acorns, holly berries, and grain of all kinds, being chiefly sought after as food. It also eats turnip-tops, clover, and other green-stuffs.

The migrants which arrive in autumn from abroad are said to be "smaller, darker in colour, and somewhat differing in the manner of flight from our home-bred birds" (Lord Lilford).

During the breeding season the male bird may be seen taking a short flight, at the same time alternately rising and descending, and occasionally producing a sharp clap by the striking together of its wings, which has been well described by Macgillivray. At this time they lose much of their usual shyness, and come to the neighbourhood of gardens and shrubberies, where the nest is often built. When on the ground Wood-Pigeons walk in rather a slow and heavy manner, quite unlike the much smarter action of the Stock-Dove when feeding, as I have noticed when the two species are together. The white ring, characteristic of both sexes when adult, is absent in the young.

Pl. 53.

Wood Pigeon   Stock_Dove.
Turtle_Dove. Pallas's Sand-Grouse. (♂ & ♀) Rock_Dove.

1/3

THE STOCK-DOVE.

Columba œnas, Linnæus.

PLATE 53.

Much smaller than the Wood-Pigeon, and said to take its name from its habits of breeding in the "stocks" of trees, this species, though plentiful in many parts of the British Islands, is not nearly so common as its larger relation just described. Within recent years, however, the Stock-Dove has greatly extended its breeding range, and now nests as far north in Scotland as Sutherlandshire. It is widely distributed over Europe and Western Asia to Turkestan.

Besides occupying hollow trees as breeding places, the Stock-Dove makes its nest in rabbit-burrows or under the shelter of thick furze-bushes, and often in cliffs. When breeding in tree-holes it appears usually to lay its eggs on the bare wood, but otherwise a slight nest of twigs and rootlets is built. The two eggs are of a delicate creamy-white colour.

The voice of the Stock-Dove differs from that of the Wood-Pigeon, consisting of a rapid succession of less distinct and agreeable notes.

In their habits the two species have much in common. According to Lord Lilford (*Birds of Northamptonshire and Neighbourhood*), the Stock-Dove appears to be more addicted to green food than its congener, but it is also very fond of beech-mast. It is quicker in its motions, turning and twisting in the air with great rapidity.

It is at all times a rather shy and wary bird, and is not easily approached, especially when feeding in the open.

63

THE ROCK-DOVE.

Columba livia, J. F. Gmelin.

PLATE 53.

This species, which appears to be the origin of all our domestic races of Pigeon, though breeding in small numbers on some of the rocky parts of the coasts of England and Wales, is not abundant, and no doubt a good many of these individuals are descended from the birds inhabiting our dove-cots. Along the Scottish coasts, and on the northern and western islands, where high and broken cliffs tower above the ocean, it is a common bird, haunting the rocky caverns and fissures overhanging the sea. Within these recesses the rather scanty nest, composed of bents or pieces of other plants, is built, in which the female deposits her two white eggs.

The food consists of seeds of various kinds, especially grain when it can be obtained, but those of weeds are also eaten.

The notes closely resemble the cooing of our domestic Pigeon.

Macgillivray, who has given the best description I can find of the habits of this species, says: "When searching for food, they walk about with great celerity, moving the head backwards and forwards at each step, the tail sloping towards the ground, and the tips of the wings tucked up over it. In windy weather they usually move in a direction more or less opposite to the blast, and keep their body nearer to the ground than when it is calm, the whole flock going together. When startled they rise suddenly, and by striking the ground with their wings produce a crackling noise. When at full speed they fly with great celerity, the air whistling against their pinions. Their flight is very similar to that of the Ringed and Golden Plovers, birds which in form approach very nearly to the Pigeons, as may be seen more especially on comparing their skeletons; and as this affinity has not been observed by any other person, I would direct the attention of ornithologists to it."

The bird represented in the plate was drawn from a specimen obtained on the coast of Ross-shire.

THE TURTLE-DOVE.

Turtur communis, Selby.

PLATE 53.

This beautiful little dove, the smallest of our British species, is a common summer visitant to England, being more plentiful in the southern, eastern, and midland counties than in other parts. It is rare in Scotland, where it has never been known to breed, and although also scarce in Ireland, it is said to have nested there.

The Turtle-Dove is found during summer over the greater part of Europe and also in Western Asia, whilst in winter it retires to Africa. It arrives in England about the end of April or early in May, where its presence is soon revealed by its pleasing though rather monotonous love-notes.

The food consists of various seeds, including those of weeds, as well as the leaves of plants.

The nest, which is nothing more than a lightly constructed platform of twigs, containing the two white eggs, is built in tall hedges or on trees. In my own neighbourhood, where the bird is common, I have more often found it in young larches than in others, but have seen it among old furze-bushes overgrown with brambles.

When the female is sitting, her mate often perches not far off on the bare bough of some favourite tree. At times he will leave his perch and fly upwards till a certain height is reached, when, stretching out his wings and sailing downwards with a gliding motion, he again alights. On ordinary occasions the flight is very swift and direct.

An example of the Rufous Turtle-Dove, *Turtur orientalis*, an immature bird, was obtained near Scarborough, Yorkshire, in October 1889. It inhabits south-eastern Siberia, eastwards to Korea and Japan, and southwards to China and India.

This species is larger and darker than our bird, and has the light edges of the black feathers on the collar of an ashy-blue instead of white.

Several examples of the American Passenger Pigeon, *Ectopistes migratorius*, have been obtained in Great Britain, but these, no doubt, had escaped from captivity. I may mention here that this species is now quite extinct, the last of her race, a very old bird, having died recently in captivity.

Pl. 54.

A.Thorburn. 1915.

Capercaillie (♂ & ♀)

5

Order PTEROCLETES.

Family PTEROCLIDÆ.

PALLAS'S SAND-GROUSE.

Syrrhaptes paradoxus, Pallas.

PLATE 53.

Periodical invasions of the British Islands by this beautiful desert species from the steppes of Central Asia have occurred from time to time, the greatest irruptions being those of the summers of 1863 and 1888, when vast numbers of the birds visited our eastern shores, and soon spread over the greater part of the country, many reaching Ireland, the Orkneys, and even the remote Hebrides. It was fondly hoped that the birds might remain and breed, but they are only known to have done so among the sandhills of the Moray Firth and in Yorkshire, a young bird having been found in the first-mentioned district in the summer of 1888, and another in the following year, whilst eggs were discovered in Yorkshire in 1888. The birds, however, all soon disappeared, a good many having been shot, and others no doubt died, owing to the unaccustomed climate.

The nest is a mere hollow in the sand, and contains three eggs, in colour a dull buff marked with purplish-brown.

The food consists chiefly of the seeds of various plants.

The home of Pallas's Sand-Grouse is among the deserts of Central Asia; it is difficult to account for the periodical migrations of such large numbers, unless it be due to overcrowding. This is no doubt the species mentioned by Marco Polo, under the name *Barguerlac*, which he met with on his travels through this wild country in the thirteenth century.

According to Millais, who had opportunities of observing the birds during the visitation of 1888, "the flight is very swift, direct, and like that of the Golden Plover. When on the wing they constantly cry "Kit-id-dee."

Order GALLINÆ.

Family TETRAONIDÆ.

THE CAPERCAILLIE.

Tetrao urogallus, Linnæus.

PLATE 54.

In former times the Capercaillie or Wood-Grouse inhabited to some extent the pine-forests of England, as is proved by the discovery of its bones among Roman remains and in caves in Yorkshire. According to Pennant, it also occurred in Wales.

This fine bird lingered to a much later date in Scotland and Ireland, and is supposed to have become extinct in the two last-mentioned countries during the last half of the eighteenth century, perhaps sometime between 1760 and 1770.

In the autumn of 1837 and in the following spring it was successfully re-introduced to Scotland by Lord Breadalbane, who imported birds from Sweden and established them at Taymouth, whence they have spread far and wide over the country.

The Capercaillie is widely distributed over Europe, where there are tracts of pine-forest large enough to meet its requirements, from Scandinavia and Russia, to the mountain ranges of northern Spain and Italy, as well as the Carpathians. In Asia it ranges eastwards as far as Lake Baikal.

The nest, a mere hollow in the ground among trees, and lined with bits of grass and pine-needles, usually contains from six to ten eggs, of a pale brownish-buff colour blotched with reddish-brown.

The food consists of various wild berries, buds and shoots of trees, pine-needles, and also insects.

The remarkable display of the cock Capercaillie in spring, when the bird, perched on the bare bough of some pine, utters his weird love-song, has been graphically described from personal observation by Millais in his *Natural History of British Game Birds* (p. 10) as follows: "When in the act of display the male stretches out the neck, spreads the tail and lowers the wings, and utters a note something like the words 'Klick-kleck,' repeated at intervals. It then turns the

67

head upwards and backwards, uttering a variety of extraordinary noises or squalls, more like two cats fighting at a distance than anything else. During the performance of the culmination of his display the bird seems to be thrown into a kind of ecstasy of excitement, and to be quite oblivious to all sounds or movements in its immediate neighbourhood."

The Capercaillie is polygamous, and fierce battles often take place between rival males; according to the authority just quoted, these fights are sometimes carried to such a length as to cause the death of one of the combatants.

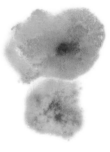

Pl. 55.

A. Thorburn. 1915.

Red Grouse. (♂ & ♀)
Black Grouse. (♂ & ♀).

⅓

THE BLACK GROUSE.

Tetrao tetrix, Linnæus.

PLATE 55.

Commonly known as Black-game when both sexes are included, and respectively as Blackcock and Greyhen, this species is still fairly plentiful in the north of England, becoming less frequent in some of the midland counties, and though still found in Wales, Somersetshire, and North Devon, exists only in small and diminishing numbers in other parts of south-western England. Formerly it inhabited Kent, Hampshire, Surrey, and Sussex, but in those counties it is now quite extinct. The Black Grouse is widely distributed over Scotland, being a common species in many parts, but it is not indigenous in Ireland. It is well known on the Continent of Europe, and ranges eastwards into Siberia.

In March and April, and sometime onwards until summer, the males assemble soon after daybreak on some favourite open spot, when they perform their striking love-display, known as the *lek*, and engage in battle—never, as far as I have seen, with any very serious results—for possession of the females. I have often watched these meetings on grassy "knowes" by the Helmsdale in Sutherland, where the sketches were made for the birds in the picture, which show the Blackcock's attitude when courting. He produces at the time a succession of soft notes, which have been described as "whirring" or "bubbling," and these may be heard at times during the day; when sparring with an antagonist, the cocks often emit a rather harsh cry.

The nest is merely some small cavity in the ground, with a scanty lining of dry herbage, and contains from six to ten eggs, in ground colour yellowish-white spotted and marked with brownish-red.

Black-game feed chiefly on various wild fruits, such as rowan berries, blackberries, heps and haws, as well as on buds of the birch and other trees, and, when young, more or less on insects.

THE RED GROUSE.

Lagopus scoticus, Latham.

PLATE 55.

Confined entirely to our islands, this truly British species is plentiful on ground suited to its habits in many parts of England and Wales, being more numerous in the northern counties, whilst it abounds on the hill-sides and heathery moors of Scotland, from the sea-coast up to the Ptarmigan ground on the mountains. In Ireland it is less in evidence, chiefly owing to the want of protection.

The nest, composed of small sticks, grass, or moss, is placed in a slight hollow under branching heather or tufts of grass, and usually holds from seven to twelve, or occasionally more, eggs, creamy-white in ground-colour blotched with rich reddish-brown.

The staple food of the Red Grouse on most moors consists of the green shoots of the common heather or ling, the bell-heather and cross-leaved heath, besides the fruit and leaves of other plants, and the seeds of grass and rushes. The out-lying oat-fields are a great temptation to the birds in autumn, when they visit the stooks in large numbers, and I have found that the best means of studying the grouse at close quarters is to conceal oneself in a hiding-place among the sheaves, when they will approach within a few feet, or even alight on the straw above the watcher's head. I have noticed on one of these occasions how terrified the birds become on the approach of a Peregrine Falcon, when they will crouch low down among the stubble, well aware of the danger of any attempt to escape by flight, and of the Falcon's dislike to attack her quarry on the ground.

In winter, when the higher feeding grounds are often covered with frozen snow, which cuts off their food supply, the birds suffer accordingly, and migrate in large packs from the higher moors to less exposed situations.

The loud, cheery call of the cock Grouse, often heard at dawn as the bird stands on a stone or grassy hillock, beginning with what may be syllabled as *kok, kok, kok*, and ending with *gobak, gobak, gobak*, is a characteristic sound on the moors in early spring.

Apart from man, the Red Grouse has many enemies, the Hooded Crows causing great destruction to their eggs and young, while the Peregrine and Golden Eagle also take their toll of the older or sickly birds, but the depredations of the nobler birds of prey are no doubt beneficial in some measure, as the well-known and much discussed Grouse disease is probably due to overcrowding.

THE PTARMIGAN.

Lagopus mutus (Montin).

PLATE 56.

The Ptarmigan inhabits the higher mountain tops of the Scottish Highlands, being plentiful on many of their stony summits at an altitude above two thousand feet, ranging as far south as Ben Lomond, and is found also in small numbers on some of the Western Islands, viz. in Mull, Islay, Jura, Skye, and also in Rum, in which island some are said still to linger, after having been re-introduced some years ago. According to the late Robert Service (*Zoologist*, 1887, pp. 81–89), a few still existed on some of the Dumfriesshire and Galloway hills until about 1822, when the last survivors were obtained near Sanquhar, and although re-introduced by the Duke of Buccleuch, failed to establish themselves. Tales have been handed down of its occurrence on the Cumberland and Westmorland fells in olden times, but it never inhabited Ireland.

The Ptarmigan is numerous on the high fjelds of Scandinavia, ranging southwards to the mountains of Central and Southern Europe, and eastwards as far, or perhaps farther, than the Ural Mountains, while closely allied forms are found in Iceland, Greenland, North America, and Northern Asia.

The female scrapes a hollow in the ground to serve as a nest, seldom lining it with more than a few bents and some of her own feathers, and here she lays her eight or nine eggs. These have a ground colour of yellowish-white or reddish-buff blotched with rich brown.

The Ptarmigan's food consists of the young shoots of heather and various mountain plants, as well as berries. Macgillivray has shown that the birds pick up numerous particles of quartz, by which means the food is ground and pounded in the gizzard.

In autumn, after a long tiring climb to the Ptarmigan ground, usually not much under some two thousand feet above sea-level, the only intimation of the presence of a covey may be the low jarring notes of the old cock bird in charge, heard close by, but very difficult to locate, and so closely does the plumage of these hardy mountaineers match the grey stones and lichen of their surroundings, that often the flash of their snowy pinions as they rise is the first glimpse obtained of them, and, when once started, few birds can disappear more quickly than Ptarmigan, as they wheel over the brink of a precipice and dive into space.

They are much affected by weather conditions, being more easily approached on still sunny days, when they will often run before the intruder without taking wing; on the other hand, when a change to wind and rain takes place, they become wild and suspicious.

Ptarmigan seem well aware of the safety afforded by their highly protective colouring. I once observed an instance of this when watching some birds feeding on an eagle-haunted hill on the forest of Gaick; they hurriedly crossed open patches of stunted heather and blaeberry in a rather nervous manner, but appeared quite at home when they reached the shelter of broken stones and rocky debris.

The Golden Eagle and Hill Fox are their chief enemies; these appear to be the cause of the scarcity of this species on many hills where it was once common.

They are hardy birds, and brave extreme cold and very severe weather as long as they can get at their food on snow-slips and wind-swept stretches on mountain sides.

In the plate the lower figures represent the birds in late autumn, the more distant one showing the intermediate stage of plumage between that season and the snowy white of mid-winter.

The male may always be distinguished from the female by the black band of feathers, reaching from the bill through the eye to the ear-coverts.

Family **PHASIANIDÆ.**

THE PHEASANT.

Phasianus colchicus (Linnæus).

PLATE 57.

When and by whom the Pheasant was originally introduced into England is unknown, but it probably existed there long before it was first mentioned in a document in the reign of King Harold in A.D. 1059.

It is not heard of in Scotland until 1594, although, according to Thompson, it was common in Ireland in 1589.

About the end of the eighteenth century the Ring-necked Pheasant, *P. torquatus*, was introduced from China, and later other varieties from Asia, so that practically none of our wild birds are now pure bred.

At the present time the Common Pheasant, the wild *P. colchicus*, according to the B.O.U. "List of British Birds" (1915, p. 312), "inhabits the western parts of Transcaucasia bordering the eastern and south-eastern shores of the Black Sea. It is also found in a wild state in the northern parts of Asia Minor, Greece, south Turkey, and along the western shores of the Black Sea as far as the Balkans, and in Albania, but in those places it may have been introduced at some remote period."

In April or May the female lays her eight to twelve eggs, of a pale greenish-brown colour occasionally tinged with bluish, the nest being only a slight hollow in the soil, lined with dead leaves or pieces of herbage placed under the protection of a fallen branch, or hidden among brambles or some such cover.

The food consists of grain and various wild fruits and seeds, including black-berries, acorns, beech-mast, and others, as well as snails, insects and grubs, the young at first feeding mostly on ants and their pupæ.

The Pheasant is polygamous, and the harsh challenging crow of the cock, followed by an audible flutter of his wings, may constantly be heard in the coverts in spring, especially on fine sunny mornings, but what seems to be the true love-note, uttered by the male when near the hens, is a very soft clucking sound, delivered with head bent low as he walks with slow, dainty steps along the ground.

Pl. 56.

A. Thorburn
1915

Ptarmigan (♂&♀): winter & autumn.

⅓

Cock Pheasants appear to be susceptible in an extraordinary degree to any air concussions or unaccustomed sounds, which they will at once challenge.

Interesting letters were written to the *Times* and *Field* in January 1915, after Admiral Sir David Beatty's fight in the North Sea, describing how the Pheasants in Norfolk and Lincolnshire were all crowing, and how they foretold the news of battle. Night raids by Zeppelins will also thoroughly upset Pheasants, as was observed during such attacks lately.

The other species represented on Plate 57 are:

The Chinese Ring-necked Pheasant, *P. torquatus*, a native of southern China, which was first introduced to Great Britain, as already mentioned, about the close of the eighteenth century, and its blood can be traced in most of our cock birds now, even when lacking the white collar, by the lighter and bluer upper tail-coverts.

The Japanese Pheasant, *P. versicolor*, brought here about 1840, inhabits all the islands of Japan with the exception of Yezo.

According to Millais (*The Natural History of British Game Birds*), the general habits of this species "are very similar to those of the Common Pheasant. The spring crow is, however, quite distinct from the typical species or its other allied forms. It is shriller, sharper, and more strained—seemingly somewhat of an effort on the part of the bird. In the spring, at roosting time, they keep calling repeatedly almost like a Peacock."

The last species is the splendid Mongolian Pheasant, *P. mongolicus*, which was brought to England as recently as 1901, and has now established itself in our coverts. At the present time, owing to the importation of these and other varieties, the greater part, if not all, of our birds are hybrids.

THE COMMON PARTRIDGE.

Perdix cinerea, Latham.

PLATE 58.

There is hardly a more popular bird in our islands than the Partridge, which is resident and widely distributed over Great Britain, and although also found in Ireland, it is said to be yearly becoming scarcer in that country. It inhabits the greater part of Europe, from Scandinavia to the Mediterranean regions, and ranges eastwards across Asia to the Altai Mountains.

The nest is a slight hollow in the ground, scratched out by the parent bird, scantily lined with dry grass, and contains from a dozen to twenty eggs, which are usually an olive-brown, but sometimes may be bluish or nearly white in colour. On examining a nest, which the young had just left, a summer or two ago, I was struck with the tidy appearance of the egg-shells, each half having been neatly fitted into the corresponding portion of the other, but whether this is always done I am unable to say.

When a pair of Partridges have once settled on a suitable piece of ground, I have found, as far as my experience goes, that they or their successors will nest there year after year, not actually on the same spot, but not far away, the most favourable conditions being a light soil and an open aspect, with sheltering banks and hedgerows, where they can dust and take their pleasure.

The food consists chiefly of grasses and other herbage, grain, and insects, especially ants and their pupæ, on which the young are principally fed.

The cheerful jarring notes of the male are a familiar country sound, heard most often in the early morning and towards sundown in spring, but also at other times of the year.

At night the covey sleeps in the open, the birds bunched closely together, lying in a circular formation, with their heads pointing outwards.

The Partridge is monogamous, the birds pairing in February, when the males fight fiercely for their chosen partners. In the female, the chestnut horse-shoe, so characteristic of the other sex, is either absent or only partly developed, and Mr. Ogilvie Grant has shown (*Field*, November 21, 1891, and April 9, 1892) that another distinction is apparent, the hen bird having the lesser and median wing-coverts and scapulars crossed with buff-coloured bars on a dark ground, these being absent in the male.

If a pair of live Partridges are studied at close quarters, it will be seen that the male has the lines of the brow more angular than the corresponding parts of the female, at least it was so in a brace I kept for some time in an aviary.

75

THE RED-LEGGED PARTRIDGE.

Caccabis rufa (Linnæus).

PLATE 58.

The Red-legged or French Partridge was introduced into England before the end of the eighteenth century, and the birds, first turned out in Suffolk in 1770, have spread freely over the southern and eastern counties as well as the midlands, and are now found in Yorkshire and in Wales.

This species, which is most at home on dry and sandy soils, where it obtains its food of various seeds, herbage, and insects, is a native of Southern and Western Europe.

The female scrapes a slight hollow in the soil, concealed by long grass or other vegetation, often under a furze-bush or among brushwood, and in this nest she lays from ten to eighteen eggs, of a pale buff colour spotted and marked with rust-coloured freckles.

The call of the Red-legged Partridge differs from that of the Common species, having a much less clear and ringing sound. It has been syllabled by Howard Saunders in his *Manual of British Birds* as *chuk, chuk, chukar.*

Unlike our Grey Partridge, this species will sometimes perch on trees or walls, and often trusts to its running powers as a means of escape instead of taking flight.

Pl. 57.

Mongolian Pheasant.(♂&♀).   *Pheasant.(♂&♀).*   *Japanese Pheasant.(♂)*

Chinese Ring-necked Pheasant.(♂).

THE QUAIL.

Coturnix communis, Bonnaterre.

PLATE 58.

This dainty little game-bird, although best known as a summer visitant to the British Islands, sometimes remains with us throughout the winter, but is at the present day much less plentiful than it used to be, the cause of its decrease as regards England being attributed to the higher farming of the land, which has deprived the birds of their former rougher but more congenial breeding grounds.

The Quail appears to visit Scotland in smaller numbers than the more southern parts of Great Britain, and in Ireland was common as a resident until almost the middle of last century, but its numbers there have now greatly diminished.

It is plentiful as a breeding species over the greater part of Europe, Asia, and Northern Africa, and in winter visits South Africa.

The food, nest, and habits in general of this species closely resemble those of its near relation the Partridge.

The seven to twelve eggs, creamy-white in ground-colour and blotched with rich blackish-brown, are laid in some depression in the soil, lined with a few bents, and situated among corn or in grass or clover fields.

The cry of the male, consisting of three shrill notes, is usually rendered as "Wet-my-lips."

Order GRALLÆ. Sub-order FULICARIÆ.

Family RALLIDÆ.

THE LAND-RAIL.

Crex pratensis, Bechstein.

PLATE 59.

The Land-Rail or Corn-Crake is a regular summer visitant to the British Islands, usually arriving in the southern parts of England towards the end of April, and in Scotland, including the Shetlands and Outer Hebrides, in May. It appears to be less common now than it was some years ago, especially in south-eastern England, without any apparent cause for this diminution.

In summer the Land-Rail has a wide range over Europe, migrating as far to the north as Scandinavia, and eastwards to the Yenisei, and possibly as far as the Lena, in Siberia, whilst in winter it retires to Africa.

The nest, composed of a few stalks of dead grass or other herbage, and placed in some depression in the ground, amidst growing corn, hay-fields or other thick cover, contains from eight to twelve eggs, creamy-white in colour, spotted and marked with reddish-brown and grey.

This species feeds chiefly on slugs, worms, and various insects, varying its diet with seeds and plants.

The harsh and rather monotonous cry, often heard during the daytime as well as by night, can be so closely imitated by drawing a quill rapidly over the teeth of a comb, that the bird may sometimes be lured from its hiding-place.

In its habits the Land-Rail is shy and retiring, and is comparatively seldom seen. In the lowlands of Scotland, its favourite haunts are the hay-fields of tall rye-grass or growing corn, where it finds concealment, and seldom flies unless compelled to do so by necessity.

THE SPOTTED CRAKE.

Porzana maruetta (Leach).

PLATE 59.

The Spotted Crake is best known as a summer visitant to our islands; a few remain, however, throughout the winter months.

In Europe it breeds in localities suited to its habits, from Norway and Russia, southwards to the Mediterranean countries, also in North Africa and many parts of Asia, whilst it spends the winter in Africa and India.

The nest is built among dense aquatic vegetation in swamps, and is composed of flags and such-like material, with a lining of fine grasses; it contains from eight to ten eggs, usually a pale buff in ground-colour, blotched and spotted with rusty-brown and marked with shades of grey.

The late Lord Lilford says (*Birds of Northamptonshire and Neighbourhood*), "In general habits of skulking and concealment this Crake much resembles the Land-Rail, but it is more strictly aquatic, swimming, and even diving, when pressed by a dog, with great ease and rapidity; its flight also is quicker than that of the Corn-Crake, and it takes wing more readily than that bird."

The female resembles the male in colour, but is slightly duller.

Pl. 58.

Common Partridge. (♂ & ♀)

Red-legged Partridge. (♂ & ♀)

Quail. (♂ & ♀)

⅓

THE CAROLINA CRAKE.

Porzana carolina (Linnæus).

PLATE 59.

A native of America, and differing chiefly from our European bird in having a black face and throat, this species has been recorded four times in Great Britain, the first in Berkshire, October 1864, the next in Glamorgan, 1888, the third on Tiree, Inner Hebrides, October 1901, and the last obtained on the island of Lewis, Outer Hebrides, in November 1913.

THE LITTLE CRAKE.

Porzana parva (Scopoli).

PLATE 59.

This small species is a rare visitant to the British Islands, some forty records, mostly occurring in the southern and eastern districts, having been noted in England, but only two in Scotland, and a like number in Ireland.

It inhabits the marshes of Central and Southern Europe, ranging as far north as the southern parts of Sweden and eastwards into Asia. It is also found in North Africa, and in winter visits the more southern portions of that country and India.

Mr. W. Eagle Clarke, as quoted in Seebohm's *British Birds* (p. 549), says: "The nest (discovered on the 24th of May) was in an extensive and particularly secluded shallow marsh near the village of Obrez. The surface of this marsh was clothed with sallow brakes, reed-beds, and areas covered with tussocks of sedge. The nest, containing seven eggs, was placed on the side, not in the centre, of one of these tussocks of medium size. It was merely a depression, amply lined with short, broad pieces of withered reed-blades, and was about six inches above the surface of the water, which was here about eighteen inches deep."

The colour of the eggs is a pale yellow-brown blotched and marked with a darker brown.

The food consists chiefly of various water-insects and their larvæ.

Though shy and retiring in its habits, the Little Crake is said to frequent open pools of water when undisturbed, and its actions when swimming closely resemble those of our Moor-Hen.

The notes have been syllabled as *kik-kik, kik* (Naumann).

According to Dresser (*A Manual of Palæarctic Birds*), "the female differs from the male in having the chin, lower cheeks, and throat white, the sides of the head only greyish slate-blue; lower throat, breast, and abdomen pinkish-buff, the lower abdomen and under tail-coverts as in the male, but paler."

BAILLON'S CRAKE.

Porzana bailloni (Vieillot).

PLATE 59.

Baillon's Crake is only an occasional visitant to our islands, and although very irregular in its appearances, has been known to breed in Cambridgeshire and in Norfolk, visiting the latter county more often than other parts of England. It is very rare in Scotland, and still more so in Ireland.

The home of this species is in Central and Southern Europe, also Asia Minor, Asia, Africa, and Madagascar.

The late Lord Lilford says (*Coloured Figures of the Birds of the British Islands*): "In general habits this Crake much resembles the better-known Spotted Crake, but it is decidedly more aquatic and less often met with in open marsh-lands than that bird. The nests that we found were always concealed amongst the dense masses of reeds and sedge that fringe and often conceal the runs of fresh water that meander through the vast open 'marisma'—a district that in rainy seasons or very high tides is frequently entirely submerged. The nests that I examined were exact miniature copies of those of the common Water-Hen, being loosely composed of reed-leaves, flags, and sedge. The usual full complement of eggs was seven; but we occasionally met with five or six partially 'set,' and, in one instance, with eight. These eggs vary in colour from a very pale green to a dark olive ground, but are always very closely streaked and spotted with brown."

In disposition this bird is extremely shy, and will hardly leave the protection of the dense reed-coverts among which it lives.

The food consists chiefly of insects and their larvæ, and its call-note is said to resemble that of the Little Crake.

Pl. 59.

½

Moor-hen.   Coot.
Baillon's Crake.   Water-Rail.   Carolina Crake. Spotted Crake.
                              Little Crake.   Land-Rail.

THE WATER-RAIL.

Rallus aquaticus, Linnæus.

PLATE 59.

The Water-Rail is not uncommon as a resident in marshy places in England, where it breeds in some numbers, and during winter others put in an appearance, arriving from more northerly countries, whilst some of our home-bred birds move southwards at the same time.

It is less well known as a breeding species in Scotland, although occurring in winter, but may be found at all times of the year in Ireland. It is also widely distributed over Europe, Asia, and Africa.

The nest, composed of the leaves of withered reeds or sedge, and hidden amongst dense reed-beds or rushes, contains from eight to ten eggs, of a pale-cream colour marked with reddish-brown and purplish-grey.

In the breeding season this species utters loud, clamorous notes.

Owing to its extremely shy habits the Water-Rail is seldom seen, unless for a moment as it crouches and glides across some small opening among the reeds or rushes.

The food consists of worms, molluscs, and various insects, also the young shoots of water-plants.

The female resembles the male, being only slightly duller in colour.

THE MOOR-HEN.

Gallinula chloropus (Linnæus).

PLATE 59.

Known also as the Water-Hen, this very common bird is widely spread over the British Islands, being also distributed far and wide over Europe, Asia, and Africa.

The rather large and bulky nest, begun early in the year, and composed of the dry blades of sedge and flags, is usually placed amongst the cover of marsh vegetation, and often, but not always, low down on the branches of thorn, alder, or other trees overhanging the water. The seven to nine eggs are pale buff in ground-colour, spotted and marked with reddish-brown and grey.

The food consists of worms, slugs, insects and their larvæ, as well as shoots and seeds of plants.

The birds may often be seen on meadows near water, on the least alarm usually running for cover, as they are by nature shy and timid.

Their call-note is a loud and shrill cry, which may often be heard in the evening.

In the male bird, used for the drawing on Plate 59, the scarlet colour of the garter, usually only a band on the upper part of leg, was extended downwards along the middle of each side of the tarsus.

Mr. Robert J. Howard has drawn my attention to the fact that the female is not, "as a rule, rather larger and more vividly coloured than the male," as stated in *Yarrell* (vol. iii. p. 169), the average length of eleven males he measured being 14.26 inches, whilst the measurements of eight females averaged 13.14 inches, and not only is the shield of the cock larger than that of the hen, but the colour is brighter.

THE COOT.

Fulica atra, Linnæus.

PLATE 59.

This species is common in the British Islands, for the most part haunting wide sheets of sheltered inland water, where it can nest amongst the cover of reeds and bull-rushes, but in winter, under stress of weather, it may often be found on the salt-water estuaries of the coast, where it is said to feed on the sea-grass.

The nest is a large, piled-up structure of dead flags, reed-stems, or sedges, and contains from seven to ten eggs, yellowish-grey in ground-colour, marked with small dark brown specks.

The Coot is an expert diver, and obtains a large part of its food, consisting of shoots and buds of aquatic plants, insects and molluscs, under water, as well as slugs and worms on land.

The call-note is a loud, clear cry.

This species is still plentiful on the Broads of Norfolk, but in old days appears to have been much more numerous in those waters.

Sir Thomas Browne, describing how these birds defend themselves against their enemies, says in his *Notes and Letters on the Natural History of Norfolk* (Jarrold and Sons, p. 15), " I have seen them vnite from all parts of the shoare in strange numbers when if the Kite stoopes neare them they will fling up [and] spred such a flash of water up with there wings that they will endanger the Kite."

No doubt the " flash of water " was thrown up by their large lobed feet as described by Lord Lilford in his work on British Birds as follows : " In Epirus, where the Coot is exceedingly abundant, I several times witnessed the curious manner in which these birds defend themselves from the assaults of feathered enemies by gathering together in a compact mass and simultaneously throwing up a sheet of water with their feet when the *raptor* made its stoop. On one occasion of this sort, the assailant, an adult White-tailed Eagle, was so thoroughly drenched, that it had great difficulty in flapping along to a tree at not more than a hundred yards from the point of attack."

Pl. 60.

Great Bustard. (♂ & ♀.)

5.

Sub-order OTIDES.

Family OTIDIDÆ.

THE GREAT BUSTARD.

Otis tarda, Linnæus.

PLATE 60.

By rights the Crane ought to have followed the Coot in this work instead of the Great Bustard, but in order to allow a whole plate for this magnificent species, now, alas! no longer found in our islands, except occasionally as a rare straggler from the Continent of Europe, I have thought it best to give its picture as a frontispiece to the third volume.

Formerly the Great Bustard, the largest of our land-birds, inhabited open country in many parts of England, and also the Merse in south-eastern Scotland. Writing in 1770, Gilbert White mentions that "there are Bustards on the wide downs near Brighthelmstone" (Brighton), and noticed they looked like fallow deer at a distance; and the late Mr. Borrer in his *Birds of Sussex* stated that his father had come across a flock—or "drove," as they used to be called in Norfolk—of nine birds in a turnip-field when riding on these downs about 1810. Salisbury Plain was another of their well-known haunts up to the beginning of the nineteenth century, and on the Yorkshire wolds they survived until about 1832, while their latest stronghold in England was in Suffolk and Norfolk.

The last nest in Suffolk, according to Stevenson's *Birds of Norfolk*, was found on the borders of Thetford Warren in 1832, and the last bird in this county was observed on Icklingham Heath the same year. Some females lingered on for some time longer in Norfolk, where the only survivors were killed in 1838, completing the tragic history of the Bustard as an indigenous British bird.

The new system of farming which came in some time before the extinction of this fine species no doubt hastened its end, as the hens in later years usually laid their eggs in the young corn, thus exposing them to the danger of being broken or carried away by the labourers during the process of cleaning and weeding the land.

The Bustard is still found in some numbers on the plains of Europe, from

THE GREAT BUSTARD

central Germany to Spain, and ranges eastwards to Central Asia; it also visits North Africa, but rarely North-west India.

The two to three eggs, of a dull olive colour blotched with deep brown, are laid in a hollow in the soil scratched out by the parent bird.

The food consists of various greenstuffs, such as clover leaves and the blades of young corn, besides insects, worms, mice, and reptiles.

The striking attitudes assumed by the males in spring when courting are shown in the picture.

Lord Lilford, describing their habits at this time of the year on the great plains and marshes of the "marisma" in Spain, says (*Birds of Northamptonshire and Neighbourhood*): "Here these splendid birds may be observed in all their glory of perfect nuptial plumage and conscious strength and beauty, stalking about with a stately and deliberate gait, the body always carried horizontally, and occasionally showing off, apparently from pure 'pride of life,' in the Turkey-cock fashion above described. Towards evening, and in the early morning, they go off to feed in some favourite '*querencia*,' a Spanish word difficult to translate briefly, but implying a haunt which supplies a want, generally a piece of land sown with chick-peas, clover, or vetches; but they seem always to return to the marshes for the night, and, I believe, spend the dark hours in the same formation as that of a covey of Grey Partridges, viz. squatting on the ground in a closely-packed circle, with their heads outwards."

END OF VOL. III.

CONTENTS OF VOL. IV.

CONTENTS

CONTENTS

Sub-Order OTIDES.

FAMILY OTIDIDÆ.

THE LITTLE BUSTARD.

Otis tetrax, Linnæus.

PLATE 61.

The Little Bustard is an irregular straggler to the British Islands, usually arriving during the winter months, and although found occasionally on the southern coast of England, it occurs with greater frequency in the counties of Yorkshire, Norfolk and Suffolk, whilst it has been recorded five times in Scotland and eight times in Ireland. This species breeds in Central and Southern Europe and North Africa, ranging eastwards as far as Western Siberia, and in winter reaches North-west India. Usually inhabiting more southerly regions than its larger congener the Great Bustard, it shows a partiality for rolling grass-lands and corn-fields during the breeding season, where the nest, a slight hollow in the soil, lined with a few straws or bents, is hidden among growing corn or some similar cover affording concealment. The three or four eggs, usually a glossy olive-green, blotched with dark brown, are laid early in May.

The food consists of various herbs, seeds, insects, small mammals, and reptiles. Colonel Irby, in his *Ornithology of the Straits of Gibraltar*, 2nd ed. pp. 259–260, says: "The male Little Bustard in the breeding-season has a most peculiar call, which can be easily imitated by pouting out and pressing the lips tight together and then blowing through them; the birds when thus calling seem to be close to you, but are often in reality half a mile off. They must possess powers of ventriloquism, as I have often imagined that they were quite close to me, and upon hunting the spot with a dog found no signs of them anywhere near; indeed, at that season it is sometimes as difficult to make them rise as a Landrail."

Lord Lilford describes the nuptial display of the male in spring, when the bird with dilated throat and partially extended wings may constantly be seen springing two or three feet from the ground. After the nesting season the birds often congregate in large flocks, and, except during the hot days of August and September, are then usually very shy and wary. In autumn the male Little Bustard loses the distinctive black and white gorget on the throat, when his colour in general resembles that of the female, except that the black vermiculations are finer and less blotched.

MACQUEEN'S BUSTARD.

Otis macqueeni, J. E. Gray.

PLATE 61.

This rare visitant has only been obtained four times in the British Islands, the first having been shot near Kirton-in-Lindsey, Lincolnshire, in October 1847, the next in 1892 in Yorkshire, another in the same county in 1896, whilst the last was obtained as far north as Aberdeenshire in 1898. All these birds occurred during the month of October. Macqueen's Bustard inhabits the western part of Siberia, Turkestan, Persia, Afghanistan, Baluchistan, and North-western India. In the last mentioned country, where it occurs as a winter visitor, it is known as " Houbara," which name is also applied to a closely allied species, *Otis undulata*, inhabiting Africa.

The nest consists of a slight hollow scratched in the sand, in which the female lays her eggs; these are olive-brown in colour, blotched with shades of darker brown. According to Blandford (*The Fauna of British India*, vol. iv. pp. 197–198), "This Bustard is generally found solitary or in small parties on open sandy semi-desert plains, very often in the neighbourhood of mustard-fields. It feeds on seeds, small fruits, shoots of plants, and insects. It runs quickly and is difficult to approach on foot, but it is generally shot from a camel. I have repeatedly shot Houbara (from horseback) by circling round, never going directly towards the bird until it squats down. When thus lying down, even in bare ground, only a trained eye can detect it; this resemblance to a stone or a small heap of sand is remarkable, and the transformation that takes place when a Houbara, or, as sometimes happens, two, three, or more, spring into flight from the apparently lifeless waste, is not easily forgotten by anyone who has witnessed it. Houbara are excellent eating as a rule, but they contract a strong and unpleasant flavour at times from feeding on shoots of mustard and other allied plants grown as oil-seeds."

The female is hardly so large as the male, and although the colour in general is similar in both sexes, her crest and neck plumes are less developed than those of her mate.

Pl. 61.

Little Bustard &♀.

Crane.

Stone-Curlew.

Macqeen's Bustard ♂.

Sub-Order GRUES.

Family GRUIDÆ.

THE CRANE.

Grus communis, Bechstein.

PLATE 61.

From an old Act of Parliament, protecting the eggs of the Crane, passed about the year 1533, it is evident that this fine species nested regularly in the fens of our eastern counties at that period and for some time onwards, but it is not known to have bred in England later than 1590, though flocks regularly visited this country in winter to a much later date. Now it is only known as a bird of passage, and is rarely seen in our islands.

In spring large flocks leave their winter quarters in Africa and travel northward to breed in various parts of Europe, from Scandinavia, Russia, and Northern Germany, southwards to Spain, Italy, and the Balkan Peninsula, also possibly in Western Siberia and Turkestan, whilst a paler race breeds in Eastern Siberia and winters in North-west India.

Wooley, who has given a charming account of the breeding of the Crane in Lapland (*Ibis*, 1859), says: "The two eggs lay with their long diameters parallel to one another, and there was just room for a third egg to be placed between them. The nest, about two feet across, was nearly flat, made chiefly of light-coloured grass or hay loosely matted together, scarcely more than two inches in depth, and raised only two or three inches from the general level of the swamp. There were higher sites close by; and many of them would have seemed more eligible. . . . At length, as I had my glass in the direction of the nest, which was three or four hundred yards off, I saw a tall grey figure emerging from amongst the birch-trees, just beyond where I knew the nest must be; and there stood the Crane in all the beauty of nature, in the full side-light of an Arctic summer night. She came on with her graceful walk, her head up, and she raised it a little higher and turned her beak sideways and upwards as she passed round the tree. . . . At length she turned back and passed her nest a few paces in the opposite direction, but soon came into it; she arranged with her beak the materials of the nest, or the eggs, or

3

both; she dropped her breast gently forwards; and as soon as it touched, she let the rest of her body sink gradually down. And so she sits with her neck up and her body full in my sight, sometimes preening her feathers, especially of the neck, sometimes lazily pecking about, and for a long time she sits with her neck curved like a Swan's, though principally at its upper part."

The eggs vary in colour from pale buff to olive-brown, blotched with reddish-brown.

The Crane feeds chiefly on vegetable food, grass of all kinds forming a large part of its diet, as well as the green shoots of water-plants; it also eats worms, insects, and reptiles.

Col. Irby, describing the migration of this species as witnessed in Spain, states (*The Ornithology of the Straits of Gibraltar*, 2nd ed. p. 251): "These Andalucian-breeding Cranes are very largely reinforced by the autumn migration, which arrives early in October; and they then form immense bands of from two to three hundred in number, though generally they keep in smaller lots of from five to thirty or forty. Those which do not remain to nest, pass north in March. On the 11th of that month, in 1874, Mr. Stark and myself had the pleasure of seeing them on passage; and a grand and extraordinary sight it was, as flock after flock passed over at a height of about two hundred yards—some in single line, some in a **V**-shape, others in **Y**-formation, all from time to time trumpeting loudly."

The long convoluted trachea or windpipe and hollow keel to the sternum of the Crane no doubt enable the bird to utter its loud trumpet-like notes.

The sexes are much alike in colour, but the male is said to be darker.

An example of the Demoiselle Crane, *Grus virgo*, was shot in the Orkneys in May 1863, and another is said to have been picked up dead in Somersetshire, but these are supposed to have escaped from captivity. During summer this species occurs in Southern Europe, ranging eastwards into Asia, and winters in Africa and India.

Order LIMICOLÆ.

Family ŒDICNEMIDÆ.

THE STONE-CURLEW.

Œdicnemus scolopax (S. G. Gmelin).

PLATE 61.

The Stone-Curlew, distinguished also by the various names of Great Plover, Stone-Plover, Norfolk Plover, and Thick-Knee, the last having been applied to it on account of the swollen tibio-tarsal joint, noticeable in the immature birds, is best known as a summer visitor to England, though a few remain during the winter, especially in Devonshire and Cornwall. Its favourite haunts are the chalk-downs and barren sandy warrens of the southern and eastern counties, and though it is known to breed as far north as Yorkshire, it is only an occasional visitor to the other parts of England and Wales, and rarely occurs either in Scotland or Ireland.

Inhabiting Central and Southern Europe and ranging eastwards as far as Central Asia, this partially migratory species is also found in North Africa, Abyssinia, India, Burma, and Ceylon.

In England, the birds usually arrive at their breeding-stations in April, and the nest, consisting only of a slight hollow in the sand or chalky soil, generally contains two eggs; these are yellowish-buff in ground colour, blotched and streaked with brown, with underlying grey shell-markings, and closely resemble the stones and flints scattered around.

The Stone-Curlew is nocturnal in its habits, and after dark usually leaves the higher barren uplands to forage among the fields and pastures for worms, slugs, beetles, and other insects on which it feeds. It will also capture mice and reptiles.

When passing to their feeding grounds the birds are very noisy and clamorous, their note, according to Stevenson (*Birds of Norfolk*), being a " loud vibratory whistle which may be heard at all times of the night. By moonlight their cries become even more incessant. . . ."

If approached by day they endeavour to escape observation by squatting, when they are not easily seen owing to their colour matching so closely the surrounding sand and pebbles, although their large yellow eye will often betray them.

Before leaving us in autumn, Stone-Curlews congregate in large flocks, but since the cultivation of so much waste land and the increase of plantations, they are not now so numerous as in former days.

The sexes do not differ in plumage.

5

Family **GLAREOLIDÆ**.

THE PRATINCOLE.

Glareola pratincola (Linnæus).

PLATE 62.

This beautiful species, which in some of its habits takes after the Plovers, though its manner of flight resembles that of the Swallows and also the smaller Terns, is a rare straggler to the British Islands, some twenty occurrences having been recorded in England, mostly in the eastern, southern, and south-western counties. It seldom visits Scotland, where only four have been noted, whilst one is said to have been shot in Ireland.

The Pratincole is a common bird in many parts of Southern Europe, breeding in Spain, South-eastern France, Sicily, and eastwards as far as the Black and Caspian Seas; it also inhabits North Africa, and ranges to Turkestan, Persia, and India.

The two or three eggs, which are thin-shelled and extremely fragile, are in ground colour buff or slaty-grey, spotted and streaked with very dark brown. They are usually laid on the open expanses of hard and sun-baked mud left exposed after the waters of the previous winter have dried up. At this time the birds are bold and fearless and allow a close approach, but otherwise are generally shy and take wing at some distance.

Lord Lilford says (*Coloured Figures of the Birds of the British Islands*): "In flight, cry, and general habit of life the present bird much resembles the Marsh-Terns, and its eggs have a certain resemblance to those of some of that group," whilst it "frequently cowers with extended wings on the bare ground without any apparent cause, and as frequently lies upon its side with one wing partially elevated." Towards dusk the birds become very active, and continue hawking till long after dusk for the beetles, grasshoppers, and other insects on which they feed. Seebohm describes their note as "a peculiar rattle, impossible to express on paper; but the principal sound may be represented by *kr* rapidly repeated." The young, like the Plovers, are active, and can run about shortly after leaving the egg. At first they are mottled brown and buff above, with white underparts.

The adult male and female are alike in colour.

6

THE BLACK-WINGED PRATINCOLE.

Glareola melanoptera, Nordmann.

PLATE 62.

This species inhabits the steppes of Southern Russia, ranging westwards to Hungary and eastwards as far as Turkestan, and migrates for the winter to tropical and South Africa. The Black-winged Pratincole is a very rare visitor to England, where it has only been obtained four times, the first on Romney Marsh, Kent, May 30th, 1903, the next in the same locality, June 17, 1903, another at Rye on the following day, and the last near Northallerton, Yorkshire, on August 17th, 1909. It differs chiefly from the Common Pratincole in having the under wing-coverts and axillaries black instead of chestnut, and has no white on the secondaries.

According to the late H. E. Dresser's *Birds of Europe*, "In its habits and mode of nidification, the present species closely agrees with *Glareola pratincola*, and like that bird it frequents the open steppes and treeless localities."

The eggs are not unlike those of the Common Pratincole, but the ground-colour is usually a rather deeper ochre, with bolder markings.

THE CREAM-COLOURED COURSER.

Cursorius gallicus (J. F. Gmelin).

PLATE 62.

The Cream-coloured Courser is a rare straggler to Great Britain, some twenty occurrences having been recorded in England and Wales and one in Scotland. The habitat of this desert bird stretches from the Canaries and Cape Verde Islands, across the sands of North Africa, Arabia, and Persia, and in winter includes North-west India.

No nest is made, the two eggs, of a yellowish stone-colour, marbled and dotted with markings of brown and grey, are laid in some slight depression among the stones and sand, and owing to their colour are very difficult to find. Mr. E. G. Meade-Waldo, in his "Notes on the Birds of the Canary Islands," published in *The Ibis* for 1889, says: "The young are much easier to find than the eggs. The hen only remains at the nest whilst she is sitting; the cocks either go about in little

7

Pl. 62.

Black winged Pratincole.   Pratincole.
Caspian Plover. (adult & young).   Cream. coloured Courser.
                                           Ringed Plover.
Dotterel.   Little Ringed Plover.   Kentish Plover.

2/5

parties or mix with birds that are not breeding. When the young are hatched, however, both parents care for them, the male being rather more shy than the hen. It is easy to tell the cock from the hen while running about; he carries himself much higher and seems to have a bigger head; when shot, this difference vanishes. The males breed in their first year, as two that I shot were in partly spotted plumage. Nevertheless, many do not breed at all, as I saw flocks of some fifteen to forty birds, while others had eggs or small young. In flocks they were very wild, and reminded one generally of Lapwings; they skim a great deal with outstretched, motionless wings. 'Their note is a low *qua qua* when they have young."

The food consists chiefly of grasshoppers and other insects.

In colour the sexes are alike.

Family **CHARADRIIDÆ**.

THE DOTTEREL.

Eudromias morinellus (Linnæus).

PLATE 62.

A summer visitor to Great Britain, this beautiful Plover usually reaches the southern and eastern parts of England and Southern Scotland about the end of April or beginning of May, when small parties or "trips" may be seen on the open downs and fallows as they make their way to their breeding stations on the northern hills.

Though now very rare, the Dotterel has long been known to nest on the hills of the Lake District, but its chief breeding haunts in the British Islands are the mountains of the Scottish Highlands, where in summer at high elevations it nests among the mists of the Grampians and in a few other favourable localities. This species occasionally visits Ireland on passage, chiefly in the autumn months.

It breeds in Scandinavia and as far north as Novaya Zemlya, and, according to Howard Saunders' *Manual*, "on the highlands of Transylvania, Styria, and Bohemia," whilst it also ranges in summer to Northern Asia. In winter it migrates to North Africa, Turkestan, and Persia.

The nest, consisting of nothing more than a slight hollow in the moss-covered ground, contains three eggs, of a pale greyish-buff colour, blotched and spotted with blackish-brown. The food consists of grasshoppers, beetles, and other insects, as well as of worms and grubs.

The Dotterel, which in its habits has much in common with the Golden Plover, is, however, much less wary than that bird, and will usually allow a close approach. Macgillivray thus describes a flock he came across in the parish of Towie, Aberdeenshire, in September: " Not having been molested, the birds merely ran along before us as we approached them. Several, on being first roused, stretched up their wings, as is customary with all birds of this group, and moved about in a lifeless sort of way, seeming to entertain little apprehension of danger. On being urged, they rose on wing, but presently alighted in the neighbourhood. It is this insensibility to danger which has procured for them the names of Dotterels and Morinelli, or little fools. It has been alleged, too, that by stupidly looking on, and imitating the

9

gestures of the fowler, they suffered themselves to be driven into the net; but this propensity to imitate is probably imaginary, although it is certain the bird runs along with an outstretched wing, which might be supposed to be in imitation of an elevated arm."

Heysham's account of this bird in the Lake District, published in the *Magazine of Natural History*, has been often quoted; he says: "In the neighbourhood of Carlisle Dotterels seldom make their appearance before the middle of May, about which time they are occasionally seen in different localities, in flocks which vary in number from five to fifteen, and almost invariably resort to heaths, barren pastures, fallow grounds, etc., in open and exposed situations, where they continue, if unmolested, from ten days to a fortnight, and then retire to the mountains in the vicinity of the lakes to breed. The most favourite breeding haunts of these birds are always near to or on the summits of the highest mountains, particularly those that are densely covered with the woolly fringe moss (*Trichostomum lanuginosum*, Hedw.), which indeed grows more or less profusely on nearly all the most elevated parts of this alpine district. In these lonely places they constantly reside the whole of the breeding season, a considerable part of the time enveloped in clouds, and almost daily drenched with rain or wetting mists, so extremely prevalent in those dreary regions; and there can be little doubt that it is owing to this peculiar feature in their economy, that they have remained so long in obscurity during the period of incubation."

The female is the larger bird, and is said to be more brightly coloured than her mate.

THE CASPIAN PLOVER.

Ægialitis asiatica (Pallas).

PLATE 62.

The first occurrence of this rare species in the British Islands was on May 20th, 1890, when two birds were seen in a market garden at Great Yarmouth, Norfolk, and later in the day one of these was shot on the denes. Two more were obtained in Sussex, July 13, 1911.

During the breeding season this Plover inhabits South-eastern Russia, from where the Volga joins the Caspian Sea eastwards to the Altai mountains, and southwards to the desert lakes of Turkestan and the Amu-Daria. It migrates for the winter to Africa, reaching Cape Colony, and has been recorded in Western India.

THE CASPIAN PLOVER

When nesting, the birds frequent the neighbourhood of salt-lakes and lay three eggs, which are in ground-colour ochreous, blotched and spotted with blackish-brown, in a slight hollow in the ground.

THE RINGED PLOVER.

Ægialitis hiaticola (Linnæus).

PLATE 62.

The Ringed Plover or Ringed Dotterel is very plentiful on stretches of sand and shingle along the coasts of the British Islands, and in the breeding season it also frequents the margins of many inland lakes and rivers, the sandy warrens of Norfolk, and other localities suited to its habits. Two forms of this species have been recognised, one rather larger and duller in colour, resident in our islands and on the coasts of France and Holland, and the other smaller, which visits England in spring (not to be confounded with the Little Ringed Plover, *Æ. curonica*). Abroad the Ringed Plover is widely distributed, breeding as far north as Spitsbergen and southwards to Central Europe and Central Asia, also in Greenland and the eastern parts of North America. In winter it ranges to the Mediterranean countries, and southwards to Cape Colony in Africa.

The nest consists of a hollow in the sand or pebbly beach, occasionally with a lining of small stones, and contains four eggs, generally laid about the middle of April, of a yellowish-buff, spotted and blotched with brownish-black and shades of purplish-grey. This species generally breeds twice in the season. When the eggs or young are approached the parent bird shows great anxiety, and will endeavour to lead away the intruder by feigning lameness or a broken wing. Though without bright colouring, few birds are so attractive as this dainty little wader, with its strongly contrasted markings of black and white and grey-brown mantle.

Flocks of varying size may be seen scattered along our shores in autumn and winter, and when feeding on the flats left bare by the receding tide they spread out, and, keeping a little apart, run a few paces, quickly pick up some small sea-worm, shrimp, or other marine creature, then pausing for a moment or two proceed in their quest. When thus engaged they usually keep near the margin of the waves, where a larger supply of food is obtained, and now and again, as they move along, they utter their soft and plaintive whistle, one of the most pleasing sounds in nature.

When their feeding grounds are covered, the birds retire to some quiet spot above high-water mark, when they rest and preen their feathers. Macgillivray says : "Their flight is rapid, even, performed by regularly-timed beats, and they glide along, often at a very small height, or ascend, and perform various evolutions before alighting, sometimes all the individuals in a flock inclining to one side, so as to expose now their upper and again their lower surface to the spectator. Frequently when feeding they intermix with Sandpipers, Turnstones, Redshanks, and other species ; but in flying they generally keep apart. At high water they repose on the sands or on the pastures, usually in a crouching posture. They are partly nocturnal, and I have often found them searching for food by moonlight. As the autumn advances, they collect into larger flocks, and at the mouths of rivers may often be seen in very numerous bands. During winter and the greater part of spring they continue along the sea-shore, none then being found by the rivers or lakes."

The young, which leave the nest as soon as hatched, are at first clothed in down of a mottled greyish-brown above and white beneath. In the immature birds, the black bands on the forehead and breast are absent and the dark parts of the head are brown, while the bill is blackish without any orange at the base, and the legs and feet are dull yellow.

The female resembles the male in colour, but is rather duller, while in winter both sexes have the black markings less distinct.

THE LITTLE RINGED PLOVER.

Ægialitis curonica (J. F. Gmelin).

PLATE 62.

This species, smaller than our common Ringed Plover, differs also in having all the shafts of the primaries dark, except the outer one, which is white. These shafts in the larger bird are all marked with white, whilst the only yellow on the bill of the present species is at the base of the lower mandible, and the legs and feet are of an ochre colour instead of orange.

The Little Ringed Plover is a rare straggler to the British Islands, eight having been recorded in England and one in the Outer Hebrides.

It nests in Spain and other parts of Southern Europe, ranging as far north as Scandinavia, and eastwards throughout a great part of Asia to Japan. During the breeding season it is also found in North-west Africa, and in winter visits Africa, India, the Malay Archipelago, and wanders to New Guinea.

According to Lord Lilford (*Coloured Figures of the Birds of the British Islands*), "Except in the matter of its preference for the sandy banks of fresh-

12

water lakes, ponds, and streams, to the sea-shore, this species differs but little in habits from the common Ringed Plover, but it is considerably smaller and proportionately much more slenderly built than that bird. The eggs of the present species, found by us in Spain were laid in slight depressions of the sand amongst stones and stunted vegetation, without any attempt at a nest; the complement is four, they are, of course, smaller, and more elongated and thickly speckled, than those of the Ringed Plover. In one instance I came upon three of these eggs on the sand between the wheel-ruts of a rough cart-road."

Seebohm says (*British Birds*, vol. iii. pp. 17-18), "It is rather more shy than its larger ally and takes wing more readily. In its flight it is very similar to the Ringed Plover, but its notes are very different from that of either of its near allies.

"Its ordinary call-note is a loud, clear, plaintive, and monotonous *pee*, almost lengthened into two syllables. When alarmed the note is pronounced much shorter and repeated more rapidly; and in spring it is uttered still more rapidly, so as to become continuous, especially at the close of its love song, when it becomes a trill."

THE KENTISH PLOVER.

Ægialitis cantiana (Latham).

PLATE 62.

A summer visitant to our coasts, this species, which is very local in its distribution, breeds regularly on the shores of Kent and Sussex, but elsewhere in England has occurred only as a more or less rare straggler from as far north as Teesmouth, Durham, southwards to the coasts of Devonshire and Cornwall. It is hardly known in Ireland, not having occurred there for many years, but is fairly common in the Channel Islands.

In Europe it breeds in Southern Sweden, southwards to Spain and the Mediterranean, also in North Africa, the Azores, Madeira, Canaries, and Cape Verde Islands. Eastwards it is found during summer frequenting the margins of the Black and Caspian Seas, and ranges across Central Asia as far as Japan. In winter it migrates to Africa, India, Ceylon, Burmah, and the Malay Peninsula.

The Kentish Plover was first brought to notice by Latham, who described specimens obtained at Sandwich by Dr. Boys in 1787 and 1791. In its habits this species resembles the Ringed Plover, but according to Lord Lilford "appears to be more exclusively addicted to shingle and hard sands than that bird." Well on in May, the eggs, usually three in number, are laid in a depression in the sand or

13

shell-strewn pebbly beach. In ground-colour they are yellowish-buff, of a deeper tint than the Ringed Plover's, irregularly marked with scratches and spots of blackish-brown. During the breeding season the birds are very tame and fearless, and may easily be approached. They seek their food along the margin of the tide, running hither and thither on the wet surface to secure the tiny shell-fish and other marine animals stranded by the waves.

The female differs somewhat from the male in colour, having the dark markings less distinct and browner, and the buff tint on the head duller.

THE KILLDEER PLOVER.

Ægialitis vocifera (Linnæus).

PLATE 63.

This rare species, a wanderer from America, has been recorded half-a-dozen times in the British Islands, viz. in Hampshire, April 1859; Aberdeenshire, 1867; Tresco, Isles of Scilly, January 15, 1885; and three on Romney Marsh, Kent, April 1908.

According to the B.O.U. *List of British Birds* (2nd ed. 1915), "The Killdeer Plover breeds in North America, from central British Columbia and central Quebec southwards to central Mexico. It winters from California, New Jersey, and the Bermudas, southwards to Venezuela and Peru, and has occurred in Chile and Paraguay."

Inhabiting the coast in winter, and at other times usually found on inland swamps or pastures, the Killdeer Plover makes no nest beyond a mere hollow in the ground, lined with a few dry bents, in which it lays its four eggs, in colour yellowish-buff, with spots and blotches of black.

This bird is noisy and restless, running with great rapidity and possessing great power of flight, whilst it owes its name of "Killdeer" to its loud clear call.

The food consists of insects, worms, and small crustaceans. Larger than our Ringed Plover, it is easily distinguished by its long rufous tail, double band of black across the chest, and longer legs.

Pl. 63

Sociable Plover (adult & young).   Killdeer Plover.
Golden Plover (summer & winter).   Asiatic Golden Plover.
Grey Plover (summer & winter).   Lapwing.

THE GOLDEN PLOVER

THE GOLDEN PLOVER.

Charadrius pluvialis, Linnæus.

PLATE 63.

The Golden Plover may be found at all times of the year in the British Islands, where it breeds freely on the moors of Northern England, in smaller numbers in Devonshire and Somersetshire, while in Scotland and Ireland it is plentiful in summer on the mountain sides and heathery bogs. In autumn and winter it seeks the low-ground pastures and mud-flats on the shores, when its numbers are increased by flocks arriving from the Continent of Europe, which remain with us till spring. This species has a wide distribution over Central and Northern Europe, and ranges as far east as the Yenesei in Siberia. In winter it visits Southern Europe, Africa, the Azores, and Canaries, and has wandered to India.

The nest consists of a slight depression in the ground, sparsely lined with bents and bits of heath, and generally situated among stunted grass or heather. It contains four eggs, arranged with their pointed ends together, which in colour are buff or yellowish-grey, blotched and spotted with deep rich brown and purplish-brown markings. In the breeding season the Golden Plover loses much of its usual wariness, and may then be watched at fairly close quarters.

The bird represented in the plate in full summer plumage, showing the characteristic black breast only assumed in the breeding season, was painted from a sketch made in the month of April on a heathy flat by the Helmsdale in Sutherland, when the birds were returning to their nesting haunts. After their usual manner when feeding, they were scattered over the moor, some yards apart from each other, at one time standing motionless, then again running forwards a few paces to pick up some grub or worm, while at intervals they uttered that soft and melodious whistle which harmonizes so well with their wild surroundings. In autumn and winter, when the flocks come down to the fields and tidal estuaries, they are much sought after by gunners, when the birds become very wary and difficult to approach. In flight they move with great speed, progressing with steady beats of their long pointed wings.

The female resembles the male in colour, but in summer the white parts of the plumage are less pure and the black duller and not so extensive.

15

THE ASIATIC GOLDEN PLOVER.

Charadrius dominicus, P. L. S. Müller.

PLATE 63.

This species, also known as the Lesser Golden Plover and the Eastern Golden Plover, is represented by two forms, only slightly differing from each other. One inhabits in the breeding season Northern Asia, from the Yenesei to Bering Sea and south to Mongolia, and is also found at that time in Alaska, while in winter it migrates to China, Japan, Southern Asia, and the countries of the Pacific Ocean.

The other, which is usually slightly larger than the Asiatic race, and has been distinguished under the name of the American Golden Plover, breeds in the Arctic parts of North America, and winters in the south of that continent. This bird, including both the above-mentioned forms, has occurred about eight times in the British Islands. The specimen shown in the plate, kindly lent to me for the purpose by Lt.-Commander Millais, is of the Asiatic race, and was obtained at Loch Stennis, the Orkneys, in November 1887. It is apparently a young bird in first plumage. The Asiatic Golden Plover, which in summer has the colour in general brighter and the black and white on the breast more richly marked than our bird, may at all seasons be distinguished from the other by the smoke-grey axillaries, which may be seen when the wing is extended. These in the common Golden Plover are white. The present species is also a smaller bird.

Miss Maud D. Haviland, who found the Asiatic Golden Plover breeding in numbers by the Yenesei in Siberia in the summer of 1914, says (Witherby's *British Birds*, vol. ix. pp. 82-83), " I first saw a few birds at Dudinka, where they were probably on migration, and afterwards the species was common all the way down to Golchika. Each pair occupied perhaps two furlongs of tundra. I should think that every acre of moss and lichen from the Yenesei to the Lena in summer is thus parcelled out. Your progress across the tundra in July is heralded and attended by a chorus of plaintive cries. Both birds meet you a quarter of a mile from the nest, and never leave you until you are at the boundaries of their own territory, and they can safely hand you over to their next neighbours for espionage. Covert, of course, there is none—but it is needless to say more. The suspiciousness and patience of the Golden Plover are the same all the world over ; and I will not dwell upon them to those who themselves have no doubt walked vainly for half a day about the bird's breeding grounds in this country, and listened to its maddening but at the same time most musical protests."

16

THE ASIATIC GOLDEN PLOVER

Seebohm describes the nest in his work on *British Birds* (vol. iii. p. 42) as "merely a hollow in the ground, upon a piece of turfy land, overgrown with moss and lichen," and this was "lined with broken stalks of reindeer-moss." According to the same authority, the four eggs "vary in ground-colour from light buff to very pale buff with a slight olive tinge, blotched and spotted with rich brown." He describes the note as "very similar to that of the Grey Plover. Its commonest note is a plaintive *kö*; occasionally the double note *kl-ēē* is heard, but more often the treble note *kl-ēē-kö* is uttered."

THE GREY PLOVER.

Squatarola helvetica (Linnæus).

PLATE 63.

This beautiful Plover visits our shores in late summer and autumn, some only as birds of passage, while others spend the winter and leave for their northern breeding quarters in the spring. Sometimes individuals in full breeding plumage may be seen on the coast as late as the end of May. It is more numerous on the southern and eastern shores of England and east coast of Scotland as far north as the Moray Firth, where I have seen it in autumn near Lossiemouth, than in the west.

It visits Ireland in small numbers during the winter, but, according to Lord Lilford, the term "Grey" is applied there to the Golden Plover, to distinguish the latter from the Peewit, which has caused confusion.

The late H. E. Dresser, in his *Manual of Palæarctic Birds*, gives the habitat of the Grey Plover as "the extreme northern parts of Europe, Asia, and America; in winter migrating south throughout Europe, Africa, Asia, Australia, North and South America."

Seebohm describes the nest (*British Birds*, vol. iii. p. 47) as "a hollow, evidently scratched, perfectly round, somewhat deep, and containing a handful of broken slender twigs and reindeer-moss." He states that the eggs are "four in number, intermediate in colour between those of the Golden Plover and the Lapwing, and subject to variation, some being much browner, and others more olive, none quite as olive as typical Lapwing's eggs or as buff as typical ones of the Golden Plover, but the blotching is in every respect the same; the underlying spots are equally indistinct, the surface-spots are generally large, especially at the large end, but occasionally very small and scattered, and sometimes taking the form of thin streaks."

The plaintive call-note differs from that of the Golden Plover. Although the winter plumage of both species has some resemblance, the birds may easily be distinguished by the larger size of the Grey Plover, its longer and heavier bill, and the presence of a small hind-toe, which is absent in the Golden Plover, and also by the black axillaries, seen under the wing in the second figure in the plate. Their habits in general, and also their food, are much alike, although in our country the Grey Plover is seldom met with away from the coast, while the other frequently occurs inland.

THE SOCIABLE PLOVER.

Vanellus gregarius (Pallas).

PLATE 63.

About the year 1860 a specimen of this rare Plover, accompanying a flock of Peewits, was shot in the neighbourhood of St. Michael's-on-Wyre, Lancashire, but was not identified till many years later. Another was obtained at Meath in August 1899, six in Kent, May 1907, and four near Winchelsea, Sussex, in May 1910.

A rare straggler to Central and Southern Europe, this species breeds in Southern and South-eastern Russia, eastwards through Western Siberia and Turkestan to Mongolia, migrating in winter to North-eastern Africa, Arabia, North-western India, and Ceylon.

Regarding the habits of the Sociable Plover, von Heuglin, as quoted in Dresser's *Birds of Europe*, writes (*Orn. N.O. Afr.* p. 997), "During autumn and winter it regularly visits the localities we explored; it appears in Egypt early in October, and migrates southwards to the savannas of Kordofan, Takah, and Senaar, usually in flocks of from five to fifteen individuals, each flock keeping close together; and generally they are extremely shy. I observed it during the month of December in places where the plains had been burnt, and in sandy places around Rahad and Atbara. It appears seldom to settle on the ground, but is usually seen flying swiftly near the ground over the plains, now and again crossing the caravan roads; and I succeeded in shooting several from horseback as they crossed the road; for I could not otherwise get within range. Sometimes we heard it utter a shrill, short whistle; but otherwise it uttered no sound."

It resembles the Peewit in its habits, making its nest, a mere hollow lined with bents, among the steppes. The four eggs are somewhat paler in colour than those of the last-mentioned bird, and less boldly marked.

THE LAPWING

THE LAPWING.

Vanellus vulgaris, Bechstein.

PLATE 63.

The Lapwing, Peewit, or Green Plover, as it is variously called, is resident and widely distributed throughout many parts of England, and is even more numerous in Scotland and Ireland, whilst in autumn its numbers are increased by the arrival of flocks from the continent of Europe. This species is found breeding more or less over the whole of Europe, from the Arctic Circle, southwards to Spain, also in small numbers in North Africa and Egypt, and across Asia eastwards to Japan. In winter its migrations extend as far as Southern China and North-west India.

The nest, which is only a depression in the ground lined with a few bents and usually situated in rough pastures, moorland wastes, or on fallows, contains four eggs. These vary somewhat in colour, but are generally brownish, yellow, or olive, blotched and spotted with blackish-brown. When their treasures are approached, the parent birds show great anxiety and distress, uttering their loud peevish cries and attempting to lure aside the intruder by feigning lameness or a broken wing.

I know no bird which excels the Lapwing in its marvellous powers of twisting, turning, and diving in the air, and in the breeding season they may constantly be seen performing these aerial evolutions, while their notes at this time are more modulated and varied, and blend with the vibrating sound made by their wings.

The food consists chiefly of earthworms, grubs, and insects. The female is duller in colour than the male, and has the crest less developed. In winter the black on the throat in both sexes changes to white.

THE TURNSTONE.

Strepsilas interpres (Linnæus).

PLATE 64.

The Turnstone, though mostly occurring on our coasts during autumn and winter, partly as a visitor and also on passage, remains throughout the year in some localities, though it has never been known to breed in the British Islands. I have seen small parties, including birds in full breeding plumage, on the shores of Tresco, Isles of Scilly, about the middle of May, which were easily approached, as they worked their way along the edge of the sea, probing and searching the wet shingle for their food.

The Turnstone breeds in Northern Europe and the lands within the Arctic Circle, from Northern Siberia to the Arctic regions of North America. In winter it migrates to the warmer shores of Europe, Africa, Asia, South America, and the countries of the Pacific Ocean, and, according to Gould, " it inhabits the sea-shores of every part of the globe."

The nest, placed on the shore, near salt-water, consists of a slight hollow scantily lined with herbage, and generally sheltered by a stone or low bush. The four eggs are greenish-grey in ground-colour, blotched and spotted with brown and grey. In our islands this species is mostly found on rocky shores or beaches of shingle, and avoids the bare sands and mud-flats. Running hither and thither among the stones and sea-weed, it seeks the small crustaceans and other marine animals which compose its food, deftly turning over the pebbles in its search or exploring likely crevices where its prey may be concealed. Their long and pointed wings enable them to fly with great power and speed, when the pure white of their rumps and underparts show conspicuously.

The usual cry is a shrill clear whistle, but, according to Macgillivray, they occasionally utter a mellow note. The female is less richly coloured than the male, and is said by Howard Saunders to be a trifle larger.

THE OYSTER-CATCHER.

Hæmatopus ostralegus, Linnæus.

PLATE 64.

The Oyster-Catcher or Sea-pie is a common bird, inhabiting the greater part of the British coasts throughout the year, where it nests on the sand dunes and stony beaches, or higher up on the lichen-covered rocks, among tufts of flowering thrift.

On the eastern side of Scotland, many pairs leave the sea at the beginning of the breeding season and make their way up the larger streams and rivers, laying their eggs among the sand and shingle of the river-beds, or by the side of lochs far inland, sometimes at a considerable elevation.

This species has a wide range over Europe and Asia, breeding as far north as the Arctic Circle, and visiting the Mediterranean coasts in winter, when its migrations extend to Africa, North-west India, and Ceylon.

The three or occasionally four eggs, deposited not far above high-water mark, are greyish-buff in ground-colour, marked with blotches, dots, and streaks of blackish-brown and with grey shell-markings.

The Oyster-Catcher is extremely shy and difficult of approach, and when its feeding grounds are covered by the tide the flocks betake themselves to quiet stretches of sand or flat rocky islets, where they while away the time, standing on one leg with their long bills hidden under the feathers of their shoulders, or preening their showy black-and-white plumage. The rather unfortunate name of this species is misleading, as it certainly does not catch oysters, but feeds chiefly on limpets, mussels, and other shell-fish, which it wrenches off the rocks or picks up among the ripples of the incoming or receding tide.

The name is no doubt derived from the Dutch word for Magpie, *aekster* or *ackster* (see Howard Saunders' *Manual* and Canon Rawnsley's *Round the Lake Country*), and must originally have signified Oyster-magpie.

The cry or alarm-note is shrill and penetrating, and when heard at night on approaching their haunts is very striking.

The sexes are alike in colour.

THE AVOCET.

Recurvirostra avocetta, Linnæus.

PLATE 64.

In former days this species annually visited in spring the eastern and southern counties of England, where it nested on the mud-flats and estuaries; but now it is a rarity and no longer breeds, though still seen occasionally at the time of the vernal migration and also in autumn. During summer the Avocet inhabits various parts of Europe, where it can find suitable breeding grounds, from as far north as Denmark southwards to Spain and also Africa. Eastwards it ranges over a great part of Asia, the birds nesting in the colder regions, migrating to warmer latitudes in winter.

The three or four eggs are laid on dry expanses of mud or sand in the neighbourhood of water, and in colour are pale yellowish-brown, blotched and spotted with blackish-brown and marked with shades of grey. The birds are very noisy when their territory is invaded, and their clamour, according to Lord Lilford, "is almost deafening, consisting of a continued series of shrill yelps, from which the Avocet derived some of its most common English designations, such as 'Yelper' and 'Clinker.'"

21

Pl. 64.

Grey Phalarope (winter & summer).
Oyster catcher (summer & winter).
Turnstone. (summer & winter).
Avocet.
Black-winged Stilt.
Red-necked Phalarope (summer & winter)

Referring to the extinction of this bird as a breeding species in England, Stevenson says (*Birds of Norfolk*, vol. ii. p. 240), "At Salthouse, long prior to the drainage of the marshes and the erection of a raised sea-bank, the Avocets had become exterminated by the same wanton destruction of both birds and eggs as is yearly diminishing the numbers of Lesser Terns and Ringed Plover on the adjacent beach. I have conversed with an octogenarian fowler and marshman named Piggott, who remembered the 'Clinkers' (as the Avocet was there called), breeding in the marshes 'by hundreds,' and used constantly to gather their eggs. Mr. Dowell, also, was informed by the late Harry Overton, a well-known gunner in that neighbourhood, that in his young time he used to gather the Avocet's eggs, filling his cap, coat pockets, and even his stockings; and the poor people thereabouts made *puddings* and *pancakes* of *them.*"

The manner of feeding of the Avocet is peculiar, the long flexible recurved bill is swept from side to side across the surface of the mud or shallow pools, as a mower uses his scythe. The food consists chiefly of small crustaceans, water-insects, and their larvæ, secured by this method.

The female resembles the male in colour, but has the black rather browner and the white duller.

THE BLACK-WINGED STILT.

Himantopus candidus, Bonnaterre.

PLATE 64.

The Stilt is a rare wanderer to the British Islands, and has been recorded more often in the eastern and southern counties than in other parts of England, and less frequently in Scotland and Ireland. In the breeding season it is plentiful on many of the marshes of Southern Europe, thence eastwards through Central Asia to China and southwards to India and Ceylon, and also in suitable localities all over Africa.

In winter the birds which have bred in the more northerly regions migrate to warmer climates. The nest, composed of dry bents or fragments of withered reeds, and placed amongst the surface vegetation of swamps or on the bare partially dry mud near pools of water, contains four eggs, pale sandy-brown in ground-colour, with blotches and scrolls of blackish-brown.

The extraordinarily long legs of this graceful species allow it to wade with ease among the pools and swamps, where it picks up water-beetles, small shell-fish, and tadpoles from the surface of the water, or catches winged insects as they hover near. When disturbed at their breeding grounds, the birds fly around overhead, making a great outcry.

The fully adult birds of both sexes have the head and neck pure white, though the younger males are found breeding before they lose the black nape and hind neck of immaturity.

THE GREY PHALAROPE.

Phalaropus fulicarius (Linnæus).

PLATE 64.

Chiefly visiting the south-western coast of England in autumn and very rarely in winter and spring, this circumpolar bird, best known to us in its grey winter plumage, occurs here and there at irregular intervals, though at times, as in the visitations of 1866, 1869, 1886, and 1891, in much larger numbers, so that, according to Mr. J. H. Gurney, over four hundred were accounted for in the first-mentioned year.

The Grey Phalarope nests sparingly in Iceland, which appears to be its most southerly breeding range, and more plentifully in Spitsbergen and Novaya Zemlya, and through the Arctic regions of Northern Asia and America, as well as in Greenland. In winter the migrations of this species extend far and wide over the Old and New Worlds, when it visits the shores of Southern Europe, North Africa, China, Japan, South America, and even New Zealand.

The nest, placed on the ground among withered grass or moss, and often situated in wet places, usually contains four eggs, pale buffish-olive in ground colour, and thickly spotted and blotched with dark brown.

Miss Maud D. Haviland, describing the habits of this bird on the Yenesei, Siberia (Witherby's *British Birds*, vol. ix. p. 12), says, "I found the first nest on Golchika Island early in July. My attention was called to it by the male bird, which flew round uneasily. Even when the nesting-ground is invaded, this Phalarope is very quiet and not very demonstrative. He flits round the intruder with a peculiar silent flight, rather like a big red moth, while he utters his chirruping alarm note—*zhit zhit*. This call is shriller than that of *Phalaropus lobatus*, and quite recognisable when the two species breed side by side."

Like the Red-necked Phalarope, the male in the present species is smaller and duller in colour than the female, is courted by her, and carries out the duties of

23

incubation as well as attending to the young, but, according to the authority above quoted, when the breeding ground is approached both sexes "fly around and call anxiously."

The Grey Phalarope, owing to its curiously lobed feet, is a powerful swimmer, and flocks are often met with far out at sea, even among icebergs. The food consists of gnats, water-insects, and small marine animals, sometimes obtained from stretches of floating sea-weed, sometimes by following the schools of whales, which seem to bring a supply to the surface.

At all times these birds are tame and unsuspicious, and show little fear of man.

THE RED-NECKED PHALAROPE.

Phalaropus hyperboreus (Linnæus).

PLATE 64.

The Red-necked Phalarope visits our islands in summer to breed in the Orkneys and Shetlands, on some of the Outer Hebrides, and in one district in Western Ireland. It is known in England only as a passage migrant, more often seen in autumn than at other seasons, but never in any numbers. This species breeds in Iceland and Northern Europe, thence across Northern Asia and Arctic America, and also in Greenland; and migrates southwards in winter to warmer regions, in Europe ranging as far as the Mediterranean, and also to Arabia, India, China, Japan, the Malay Archipelago, and Central America.

The birds, which usually breed in small companies, select for their nest a tussock of grass in boggy ground, intersected with pools of water, and lay four eggs, in ground-colour yellowish or olive, blotched and spotted with dark blackish-brown or umber.

Before pairing, the larger and more brightly coloured female woos the husband of her choice, resembling the Grey Phalarope in this respect, and, like the other, this charming little bird is extremely fearless and confiding, and may be seen swimming or floating lightly on the water, from the surface of which it obtains a good deal of the insect food on which it lives.

Seebohm describes the note as "a clear sharp *wick*."

Pl. 65.

Common Snipe.   Woodcock.   2/5

Jack Snipe.   Great Snipe.

road-billed Sandpiper.   Terek Sandpiper.   Pectoral Sandpiper.   Baird's Sandpiper.

THE WOODCOCK.

Scolopax rusticula, Linnæus.

PLATE 65.

The Woodcock, at one time considered to be chiefly a winter visitor, breeding rather rarely in the British Islands, is now known to nest regularly and in increasing numbers in favourable localities in many parts of the three kingdoms, though the majority of the birds found here, from October onwards until spring, have undoubtedly travelled from overseas. Our home-bred Woodcocks and their parents disappear early in September, and whither these birds go seems to be unknown. Howard Saunders considered (*Manual of British Birds*, 2nd ed. p. 569) that "their disappearance is partially attributable to self-effacement during the moult, for many birds which had been captured and marked with metal rings in the spring in Northumberland, have been shot in the same county in autumn."

In the breeding season the Woodcock has a very extensive range over Europe and Asia, from the Arctic Circle southwards to the Pyrenees and Himalayas, and eastwards to Japan, whilst in winter numbers migrate to the countries on both sides of the Mediterranean and Southern Asia.

Very early in the year, generally about the middle of March, the Woodcock lays her four eggs within the shelter of some dry coppice or similar cover, the nest being merely a slight depression in the ground among withered leaves or bracken, which form a lining. In colour the eggs are pale yellowish-buff, blotched and spotted with shades of reddish-brown and grey. The young, which are able to run soon after being hatched, are often carried by the mother to and from their feeding-grounds in marshy places, and sometimes are caught up and removed to a place of safety when in danger. There has been much difference of opinion as to how this singular action is carried out, and I have never had an opportunity of witnessing it myself, but from the evidence of competent observers it appears that the nestling is usually carried clasped by the feet of the parent bird.

St. John, in his *Wild Sports and Natural History of the Highlands*, p. 264 (ed. 1878), says, "In the woods of Altyre and Darnaway (as well as in all the other extensive plantations in the country), during the whole spring and summer, I see the Woodcocks flying to and fro every evening in considerable numbers. As early as six or seven o'clock they begin to fly, uttering their curious cry, which resembles more the croak of a frog than anything else, varied, however, by a short shrill chirp. Down the shaded course of the river, or through the avenues and glades of the forest, already dark from the shadow of the pine trees, the Woodcocks keep up a continual flight, passing and repassing in all directions, as if in search of each other. As the twilight comes on, in the open parts of the country, they leave the shade of the woods and fly down to the swamps and pools near the sea-shore and elsewhere, to feed during the night. . . . In the evening the Woodcock's flight is rapid and steady, instead of being uncertain and owl-like, as it often is in the bright sunshine. I consider their vision to be peculiarly adapted to the twilight, and even to the darker hours of night—this being the bird's feeding-time."

Woodcocks eat enormous quantities of worms, grubs, and insects to satisfy their ravenous appetite.

THE GREAT SNIPE.

Gallinago major (J. F. Gmelin).

PLATE 65.

This species, also known as Solitary or Double Snipe, visits our islands in autumn, but never in any numbers, and is more frequently seen in the eastern and southern counties than elsewhere in England, while it is rare in Scotland and in Ireland. It breeds in the northern and north-eastern parts of Europe and in Northern Asia as far east as the Yenesei, and migrates southwards in winter, when it visits Southern Europe and Africa, ranging as far south as Cape Colony in the latter country.

The nest, consisting of a slight hollow in the ground among grass or rushes, contains four eggs, in colour a greyish- or olive-buff, blotched and spotted with deep brown and with purplish shell-markings. The food consists of worms, insects and their larvæ, and slugs.

The late H. E. Dresser, in his *Birds of Europe*, quoting some notes from Professor Collett, states that the Double Snipe "is chiefly a nocturnal bird. Not only does it migrate at night, but it is in motion almost solely after twilight, when its peculiar 'spil' or drumming takes place; and it also searches after food chiefly during this time of the evening, remaining quiet and hidden during the day time, seldom or never taking wing unless flushed, but sitting well hidden amongst dense grass. On the whole, it is an unsociable bird; yet each pair has its own small district, where they appear to take but little notice of their neighbours. They also rise singly; and it is one of the most uncommon occurrences if two are killed by the same discharge.

THE GREAT SNIPE

"It is not a shy bird, and may usually be approached within a few paces distance; and when it rises it flies but a short distance and drops again. . . . During the pairing season the habits of this bird are very peculiar; for it has a so-called 'Lek' or 'Spil,' like some of the Grouse tribe, a sort of meeting place, where they collect to 'drum,' and often engage in combat for the possession of the females: and in this respect it differs widely from its allies; for it does not engage in aerial evolutions, but remains on the ground. Though its habits are so peculiar at this season, they are, comparatively speaking, seldom observed, as its note, or song as it may be called, is very low in tone. . . .

"The drumming place (Spil-plads) is usually in some damp place in the marsh, where there is water between the tussocks; and the number of pairs resorting to the same drumming place is usually eight or ten, frequently less and often more."

This species is always distinguishable from our Common Snipe, not only by its larger size, but in having sixteen, and occasionally eighteen, tail-feathers, instead of the fourteen possessed by the latter. The tail has also a larger amount of white, whilst the dark bars on the flanks are broader and more distinct.

THE COMMON SNIPE.

Gallinago cœlestis (Frenzel).

PLATE 65.

The Common Snipe breeds in localities suited to its marsh-loving habits throughout the greater part of the British Islands, whilst in winter, especially during severe weather, its numbers are much increased by birds reaching our shores from the Continent of Europe. The Western Islands of Scotland are a great resort of this species, where large bags have been obtained by sportsmen. In the breeding season it has a wide range over northern and temperate Europe and Asia, while later in the year many birds move southwards to warmer latitudes in Africa and Asia.

The nest is situated among tussocks of grass or rushes in wet ground, and consists of a slight depression, with a scanty lining of withered grasses, and contains four eggs, laid usually in April, which in colour are pale greenish-olive, blotched with shades of brown. Late in the evening or at night the Snipe seeks its feeding grounds among the bogs, probing the soft surface with its sensitive bill, which is sometimes so deeply plunged that the mud may be found adhering to the bird's forehead. If the wet ground be closely examined, the footprints may be seen and the small borings with irregular crater-like edges, made by the working of the bill, which is so wonderfully adapted to secure the worms, larvæ, and insects on which this species feeds. When put up, the usual cry, which has been syllabled as "scape, scape," is uttered, and when the young have left the nest I have noticed a softer double chuckling note emitted by the parent bird as it circled round the marsh at a considerable height.

By what means the "drumming" or "bleating" of the Snipe—which has given the bird its name of "heather-bleater" in Scotland—is produced, has for long been a puzzle to naturalists; it is certainly not vocal like the other notes, but is apparently caused by the vibration of the two stiff and peculiarly shaped outer tail-feathers, though I should not like to say that the wings may not have some connection with the sound produced, as they appear to quiver during the performance. Rising to a height, the bird swings around in wide circles, shooting downwards and again ascending, and it is during this downward stoop that the sound, which has some resemblance to the bleating of a goat, is heard.

The drawing on Plate 65, made from sketches taken in the spring of 1914 after watching the bird, shows the position of the outer tail-feathers, spread out and separated only during the descent.

Snipe are much affected by weather conditions, and in times of severe frost suffer considerably, when they frequent the open spring-heads or leave the locality altogether.

A dark form of the present bird, known as Sabine's Snipe, was formerly considered to be a distinct species, but is now known to be only a variety of the Common Snipe. This has very seldom been obtained except in the British Islands.

THE JACK SNIPE.

Gallinago gallinula, Linnæus.

PLATE 65.

This little bird usually arrives in the British Islands in September and October and remains till March or April, when it leaves for its breeding haunts among the swamps of Northern Europe and Asia, chiefly within the Arctic Circle. It has never been known to nest with us. In winter it migrates southwards to the Mediterranean countries, when it also visits Africa, India, and China.

THE JACK SNIPE

The first authentic account of the nest of this species was given by Wooley, who found the bird breeding at Muonioniska in Lapland in June 1853. In a communication to Hewitson (*Eggs Brit. Birds*, ed. 3, ii. p. 357) he describes the nest as "all alike in structure, made loosely of little pieces of grass and *equisetum* not all woven together, with a few old leaves of the dwarf birch, placed in a dry sedgy or grassy spot close to more open swamp." The four eggs, which are very large in proportion to the bird, are of a yellowish-olive colour, blotched and spotted with dark brown.

The food is similar to that of the Common Snipe. Wooley, in his letter to Hewitson, alludes to the curious "drumming" made by the Jack Snipe in spring. He says, "I know not better how to describe the noise than by likening it to the cantering of a horse in the distance, over a hard hollow road; it came in fours with a similar cadence, and a like clear but hollow sound." Besides being much smaller, the Jack Snipe differs considerably from the Common Snipe in colour, having a glossy sheen of green and purple on the upper parts, and it lacks the pale buffish streak on the centre of the crown and forehead of the larger species. The tail is sharply pointed.

The two birds also differ in character, the present species being rather solitary in its habits and more sluggish than the other, while it is much less affected by severe weather, due doubtless to the fact, as Mr. R. J. Howard informs me, that it adds vegetable matter to its diet of worms and larvæ.

THE BROAD-BILLED SANDPIPER.

Limicola platyrhyncha (Temminck).

PLATE 65.

The Broad-billed Sandpiper, represented in the plate in summer plumage, is a rare straggler to our shores, about sixteen having been recorded in Great Britain, mostly on the southern and eastern coasts, and only one in Ireland.

It breeds on the mountains in Scandinavia, in Northern Russia, and probably in Siberia, and migrates in winter, when it visits most of the European countries, Egypt, Southern Asia, the Philippines, and Madagascar.

Quoting some notes on this species by the late Richard Dann, "Yarrell" (4th ed. vol. iii. p. 365) states, "This Sandpiper is by no means uncommon during the breeding-season in Lulea and Tornea Lapmark, frequenting grassy morasses and swamps in small colonies, generally in the same places as those frequented by the

Totanus glareola, our Wood Sandpiper. It breeds also at Fokstuen on the Dovre Fjeld mountains, about three thousand feet above the level of the sea, in Norway, where it arrives at the latter end of May. On its first appearance, it is wild and shy, and similar in its habits to the other species of the genus, feeding on the grassy borders of the small pools and lakes in the morasses. On being disturbed it soars to a great height in the air, rising and falling suddenly like the Snipe, uttering the notes *two woo*, which are rapidly repeated. . . . It seems to lay its eggs later than others of this tribe generally. I found the eggs not sat upon on the 24th June, and the last week in July the young were unable to fly; a period when all the other Sandpipers are on the move south. The eggs were of a deep chocolate colour, and its nest, like that of the Snipe, was on a hummocky tuft of grass."

The Broad-billed Sandpiper feeds chiefly on insects and larvæ, and is more partial to fresh-water marshes than to the coast. In winter the general colour of the upper parts is ashy-grey, when, except for its singularly broad bill, it is not unlike the Dunlin at that season.

A paler form of this species is found inhabiting Eastern Siberia.

THE TEREK SANDPIPER.

Terekia cinerea (Güldenstädt).

PLATE 65.

Two pairs of this rare species, which has never before been known to visit the British Islands, were obtained on Romney Marsh, Kent, in May 1912.

According to the *List of British Birds*, published by the British Ornithologists' Union (2nd ed. 1915), "The Terek Sandpiper breeds in north-eastern Europe and north Siberia from the valley of the Onega in Russia, to the valley of the Kolyma, in east Siberia, and probably to the Anadyr Peninsula; on the Yenesei it ranges to 70° N. latitude, southwards it breeds to about 51° N. in the Ural Mountains and Central Asia, but has not been found breeding on the shores of the sea of Okhotsk. In winter it visits the coasts of Africa, ranging south to Damaraland and Natal, southern Asia, and the Malay Archipelago to Australia."

This species is found along the courses of rivers and on the shores of fresh-water lakes, it takes after the Common Sandpiper in its habits and food, and utters a loud clear call-note.

It lays four eggs in a slight hollow in the ground; these are greyish-buff in ground-colour, blotched and spotted with brown and purplish-grey.

THE PECTORAL SANDPIPER.

Tringa maculata, Vieillot.

PLATE 65.

This American species, which visits our shores more often than any other wanderer from the Western World, has been recorded about fifty times in the British Islands, ten of these having occurred in the Isles of Scilly, which seem to have a strong attraction for American waders.

The Pectoral Sandpiper breeds in the Arctic regions of North America, and winters in the southern part of that continent, ranging as far as Patagonia. The nest is placed on the ground amongst grass, and contains four eggs, either buffish or pale greenish-brown in ground-colour, blotched with deep warm brown.

The food consists of insects, tiny shell-fish, etc., and also, according to Howard Saunders, of sea-weed. Various authors have referred to the remarkable display performed by the male during the breeding season, which seems peculiar to this species. Inflating his throat, he utters deep reverberating notes, sometimes delivered in the air, sometimes on the ground. The sexes are alike in plumage. The bird represented in the plate was drawn from a specimen obtained at Buenos Aires, Argentina, in winter plumage, kindly lent by Lord Rothschild.

An example of the Siberian Pectoral Sandpiper, *Tringa acuminata* (Horsfield), was obtained at Breydon, Norfolk, in August 1892, and another is said to have been taken near Yarmouth in September 1848. This Sandpiper breeds in North-eastern Asia, and migrates southwards in winter, when it visits Japan and China, ranging as far as Australia and New Zealand.

In general the colour of the upper parts in this bird is more rufous than in the other just described, and the tail feathers are more pointed.

BAIRD'S SANDPIPER.

Tringa bairdi (Coues).

PLATE 65.

Baird's Sandpiper is another rare American visitor to Great Britain. The first was obtained in Sussex in October 1900, the next in Norfolk in September 1903, a third on St. Kilda, Outer Hebrides, in September 1911, while two more were taken in Sussex in 1912 and 1914, both in the month of September. Baird's Sandpiper inhabits the Arctic shores of North America during the breeding season, whence it migrates in winter to the southern parts of the New World, ranging as far as Argentina and Chili.

In habits this bird does not appear to differ from others of the genus, and nests on the ground amongst grass. According to the late H. E. Dresser (*A Manual of Palæarctic Birds*, vol. ii. p. 768) it lays four eggs of "a light creamy buff, sometimes tinged with rusty, thickly speckled and spotted with deep reddish brown or chestnut."

The specimen shown in the plate was painted from a bird in Lord Rothschild's collection, obtained in British Columbia in August. In winter the colour of the upper parts becomes greyer, with dusky central streaks on the feathers.

BONAPARTE'S SANDPIPER.

Tringa fuscicollis, Vieillot.

PLATE 66.

Bonaparte's Sandpiper only occasionally wanders to our country from America, having been obtained fourteen times in England, and once or possibly twice in Ireland. It breeds far northwards in the Arctic wastes of America, and in winter migrates to the southern parts of the Continent and to the Falkland Islands.

The nest, a slight depression in the ground, with a scanty lining of withered leaves, contains four eggs of a dull rufous or greyish-buff colour, blotched with deep brown.

Dr. E. Coues observed this species on rocky coasts, and describes its note as a soft low *weet*, differing from that of other Sandpipers. The food consists chiefly of insects and tiny shell-fish.

The bird in the plate was drawn from a male in summer plumage, obtained at Pt. Barrow, Alaska, early in July. In winter the upper parts become greyer, with dusky streaks in the centre of the feathers, and the dark marks on the breast are paler. The female, according to Howard Saunders' *Manual*, is "a trifle larger and more richly coloured."

THE DUNLIN

THE DUNLIN.

Tringa alpina, Linnæus.

PLATE 66.

Frequenting our shores in large numbers during the autumn and winter months, especially mud-flats and estuaries, this wader breeds regularly in suitable localities in the British Islands, though many leave us in spring for their summer quarters in other lands.

The Dunlin is more plentiful in the breeding season on the moors of the northern counties of England than in the south, and nests in some favourable districts in Wales, but is still more numerous in the wilder parts of Scotland and its islands, where it often associates with the Golden Plover, hence its name of "Plover's Page." A few pairs breed in Ireland.

In summer this species inhabits many parts of Northern Europe and Asia, and in winter visits the Mediterranean, as well as Africa and India.

The nest, lined with a few dry bents, is placed in a tuft of grass or in some slight hollow in the ground, and contains four eggs which vary in ground-colour from a light greyish-green to a pale brown, blotched and spotted with rich warm brown and purplish-grey shell-markings. The food consists of worms, insects, and small marine animals.

The striking effect produced by a flock of Dunlin in their ordered masses when in flight, as the birds incline first to one side and then the other, flashing as their snowy underparts catch the light or melting into the background as they turn, has often afforded delight to lovers of nature and has been alluded to by most authors who have described this bird.

Macgillivray thus describes their habits, "If it be pleasant to gaze upon the flocks as they sweep over the water, it is not less so to watch them searching the shores. They are seen moving about in a quiet manner, never interfering with each other, but busily picking up the food which comes in their way, or which they discover by tapping or probing, without, however, thrusting their bills deep into the sand or mud. Frequently, keeping along the edge of the water, they are seen to run out as the wave retires, and retreat as it advances on the beach. In still shallow water they may often be seen wading, and it is observable that their bills are just about the length of their tarsi and the exposed part of the tibia; but they never go beyond their depth or resort to swimming, although when wounded, should one drop into the water, it floats buoyantly, and is capable of advancing.

33

Their ordinary cry when on wing is a single shrill peep, and when feeding a softer and less loud note. Very frequently they associate with Sanderlings, sometimes with Ring-Plovers; but although while feeding they may often be seen mingling with Curlews, Redshanks, Godwits, or Oyster-Catchers, they separate from these birds when put up, as their mode of flight is different."

THE LITTLE STINT.

Tringa minuta, Leisler.

PLATE 66.

The Little Stint visits the British Islands on passage in the autumn and again in spring on its way from and to its breeding grounds in Northern Europe and Western Siberia. In winter it ranges far and wide, when it visits Africa, India, and Ceylon.

The eggs of this little wader were unknown until Middendorf found it breeding in Siberia, and the late Henry Seebohm and Mr. Harvie-Brown were the first to discover the nest in Europe, near the Petchora river, in July 1875. The nest is only a slight hollow in the ground, with a lining of dry leaves, etc., and contains four eggs, which, except for their smaller size, are indistinguishable from the Dunlin's. When on our shores in autumn the habits and manner of feeding of the Little Stint are very like those of the latter bird, as it runs along the sand by the water's edge in search of the small marine animals on which it lives.

In winter the general colour of the upper parts is greyish-brown, with dusky markings caused by the darker centres of the feathers.

THE AMERICAN STINT.

Tringa minutilla, Vieillot.

PLATE 66.

There are only four recorded visits of this small species to England, two having been obtained in Cornwall—October 1853 and September 1890, and the same number in Devonshire, September 1869 and August 1892. It breeds in Arctic America, and migrates in winter as far as Chili in South America.

34

THE AMERICAN STINT

The present species is rather smaller than the Little Stint, and differs only slightly in colour, though if a series of specimens of the two in summer plumage be compared, the American bird is seen to be generally blacker on the upper parts.

The nest is merely a slight hollow in the ground, scantily lined with withered leaves, and contains four eggs, similar in colour to those of the Little Stint.

TEMMINCK'S STINT.

Tringa temmincki, Leisler.

PLATE 66.

Like the Little Stint, this small bird of passage visits the British Islands in autumn and again in spring, but is much rarer and less regular in its appearances on our shores than its congener. It breeds in Northern Europe and Asia, and migrates southwards in winter, when its range extends to Africa and India.

Wooley, in a communication regarding Temminck's Stint, published by Hewitson in his *Eggs of British Birds* (3rd ed. vol. ii. p. 362), says: "Grassy banks and pastures by the water-side are the kind of places where it takes up its breeding quarters; and it seems to like to be near houses. Nothing could be more interesting and pretty than this little bird in the early part of summer; it is so tame one could often catch it in a net at the end of a stick. At one time it is hovering with its wings raised over its back, or floating about, and it reminds me rather of some insect than any other bird; at another time it will be standing on the top of a stone or stake, or the gable end of a cottage; and whether hovering or standing on its perch, it utters a constant trilling note, of which I can best give an idea by saying that it brought to my recollection the Grasshopper Warbler, though the resemblance is perhaps slight.

"When its eggs are very near, it sometimes runs about one's feet, and though it cannot but be anxious, it seems as busy as ever, picking gnats and other insects off the grass. . . . The nest is very simple—a few short bits of hay, in a little saucer-shaped hollow, placed amongst thin grass or sedge, generally not far from the water's edge, but sometimes in the middle of a meadow."

The eggs are four in number, and are of a pale greenish or buffish stone-colour, blotched with shades of brown.

In winter the colour of the upper parts of the bird is a dull greyish-brown with dusky streaks.

35

Pl. 66.

Sanderling (winter & summer).   Dunlin. (winter & summer.)
onaparte's Sandpiper.   Little Stint (summer & autumn)
                              Knot. (winter & summer).
                                                                          Temminck's Stint.   2
Purple Sandpiper (winter & summer)   American Stint.   5
                                          Curlew Sandpiper (summer & autumn)

THE CURLEW-SANDPIPER.

Tringa subarquata (Güldenstädt).

PLATE 66.

This wader visits our shores on passage in autumn and spring, showing a preference for those of the eastern and southern counties of England and east coast of Scotland. Though seldom seen on the western side of Great Britain, in autumn it is found in favourable localities in Ireland, where it has been known to linger till December. It breeds on the tundras of Northern Siberia, and migrates southward in winter to Africa, Southern Asia, and Australia.

The nest of the Curlew-Sandpiper appears to have been unknown to zoologists till Mr. H. L. Popham described one containing four eggs, which he discovered in July 1897 at the mouth of the river Yenesei in Siberia. This nest was a somewhat deep hollow in the moss, and the eggs, though smaller, were very like those of the Snipe (see *Proceedings of the Zoological Society*, 1897, p. 490).

While tarrying with us, this Sandpiper often associates with others of its kind, and in its actions is very like the Dunlin, tripping hither and thither and dabbling with its curved bill on the sand and mud in search of its food, which does not differ from that of its allies.

The deep russet of its summer dress is very striking, but in winter this colour changes to a sober grey, streaked with darker tones.

The second figure in the plate represents a young bird in autumn.

THE PURPLE SANDPIPER.

Tringa striata, Linnæus.

PLATE 66.

The Purple Sandpiper is a fairly common winter visitant to the rocky parts of our coasts, arriving in autumn and departing in spring. Its nest has never been discovered in the British Islands, though Lord Lilford and others had a suspicion that it might be found breeding in some localities.

In summer it inhabits the Færoes, Iceland, Northern Europe, Asia, and Arctic America, and leaves the colder portion of its territory in winter, when it ranges to the Mediterranean and in the American continent as far south as Florida.

THE PURPLE SANDPIPER

The four eggs are laid in some hollow in the ground, which is lined with pieces of moss or dry leaves, and vary in colour from a pale olive-green to buffish-stone colour, with underlying shell markings of purplish-grey and blotches of reddish-brown.

The Purple Sandpiper is very tame and confiding, and when feeding among the sea-weed is easily approached, and can be watched at very close quarters. They show little fear of the waves as they break against the rocks, and are able to swim easily, and on passing across the water from one group of rocks to a fresh feeding ground fly swiftly, usually keeping together in a flock. When unemployed at high-tide, they loiter on the drier places, quietly resting or preening their feathers.

THE KNOT.

Tringa canutus, Linnæus.

PLATE 66.

The Knot is another of our birds of passage, occurring in numbers on many parts of the British coasts and tidal estuaries in autumn and spring. This species breeds in the remote Arctic solitudes of Parry's Islands, Melville Peninsula, Grinnel Land, and Greenland, and ranges very far southwards in winter, occurring at that season in South Africa, India, as well as in Australia, New Zealand, and South America.

Although in the summer of 1876 Col. Feilden and Mr. Chichester Hart obtained nestlings of the Knot in latitudes 82° 33′ and 81° 44′ N., when Sir George Nares made his voyage to the Polar seas, no authentic eggs appear to be known, but, according to Dresser's *Manual of Palæarctic Birds*, there "is said to be a specimen in the Smithsonian Museum at Washington."

At one time the late Lord Lilford possessed a number of these birds, and by keeping them in a warm aviary in winter and then transferring them to a colder one in spring, hoped by this means to induce them to breed. At last an egg, which I believe is now in the museum at Cambridge, was found in the enclosure, but some doubt occurred regarding the origin of this egg owing to the discovery in the aviary of a Wader of another species, which had unfortunately been overlooked when the place was prepared.

When on our shores the habits of the Knot are very much like those of its congeners ; it frequents the sands and mudflats at low-tide, usually seeking its food of sand-worms, small crustaceans, and other marine creatures by the sea-margin, but on its breeding grounds in Grinnel Land, Col. Feilden noticed that the birds fed largely on the buds of the little rock-plant, *saxifraga oppositifolia.*

Describing this species at its breeding stations, he states (" Notes from an Arctic Journal," *Zoologist,* 1879, pp. 102, 103), " The Knot has not the power of drumming like the Common Snipe, but, after soaring in mid-air with outspread pinions, they frequently descended to the ground. During this descent the wings were beaten over the back with such rapid motion that a loud whirring noise was produced, which might be heard at some distance. According to my observations, this action was confined to the males and to the period of courtship."

The sexes are much the same in colour.

THE SANDERLING.

Calidris arenaria, Linnæus.

PLATE 66.

This restless little wader is common on the sandy parts of our shores in autumn and also in spring, before leaving for its summer quarters in the far north. It breeds in the Arctic portions of Siberia, in Greenland, and also in the circumpolar regions of the New World, migrating southwards in autumn to spend the winter in warmer lands, when it visits the southern parts of Africa, Asia, and America, and also Australia.

The nest is a slight depression in the ground, scantily lined with dry grass or leaves, and contains four eggs. These, according to Seebohm (*British Birds,* vol. iii. pp. 223, 224), are " buffish olive in ground-colour, thickly spotted with pale olive brown, and with a few indistinct underlying markings of violet-grey."

Like the Dunlin and other members of this family, the Sanderling may usually be seen feeding close to the water's edge, nimbly running after the receding waves and picking up tiny marine animals.

It differs from its allies in having no hind toe, and when in the pale winter dress of white and grey it is easily recognised even at a distance.

This species shows a strong partiality for stretches of pure sand.

Pl. 67.

Common Sandpiper.   Spotted Sandpiper.   Wood-Sandpiper.

Buff-breasted Sandpiper.   Bartram's Sandpiper.

Semi-palmated Sandpiper.

Ruff (Brudatus) & Reeve.

THE SEMI-PALMATED SANDPIPER.

Tringa pusilla, Linnæus.

PLATE 67.

A specimen of this Sandpiper, a young bird in autumn plumage, was obtained on Romney Marsh, Kent, on September 12th, 1907. In summer it inhabits the Arctic regions of North America southwards to the mouth of the Yukon river on the eastern, and Labrador on the western sides of the continent, whilst in winter it migrates as far south as Patagonia.

In its habits this species does not appear to differ from its allies, but is distinguished by the webbing at the base of the front toes.

The eggs are of a yellowish or greenish stone-colour, blotched and spotted with dark brown.

THE RUFF.

Machetes pugnax, Linnæus.

PLATE 67.

This species, noted for the remarkable feathered shield which adorns the necks of the males during the nuptial season, was once a common summer visitant to our English fens, but owing to the draining and enclosure of its favourite haunts, and also to the value put upon the eggs by unscrupulous collectors, it is now almost banished from the land, except as a bird of passage. In summer the Ruff inhabits localities suited to its marsh-loving habits in various parts of Europe and Western Asia, and in winter visits Africa and Southern Asia.

The plainly coloured female, known as the Reeve, builds her scanty nest on the ground among grass or rushes, and lays four eggs, in colour pale greyish-green, blotched with umber-brown.

The food consists chiefly of various insects, worms, slugs, etc.

In former days, when this polygamous species was so plentiful in the fens of the eastern counties, the males soon after their arrival in spring betook themselves to their breeding stations, and, collecting on some piece of ground a little above the level of the marsh, known to fowlers as a "hill," fought for possession of the Reeves.

As the Ruff was held in high estimation for the table, large numbers were regularly netted or taken in snares of horsehair at these places, and after having been fattened in confinement were sold at high prices.

The singular variety of pattern and colour in the plumage of the male birds is extraordinary.

The late Professor Newton, in his *Dictionary of Birds*, pp. 799-800, says : " It has often been said that no one ever saw two Ruffs alike. That is perhaps an over-statement; but, considering the really few colours that the birds.exhibit, the variation is something marvellous, so that fifty examples or more may be compared without finding a very close resemblance between any two of them, while the individual variation is increased by the 'ear-tufts,' which generally differ in colour from the frill, and thus produce a combination of diversity." Birds which are decorated with a white tippet are said to be the rarest; one of these is shown in the background of the plate, taken from a specimen in the collection of Lieut.-Commander Millais.

Before summer is far advanced, all the variously coloured feathers of these decorative shields are shed, when the bird is not unlike the Reeve in appearance, though larger.

THE BUFF-BREASTED SANDPIPER.

Tringites rufescens (Vieillot).

PLATE 67.

The Buff-breasted Sandpiper, a native of America, seldom visits the British Islands, only about eighteen having been recorded in England, and two or three in Ireland. It breeds in the Arctic regions of North America and Asia, and ranges far southward in winter to the warmer parts of America, Asia, and Africa. The nest, placed on the ground, and, according to Macfarlane, hardly to be distinguished from the Golden Plover's, contains four eggs, in colour buffish, occasionally tinged with pale-olive, and blotched with deep umber and shell-markings of purplish grey.

The food consists chiefly of grasshoppers and other insects. The late H. E. Dresser, in his *Birds of Europe*, says : " We generally met with them in small flocks of from five or six to a dozen individuals, never near or on the edge of water, though in some cases there were small ponds which swarmed with waders; but they frequented the grassy places, if any such were to be found, or were seen running along in an irregular wavy line on the road or track made by the cotton-teams. . . .

40

THE BUFF-BREASTED SANDPIPER

Its call-note is low and weak and is repeated several times in succession, either as it trips along or else as its rises to fly away."

The beautiful pencilled markings to be seen on the under surface of the wing in this species serve to distinguish it.

The bird in the plate was taken from a specimen in Lord Rothschild's collection, obtained in Kansas, in May.

BARTRAM'S SANDPIPER.

Bartramia longicauda (Bechstein).

PLATE 67.

Bartram's Sandpiper, which, according to Lord Lilford, resembles the Plovers much more closely in its habits than the Sandpipers, has been recorded about eleven times in the British Islands. It breeds on the grassy uplands of North America, and migrates in winter to South America.

The four eggs are laid in some depression in the ground, which is scantily lined with bents or dry leaves, and in colour are pale buffish, blotched and marked with reddish-brown, and purplish-grey.

Seebohm describes the ordinary note of this bird as "a soft mellow whistle," and its food appears to consist chiefly of beetles, grasshoppers, and other insects obtained on the prairies it frequents.

THE GREY-RUMPED SANDPIPER.

Totanus brevipes, Vieillot.

Two examples of this Sandpiper, a male and female, according to Mr. H. W. Ford-Lindsay (*vide* Witherby's *British Birds*, vol. ix. p. 205), were obtained at Rye Harbour, Sussex, in September 1914. The late H. E. Dresser (*A Manual of Palæarctic Birds*, vol. ii. p. 793) gives the habitat of this species as "Kamchatka, Eastern Siberia, and Japan, migrating south for the winter to China, the Malay Archipelago, the Papuan Islands, and Australia."

In summer the general colour of the upper parts is ashy-grey, of the lower white, while the cheeks and neck are streaked with dark markings, and the breast and flanks barred with greyish-black. In winter the colour is more uniform, the dark markings being then less distinct.

The habits and nest of this species appear to be unknown.

THE COMMON SANDPIPER.

Totanus hypoleucus (Linnæus).

PLATE 67.

This attractive little wader, also known as the Summer-Snipe, is a common visitor in spring to the British Islands, arriving in April and taking its departure in September. During summer it is found over the whole of Europe and a great part of Asia, while in winter it migrates to Africa, India, and as far south as Tasmania.

The nest of the Common Sandpiper is usually placed near the water on the banks of some clear running stream, or often, as in the Highlands of Scotland, among the stones and herbage by the side of a loch. It is merely a slight depression, lined with dry grass, rushes, and similar material, in which the four eggs are laid. These in ground-colour are usually creamy-buff, with blotches and spots of purplish-brown and grey.

The food consists of worms, grubs, and various insects. In summer the clear piping note of the Sandpiper may often be heard as it runs along the gravelly margins of lakes and streams with dainty steps and a graceful vertical swing of the tail. On taking flight, it skims near the surface of the water, gliding at times without any movement of the wings, then again proceeding with steady strokes. There is no difference in the colour of the sexes, but in winter the dark markings on the upper parts are less distinct.

THE SPOTTED SANDPIPER.

Totanus macularius (Linnæus).

PLATE 67.

This species is the representative of our Common Sandpiper in America, distinguished, according to Howard Saunders' *Manual of British Birds*, 2nd ed. p. 606, by having "*all* the secondaries broadly barred with ash-brown, while in the

Common Sandpiper, the 8th and 9th are nearly white." It is an uncommon visitor to the British Islands, some seven or eight examples having been obtained, the last of these in Sussex in May 1913.

In summer it inhabits the northern parts of the New World, and migrates in winter to Central and South America. In its general habits this species does not appear to differ from our Common Sandpiper, and the four eggs are light buff or cream colour, blotched and spotted with deep brown and underlying shell-markings of grey.

THE WOOD-SANDPIPER.

Totanus glareola (J. F. Gmelin).

PLATE 67.

The Wood-Sandpiper visits England more or less regularly in autumn and in smaller numbers in spring, though on the mainlands of Scotland and Ireland it is seldom seen. Usually a bird of passage, it is supposed to have bred more than once in Great Britain, but the only authentic nest known in this country was one obtained by the late John Hancock on Prestwick Car, Northumberland, on June 3rd, 1853.

The Wood-Sandpiper breeds in various parts of Europe from Scandinavia southwards to Spain, and in Northern Asia south to China and Japan, in the winter season migrating to the Mediterranean, Africa (as far as Cape Colony), India, Ceylon, the Malay Archipelago, and Australia.

The nest, placed on the ground generally in open moorland diversified by bogs and marshy places, is usually nothing more than a little hollow in the soil, with a scanty lining of bents. The four eggs are pale buff or light pale olive-green in ground-colour, spotted and blotched with deep warm brown.

Although this species will often perch on a post or dead bough of a tree, its name seems inappropriate, as the bird is much less arboreal than its congener the Green Sandpiper, to which in appearance it has a good deal of resemblance, yet the birds may always be distinguished not only by the difference in the markings of the tail, but by the axillaries, these in the Green Sandpiper being dark with narrow bars of white, whereas in the present species they are white with dusky markings.

In the breeding season the bird utters a succession of trilling notes, and performs a courtship display; commencing in the air and continued after settling on its perch or on the ground.

THE GREEN SANDPIPER.

Totanus ochropus (Linnæus).

PLATE 68.

The Green Sandpiper is fairly common on passage in some localities in the British Islands, where a few birds remain during the winter, though seldom throughout the summer months.

It breeds in the northern parts of Europe and Asia, migrating southwards when winter approaches as far as Africa, Southern Asia, the Malay Archipelago, and even on rare occasions to Australia.

The breeding habits of this Sandpiper are noteworthy, insomuch as this species and its near relation the Solitary Sandpiper are apparently the only members of the group which nest in trees, sometimes at some considerable height from the ground, and, at least as regards the present species, always in the neighbourhood of water.

The four eggs, in colour a delicate greenish-grey, spotted with purplish-brown, are usually deposited in the abandoned nests of various birds, such as Thrushes, Jays, and Wood-pigeons, or in Squirrels' "dreys." At other times the eggs are laid on mossy stumps of trees or even on the ground.

The late Lord Lilford, in his *Birds of Northamptonshire and Neighbourhood* (vol. ii. p. 89), says: "The Green Sandpiper is, in my experience, a very wary bird, and a very great nuisance to the Snipe-shooter, as, rising wildly, it darts up into the air, with a shrill trisyllabic whistle, which puts all the Snipes within hearing on the alert; in common with most of our waders, however, it soon becomes reconciled to captivity, and feeds readily on small worms and chopped meat; it is a good swimmer, but I have never seen one of this species attempt to dive as the Common Sandpiper often does when wounded and fallen into water and chased by a dog."

On rising from the ground the white upper-tail coverts are very conspicuous in this bird, which help to identify it.

THE SOLITARY SANDPIPER.

Totanus solitarius (Wilson).

PLATE 68.

This species has a good deal of resemblance to the Green Sandpiper in appearance and habits, but may always be recognized by the dark ground-colour of the lower back and tail feathers. A native of America, breeding in the northern parts of that continent and migrating southwards in winter, it has wandered on rare occasions to our islands, having been recorded five times, viz. in Lanarkshire, Scilly Islands, Cornwall, Sussex, and Kent.

The Solitary Sandpiper owes its name to its more or less unsocial habits, and until only a few years ago no authentic information regarding its nest and eggs had been published. According to a communication to *The Ibis* for April 1905, by the Rev. Francis C. R. Jourdain, the eggs were first discovered in North Alberta in 1903 by Mr. Evan Thomson, who was collecting for Mr. Walter Raine of Toronto. The eggs were found in an old nest of the American Robin, *Turdus migratorius*, in a tree, and in the following year some more were obtained by the same collector in the nests of other birds. Four seems to be the usual complement of eggs ; these vary in ground-colour from a pale greenish-white to a warmer tint, with spots and blotches of rich dark brown and purplish-grey.

THE GREATER YELLOWSHANK.

Totanus melanoleucus (Gmelin).

PLATE 68.

The Greater Yellowshank has twice been recorded in the British Islands, the first having been obtained at Tresco Abbey, Isles of Scilly, in September 1906, and another at Winchelsea, Sussex, in October 1915.

This species inhabits the continent of America, breeding in the northern portions and migrating to the south in winter, when it also visits the Bermudas and West Indian Islands.

It frequents the margins of water-pools, marshes, and estuaries, where its loud thrice-repeated alarm note may often be heard. According to Dr. Elliott Coues'

Pl. 68.

Green Sandpiper.   Spotted Redshank. (Summer & winter).

Redshank.

Solitary Sandpiper.   Greenshank.   Red-breasted Snipe.   Marsh Sandpiper.   2/5

Greater Yellowshank.

Key to North American Birds, the eggs are "greyish or deep buff, irregularly spotted with rich dark brown."

The specimen shown in the plate, kindly lent by Lord Rothschild, was obtained at Buenos Aires, Argentina, and represents a male in winter plumage. In summer the upper parts are more strongly marked with black, whilst the under parts are whiter.

THE YELLOWSHANK.

Totanus flavipes (J. F. Gmelin).

This species has occurred thrice in the British Islands, the first having been obtained in Nottinghamshire about 1854, the second in Cornwall in September 1871, and the last on Fair Isle, Shetlands, in September 1910.

In the breeding season the Yellowshank inhabits the greater part of North America, where it is a common bird, and in winter ranges southwards to the West Indian Islands and South America as far as Patagonia. The nest is a slight depression in the ground, sometimes with, sometimes without a scanty lining of grasses, etc., and contains four eggs, in ground-colour pale cream or pale drab, blotched with deep reddish-brown.

The habits in general of the Yellowshank appear to be much like those of its congeners.

In summer the head and neck are dull white with dark streaks, the upper parts greyish-brown, blotched and marked with black and spotted with white, tail dull grey and white with dusky bars, under parts white, flanks darkly barred. The axillaries, which are also white, are marked with greyish-brown. Legs and feet yellow. In winter the plumage is less distinctly marked.

THE REDSHANK.

Totanus calidris (Linnæus).

PLATE 68.

This well-known bird is a common resident in the British Islands, breeding abundantly in many localities and haunting the coast and mudflats of the estuaries in autumn and winter. It breeds throughout Europe from Scandinavia southwards to the countries of the Mediterranean, and eastwards through Asia Minor to Siberia, ranging in winter to Africa, Southern and Eastern Asia, and the Malay Archipelago.

The nest is generally well concealed in a tussock of coarse grass or rushes among the marshes or rough pastures the Redshank is so partial to in summer, and contains four eggs, in ground-colour a pale yellowish-olive, blotched and spotted with purplish-brown. The Redshank feeds on worms, water-insects, small crustaceans, and other sea animals, which the bird secures as it probes the bottom of the shallow pools of the sea-shore or marshes. This species is one of the shyest and most wary of our waders, and usually acts as a sentinel to other birds near by, when its clear and clamorous whistle, uttered when rising and often continued as it flies around, serves as a warning signal to its companions.

Macgillivray, in his work on *British Birds*, gives the following accurate description of the habits of this species: "Its flight is light, rapid, wavering, and as if undecided, and being performed by quick jerks of the wings, bears some resemblance to that of a pigeon. Alighting again at a great distance, along the edge of the water, it runs a short way, stands, vibrates its body, utters its cry, and thus continues until its alarm has subsided. It runs with great celerity, and is in every way remarkable for its activity, which becomes almost ludicrous when it is picking up its food on a beach washed by a high surf, its movements being then executed with astonishing rapidity, as it follows the retiring and retreats before the advancing waves."

The bird represented in the plate is in breeding plumage; in winter the upper parts are of an ashen-grey colour and the under parts lose more or less the dark markings, whilst the neck and breast are only slightly streaked, and the legs of an orange-red.

THE SPOTTED REDSHANK.

Totanus fuscus (Linnæus).

PLATE 68.

The Spotted Redshank is rare in the British Islands, only occasionally visiting our shores when passing to and fro between its breeding quarters in Northern Europe and Asia and the warmer regions which it seeks in winter, when it visits Southern Europe, Northern Africa, India, China, and Japan.

The nesting habits of this species in Finland were first described by Wooley (see Hewitson's *Eggs of British Birds*, 3rd ed. pp. 326–328, and Dresser's *Birds of Europe*). He found the birds nesting in dry places near the tops of long hills amongst forests, far away from marshes, and often, curiously enough, on black ground where the trees had been burnt, which made it difficult to see the bird when sitting on her nest amidst these surroundings.

The four eggs are laid in some small depression in the ground—those found by Wooley being bedded with a few needles of the Scotch fir—and in colour vary from a delicate green to a pale brownish tint, blotched and spotted with deep brown and having shell-markings of purplish-grey.

Like the Redshank, this species is very alert and wary, and lives on much the same kind of food, though it shows more partiality for fresh water than the other. When its breeding ground is invaded the bird utters loud cries, but the late Lord Lilford considered it less noisy on ordinary occasions than our Common Redshank. The remarkable difference between the dark nuptial plumage and the white and silvery grey of winter is shown in the plate.

THE GREENSHANK.

Totanus canescens (J. F. Gmelin).

PLATE 68.

This species, which is a good deal larger than the Redshank, visits the British Islands in autumn and spring, occasionally staying during the winter months, especially in Ireland. It has long been known to breed on the moorlands and hillsides of Scotland and the western islands, where the bird is found in summer in many localities. It also breeds in Northern Europe and Asia, migrating southwards in winter to Africa, the warmer parts of Asia, the Malay Archipelago, and even down to Australia.

The nest is placed on the ground, sometimes on a hillside among heather or by a fresh-water loch, and is merely a slight hollow lined with pieces of heath, dry grass, etc. The four eggs are pale buff or stone-colour, blotched with pale purplish-grey, and dotted with dark brown.

In April I have seen the Greenshank by the River Ewe in Ross-shire feeding among the stones and mud on the margin of the stream, when its loud musical whistle could frequently be heard. The food consists of worms, insects, molluscs, tiny fishes, etc.

48

THE GREENSHANK

The bird in the plate shows the dark markings on the mantle and scapulars assumed in the breeding season. In winter the upper parts in general are a paler grey, when, excepting the colour of the feet and legs, the present species resembles the Greater Yellowshank, both species having a slight upward curve in their bills.

THE MARSH-SANDPIPER.

Totanus stagnatilis, Bechstein.

PLATE 68.

This species, which is very like a diminutive Greenshank, though its legs are proportionately longer and its body more slenderly built, is a very rare wanderer to Great Britain, where only four occurrences have been noted, the first at Tring, Hertfordshire, October 1887, two at Rye Harbour, Sussex, June 1909, and the last at Bodiam Marsh, in the same county, in July 1910. In summer the Marsh-Sandpiper inhabits the south-eastern parts of Europe, ranging eastwards to Turkestan and Siberia, while in the winter season it retires southwards to Africa, India, Ceylon, the Malay Archipelago, and Australia.

According to the late H. E. Dresser's *Manual of Palæarctic Birds*, vol. ii. p. 788, "It usually breeds near, but occasionally at some distance from water, in grassy places, its nest resembling that of its congeners, and its eggs, four in number, are usually laid in June or July, and are ochreous buff, sometimes with a faint olivaceous tinge, with pale purplish-brown shell-markings and rich dark brown surface spots and blotches."

The bird represented in the plate is in summer plumage. According to Dresser, in the work referred to above, "in winter the upper parts are brownish-grey, somewhat marked with white, the wing coverts darker; under parts and axillaries pure white."

THE RED-BREASTED SNIPE.

Macrorhamphus griseus (J. F. Gmelin).

PLATE 68.

This so-called Snipe, which is now known to have more affinity to the Sandpipers, occasionally straggles to the British Islands in autumn, some twenty-two occurrences having been recorded. It breeds in high northern latitudes in America,

49

migrating in winter to the central and southern parts of that Continent and the West Indian Islands. The nest is placed on the ground among marshes, and contains four eggs, which, according to Seebohm's *British Birds*, " vary in ground-colour from pale buffish-brown to pale greenish-brown, spotted and blotched with dark reddish-brown, and with well-marked pale greyish-brown underlying spots." This species obtains its food like the Sandpipers, by probing the sand and mud with its long bill.

The specimen in the plate is shown in full summer dress; in winter the colour of the upper parts in general becomes a dull ashen-grey, whilst during the intermediate stage of plumage in autumn, when the bird visits the British Islands, the colour is more or less brown. It is, therefore, sometimes known as the Brown Snipe.

THE BAR-TAILED GODWIT.

Limosa lapponica (Linnæus).

PLATE 69.

This bird of passage visits our shores in some numbers every year in spring and autumn, often frequenting suitable localities throughout the winter, and even at times lingering during the summer months, but it has never been known to nest in the British Islands.

The Bar-tailed Godwit breeds in the northern parts of Europe and in Siberia, where it ranges as far east as the Yenesei, while in winter it migrates to Southern Europe, Africa, and South-western Asia.

The nest is merely a small hollow in the ground, and the four eggs are pale olive-green, with dark markings of brown.

When on our coasts this species often associates with other waders, and may be seen on the wet sands and mud-flats of estuaries and other parts of the shore searching the pools and probing the soft ground with its long, slightly upcurved bill in quest of the worms, insects, and small marine creatures on which it lives.

Macgillivray says their note is a loud shrill whistle. According to Stevenson's *Birds of Norfolk*, vol. ii. p. 253, the Bar-tailed Godwit arrives so punctually on the Norfolk coast, on its vernal passage in May, that the 12th of that month is known to the gunners as " Godwit day."

The birds are then usually in their beautiful russet summer-dress, which changes in the winter to sober brown and grey.

The female, though less brightly coloured, is considerably larger than the male.

THE BLACK-TAILED GODWIT.

Limosa belgica (J. F. Gmelin).

PLATE 69.

The Black-tailed Godwit, unlike the preceding species, used formerly to breed regularly in the fens of our eastern counties, the eggs, according to Stevenson (*Birds of Norfolk*, vol. ii. p. 250), having been taken at Reedham as late as 1857. A few birds appear still to visit our country on passage, when they are more often seen on the eastern and southern shores than elsewhere in England, while they are rare in Scotland, though often visiting Ireland in autumn.

The Black-tailed Godwit still breeds among the marshes of Holland and in favourable localities in other parts of Central and Northern Europe, in Iceland, the Færoes, Siberia, and Turkestan, and retires southwards in winter to Southern Europe, Africa, and Southern Asia.

The nest is only a slight depression among the vegetation of the marsh or tundra, and contains four eggs, in ground-colour a pale dull green, blotched and spotted with olive-brown.

This species is very noisy on its breeding ground being approached by anyone, when it flies around the intruder, uttering loud cries, hence its local name of "barker" or "yarwhelp," mentioned by Sir Thomas Browne of Norwich, who also alludes to the reputation this bird had as "the dayntiest dish in England & I think for the bignesse, of the biggest price" (see *Notes on the Natural History of Norfolk*, by Sir Thomas Browne. Jarrold & Sons).

As with the Ruff, it was formerly the custom to keep the birds in confinement and fatten them for the table.

The male is brighter in colour than the female, but she is the larger bird.

THE COMMON CURLEW.

Numenius arquata (Linnæus).

PLATE 69.

The Curlew, known in Scotland as "Whaup," is a very common bird on our shores and estuaries in autumn and winter, and breeds plentifully among the heather of the moorlands, especially in Scotland and Ireland.

51

In August and September, as they move down from their breeding grounds to the coast, their well-known cry may be heard, often in the stillness of the night, over towns and cities, even in the outskirts of London. This bird has a wide range during the nesting season over Northern and Central Europe and Northern Asia, and migrates southwards from the more northern parts of its habitat in winter, when it visits the Mediterranean countries, Africa, South Asia, and Japan.

The nest is a shallow depression amongst the grass and heather of the moorland, scantily lined with dry bents or twigs of heath, and contains four eggs—large for the size of the bird—in ground-colour pale brownish-green, blotched and spotted with brown. The usual call-note of this species, from which the bird has probably derived its name, is clear and loud, but in the breeding season a succession of soft warbling notes are uttered during flight, which are extremely pleasing to the ear. Though sometimes showing great boldness when its eggs or young are threatened, there is no more wary bird than the Curlew, and it is practically unapproachable on the mud-flats and open sandy shore where it seeks its food, consisting then chiefly of crustaceans and various small sea animals, or of earth-worms, insects, and wild fruits, when inland on the moors.

THE WHIMBREL.

Numenius phæopus (Linnæus).

PLATE 69.

The Whimbrel is a regular visitor to the British Islands on passage in spring and autumn, while a few stay throughout the winter on our shores. It breeds in the Orkneys and Shetlands, and, according to the B.O.U. *List of British Birds* (2nd ed. 1915), it has nested in St. Kilda and apparently on North Rona, though never known to nest on the mainland of Great Britain or Ireland. It inhabits Northern Europe and Asia in the nesting season, and migrates southwards for the winter to Africa, India, and the Malay Peninsula. The Whimbrel is known by various names to the gunners on the coast, among others " May-bird," on account of the numbers seen during that month, when the bulk of these migrants appears, and " Half-Curlew," in allusion to its resemblance to the larger species. In its habits it does not appear to differ much from the Curlew, nor in its nidification. The four eggs are dull olive-green, marked with umber-brown.

Pl. 69.

Bar-tailed Godwit. (summer & winter)   Black-tailed Godwit. (summer & winter)
Eskimo Curlew.   Slender-billed Curlew.
Whimbrel.   Common Curlew.

THE WHIMBREL

The voice of the Whimbrel is, however, quite distinct, the birds having, according to the late Lord Lilford, acquired the local name of "Seven-whistlers" owing to their peculiar cry of seven distinct notes.

THE ESKIMO CURLEW.

Numenius borealis (J. R. Forster).

PLATE 69.

The Eskimo Curlew, a native of America, and now supposed to be almost extinct, has been obtained about eight times in our islands, the first in Kincardine-shire in September 1855, and the last on Tresco, Isles of Scilly, in September 1887.

This species breeds in Arctic America, whence it migrates in autumn to spend the winter in South America.

I have copied the following notes on its habits from Dresser's *Birds of Europe*, vol. viii.: "Audubon, who met with this Curlew in numbers in Labrador, writes that, 'wherever there was a spot that seemed likely to afford a good supply of food, there the Curlews abounded, and were easily approached. By the 12th of August, however, they had all left the country. In Labrador they feed on what the fisher-men call the Curlew-berry (*crow-berry?*), a small black fruit growing on a creeping shrub not more than an inch or two in height, and so abundant that patches of several acres covered the rocks here and there. When the birds were in search of these feeding-grounds they flew in close masses, sometimes high, at other times low, but always with remarkable speed, and performing beautiful evolutions in the air. . . . While on the wing they emitted an oft-repeated whistling note; but the moment they alighted they became silent.'"

In his *Manual of Palæarctic Birds*, Dresser states that the four eggs "vary from light greenish to dark olivaceous in ground-colour, and marked with purplish-brown shell-markings and dark umber-brown surface spots and blotches."

The size of the Eskimo Curlew is much less than that of our common species, while the bill is proportionately shorter.

THE SLENDER-BILLED CURLEW.

Numenius tenuirostris, Vieillot.

PLATE 69.

Three examples of this rare bird were obtained on Romney Marsh, Kent, in September 1910, and recorded by Mr. M. J. Nicoll in Witherby's *British Birds*, vol: v. p. 124. This species breeds in Western Siberia, and in winter visits Southern Europe and North Africa.

The late H. E. Dresser, in his *Eggs of the Birds of Europe*, has given the following notes on the breeding habits of the Slender-billed Curlew, received from Mr. Buturlin: "The present species inhabits fenlands, either such as are open or such as are covered with birch trees, or sometimes marshes adjoining the pine forests. Its nest is placed on a large hillock, or on a small dry island, often on one ten to fifteen yards square. Mr. Ushakov always found it nesting in single pairs, and often side by side with *Numenius arquata*, but he was informed by local sportsmen that it also breeds in colonies of several dozen pairs. . . . The nest is a mere depression in the ground, not more than an inch deep, scantily lined with dry grass, or sometimes with a low border of dry grass, in which case the nest takes the form of a somewhat deep cup.

"The full clutch of four eggs may be found from the 30th of May to the 10th of June, and the young are hatched about the end of June, but the birds remain for some time at their nesting place, then undertake short wanderings till about the middle of August, and finally leave for the south in the latter half of that month." The eggs "vary in ground-colour from greyish-olivaceous to ochreous brown, or occasionally reddish-brown, but always with a greenish tinge, and are marked with ashy-grey or pale olivaceous underlying shell-spots and greyish-brown and dark olivaceous surface-dots, spots, lines, streaks, and irregular blotches."

This species is smaller than our Curlew, has a shorter and more slender bill, and may also be distinguished by the distinct spade-like dark markings on the flanks.

Order GAVIÆ.

FAMILY **LARIDÆ.**

SUBFAMILY *STERNINÆ.*

THE BLACK TERN.

Hydrochelidon nigra (Linnæus).

PLATE 70.

Owing to the extensive drainage of the fens and marshy places in our eastern counties and other localities, the Black Tern, or " Blue Darr," as it was called in Norfolk, has long ceased to nest in the British Islands, where it once was a common summer visitant, and at the present time only visits its old haunts in small numbers on passage, the last record of its breeding in Norfolk having been in 1858, according to Stevenson.

This species breeds in many parts of Europe, but apparently not beyond 60° N. latitude, whilst it ranges as far east as Siberia and Turkestan, and in winter migrates to Africa. It is purely a fresh-water species, frequenting reedy lakes and marshes, and feeds on various winged insects, including dragon-flies, and also on worms, leeches, small fishes, etc.

The nest, built of dead reeds and other plants, is placed in wet places in morasses, and contains three eggs, in ground-colour dull buff or olive, blotched and spotted with dark brown and purplish-grey. The birds, which breed in colonies, are very noisy when disturbed, their notes being loud and shrill.

The sexes are alike in colour, and the immature bird is very much the same as that of the White-winged Black Tern, shown on plate 70.

THE WHITE-WINGED BLACK TERN.

Hydrochelidon leucoptera (Schinz).

PLATE 70.

Though never known to have bred in our islands, this species occasionally visits England and Ireland in spring and autumn when on passage. It nests

55

Pl. 70.

Whiskered Tern. (adult & young).   *White-winged Black Tern. (adult & young)*

Black Tern.

Sooty Tern.   *Gull-billed Tern (adult & young)* 2/7

Caspian Tern.

among the marshes of Central and Southern Europe, and in Asia ranges as far east as China and south to Turkestan. In the winter season it migrates to Africa, Southern Asia, and as far south as Australia and New Zealand. Like the Black Tern, the present species breeds in colonies, the nest and eggs resembling those of its congener, nor does it differ much in food or habits, though the late Lord Lilford considered that its flight is somewhat less wavering and indirect than that of the Black Tern.

THE WHISKERED TERN.

Hydrochelidon hybrida (Pallas).

PLATE 70.

This southern species is a very rare visitor to England, where about a dozen have occurred at different times, while one has been recorded in Scotland and one in Ireland. It breeds in the marshes of Spain and in suitable localities in Central, Southern, and South-eastern Europe, also in North Africa and in many parts of Asia, including India. It migrates in winter as far as South Africa, when it also visits Southern Asia, the Malay Archipelago, and Australia.

The nest, generally consisting of a heap of water-plants collected on the surface of the lake, contains three eggs, varying in ground-colour, but generally of a delicate green, blotched and spotted with blackish-brown. The present species does not differ from the Black Tern in habits, but, according to Lord Lilford, its note is "somewhat harsher and more prolonged than that of the other."

The three different species of Marsh-Tern have the webbing of the toes much more indented than in our other Terns.

THE GULL-BILLED TERN.

Sterna Anglica (Montagu).

PLATE 70.

The Gull-billed Tern, a rare visitor to Great Britain, where some twenty-five examples have been recorded, was first described by Col. Montagu in the Supplement to his *Ornithological Dictionary* in 1813 from birds obtained in Sussex and Kent. It breeds in small numbers on the Danish coasts and islands, and also in

Spain and other parts of Southern and Western Europe, in Asia, North Africa, and the shores of North America, whilst in winter it is found throughout Africa, in favourable localities in Southern Asia and in South America.

The nest consists of a small scratching in the sand, with a scanty lining of bents, etc., and contains two or sometimes three eggs, in ground-colour light buff, stone-colour, or pale olive, with spots and blotches of various tones of brown.

According to "Yarrel" (4th ed. vol. iii. p. 534), "In its partiality for lagoons, tidal rivers, and inland lakes of fresh or brackish water, and in its comparatively short although distinctly forked tail and moderately-webbed feet, this species forms a natural link between the Marsh Tern and those which frequent the sea-coast."

The food consists of various insects, including locusts, grasshoppers, and beetles, often taken on the wing, and according to Col. Irby green frogs are also eaten.

THE CASPIAN TERN.

Sterna caspia, Pallas.

PLATE 70.

This large Tern is an uncommon straggler to the English coasts, mostly those of the eastern and southern counties, where some twenty examples have been recorded. In Europe it breeds from as far north as the Gulf of Bothnia southwards to the Mediterranean and eastwards to the Caspian Sea, also throughout a great part of Asia, Africa, Australia, New Zealand, and America. The birds which breed in the colder parts of their range move southwards in winter. The nest is only a small depression in the sand, with a slight lining of bents or sea-weed, and contains from two to three eggs, in ground-colour pale buff or greyish-brown, spotted and marked with purplish-grey and brown.

The food, consisting almost entirely of fish, is obtained by a sudden and headlong plunge into the sea, after the bird has located its prey from above. The cry of this species, like that of all the Terns, is harsh and strident. In winter the black on the head of the bird is streaked with white.

THE SOOTY TERN.

Sterna fuliginosa, J. F. Gmelin.

PLATE 70.

The Sooty Tern shown on this plate, with other species which occasionally or only rarely visit the British Islands, has occurred half-a-dozen times, the first in Staffordshire in October 1852, and the last in Sussex in April 1911. It inhabits the tropical seas throughout the greater part of the world, and breeds in large colonies on various islands, notably Ascension.

According to Dresser's *Manual of Palæarctic Birds*, it usually lays only one egg, "white or cream-buff in ground-colour, the shell-markings purplish-grey, and the surface spots and blotches deep red."

The Lesser Sooty Tern, *S. anæstetha*, Scopoli, and the Noddy Tern, *Anous stolidus* (Linnæus), are said to have occurred in British waters, but the records are not now considered satisfactory.

THE SANDWICH TERN.

Sterna cantiaca, J. F. Gmelin.

PLATE 71.

This species, first recognized near Sandwich in 1784, is a regular summer visitant to the British Islands, breeding chiefly on the eastern coasts of Great Britain and on some of the loughs in Ireland. In Europe the Sandwich Tern nests on the coasts of Denmark, the Netherlands, and in some parts of the Mediterranean, ranging eastwards to the Caspian Sea, while in winter its visits extend over a great part of Africa and South-western Asia. It also inhabits America.

The nest is a slight hollow scraped in the sand, and contains two or occasionally three eggs, varying in ground-colour between a pale yellowish-white and buffish stone-colour, spotted and marked with dark brown and pale grey.

In habits, the present species does not appear to differ from the other salt-water Terns, but, compared with the Common and Arctic Terns, its larger size and bolder

58

Pl. 71.

Roseate Tern.

Arctic Tern.

Common Tern.

Sandwich Tern.

Little Tern.

(Adults & young.)

$\frac{2}{7}$.

style of flight serve to distinguish it. The food, consisting chiefly of sand-eels and other small fishes, is sought for by hovering above the water, and then secured by a sudden downward swoop.

The cry of this bird is harsh and grating, and is especially noticeable when its breeding territory is invaded.

THE ROSEATE TERN.

Sterna dougalli, Montagu.

PLATE 71.

This extremely graceful and delicately coloured species was first noticed by Dr. MacDougall of Glasgow, on the Cumbraes, Firth of Clyde, over a hundred years ago, when it appears to have been more numerous than at the present day. A few colonies, however, are still to be found off the English and Welsh coasts, and some pairs are said to nest in Scotland and in Ireland. During summer it is found locally in some parts of Europe, but not apparently beyond 57° north latitude. It frequents the coasts of Africa, Asia, Australia, and America, being migratory in the colder parts of its habitat.

The nest, like that of its allies, is a mere depression in the sand, occasionally surrounded by some dry grass-stalks, and contains two or three eggs, resembling those of the Common Tern.

The habits of this species appear to be the same as those of the latter, although their cries are said to differ, while the slender form and long tail of the Roseate Tern distinguish it from other species when on the wing.

THE COMMON TERN.

Sterna fluviatilis, Naumann.

PLATE 71.

The Common Tern is a summer visitant to the British Islands, breeding abundantly on many parts of our coasts and sometimes on the shores of inland lakes, but becoming less numerous towards the north of Scotland, where the Arctic Tern predominates. It breeds in favourable localities throughout Europe, from as far north as Norway, also in many parts of temperate Asia, in Northern Africa, and North America, and in winter migrates southwards to warmer climates. The nest consists of a hollow in the sand or shingle, and is often situated on some low-lying island off the shore; it usually contains three eggs, in colour greyish-buff or pale olive, with blotches of brown and purplish-grey.

The Sea-swallow, as this species is sometimes called, is usually seen in parties flitting to and fro over the sea or shallows on sandy shores with an unsteady wavering flight, sometimes hovering and then plunging into the water after the small fish on which it lives. When at rest the birds are fond of basking in the sun on some sloping bed of shingle near the water, and lie with their breasts touching the warm stones.

In autumn, on the shores of the Moray Firth, I have often watched large flocks of Terns before they started on their journey south; in these companies were many young birds, some of which were still fed by their parents as they perched on the tops of posts supporting salmon nets, or waited on the beach. On such occasions it is hardly possible to distinguish the Common from the Arctic Tern, so much are they alike, but the larger and whiter-breasted Sandwich Terns are always easily made out.

THE ARCTIC TERN.

Sterna macrura, Naumann.

PLATE 71.

Although colonies of the Arctic and Common Terns are found nesting in the same territory on some parts of our coasts, as on the Farnes, Northumberland, Walney Island, Lancashire, and Isles of Scilly, for instance, yet the breeding range of the first-mentioned species is in general much farther north, extending to the unexplored lands of the Arctic Ocean in both hemispheres, whence the birds migrate in winter to the southern parts of Africa, Asia, and America.

The nest, like that of the Common Tern, is a mere hollow in the sand or shingle, and the eggs of the two species do not differ in colour, though those of the Arctic Tern are, according to Howard Saunders' *Manual*, slightly smaller.

The habits of the two birds are much alike, and, in fact, they are difficult to distinguish except when closely examined. Macgillivray gives as easily observed characteristics of the Arctic Tern, "the bluish colour of the lower parts, the much shorter tarsus, the greater extent of tail beyond the wings, and the uniform deep red tint of the bill, though the tip is sometimes more or less dusky." Howard Saunders, in his *Manual of British Birds*, already quoted, has shown that there is a difference in the width and colour of the dark line extending along the shaft on the inner webs of the primaries; this line is wider and darker in the Common Tern.

THE LITTLE TERN.

Sterna minuta, Linnæus.

PLATE 71.

This beautiful little bird visits its breeding stations in the British Islands every summer, arriving at the end of April or early in May, and departing in autumn. In Europe it breeds as far north as the Baltic and south to the Mediterranean, also in North Africa, and eastwards in Asia to Northern India, whilst in winter it ranges to Cape Colony and as far south as Java.

The two or three eggs, laid on the sand or shingle, are yellowish-grey in ground-colour, blotched and spotted with dark brown and purplish-grey. The late Lord Lilford, in his work on *British Birds*, refers to the extraordinary tameness of the birds when at their nests, and says they "often remain on the eggs till the intruder is within a few feet, when they usually walk off a few yards distance, or take wing and hover closely around, uttering a short grating note."

The food of the Little Tern consists of small fishes obtained from the water along the sandy shores it frequents.

Macgillivray thus describes its habits: "You may see a pair coming up from a distance, flying at the height of a few yards over the waves, their long wings winnowing the air, and impelling them in starts, as it were, as they wend their way in undulating and wavering movements. Suddenly their flight is arrested over a large pool left on the sands by the retiring tide; with quick beats of their wings they hover stationary, or but slightly shifting place, and with downward-pointed bill seem intent on something which they perceive in the water. One drops, but not like a stone, dips, but with upraised wings, and rises with a small fish in its bill. The other is similarly successful. Onward they proceed, now and then emitting a shrill cry, and with gentle beats of their wings."

SUBFAMILY *LARINÆ.*

SABINE'S GULL.

Xema sabinii (Joseph Sabine).

PLATE 72.

This rare Arctic Gull occasionally reaches the British Islands, particularly the shores of the eastern counties of England, most of the birds recorded having been in winter plumage. A few adults in summer dress have been obtained from time to time; the example from which the drawing in the plate was taken, showing the dark slaty head bordered by a black line, was purchased in the fishing village of Porthgwarra, Cornwall, from Mr. John Jackson, who informed me it had been shot near the Wolf Rock Lighthouse in September 1894.

Sabine's Gull breeds in the high northern latitudes of the Old and New Worlds, and was first discovered by Captain Sabine, from whom it takes its name. He found the birds, which showed great boldness in defence of their young, breeding on low rocky islands in company with the Arctic Tern. The eggs, placed on the bare ground, were two in number. In ground-colour these are dull brown or olive, with indistinct blotches of darker brown. The food consists of various insects, fish, and crustaceans.

In winter the ear-coverts and nape retain the dark colour, but the rest of the head is then white. Immature birds have the upper parts dull brownish-grey, with lighter edges to the feathers, while the tail has a dark subterminal band.

In this species the tail is distinctly forked.

ROSS'S GULL.

Rhodostethia rosea, Macgillivray.

PLATE 72.

A specimen of this small and very beautiful species, known also as the Wedge-tailed Gull, is said to have been obtained near Tadcaster, Yorkshire, in December 1846, or February 1847. It inhabits the seas of the Polar regions, and nothing appears to have been known of its breeding habits until Mr. S. A. Buturlin discovered the birds nesting in colonies of from two or three to ten or fifteen pairs, in company with Terns—apparently the Arctic Tern—on the Kolymá Delta, in North-eastern Siberia, during the summer of 1905. A full and most interesting account of the Gulls and their nests has been given by this explorer in a communication to *The Ibis* for January 1906, pp. 131–139, from which I have taken the following extracts and notes :

"The delta of the Kolymá, which is the easternmost of the great rivers of the North Polar basin, lies, roughly speaking, between 68½° and 69¾° N. lat. and from 159° to 161½° E. long.

"This vast area, at least 15,000 square kilometres in extent, consists of a liberal admixture of lakes, lagoons, channels, rivulets ('viska'), swamps, moors, and damp ground of every description, with dry places only at intervals. . . . On the morning of May 31st one of my men saw a pair, and during the day I went on the river—where the fathom-thick ice was still quite safe—and came across several dozens. The sun was shining brightly, and in the distance each pair appeared like so many roseate points on the bluish ice of the great stream. I say 'pair,' as from their first arrival the birds were constantly seen in pairs. They had evidently just finished their migration, and were tired after their exertions ; for they sat very quietly on the ice, and though all attempts to stalk them were unavailing, they would not fly far, but only shifted from place to place with a lazy and somewhat uneasy motion of their wings, which made me jot down in my note-book on the spur of the moment that the flight was more Fulmar-like than Gull-like.

"Several hours later they had evidently recovered from their fatigues, and then I saw that their flight, far from being Fulmar-like, was really much more Tern-like." Mr. Buturlin observed the birds hovering over a shallow lake, and noticed that when resting and in pairs the male could always be distinguished, even at a distance, by his brighter colouring.

He mentions that the note of this species is peculiar, "being high and more melodious than that of Gulls in general, and very variable." The cries he most often heard "resembled" "á-wo, á-wo, á-wo" and "claw, claw, claw" (or "cliaw, cliaw"), but various other notes were uttered.

Some nests were placed "on little mossy swamps almost bare of grass," others "on wet grassy spots or bogs much nearer to the water, and these nests rose from four to ten inches—generally from five to eight inches—above the surface." The nest is "composed of dry grass and *Carices*, sometimes with the addition of a few dry *Betula* or *Salix* leaves, while I once saw one made of white reindeer-moss." The two, or more usually three, eggs are "of a beautiful deep rich olive-green, without any of the greyish or sandy shade so common in eggs of *Sterna* and other

Pl. 72.

Ross's Gull. (summer & winter).
  Common Gull. (adult & young).
Mediterranean Black-headed Gull.
  Little Gull (adult & young).

Sabine's Gull.
  Bonaparte's Gull.

Black-headed Gull. (summer & winter).

¼

members of the Order. They are spotted especially near the larger end with chocolate-brown (not earthy brown)."

Ross's Gull, in immature plumage, has the crown and nape tinged with grey, the wings more or less marked with dull blackish-brown and buff, and the tail with a dark terminal band.

BONAPARTE'S GULL.

Larus philadelphia (Ord).

PLATE 72.

This Gull was first obtained in the British Islands in February 1848, when a specimen was killed near Belfast; another was shot on Loch Lomond in April 1850; while some four or five have since been recorded in England, the last of these in Sussex in 1913.

Bonaparte's Gull breeds in the Arctic regions of America, and migrates south in winter to the warmer parts of that Continent.

Like our Black-headed Gull, it associates in colonies on fresh-water marshes in the breeding season, but usually builds its nest, composed of twigs, moss, etc., on bushes or trees. The eggs, generally three in number, are pale olive-brown, spotted and blotched with blackish-brown.

In winter the bird loses its dark hood.

THE LITTLE GULL.

Larus minutus, Pallas.

PLATE 72.

The Little Gull not infrequently visits our eastern and southern coasts from autumn to spring, occasionally in some numbers. It breeds in Northern Europe, and ranges eastward through Northern Asia to the Sea of Okhotsk, in winter wandering southwards, when it reaches the Mediterranean, North Africa, and sometimes the United States of America.

The nest is placed on wet masses of floating water-weeds, etc., among inland marshes, and contains three or sometimes four eggs, which in ground-colour are greenish or buffish-brown, spotted with dark brown.

This diminutive species, smaller than any other Gull, does not appear to differ from its congeners in its habits.

THE BLACK-HEADED GULL.

Larus ridibundus, Linnæus.

PLATE 72.

This bird is very common, and seems to be increasing throughout the British Islands, in summer breeding in large colonies on the margins of inland lakes and marshes, and in winter haunting the sea shore, estuaries, and rivers. Most of the Gulls which visit London in the latter season appear to be of this species, and they become very tame and fearless owing to the food and protection they receive. The nest, a collection of withered flags and rushes, is built on the ground among marsh vegetation, and usually contains three eggs, olive-green, pale brown, or occasionally bluish in colour, blotched with deep brown.

The loud harsh cry of the Black-headed Gull, which never ceases when their territory is invaded, has given to this species the name of Laughing Gull.

Its food is various, consisting of worms, larvæ, and insects obtained in the fields, or small fish, crustaceans, etc., from the rivers and sea shore.

THE MEDITERRANEAN BLACK-HEADED GULL.

Larus melanocephalus, Natterer.

PLATE 72.

This species, easily distinguished from the Common Black-headed Gull in summer plumage by its jet-black head—which in our bird is not really black but a sooty-brown—only rarely visits the British Islands, where four examples have been recorded at different times. It inhabits the Mediterranean, especially to the east of Italy, and also the Black Sea, while westwards it occurs along the coast of Spain as far as South-western France.

According to Lord Lilford's *Coloured Figures of the Birds of the British Islands*, "the present species nests in small numbers on the western coast of European Turkey and on some of the coast-marshes of the Black Sea. In habits this Black-headed Gull does not appear to differ materially from *Larus ridibundus*, but its cry is much harsher and deeper-toned than that of the latter bird, from which it is to be easily distinguished at all seasons by the greater thickness of its bill and generally more robust form."

The two or three eggs are laid in a nest made of sea-weed and grasses, and in ground-colour are dull white or pale drab, with streaks and blotches of deep brown.

In winter the head and neck are mostly white, with dark streaks of grey.

THE GREAT BLACK-HEADED GULL.

Larus ichthyaëtus, Pallas.

PLATE 73.

An example of this large Gull, the only one recorded in the British Islands, was shot near the mouth of the Exe, Devonshire, in the end of May or beginning of June 1859. It breeds on the shores and islands of the Caspian Sea and eastwards through Central Asia to Turkestan and Tibet, whilst in winter it wanders southwards to the Eastern Mediterranean, Asia Minor, India, and Ceylon. Little appears to be known about its breeding habits. According to Dresser's *Manual of Palæarctic Birds*, the eggs are " dull stone-drab in ground-colour, streaked and blotched with light and dark umber-brown."

The sketches for the specimen in the plate were taken from a live bird, at one time in the Zoological Gardens of London.

In winter the head is white, with dark streaks.

THE COMMON GULL.

Larus canus, Linnæus.

PLATE 72.

The so-called Common Gull is only plentiful in England during the winter season and in spring, though it has been known to nest on the Farne Islands, Northumberland : it moves northwards to breed on the shores and fresh-water lochs of Scotland, and also nests in some localities in Ireland. After the breeding season, it is generally distributed on the coasts as well as inland throughout the three kingdoms.

The Common Gull has a wide range over Northern Europe and Asia, migrating from the colder parts of its habitat in winter, when its visits extend to the Persian Gulf, Japan, and China.

Pl. 7.

Herring Gull.(adult & young).
Lesser Black-backed Gull.
Iceland Gull.   *Great Black-headed Gull.*   ¼.

A.Thorburn
1915.

THE COMMON GULL

The nest, composed of pieces of turf, grass, sea-weed, etc., usually contains three eggs, in ground-colour greenish-brown or yellowish-brown, marked with streaks and spots of blackish-brown and purplish-grey.

According to Macgillivray, "When feeding along with Rooks in pasture ground, they are often found to be less wary than these birds, especially in places where they are not much liable to be molested. They never, I think, molest any other bird, nor are they at all addicted to quarrelling among themselves. Their food consists of small fishes, such as sand-eels and young herrings, which they pick from the water, first hovering with extended and elevated wings, then descending, spreading their tail, and letting down their feet, with which I have often seen them pat the water as if they were running on land. They never plunge so as to be immersed, but merely seize on what comes close to the surface. They also feed upon stranded fishes of large size, asteriæ, mollusca, shrimps, and other small crustacea. Sometimes also they pick up grain in the fields, and in a state of domestication may be partly fed on bread."

In winter the head and neck are streaked with dusky brown.

THE HERRING-GULL.

Larus argentatus, J. F. Gmelin.

PLATE 73.

Abundant on all our coasts and estuaries throughout the year and often seen inland, this species appears to be more numerous than any other of our larger Gulls. It breeds in Northern Europe, where it ranges as far east as the White Sea, and also in Arctic America. In winter it migrates southwards to the Mediterranean, and in the New World to South America.

The Herring-Gull usually breeds on the steep faces of rocky cliffs or on islands, and makes its nest of grass and similar material. The three eggs vary very much in colour and markings, often they are greenish-brown, spotted and blotched with dark brown and purplish-grey, or the ground-colour may be light bluish-green, reddish, or yellowish-grey.

This bird is almost omnivorous, it pursues the shoals of fish, from which it takes its toll, haunts the shores at low-water in search of crabs and other crustaceans, follows in the wake of vessels in order to obtain scraps of food, or robs other species of their eggs. In fishing villages it becomes very tame, and may often be seen perched on chimneys and housetops.

Its cry is loud and harsh, and is not unlike a laugh, while, in common with the other large Gulls, it often emits a succession of yelping notes from its widely-opened mouth as it stands erect on some rock or sandbank.

A specimen of the Yellow-legged Herring-Gull, *Larus cachinnans*, Pallas, was obtained on Breydon Water, Norfolk, in November 1886. This species is common in the Mediterranean, and chiefly differs from our bird in having the legs and feet yellow instead of flesh-colour. The habits and nidification of the two species are alike.

THE LESSER BLACK-BACKED GULL.

Larus fuscus, Linnæus.

PLATE 73.

The Lesser Black-backed Gull is a well-known bird along the shores of the British Islands, breeding in large colonies in suitable localities from the Shetlands to the Scilly Islands, though it is not in general so widely distributed in summer as the species last described. It inhabits Norway, Sweden, and Northern Russia as far east as the Dwina, and breeds as far south as the Mediterranean; while in winter it visits the west coast of Africa, the Red Sea, and Persian Gulf.

The majority of the birds found on the Continent of Europe are darker on the mantle than our Gull, which is considered a subspecies by Dr. Percy R. Lowe (*vide* Witherby's *British Birds* (vol. vi. pp. 2–7)).

The Lesser Black-backed Gull, in the breeding season, shows a preference for islands, such as the Farnes, off the coast of Northumberland, or the islets which one finds in Scotland among the waters of an inland loch, although the birds also breed in bogs. The nests, which I have seen on the Scilly Islands, were composed of dry grasses, etc., and were placed in depressions among the lichen-covered rocks.

The eggs, usually three in number, vary in ground-colour from pale greenish-blue to brown, blotched and spotted with purplish-grey and deep brown. The food is similar to that of the Herring-Gull, but the present species appears to be even more destructive to the eggs of game birds and wild fowl than the other. The cries of the two species are much alike, but practised ears can detect a difference.

In winter the head and neck are marked with dusky streaks, while the young more or less resemble those of the Herring-Gull.

THE GREAT BLACK-BACKED GULL.

Larus marinus, Linnæus.

PLATE 74.

This fine species, the largest of our British Gulls, is plentiful on certain parts of our coasts and islands, and may often be seen inland. It breeds in Northern Europe and Siberia, and, according to Howard Saunders' *Manual*, in North-western France.

In winter it wanders south to the Mediterranean, while in the New World its summer quarters are in North America, whence it migrates in the cold season to the southern parts of the Continent.

The Great Black-backed Gull generally chooses for its nesting ground the level grassy top of a high rocky islet in the sea, or some lower situation surrounded by the waters of a loch. The nest is composed of dry grasses, sea-weed, etc., and contains two or three eggs, greenish or greyish-brown in ground-colour, with markings of dark brown and grey. The food is various, comprising fish, the eggs and young of other birds, and offal of all kinds, while the bird often joins the Raven and Hooded Crow when feasting on dead sheep or other carrion on the moors.

The wide stretch of wing, extending over five feet from tip to tip, enhances the grand appearance of this Gull in flight, when its loud cackling laugh can be heard afar. In character it is bold and masterful, but is usually wary and shy in the presence of human beings. The sketch for the drawing in the plate was obtained in the Scilly Isles, through the kindness of Mr. Dorrien-Smith. There the birds are plentiful, haunting not only the inhabited islands, but also the out-lying desolate rocks, where their only companions are the Cormorants, Shags, and Great Grey Seals.

THE GLAUCOUS GULL.

Larus glaucus, O. Fabricius.

PLATE 74.

This large white-winged Arctic Gull sometimes visits in numbers the shores of our northern islands and eastern coasts of Great Britain in winter, and often

Pl. 74.

Kittiwake Gull (adult & young).
Great Black-backed Gull (adult & young).
Ivory Gull.   *Glaucous Gull.*

wanders at the same time to Ireland. Breeding as near our coasts as Iceland, where it is found throughout the year, it inhabits the circumpolar seas, whence a good many birds migrate, on the approach of the northern ice, to more southerly regions. It then ranges in Europe as far as the Mediterranean and Black Seas, in Eastern Asia to Japan, and in America to Florida.

The nests have been found situated at low elevations on sandy shores, where they were mere depressions with a lining of sea-weed, at other times they are placed high up on cliffs.

The eggs, usually three in number, are pale greyish-brown, spotted with dark brown and grey.

Predatory in its habits and of a domineering disposition, this Gull had the name of "Burgomaster" applied to it by the old mariners of the Arctic seas, and, like its congeners, it utters loud and harsh cries.

The bird in the plate is shown in winter plumage; in summer the head and neck are pure white. When young, the colour is dull yellowish-white, mottled with shades of brown blended with grey.

THE ICELAND GULL.

Larus leucopterus, Faber.

PLATE 73.

Closely resembling the Glaucous Gull in colour, but smaller and relatively with much more length of wing, this species may occasionally be seen off the English coast in winter, but much more frequently in the Shetlands and on the north-eastern coast of Scotland than in other parts of the British Islands.

Jan Mayen Island, Greenland, and the Arctic regions of America appear to be its chief breeding grounds, whence it wanders to more southerly climes for the winter.

The nest, situated on the ledges of cliffs or on sandy shores, contains from two to three eggs, in ground-colour greenish-drab, marked with blotches of brown.

Mr. Harvie-Brown, as quoted in Dresser's *Birds of Europe*, says: "When flying, the action of the Iceland Gull is more airy and buoyant, less Owl-like, than that of the Glaucous Gull"; and Saxby, in his *Birds of the Shetland Isles*, p. 336, noted that it could be readily recognized at a distance "by its acutely pointed and somewhat long white wings."

The bird in the plate shows the dark streaks on the head and neck denoting winter plumage. In summer these parts are pure white.

THE KITTIWAKE GULL.

Rissa tridactyla (Linnæus).

PLATE 74.

The Kittiwake may be seen along the coast at all times of the year, but is more locally distributed though not less abundant in summer, when it is found breeding in large numbers on the steep rocky cliffs of our shores and islands.

This circumpolar species nests throughout a great part of the Arctic and sub-Arctic regions of the Old and New Worlds, and migrates from the colder portions of its range in winter. The birds breed in colonies, and the nests, rather compactly built of sea-weed and turf, are placed on ledges, sometimes so narrow that there seems scarcely room for the bird to turn. The two to three eggs are pale olive or greenish-white, blotched with dark brown and purplish-grey.

A colony of breeding Kittiwakes, such as that on the precipitous island of Handa, on the west coast of Sutherland, where the birds are seen dotted along the face of the cliffs or wheeling in thousands over the sea far below, like drifting snow-flakes, is a never-to-be-forgotten sight.

Here they can be observed at close quarters from a convenient mass of rock, in company with Puffins, Razorbills, and Guillemots, whilst little can be heard beyond the loud clear cry of the Kittiwake, which has given the bird its name.

The food consists chiefly of fish, which the bird, as Mr. R. J. Howard informs me, not only catches close to the surface of the water, but after which it frequently dives and pursues for a considerable distance.

The late Lord Lilford found that a captive bird only throve on a diet of worms, and actually starved when the supply failed.

In this species the hind toe is wanting or rudimentary.

THE IVORY GULL.

Pagophila eburnea (Phipps).

PLATE 74.

This beautiful species is a rare visitor, more often seen off our northern shores than elsewhere in the British Islands, and usually in winter. Inhabiting the icy seas of the Polar regions, where it is abundant, it wanders southwards as the cold increases, when some of the birds find their way to Europe and North America.

The nest, composed of sea-weed, lichen, splinters of drift-wood, and feathers, is placed high up on steep cliffs or on the ground, and contains one or sometimes two eggs, in ground-colour pale greenish-brown, spotted and blotched with dark brown.

These birds not only eat crustaceans and other marine creatures, but eagerly feed on the flesh of dead whales when they get the opportunity.

The drawing of this species in the plate was taken from a sketch of a living specimen in the Zoological Gardens of London.

The plumage of the young bird is spotted with black until it attains maturity.

Pl. 75.

Richardson's Skua.
Pomatorine Skua.

Great Skua.
Long-tailed or Buffon's Skua.

¼

THE GREAT SKUA.

Megalestris catarrhactes (Linnæus).

PLATE 75.

This predatory species, the largest of our "Robber" Gulls, which in Britain until a few years ago only bred on the Islands of Unst and Foula, has now extended its range in the Shetlands, and owing to careful protection appears to be increasing in numbers. During the winter it wanders far from land, but is occasionally seen off various parts of our coasts.

The breeding stations of the Great Skua in other parts of the world seem to be restricted to Iceland, the Færoes, and, according to Howard Saunders' *Manual of British Birds*, "to some islands to the north of Hudson Strait," though its migrations extend to the Mediterranean and also to American waters.

Known in the Shetlands as the "Bonxie," this species breeds high up on the moors among heather, where a slight hollow on the mossy ground, scantily lined with bents, etc., serves as a nest. This contains two eggs, in colour a pale greenish-brown, marked with deeper brown.

Like other members of this family, the Great Skua obtains a large proportion of its food by chasing the weaker and smaller Gulls and compelling them to disgorge their rightful prey, which is deftly caught by the marauder before reaching the water. This Skua also kills and devours other birds, while food, such as fish stranded on the shore, is not unwelcome.

When their eggs or young are in danger, the parent birds do not hesitate to attack human beings, and a pair have been seen, according to Macgillivray, to beat off an Eagle from their territory.

Their cry is loud and sharp, but sometimes rather plaintive.

THE POMATORHINE SKUA.

Stercorarius pomatorhinus (Temminck).

PLATE 75.

The Pomatorhine, or Twist-tailed Skua, visits our shores more or less regularly in autumn, sometimes in large flocks, and appears more often off the eastern coasts than in other parts of Great Britain. In summer it inhabits the Arctic regions of Asia and America, and moves southwards in winter, roving at that time as far as the Mediterranean, South Africa, Australia, and South America.

The two eggs, greenish-brown in ground-colour, and blotched with blackish-brown, are laid in a slight hollow in the mossy ground.

This species, like the Arctic or Richardson's Skua, is dimorphic, exhibiting in both sexes a darker and lighter phase of plumage, as shown in the plate.

It lives by plundering its neighbours, and often hunts down and kills smaller or wounded birds, and also mammals, especially the lemming.

RICHARDSON'S SKUA.

Stercorarius crepidatus (J. F. Gmelin).

PLATE 75.

This bird, also known as the Arctic Skua, is the most abundant of its kind in the British Islands, breeding not only in the Shetlands, Orkneys, and the Hebrides, but on the mainland of Scotland as well. In autumn, during migration, it is dispersed along our coasts, chiefly on the eastern shores of England and Scotland, and on the western side of the latter country.

The nest is situated among grass and heather in wet moorland places, and contains two eggs, in ground-colour a dull olive, blotched with brown.

The birds fiercely attack any intruder on their domain, and, being predatory in their habits, like the other Skuas, they chiefly live by robbing weaker Gulls.

There are two forms of this species, one with the throat and under-parts light, and the other entirely dark, as shown in the picture. Birds are found breeding indiscriminately in both these phases of plumage.

74

THE LONG-TAILED OR BUFFON'S SKUA

THE LONG-TAILED OR BUFFON'S SKUA.

Stercorarius parasiticus (Linnæus).

PLATE 75.

This slender and elegant species, which is the true Arctic Skua, is a rather rare visitor to the coasts of the British Islands, and is chiefly seen in autumn. It breeds in the high northern latitudes of Europe, Asia, and America, while in winter it seeks more southerly regions.

The nest is a mere depression among the moss and lichen of the tundra, and contains two eggs, which, according to Dresser's *Manual of Palæarctic Birds*, are similar in appearance to those of the Arctic Skua, but as a rule greener in tone and subject to considerable variation. The Long-tailed Skua takes after the other Skuas in its marauding habits, and preys largely on lemmings.

Pl. 76.

Black Guillemot. (summer & winter)   Puffin. (summer & winter)
Common Guillemot.   Brünnich's Guillemot.
Razorbill (summer & winter)
Great Auk.   Little Auk. (summer & winter)

Order ALCÆ.

THE RAZORBILL.

Alca torda, Linnæus.

PLATE 76.

Common throughout the year in British waters, the Razorbill comes inshore in spring, and breeds in vast numbers on precipitous sea-cliffs on the mainland and islands. It breeds in suitable localities in the North Atlantic Ocean, in Europe, as well as in America, and wanders southwards in winter.

The single egg is laid sometimes on an open ledge of rock, or more often in some sheltered cranny or recess, and in colour and markings it varies less than that of the Guillemot, while it is less pyriform in shape. The usual ground-colours are a pale brownish-buff or dull white, rarely showing any greenish tint, with blotches and various streaks and dashes of umber-brown and black.

Under the guidance of the parent birds, the young somehow manage to reach the water before they can fly, and soon learn to obtain their own food, which consists of fish and crustaceans secured by diving.

The Razorbill occasionally utters a low croaking note, but is otherwise a silent bird. Its flattened knife-like bill and pointed tail suffice to distinguish it from the Guillemot.

THE GREAT AUK.

Alca impennis, Linnæus.

PLATE 76.

A most interesting and concise history of this "much-lamented" bird, exterminated over seventy years ago, has been given by the late Professor Newton in his *Dictionary of Birds* under its old name of Gare-fowl, from which it appears that, contrary to a common misapprehension, the Great Auk, with perhaps one doubtful exception, never inhabited the seas within the Arctic Circle, but was found south of that line in the North Atlantic. Though occurring in the Orkneys and St. Kilda, it appears chiefly to have frequented Iceland, the Færoes, South-eastern Greenland, Newfoundland—where it was abundant—and the Labrador coast, and its destruction was ruthlessly carried out, partly in the first instance by fishermen for food and bait, and as the bird became scarcer its extermination was completed to furnish specimens and eggs for collectors and museums. Another circumstance which hastened the end appears to have been the destruction of one of its principal breeding stations off the coast of Iceland by a volcanic eruption. Unfortunately for the bird, it fell an easy prey to its enemies when it arrived at the low-lying rocks which served as nesting places, as, owing to its very diminutive wings, it was quite unable to fly.

An example taken in the Orkneys about 1813 is now in the British Museum, and two are said to have been secured at St. Kilda about 1821 and 1840, whilst a pair, the last of their race, were obtained as late as 1844 on some skerries off the coast of Iceland.

The single egg was apparently laid on the rocks, and the colour of those left to us is usually buffish-white, blotched with dark brown and grey.

According to Howard Saunders' *Manual of British Birds* (2nd ed.), about seventy-two eggs and seventy-nine specimens of the bird appear to exist.

Its food and habits in general seem to have resembled those of the Razorbill.

THE COMMON GUILLEMOT.

Uria troile (Linnæus).

PLATE 76.

This is a common bird on and off the shores of Britain throughout the greater part of the year, coming like the Razorbill, but in greater multitudes, to breed on the cliffs and precipices of our sea-coast and islands.

The Guillemot has a wide range on both sides of the Atlantic, whilst it also inhabits the Pacific Ocean, and migrates southward in winter.

The female lays her single egg on the crowded and narrow ledges of high precipitous cliffs, sometimes in such precarious situations that a sudden movement of the bird or unexpected gust of wind sends it into space, notwithstanding its pear-like shape, which no doubt helps to keep the eggs from straying.

The variety of colour, shape, and size of the eggs is wonderful. In ground-colour they range from white to bluish-green or blue, showing many variations of tint, with scribbled lines and blotches of brown and black. Some are of a deep chocolate red, but these are rare, and command a correspondingly high price at Bempton. It has been noticed that each female always produces the same type of colour and markings in her eggs. After the breeding season the Guillemots go out to sea, and, considering their vast numbers, it is difficult to say why comparatively so few are seen during winter. The food, consisting chiefly of fish, is obtained by diving.

A variety of this species, known as the Bridled or Ringed Guillemot, which only differs in having a distinct circle of white around the eye, continued in a straight line backwards, is shown behind the principal figure on the plate. In winter the throat becomes more or less white.

BRÜNNICH'S GUILLEMOT.

Uria bruennichi, E. Sabine.

PLATE 76.

This species is the Arctic representative of the Common Guillemot, and is a rare straggler in winter to our eastern coasts.

It is a larger bird, with a thicker bill, marked with a pale line on the edge of the upper mandible, whilst in summer plumage the head and upper parts are blacker than in those of the Common Guillemot. The figure in the plate is in winter dress.

THE BLACK GUILLEMOT.

Uria grylle (Linnæus).

PLATE 76.

This species, known also as the "Tystie," has a more northern range in our islands than the Common Guillemot, and does not now breed on the English mainland, though in summer a few frequent the Isle of Man for this purpose. It nests in some numbers in the Orkneys and Shetlands, the Hebrides, on the rocky

THE BLACK GUILLEMOT

shores of northern and western Scotland, and also in Ireland, and in winter is chiefly found in the waters around the Scottish and Irish coasts.

It inhabits the coasts of Northern Europe and other localities westwards to the north-eastern side of America.

The Black Guillemot differs in habits from the common species, laying two eggs instead of one, and these are placed in crevices among the rocks or under slabs of stone.

In ground colour they are more or less white, with a tinge of pale blue or green, blotched and spotted with dark brown and shades of purplish-grey.

Macgillivray says : "Their food consists of small fishes and crustacea, in search of which they frequent less the sounds and bays than the open sea. On all the coasts of Scotland, the fry of the Coal-fish is a very common article of food with them, as with many other sea-birds. About most of their breeding-places, I have not observed them to proceed daily to a great distance; but on leaving the rocks with their young they disperse over the ocean, entirely deserting their breeding-places until the next spring. Yet they do not migrate far southward with us, most of them remaining all winter in the north.

This species sits lightly on the water, on which it paddles about in a lively manner. It dives with rapidity, like a shot as it were, opening its wings a little, and under water actually flies, as I have often seen."

The remarkable difference between the summer and winter plumage is shown on the plate.

THE LITTLE AUK.

Mergulus alle (Linnæus).

PLATE 76.

The Little Auk, whose summer home is among the rocks and islands of the Arctic Ocean, as a rule only visits our coasts in winter, where it occasionally appears in large numbers, especially after stormy weather, and at such times is often found far inland.

As an instance of the destruction of bird life by weather conditions, I once counted no less than ninety remains of various species, including three of the Little Auk, during a short afternoon's walk along the shores of the Moray Firth.

This bird is more frequently seen on our northern coast-line than further south in Great Britain. At their breeding stations on Spitsbergen, Novaya Zemlya, and other lands, they congregate in multitudes, nesting within the dark recesses under loose rocks and stones, where they are safe from the depredations of foxes; they are also said to breed on very high cliffs. Only one egg is laid, which, in ground-colour, is pale greenish-blue, sometimes dotted and streaked with pale red.

Birds in full summer plumage are seldom seen in the British Islands; the one represented in the plate was drawn from a specimen kindly lent to me by Lt.-Commander Millais obtained in June 1881 in Monefeith Bay, Forfar.

SUBFAMILY **FRATERCULINÆ.**

THE PUFFIN.

Fratercula arctica (Linnæus).

PLATE 76.

This oceanic bird spends the greater part of its life at sea, and only comes ashore to breed. Vast numbers arrive about the end of March or a little later, and depart in the latter half of August.

Its breeding stations are numerous on the mainland and islands of Scotland, while on the eastern side of England colonies are found on the Farne Islands and Flamborough Head; farther south a few birds nest on the Isle of Wight and in some localities on the south-western coast, becoming numerous again on the Isles of Scilly, Lundy Island, and in Wales. It is also common in Ireland, and inhabits the North Atlantic, ranging from the coasts of Europe to those of Greenland and Labrador.

Steep grassy slopes overhanging the sea or low turf-covered islands are chosen as nurseries, where the birds dig out tunnels by means of their bills, or occupy narrow openings in the rocks or under stones, and sometimes rabbit-holes are chosen.

The single egg when first laid is dull white, faintly spotted with pale brown and grey, later becoming more or less soiled and darkened.

The young, clothed at first in soft fluffy down, used to be much esteemed as food, and the name Puffin, according to Professor Newton (*Dictionary of Birds*, p. 751), was no doubt applied to these owing to their downy covering. He also states that, "In 1345, according to a document from which an extract is given in Heath's *Islands of Scilly* (p. 190), these islands were held of the Crown at a yearly rent of 300 Puffins, or 6s. 8d., being one-sixth of their estimated annual value."

The nestlings are assiduously attended to by the parent birds, who may be seen flying constantly to and fro carrying a supply of small fishes held across the mandibles.

The curiously shaped and vividly coloured bill of this species resembles the fore iron of a plough, hence its name of Coulterneb. After the breeding season the bill is much reduced in size, owing to the shedding of the sheath on the frontal part, and at the same time the blue appendages above and below the eye are also shed.

On the ground the Puffin stands as shown in the plate, differing from the Razor-bill and Guillemot in this respect, while, unlike the other members of this group, it has the claws on the inner toes placed horizontally for some purpose, so far unexplained, but possibly to enable the bird to arrange or disengage the rows of small fishes carried in the bill to feed the young.

Pl. 77.

Great Northern Diver (summer & winter)

ed-throated Diver (summer & winter)

White-billed Northern Diver.

Black-throated Diver.

Order PYGOPODES.

Family COLYMBIDÆ.

THE GREAT NORTHERN DIVER.

Colymbus glacialis, Linnæus.

PLATE 77.

This large Diver is a winter visitor to the waters of the British coast, and has never been known to nest in our islands, though mated pairs in full breeding plumage are sometimes observed in summer.

It breeds in Iceland, Greenland, and in the colder parts of North America, whence it migrates southwards in winter.

The nest, composed of aquatic plants, is always placed either on the shores or on some small island on fresh-water lakes, so that on the least suspicion of danger the bird can slide stealthily into the water.

The two eggs, varying in ground-colour from greenish to reddish-brown, are spotted with black.

The food consists of fish and crustaceans, often obtained at a great depth, as the bird, like all the members of this family, is a splendid diver, and can remain under water for a considerable time. It has, in common with the other Divers, a habit of sinking its body when swimming, so much so that sometimes little more than its head and neck are visible.

During the breeding season it utters a strange melancholy cry, while at other times it has been heard to emit a low croaking sound, according to Macgillivray.

THE WHITE-BILLED NORTHERN DIVER.

Colymbus adamsi, G. R. Gray.

PLATE 77.

This species differs from the Great Northern Diver in having a heavier and more angular bill of a yellowish ivory colour, while another means of distinguishing them has been pointed out by Howard Saunders (*Manual of British Birds*, 2nd ed. p. 711), viz. that in the present species the upper part of the head and neck have a greenish sheen, changing to purple below, whereas in the others these colours are reversed. The streaks of white on the neck are also fewer in number and broader in the white-billed species.

Some five occurrences have been noted on the coast of England, and one in Argyllshire, Scotland. It breeds in Novaya Zemlya and Northern Asia, and ranges eastwards to the Arctic regions of the New World.

In habits the two species appear to be alike, and in their winter plumage closely resemble each other.

THE BLACK-THROATED DIVER.

Colymbus arcticus, Linnæus.

PLATE 77.

Though breeding regularly in the more northern parts of Scotland, this beautiful bird is not nearly so common off our shores in winter as the Great Northern Diver.

It inhabits the northern parts of Europe, Asia, and America, and in winter migrates to warmer waters, where in Europe it is found as far south as the Mediterranean and the seas of Southern Russia, in Asia ranging to Japan, and in America to the Eastern United States.

In Scotland it usually breeds on some island in a loch, sometimes a large sheet of fresh water, such as Loch Maree, where I have seen the nest, at other times it may be a comparatively small lake.

The two eggs, greenish or reddish-brown in ground-colour, spotted with black or brown, are laid in a slight hollow in a bed of herbage collected by the bird.

Like the other members of this genus, the Black-throated Diver makes its nest just at the water's edge, so that the bird when alarmed can quickly reach a place of safety by sliding to the water.

When watching the only nest of this species I have seen, which contained a broken egg, apparently damaged by Gulls, one of the parent birds could be observed quietly swimming around, and occasionally dipping its bill in the water.

During the breeding season the cry is loud and harsh.

The male and female are alike in colour, and in winter have the upper parts dark greyish-brown, with the chin, throat, and under parts white.

THE RED-THROATED DIVER.

Colymbus septentrionalis, Linnæus.

PLATE 77.

The Red-throated Diver is plentiful off the coasts of the British Islands throughout the autumn and winter, and in summer breeds in many localities on the northern mainland of Scotland, as well as in the Orkneys, Shetlands, and Outer Hebrides, while a few birds are said to nest in Ireland. It inhabits Iceland, Spitsbergen, Greenland, and the northern parts of Europe, Asia, and America, and visits more southern regions in winter.

Macgillivray, in his *History of British Birds*, pp. 304–305, describing the habits of this species, says : " In alighting it comes down nearly erect, ploughing up the water for a short way. Its activity in its proper element is astonishing ; it swims with extreme speed, keeping deep in the water, and sometimes only allowing its head and neck to emerge. In diving it slips as it were out of sight without noise or flutter, and under water pursues its way with great speed, using its wings as well as its feet. Its food consists of small fishes, especially sprats, young herrings, and codfish, as well as crustacea, and I have usually found numerous pebbles and bits of gravel in its stomach. . . . The nest is placed on an island, or tuft, or among the herbage near the margin, or even on the stony beach, of a lake or pool, and is composed of grass, sedge, and heath, or other easily-procured plants, generally in small quantity, and neatly put together. The eggs, in so far as I am aware, are always two ; but it is stated by some that three as frequently occur. . . . They are of a deep or pale olive-brown, or dull greenish-brown, or pale brownish-green colour, spotted and dotted with umber, more densely at the larger end."

In the nesting season, this species, like the other Divers, utters loud and harsh cries.

Pl. 78.

A.Thorburn
1916

Black-necked or Eared Grebe.

Red-necked Grebe.   Great Crested Grebe. $\frac{1}{3}$

Slavonian or Horned Grebe.(summer & winter)   Little Grebe.(summer & winter).

Family **PODICIPEDIDÆ.**

THE GREAT CRESTED GREBE.

Podicipes cristatus (Linnæus).

PLATE 78.

This beautiful species, the largest of our Grebes, is now not uncommon on many of the large reedy lakes and ponds in the British Islands, and appears to be increasing in numbers and extending its breeding range in various directions. According to the B.O.U. *List of British Birds* (2nd ed. 1915), it nested as far north as Morayshire in 1913. In winter it is often found on the coast and estuaries.

It is resident in Central and Southern Europe, and also inhabits Africa, Asia, Australia, and New Zealand.

The nest of the Great Crested Grebe is a wet and more or less floating mass of sedges and other water plants on the outskirts of beds of reed or bulrush, and on this platform the four or five eggs are laid, which at first have a ground-colour of chalky white, with an underlying tinge of green, but afterwards become stained to a yellowish-brown or buff. On leaving the nest, the parent bird generally covers the eggs with any loose material close at hand.

The food consists of various water insects, fish, reptiles, etc., and, according to Macgillivray, " along with remains of these are usually found in its stomach numerous large curved feathers, which it probably picks up as they float on the water, and which are, no doubt, intended to facilitate digestion." If pursued on the water, the bird generally attempts to escape by swimming and diving, although it can fly swiftly and at some height.

In the breeding season it utters a rather harsh cry. The female is smaller, and has the occipital tufts and ruff less pronounced than those of the male, while in winter both sexes lose these nuptial decorations.

THE RED-NECKED GREBE.

Podicipes griseigena (Boddaert).

PLATE 78.

Though never known to have nested in the British Islands, the Red-necked Grebe visits our coasts in winter, chiefly those of the eastern side of Great Britain, where it occasionally occurs in some numbers.

It inhabits various parts of Europe, breeding as far north as Scandinavia and Northern Russia, thence southwards to the Mediterranean countries and the shores of the Black and Caspian Seas. In Asia it is found in Turkestan and Siberia, while in North-eastern Asia and in America it is replaced by a larger race.

The Red-necked Grebe builds a floating nest, composed of the dead stems and the leaves of water-plants, and lays three to four eggs, resembling those of the Great Crested Grebe but smaller, and in its habits the present species is very like its larger congener.

THE SLAVONIAN OR HORNED GREBE.

Podicipes auritus (Linnæus).

PLATE 78.

This Grebe is chiefly known as a winter visitant, when it occurs not only on the sea-coast but also on waters lying inland, and has lately been discovered breeding on lochs in Northern Scotland.

It inhabits the circumpolar regions of the Northern Hemisphere, and in winter migrates southwards to warmer regions in Europe, Asia, and America.

The floating nest of this species, which, like those of its congeners, is made of water-plants, contains from two to four and occasionally five eggs, in ground-colour white, faintly tinged with blue, which, when time permits, are concealed from notice by the parent bird when compelled to leave her treasures.

Proctor, who found this species breeding in Iceland, observed that the mother endeavoured to convey her young to safety by diving under water while she held them under her wings.

In food and habits this species does not differ from the other Grebes.

THE BLACK-NECKED OR EARED GREBE.

Podicipes nigricollis, C. L. Brehm.

PLATE 78.

The Black-necked Grebe, apart from its size and colour, differs from the other species in the shape of its bill, which has a slight upward curve. Though usually only known as a winter visitant, this Grebe now breeds annually in Wales, and no doubt has done so in other parts of Great Britain.

It inhabits the countries of Central and Southern Europe, as well as North Africa, and, according to Dresser, has bred as far north as Denmark, while eastwards it ranges across Asia to Japan and China, and in winter migrates southwards to Cape Colony and India.

It breeds on fresh-water lakes, and lays four or five eggs, which do not differ from those of the Slavonian Grebe.

In winter the golden ear-tufts are absent, and the chin and throat become white.

THE LITTLE GREBE.

Podicipes fluviatilis (Tunstall).

PLATE 78.

The Little Grebe or Dabchick is a more or less common species on many of our still-flowing rivers, ponds, and other waters throughout the year, but appears to be less plentiful in the north of Scotland and its islands than in other parts of Britain, whilst in winter it often visits the tidal waters on the coast. It is widely distributed over Europe from Scandinavia to the Mediterranean countries, and through Central Asia as far as Japan.

The nest, consisting of a mass of water-weeds, contains from three to six eggs, which when newly laid are nearly white, and afterwards become stained to a dull buff or brown from contact with the wet material placed over them by the bird whenever she has occasion to leave the nest.

The tiny nestlings are sometimes removed from danger by the mother, who takes them under her wings.

The food consists of water-insects, tadpoles, and small fishes, obtained by diving, and when engaged in feeding the bird goes under very suddenly without any disturbance of the water, and reappears on the surface quite as unexpectedly.

The usual cry is a single rather plaintive note.

Pl. 79.

A. Thorburn 1916.

Storm Petrel.   Leach's Fork-tailed Petrel.

Frigate Petrel.   Madeiran Fork-tailed Petrel.

Wilson's Petrel.   Sooty Shearwater.

Little Dusky Shearwater.   Great Shearwater.

3

Order TUBINARES.

FAMILY PROCELLARIIDÆ.

THE STORM-PETREL.

Procellaria pelagica, Linnæus.

PLATE 79.

The Storm-Petrel, our smallest web-footed bird, breeds on many of the Scottish islands, including the Orkneys and Shetlands, the Hebrides, and various rocky islets on the western coast, while southwards it is found in similar situations off the coast of Wales, the Isles of Scilly, and also in Ireland.

In Europe it breeds from as far north as the Lofoten Islands in Norway, south to the Mediterranean, and, after nesting, spends the time at sea, when it roves as far as Cape Colony in Africa and westward to America.

The one egg, which is white, dotted with reddish spots, is laid in a hole in a cliff, at the end of a tunnel on some grassy slope, or under stones, where occasionally a scanty nest is formed of bents and bits of earth.

The Petrels seek their food upon the waters, skimming just above the waves, usually following their curves, while skilfully avoiding the breakers, and often touching the surface with their feet outspread. This habit has presented to the minds of sailors the experience of the Apostle Peter, and hence the name of Petrel.

Known also as Mother Carey's Chickens, they frequently accompany ships on their voyage across the ocean, following in their wake for many miles, no doubt attracted by the various oily substances and other animal matter which may be thrown overboard. They also eat small crustaceans and fishes. The presence of these little birds as they glide around a vessel is supposed by seamen to foretell the approach of stormy weather.

Macgillivray, describing them as seen in the waters around the Hebrides, says: "In the open ocean, they are met with by day as well as by night; but when breeding, they are seen in the neighbourhood of their haunts, that is, to the distance of twenty or more miles around, chiefly in the dusk and dawn, and during the day

89

remain concealed in their holes. Stormy weather does not prevent their coming abroad, nor are they less active during calms." In the breeding season, when underground, they utter, according to Hewitson (*Eggs of British Birds*), "a sort of warbling chatter."

As in all the Petrels, the male and female are alike in colour.

LEACH'S FORK-TAILED PETREL.

Oceanodroma leucorrhoa (Vieillot).

PLATE 79.

This species, first discovered by Bullock in 1818 on St. Kilda, is now known to breed on that island as well as in the Flannen Isles and the Outer Hebrides, also on islands off the Irish coast.

In autumn it often approaches the shores of England, and seems even more liable to be driven inland by storms than the Storm-Petrel. It inhabits the northern portions of the Atlantic and Pacific Oceans, breeding as far north as Greenland and Alaska, and wandering south in winter.

Like that species, it follows in the wake of vessels, when it may be distinguished from the other by its forked tail, larger size, and rather lighter colour. It breeds in colonies, and its single egg, which is deposited within a burrow, is pure white in ground-colour, marked with a zone of tiny spots of reddish-brown. Like other members of the family, Leach's Petrel is more or less nocturnal in its habits, becoming active as darkness comes on, when it flits to and fro, incessantly uttering its sharp querulous notes. The food is similar to that of the Storm-Petrel, consisting of floating molluscs, crustaceans, and oily substances on the sea.

MADEIRAN FORK-TAILED PETREL.

Oceanodroma castro (Harcourt).

PLATE 79.

This species, a rare bird in the British Islands, has been thrice recorded, the first at Littlestone, Kent, in December 1895, the second at Hythe, in the same county, in November 1906, and the last at Milford, Hampshire, November 1911.

MADEIRAN FORK-TAILED PETREL

Formerly known as Ridgway's, and now often called Harcourt's Petrel, it nests on the rocky islets of Madeira, the Salvages, Azores, and Cape Verde Islands in the Atlantic, while its breeding range extends as far as the Sandwich and Galapogos Islands in the Pacific Ocean. Like other Petrels, it breeds underground in burrows, and lays a single egg, which is, according to Mr. Ogilvie-Grant (*Ibis*, 1896, p. 54), "white, with an indistinct zone of light red and faint purplish underlying dots round the larger end." In habits this bird does not appear to differ from the other Petrels.

WILSON'S PETREL.

Oceanites oceanicus (Kuhl).

PLATE 79.

Wilson's Petrel is a rare visitor to the British Islands, though it was seen in some numbers near Land's End in May 1838, and about a dozen birds have since been obtained.

It breeds on Kerguelen and in other localities far southwards in the Antarctic regions, and wanders northwards in the cold season, when it ranges far and wide over the Atlantic, Indian, and South Pacific Oceans, visiting the Azores, Canaries, the coasts of France and Spain, and also Labrador.

The one egg, which in ground-colour is white, zoned with small reddish spots, is laid in chinks and crannies under stones or among broken rocks, and was first made known to naturalists by the Rev. A. E. Eaton, who found colonies of this species breeding on Kerguelen.

The food and habits of this long-legged Petrel appear to be very like those of its allies.

THE FRIGATE-PETREL.

Pelagodroma marina (Latham).

PLATE 79.

This rare species has only been taken twice in the British Islands, first on Walney Island, Lancashire, in November 1890, and again on the island of Colonsay, Inner Hebrides, in January 1897.

It breeds on various islands in the Southern Pacific, and in the Atlantic Ocean as near our coast as the Salvages, north of the Canaries, where Mr. Ogilvie-Grant found the birds nesting abundantly in April 1895. The one egg, in ground-colour white, minutely spotted and zoned with purplish and reddish dots, is laid in a burrow, and from this retreat the bird, being nocturnal in its habits, sallies forth at dark.

FAMILY **PUFFINIDÆ.**

THE GREAT SHEARWATER.

Puffinus gravis, O'Reilly.

PLATE 79.

The Great Shearwater visits the British Islands more or less regularly in autumn, when it is sometimes abundant off the southern and western coasts. According to the B.O.U. *List of British Birds,* 2nd ed. p. 287, " The only known breeding station of the Greater Shearwater is Tristan da Cunha, but it probably nests on other islands of the Southern Atlantic. It ranges over the Atlantic Ocean, from Southern Greenland, Iceland, and the Faeroes southwards to the Falkland Islands and the Cape of Good Hope." The late H. E. Dresser states (*Eggs of the Birds of Europe*) that the egg of this species is unknown.

The food consists of small cuttle-fish, etc., and oily animal substances obtained in the sea, over whose waves the Shearwater glides in long undulating curves, and from this peculiar style of flight the bird and its relations have taken their name.

The Mediterranean Great Shearwater, *Puffinus Kuhli* (Boie), a larger bird than ours, with a yellow bill and lighter in the colour of the upper plumage, and inhabiting the Mediterranean and Atlantic, has occurred once in the British Islands, viz. at Pevensey, Sussex, in December 1906.

The Mediterranean species breeds in crannies and in holes in cliffs, and is said to lay one white egg.

THE SOOTY SHEARWATER.

Puffinus griseus (J. F. Gmelin).

PLATE 79.

This species is occasionally seen off our coasts in autumn.

During the breeding season it inhabits the Southern Hemisphere, afterwards migrating northwards, when it roams as far as North America and the shores of Europe. It nests in burrows, lays a single white egg, and in its habits does not appear to differ from its near relatives.

93

THE LITTLE DUSKY SHEARWATER.

Puffinus assimilis, Gould.

PLATE 79.

Breeding on the Madeiras, Canaries, Cape Verde, and other islands in the North Atlantic, and also inhabiting the seas of Australia and New Zealand, this small species has occurred some half-a-dozen times on our coasts.

It nests in holes and in cavities between or under rocks, and lays a single white egg. Like its allies, it is nocturnal in its habits, and constantly flits around its breeding stations during the darkness, uttering weird cries.

THE MANX SHEARWATER.

Puffinus anglorum (Temminck).

PLATE 80.

This is a common species in British waters, breeding on various islands off the western coasts of Great Britain and Ireland, as well as in the Orkneys, Shetlands, and Isles of Scilly, and chiefly inhabits the North Sea and the North Atlantic Ocean.

Through the kindness of Mr. Dorrien-Smith, I was able to visit a notable breeding station of this Shearwater on the island of Annet, in the Scilly group, where the turf and sandy soil on the upper and flatter part of the ground were honey-combed with their burrows, so much so that it was difficult to avoid treading on these underground dwellings. If caught in these places the birds seem to be quite dazzled with the light, and flutter along the ground unable to fly, though in the daytime when at sea they are active and wide awake. On leaving the island we encountered a large flock resting on the water, which presented a charming picture as each bird rose, and, rippling the surface with its feet, skimmed for some distance just above the sea. When fairly on the wing they fly with great speed, and follow each other as they sweep onwards in undulating curves.

The Manx Shearwater lays one white egg in a slight nest of withered grass within a burrow, and in the breeding season the birds are very noisy and restless during the night.

94

THE MANX SHEARWATER

The food is chiefly fish, cuttle-fish, and other animal matter.

The Levantine Shearwater, *Puffinus yelkouanus*, which takes the place of the Manx Shearwater in the Mediterranean, where it is known to the inhabitants as *Âme damnée*, is occasionally seen off the coasts of the British Islands. It scarcely differs from our bird, being only somewhat larger and browner.

THE CAPPED PETREL.

Œstrelata hæsitata (Kuhl).

PLATE 80.

An example of this very rare, if not extinct, species was captured alive near Swaffham, Norfolk, in March or April 1850.

Formerly it inhabited the Lesser Antilles in some numbers, its last known breeding-place having been the island of Dominica, where the birds nested in holes in the ground at some considerable elevation. The egg is apparently unknown.

THE COLLARED PETREL.

Œstrelata brevipes (Peale).

PLATE 80.

About the end of November or beginning of December 1889 a specimen of this Petrel, the only one recorded in the British Islands, was obtained between Borth and Aberystwith in Wales. It breeds in the New Hebrides and Figi Islands in the Western Pacific Ocean, and appears to occur southwards as far as the limits of the Antarctic ice.

The Collared Petrel was found nesting in burrows high up on the mountains on an island of the New Hebrides by John Macgillivray, but no eggs were obtained.

Pl. 80.

A. Thorburn. 1916.

ack. browed Albatross. (scale ½)   Manx Shearwater.   Capped Petrel.

Collared Petrel.

Fulmar.   Bulwer's Petrel.   3.

Schlegel's Petrel.

SCHLEGEL'S PETREL

Œstrelata neglecta (Schlegel)

PLATE 80.

An example of Schlegel's or the Kermadec Petrel was discovered lying dead, after stormy weather, near Taporley, Cheshire, in April 1908 (see Witherby's *British Birds*, vol. ii. p. 14). It breeds on islands in the South Pacific Ocean.

Mr. F. DuCane Godman, in his *Monograph of the Petrels*, referring to this species, says: "This Fulmar is remarkable for its variable colour, some examples being for the most part white, while others are entirely grey. These two phases of plumage are so much unlike each other that the birds might very well be taken for different species."

BULWER'S PETREL.

Bulweria bulweri (Jardine and Selby).

PLATE 80.

Bulwer's Petrel has occurred on five occasions in Great Britain, most of these birds being dead when found, the first in Yorkshire in May 1837, and four others in Sussex between 1903 and 1907.

This species breeds on the Desertas, Madeira, and also inhabits islands in the Northern Pacific Ocean. According to Mr. F. DuCane Godman's *Monograph of the Petrels*, "The nest is usually concealed under boulders or in holes in the rocks, where a few old bones or feathers of a Tern frequently supply the place of sticks or grass for the nest. Here the single white egg is laid, though Mr. Fisher relates that on one occasion on Neckar Island two eggs were found in the same hole, possibly belonging to different birds."

"These birds are purely nocturnal in habits, and although very rarely found in flocks like Shearwaters, remain almost constantly at sea, except during the breeding season."

THE FULMAR.

Fulmarus glacialis (Linnæus).

PLATE 80.

Inhabiting the North Atlantic Ocean, the Fulmar, which has recently extended its breeding range in the British Islands, nests on a good many of the islands of Northern and North-western Scotland, including the Orkneys, Shetlands, St. Kilda, Outer Hebrides, and others, as well as on the mainland.

The female lays one pure white egg, presenting a chalky surface, and having a decided odour of musk, on some ledge of rock or in a depression among the short turf on the slopes of a cliff. On being handled or disturbed on their nests, the birds eject from their mouths a clear yellowish coloured oil, apparently as a means of defence. Howard Saunders (*A Manual of British Birds*, 2nd ed. p. 752) describes the note as a "low croon." After the breeding season the birds disperse, and are then found roaming far and wide at sea, and often approach fishing boats and whalers, when they feed chiefly on oily matter or offal floating on the surface of the water.

Variations of colour occur in this species; occasionally pure white birds are seen, while an entirely slaty-grey form is not uncommon. Like most, if not all, of the other Petrels, the Fulmar appears to be unable to stand on its feet, and rests when on the ground in a crouching attitude.

Family DIOMEDEIDÆ.

THE BLACK-BROWED ALBATROSS.

Diomedia melanophrys, Boie.

PLATE 80.

A specimen of this Albatross, driven inland and exhausted, was obtained near Linton, Cambridgeshire, in July 1897. It breeds on the Chatham, Campbell Islands, and others, in the Southern Hemisphere, and during its wanderings occasionally appears in the North Atlantic, one having been shot in the Færoes in 1893, where for thirty or forty years it had consorted with the Gannets.

The female usually lays one yellowish-white egg, which is speckled with reddish-brown.

THE HEBRIDEAN SONG-THRUSH.

Turdus hebridensis, Eagle Clarke.

PLATE 80a.

This local race, the resident representative of our Common Song-Thrush in the Outer Hebrides, differs chiefly from the latter in the darker olive-brown of the upper plumage, in the noticeably blacker and heavier spotting of the breast and flanks, and also in the less distinct yellowish-buff ground-colour of the chest.

Macgillivray has given us a fine description of the bird in its native islands, enlarging on the charm and beauty of its song, poured forth as the singer perches on some granite block, shaggy with grey lichens, the melody returning in sweeter modulations from the sides of the heathy mountains ; while sometimes several birds may be heard at the same time, filling a whole glen with their warblings.

According to the same authority, the Hebridean Song-Thrush frequents the shores in winter, feeding on whelks and other molluscs whose shells it batters to pieces on a stone, apparently in the same manner as the mainland birds treat the snails in our gardens.

Marsh-Titmouse. $\frac{2}{3}$

Greenland Redpoll.   Willow-Titmouse.

eater Redpoll.   Irish Coal-Titmouse.

Hebridean Song-Thrush.   St. Kilda Wren.

THE HEBRIDEAN SONG-THRUSH

Through the courtesy of Dr. Eagle Clarke I have been enabled to give a picture of the type specimen, a male from Barra, Hebrides, in the Royal Scottish Museum, Edinburgh.

I am also indebted to him for other assistance, and for kindly looking over the letterpress accompanying the two extra plates.

THE EASTERN PIED WHEATEAR.

Saxicola pleschanka (Lepech).

PLATE 80B.

On the plate is shown a figure of the female example of this species, now in the Royal Scottish Museum, Edinburgh, obtained by the Misses Baxter and Rintoul among the rocks on the eastern side of the Isle of May on October 19th, 1909.

When the bird was put up it was observed that it differed from our Common Wheatear by being considerably darker, looked smaller and seemed to show less white on the rump when in flight (v. *Annals Scottish Natural History*, 1910, p. 2).

A second specimen, also a female, was obtained on the island of Swona, Orkney, on November 1st, 1916.

No other examples are known to have occurred in the British Islands. A figure of the male in adult plumage is given in vol. i. plate 3, described p. 17.

RÜPPELL'S WARBLER.

Sylvia rüppelli, Temminck.

PLATE 80B.

Two examples of this beautiful little warbler, both males, were obtained at Hastings, Sussex, on May 5th, 1914. According to Dresser's *Birds of Europe*, it inhabits Greece, Asia Minor, Palestine, and Algeria, wintering in North Africa.

Rüppell's Warbler is partial to bushy places, either near water or in dry localities, and builds its nest, composed of dead grasses with a lining of hair, in bushes.

The eggs are dull white, with blurred brownish markings.

I have figured a male and female on the plate.

MOUSTACHED WARBLER.

Lusciniola melanogopogon (Temminck).

PLATE 80B.

A male of this species, which is related to our Sedge-Warbler, was shot at St. Leonards-on-Sea, Sussex, on April 12th, 1915.

It breeds among the reed-beds and marshes of the Mediterranean countries, being a resident in the southern parts of Europe and North Africa, whilst eastwards in Asia it ranges to Turkestan. In winter it occurs as far as N.W. India.

In habits the Moustached Warbler is shy and retiring, and builds its nest of grasses and rootlets in the dense cover of reed-beds.

According to Dresser, the four or five eggs resemble the Sedge-Warbler's, but are rather greener in colour and minutely spotted with brown.

THE OLIVACEOUS WARBLER.

Hypolais pallida (Hempr. and Ehr.).

PLATE 80B.

The Olivaceous Warbler has occurred but once in the British Islands, viz. near Hastings, on May 20th, 1915.

It breeds in the south-eastern countries of Europe, ranging still further eastwards to Turkestan and Persia, and is also found in North-east Africa. It winters in tropical Africa.

Dresser informs us (*A Manual of Palæarctic Birds*) that "it frequents groves, orchards, and bush-covered places both in the valleys and in damp localities and also to the altitude of 6000 feet."

The song is said to resemble that of the Icterine Warbler.

The nest, placed in the fork of a branch, is built of dry grasses, etc., with a few horse-hairs, and contains four to five eggs, in ground-colour grey tinged with pink, with dark spots and markings.

The various Warblers shown on this plate were drawn from specimens kindly lent by Lord Rothschild.

THE ST. KILDA WREN.

Troglodytes hirtensis, Seebohm.

PLATE 80A.

Although noted as a resident in St. Kilda by Martin as far back as 1697, this large and pale-coloured race of the Wren was unknown to science until 1884, when Seebohm described it in the *Zoologist* from examples obtained by Dixon in the same year. It is entirely confined to the islands of the St. Kilda group, and differs from our Common Wren not only in size but in the general greyer tone of its plumage, especially on the breast, which is "mealy" in colour, while the upper parts are more distinctly barred and the bill and feet are larger. According to Dr. Eagle Clarke (*Studies in Bird Migration*), "it breeds on Hirta, Soay, Dun, Boreray, and Stack an Armin."

He "found the Wren in all parts of Hirta, among the boulders that fringe the head of the bay, in the walls and cleits, among the crofts, on the screes and rocks on the hillsides, and in the faces of the great cliffs." Three nests were shown him. "One of these was placed in a hole worked in a mass of dead thrift on the face of a cliff; the other two were placed between the stones forming the inner walls of cleits, and were in excellent condition.

"All these nests were composed of the blades and stems of grasses, small tufts of grass, a little moss and dead bracken, and were lined entirely with white feathers of a gull, or with a mixture of moss and white feathers." The bird shown in the plate was painted from a specimen in the Royal Scottish Museum.

Another form of Wren is found in the Shetlands, distinguished from our common species by its larger and heavier bill and richer brown colouring.

THE IRISH COAL-TITMOUSE.

Parus hibernicus, Ogilvie-Grant.

PLATE 80A.

This bird, which is a sub-species of our well-known British Coal-Tit, is confined to Ireland, and the adults may be distinguished by having the white cheek patches and occipital spot suffused with sulphur-yellow and also by the golden russet tint

Pl. 80.^{B.}

Oliraceous Warbler.   Rüppell's Warbler.

Moustached Warbler.   Pied Wheatear.

Pine-Bunting   Yellowshank.   Scottish Crossbill.

2/3

on the sides of the breast and flanks. Mr. Ogilvie-Grant, writing in the *Ibis* for July 1911, says, "It is well known that the young of *Parus britannicus* and its near allies differ from the adult birds in having the sides of the head, as well as the breast and belly, washed with yellow. The persistency of this juvenile character in the adult of *P. hibernicus* seems to indicate that it is of very ancient origin, much more so than its British representative: it seems to represent a pre-Glacial type which has survived in the western and southern parts of Ireland."

According to the same authority the typical British Coal-Titmouse is also found in parts of Ireland.

I have already referred to the Irish race of this Titmouse in vol. i. p. 66.

THE WILLOW-TITMOUSE.

Parus kleinschmidti, Hellmyr.

Plate 80a.

This Titmouse is regarded by the latest authorities as a sub-species of the Northern Marsh-Titmouse *P. borealis*, and so closely resembles our Common Marsh-Tit that it was not distinguished till 1897. When compared, the chief difference between the two lies in the colour and texture of the feathers of the crown of the head, which in the Marsh-Titmouse is of a glossy black, while in the Willow-Tit this part is duller in tone; the variation however, although noticeable in a living specimen, is difficult to show in a colour reproduction. The tail feathers in the Willow-Titmouse also appear to be more graduated than in that of its near ally.

The distribution in the British Islands of the Willow-Titmouse does not yet appear to have been fully ascertained, but according to the B.O.U. *List of British Birds* 1915, it is "resident and confined to the mainland of Great Britain, where it is widely but locally distributed as far north as the Moray Firth."

The "Marsh-Tits" found in Scotland all appear to belong to this form (Willow-Tit), and as a good deal of interest has been raised among ornithologists by the different races, I have given on the plate pictures of both the Willow and Marsh-Titmice, for convenience of comparison. These were taken from specimens in the Royal Scottish Museum.

THE GREATER REDPOLL.

Linota rostrata (Coues).

PLATE 80A.

The Greater Redpoll is a native of Greenland, but also visits the northern parts of America in winter. It is usually considered a rare visitor to the British Islands, although found by Dr. Eagle Clarke to be extremely abundant during his visit to Fair Isle, Shetlands, in the autumn of 1905. He describes in his *Studies of Bird Migration* how the birds "moved about in large parties, and frequented the enclosures near the houses, being attracted by the seeds of numerous weeds which abounded there." In colour this species is darker and browner and has the plumage more heavily streaked than in the Greenland Redpoll.

THE GREENLAND REDPOLL.

Linota hornemanni, Holböll.

PLATE 80A.

A native of Greenland, this large pale coloured species occurs also in Iceland, Jan Mayen, Spitsbergen and Franz-Joseph Land, and visits North America in winter.

Although only a rare straggler to the mainland of Great Britain, it appears to be less so in the Shetlands where, on Fair Isle, Dr. Eagle Clarke observed no less than five during his visit there in the autumn of 1905.

I quote the following notes from his *Studies in Bird Migration*: "The first to come under notice were a party of three, consisting of an adult male and two younger birds, which appeared on 18th September.

"These birds frequented an enclosure in front of one of the crofter's houses, where they fed on the seeds of weeds for several days, and were exceedingly tame.

"On the 29th a second adult male was observed seeking food among some low herbage; and on the 10th October another young bird was found.

"In life these birds, especially the adults, appeared to be almost entirely white, and this fact and the habit of puffing out their fluffy feathers, rendered them exceedingly pretty and conspicuous objects."

The bird drawn on the plate was taken from one of the above-mentioned specimens, an adult male now in the Royal Scottish Museum.

THE SCOTTISH CROSSBILL.

Loxia scotica, Hartert.

PLATE 80B.

The Scottish form of our Common Crossbill (*v.* vol. i. plate 17) differs only in having a larger and heavier bill. It inhabits the pine woods of the Highlands of Scotland, where it breeds, occasionally wandering to the Lowlands in winter.

The principal figure in the plate shows a male in the interesting intermediate stage, the time of change from the brownish-green striped plumage of immaturity, to the red dress of the fully adult.

The second figure represents a female, both painted from specimens in the Royal Scottish Museum.

THE PINE BUNTING.

Emberiza leucocephala, S. G. Gmelin.

PLATE 80B.

On this plate is shown a sketch of the only example taken in the British Islands of this rare species, a male in winter plumage, obtained at Fair Isle, Shetlands, on October 30th, 1911. It is now in the Royal Scottish Museum.

For an adult bird in summer, see vol. i. plate 17, described page 123.

THE YELLOWSHANK.

Totanus flavipes (Gmelin).

PLATE 80B.

For description of this species see vol. iv. page 46. The bird represented in the plate was obtained at Fair Isle, Shetlands, in September 1910, and is now in the Royal Scottish Museum.

The following birds, mostly racial forms, have been recorded lately as having occurred in the British Islands, but are not figured.

They are given under binomial names.

North African Black Wheatear, *Saxicola syenitica*, Heuglin. One obtained at Pevensey, Sussex, June 7th, 1915. This bird differs from the typical European form in having the black of a browner tone and the black tips to the tail-feathers broader (*v.* Witherby's *British Birds*, January 1916).

Eastern Great Reed-Warbler, *Acrocephalus orientalis* (Temm. and Schleg.). One picked up dead, St. Leonards, Sussex, August 24th, 1916. Differs from the Great Reed-Warbler in its smaller size and in the wing formula (*v.* Witherby's *British Birds*, April 1917).

Eastern Short-toed Lark, *Alauda longipennis*, Eversmann. One obtained at Fair Isle, Shetlands, November 11th, 1907. It is paler in the colour of the upper parts and has the wings generally a little longer than in the typical form (*v. Scottish Naturalist*, 1915, p. 100).

Calandra Lark, *Melanocorypha calandra* (Linnæus). Two obtained near St. Leonards, Sussex, May 16th and 17th, 1916 (*v.* Witherby's *British Birds*, April 1917).

Semi-palmated Ringed Plover, *Ægialitis semipalmata* (Bonaparte). One obtained April 8th, 1916, at Rye, Sussex. This American form of Ringed Plover differs from our bird not only in the semi-palmation of the feet, but in having less black on the head, neck and breast (*v.* Witherby's *British Birds*, April 1917).

Cape Verde Little Shearwater, *Puffinus boydi*, Mathews. One picked up at Pevensey, Sussex, December 4th, 1914, and another obtained at St. Leonards, Sussex, January 2nd, 1915. It differs very slightly from the Little Dusky Shearwater, *Puffinus assimilis*, figured in vol. iv., plate 79, but is rather browner in the colour of the upper parts and has the under tail-coverts darker (*v.* Witherby's *British Birds*, January 1916).

North Atlantic Great Shearwater, *Puffinus borealis*, Cory. One obtained at St. Leonards, Sussex, March 14th, 1914. Differs chiefly from the Mediterranean Great Shearwater, *Puffinus kuhli*, in having a larger and heavier bill (*v.* Witherby's *British Birds*, January 1916).

END OF VOL. IV.

INDEX

INDEX

INDEX

INDEX

INDEX

INDEX

INDEX

INDEX

INDEX

INDEX